The Logic of Racial Practice

Philosophy of Race

Series Editor: George Yancy, Emory University

Editorial Board: Sybol Anderson, Barbara Applebaum, Alison Bailey, Chike Jeffers, Janine Jones, David Kim, Emily S. Lee, Zeus Leonardo, Falguni A. Sheth, Grant Silva

The Philosophy of Race book series publishes interdisciplinary projects that center upon the concept of race, a concept that continues to have very profound contemporary implications. Philosophers and other scholars, more generally, are strongly encouraged to submit book projects that seriously address race and the process of racialization as a deeply embodied, existential, political, social, and historical phenomenon. The series is open to examine monographs, edited collections, and revised dissertations that critically engage the concept of race from multiple perspectives: sociopolitical, feminist, existential, phenomenological, theological, and historical.

Recent Titles

The Logic of Racial Practice: Explorations in the Habituation of Racism, edited by Brock Bahler
Hip-Hop as Philosophical Text and Testimony: Can I Get a Witness?, by Lissa Skitolsky
The Blackness of Black: Key Concepts in Critical Discourse, by William David Hart
Self-Definition: A Philosophical Inquiry from the Global South and Global North, by Teodros Kiros
A Phenomenological Hermeneutic of Antiblack Racism in The Autobiography of Malcolm X, by David Polizzi
Buddhism and Whiteness, edited by George Yancy and Emily McRae
Black Christology and the Quest for Authenticity: A Philosophical Appraisal, by John H. McClendon III

The Logic of Racial Practice

Explorations in the Habituation of Racism

Edited by
Brock Bahler

LEXINGTON BOOKS
Lanham • Boulder • New York • London

Published by Lexington Books
An imprint of The Rowman & Littlefield Publishing Group, Inc.
4501 Forbes Boulevard, Suite 200, Lanham, Maryland 20706
www.rowman.com

6 Tinworth Street, London SE11 5AL, United Kingdom

Copyright © 2021 by The Rowman & Littlefield Publishing Group, Inc.

An earlier version of chapter 4 was previously published as Alison Bailey, "On Anger, Silence, and Epistemic Injustice," *Royal Institute of Philosophy Supplement* 84 (2018): 93–115. The version in this collection has been altered and updated. Permission from the Royal Institute of Philosophy for reprinting was obtained from Dr. James Garvey on February 12, 2020.

An earlier version of chapter 6 was previously published as Erin Beeghly, "Embodiment & Oppression: Reflections on Haslanger," *Australian Philosophical Review* 3, no. 1 (2019): 35–47. Permission for reprinting was obtained from Taylor & Francis Ltd, www.tandfonline.com, on August 15, 2020. The version in this collection has been significantly expanded, altered, and updated.

All rights reserved. No part of this book may be reproduced in any form or by any electronic or mechanical means, including information storage and retrieval systems, without written permission from the publisher, except by a reviewer who may quote passages in a review.

British Library Cataloguing in Publication Information Available

Library of Congress Cataloging-in-Publication Data

Names: Bahler, Brock, 1981– editor. | Yancy, George, writer of foreword.
Title: The logic of racial practice : explorations in the habituation of
　　racism / edited by Brock Bahler.
Other titles: Explorations in the habituation of racism
Description: Lanham : Lexington Books, [2020] | Series: Philosophy of race
　　| Includes bibliographical references and index. | Summary: "This book
　　explores how white supremacy produces a racialized orientation in our
　　lives, arguing that racism is habituated, enacting within us racialized
　　and racist dispositions and bodily comportments that inform how we
　　interact with others"—- Provided by publisher.
Identifiers: LCCN 2020045995 (print) | LCCN 2020045996 (ebook) | ISBN
　　9781793641533 (cloth) | ISBN 9781793641540 (epub) | ISBN 9781793641557 (pbk)
Subjects: LCSH: Racism—United States. | United States—Race relations. |
　　Race—Philosophy.
Classification: LCC E184.A1 L64 2020 (print) | LCC E184.A1 (ebook) | DDC
　　305.800973—dc23
LC record available at https://lccn.loc.gov/2020045995
LC ebook record available at https://lccn.loc.gov/2020045996

Contents

Foreword — vii
George Yancy

Acknowledgments — xv

Introduction — xvii
Brock Bahler

1. "The Talk": The Transference of Black Body Memory — 1
Autumn Redcross

2. Searching for Romance in the Age of Trumpism: The Impact of Race and Political Ideology in Partner Preferences among Ethno-Racial Minorities — 25
Sarah Adeyinka-Skold

3. The Asian-American Experience and the White Gaze: On the Potentiality of Naming Oneself from Nowhere — 55
Nora Tsou

4. Anger, Silence, and Epistemic Injustice — 77
Alison Bailey

5. The "What," "How," and "Why" of Racialized Seeing — 97
Katie Tullmann

6. Embodiment and Oppression: Reflections on Haslanger, Gender, and Race — 121
Erin Beeghly

7. The Embodied Practices of Whiteness: Unpacking One's White Supremacist Education — 143
Brock Bahler

8. Racialized Habitus in Criminal Immigration Defense Attorneys — 165
Jessie K. Finch

9. Three Kinds of Racialized Disgust in Film — 185
Dan Flory

10. Disappearance, or, the Neat Punctuation of an Invisible Sentence — 207
James B. Haile

Index 245
About the Editor and Contributors 249

Foreword

George Yancy

Embodied as a Black male, I move through the world on tenterhooks and experience deep anxiety, tension, dread. Judged by white gazes, accused by white gesticulations, blocked by white gated communities, excluded by white curricula, rendered strange by monochromatic white academic spaces, and bullied by weaponized white "innocence," I have acquired the embodied posture of a mannequin, which etymologically means "little man." It is fake, I know; but fake might just save my life. After all, my objective is to live *one more day*, which is perhaps still too much to ask in a social world where I was never meant *to be*. So, I self-censor to erase any semblance of "Black terror," any sense of foreboding. As the "little man," the mannequin, I am, hopefully, seen as nonthreatening, perhaps even as pretend and thereby not menacing at all. You see, the white gaze renders my Blackness hyper-visible, a racial surplus. Like Frantz Fanon, I have "shouted a greeting to the world and the world slashed away my joy."[1] Racialized as Black, there is no complete lithely movement or undertakings with total effortless grace within white dominant spaces.

I often assume a stilted walk, eyes lowered, and body comportment following a straight imaginary line in my head. After all, I need to get home. In my memory, in my body, in my gut, there is the resounding and haunting warning from the past: "Nigger, don't let the sun go down on you in this town."[2] But wait. It is still light outside. Hell, tell that to George Floyd or Ahmaud Arbery. The logics of whiteness constitute a site of imminent terror and are not temporally bound. Hence, I live on high alert regardless of the rising and setting of the sun.

James Baldwin warned his young nephew: "You can only be destroyed by believing that you really are what the white world calls a *nigger*."[3] I got it. I know that I'm not a nigger. I imagine that I have always known this. The problem is that whiteness, as a distorted epistemic structure, does not know this or does not want to know this or knows this and refuses to know that it knows this. My sense is that even if it does know, it does not give a damn about what I hold to be true about myself, the epistemic integrity of my doxastic structure, or the veracity of my actions.

Being Black in an anti-Black white world is to have one's embodied subjectivity called into question, one's perspective on the world doubted, where giving an account of oneself is belied not simply because of what Judith Butler calls opacity,[4] but because of white epistemic violence. It is to live a life where the meaning of one's being has been confiscated and phenomenologically returned as a site of feculence, dirt, the unclean, the stained. Charles Johnson writes, "Stain recalls defilement, guilt, sin, corpses that contaminate, menstruating women; and with them the theological meanings of punishment, ostracism, and the need to be 'cleansed.'"[5] So, I move through white social spaces marked, indelibly, with the curse of Ham,[6] where I'm always already guilty of some crime, where *I am*, ontologically, a misdeed, an offense and offensive.

The white racist interpellations shape me into a familiar racist *imago*. There are numerous white embodied, habitual racist iterations. Though it is a telescope, for them it is, "Look, a Black boy with a weapon!" Though it is a wallet, for them it is, "Look, a Black man with a gun!" Though it is a toy gun and he is only 12 years of age, for them it is, "Look, an *adult* Black man with a *real* gun!" Though he is in his own home, for them it is, "Look, a Black man has broken into my home." Though she is only smoking her cigarette and doing so with agency, for them it is, "Look, a Black woman, defiant, dangerous, and angry!" Perhaps Hamlet was right: to be *or* not to be. Yet, the reality of Black death on the ground (pun intended) renders questionable the disjunction. After all, we are a people who are forced to mourn our deaths in advance, who are subjected to a white necropolitical structure where Black bodies might be described as "walking corpses." Black bodies are haunted by death, haunted by sites of white violence that deny them their right to life and their biological capacity to breathe. "Look, a Black man! He's selling 'loosies'" (untaxed cigarettes). "Look, a Black man! He's got a counterfeit $20 bill." According to a white anti-Black hegemonic metanarrative, Eric Garner and George Floyd, respectively, had to be stopped dead through asphyxiation. "Do it! The Black abomination was never meant to be. Let's keep him down with a prohibited chokehold or unconcernedly keep our knee on his neck until he stops complaining, until he stops crying for life: 'I can't breathe!'" Yet, whiteness, like light, like virtue, like truth, knows what is best: "He's lying. After all, he can speak." As Judith Butler asks, "If racism pervades white perception, structuring what can and cannot appear within the horizon of white perception, then to what extent does it interpret in advance 'visual evidence'?"[7]

The above are quotidian examples of what it means to be Black in white America. They capture *not* what is spectacular about white racism, but what is *normative* about white racism, what is iterative, dispositional, stylized, historically sedimented, embodied, enfleshed, and a matter of hexis or habit. What is important within those violent contexts is the theme of racialized embodied practices, what takes place within the context of *lived* sociality and intercorporeality.

Critiquing the South within the context of the pre-1960s, white writer and social gadfly Lillian Smith understood the implicit and prereflective lessons that white people internalized and performed with absolute ease. She argues that the process of racialization is one that arrests the human spirit. It is a process that she describes as "day by day, hour by hour, year by year until the movements were reflexes and made for the rest of our life without thinking."[8] Within the context of whiteness, I have witnessed white bodies move within predominantly white academic spaces with ease, without question. They are not stopped, like Black bodies, because of racist micro-aggressions that are part of the performative DNA of white social embodiment. Although she is referring to white Southerners, Smith writes, "What white southerner of my generation ever stops to think consciously where to go or asks [themself] if it is right for [them] to go there!"[9] To be Black on such predominantly white campuses is to experience the weight of whiteness in the form of white gazes, glances, questions, silences, tugs on bookbags, subtle avoidant movements on elevators, several looks over the shoulder, and other body movements—white lessons learned day by day, hour by hour, year by year.

Such white spaces comfort white bodies, put them at ease, establishing for them a home away from home, where their bodies are validated not only by a sea of white faces, but by epistemological and curricular assumptions that "validate" their "superiority," their ontological and civilizational apex in human history. These lessons did not begin at the university but began in the laps of their white parents. Smith notes, "I do not think our [parents] were aware that they were teaching us lessons."[10] Of course, whether knowingly or not, white parents are responsible for the perpetuation of whiteness and its structural virulence and anti-Black impact on Black bodies. Such anti-Blackness, as Smith notes, was "taught us by our [parents'] voice, memorized with [their] love, patted into our lives as [they] rocked us to sleep or fed us."[11] The comingling of a white anti-Black racist pedagogy with acts of white parental love and affection speaks to the complexity, subtlety, and poisonous performance of whiteness; the hate was taught *through* the gentle voice, the loving arms, the rocking to sleep. Smith notes, "The mother who taught me what I know of tenderness and love and compassion taught me also the bleak rituals of keeping Negroes in their 'place.'"[12] The details of Smith's life demonstrate how white racism is not simply an abstract ideological system of beliefs, but that whiteness lives within and between white bodies, shared like mutually inhaled air, linked by an anti-Black social skin, an intertwined racist social integument. In stream with Shannon Sullivan, whiteness is "'in' the nose that smells, the back, neck, and other muscles that imperceptibly tighten with anxiety"[13] vis-à-vis Black people.

There are other sites where anti-Black racist pedagogy is performed within the context of subtle gestures, parental-like guidance, and professorial affection. For example, as a Black philosopher, I have also become painfully aware of how the canon of Western (white and mostly male and mostly Christian) philosophy is also taught to white students by their white professors whose voices lull them into accepting Western—white European—philosophy as *the only* legitimate form of philosophy, where there is no conceptual space for being challenged from elsewhere, from outside the embodied philosophical habits and practices of their white teachers, outside of the conceptual cartography of white supremacy. Before long, white students move within philosophical spaces with ease. Perhaps not dissimilar to the way some white people learn how to say, "Nigger" with facility and confidence.

Like whites whose muscles carried them "to the front of the bus"[14] during Jim Crow segregation, white students move within departmental philosophy seminar rooms filled with books, their muscles, through habit, reaching for David Hume's *An Enquiry Concerning Human Understanding*.[15] There is no hesitation, no doubt about who constitutes the "human." Their eyes move along the shelves, they walk slowly, the names on the spines of the books are familiar, they testify to something that the white students know without ever thinking twice about (not even once): these books are meant for me. The texts call to the white students. Yet, those books are where they are because of a long history of embodied white macro- and micro-racist practices. To produce *these* books, white hands furiously wrote, took notes, stroked beards, drank wine, gesticulated with philosophical authority, paced back and forth in deep thought, deep *white* thought, the only "real thought." There is also the "hidden" or unmentioned/unmentionable long history of canonical formation established by white gatekeepers who saw it as their "divine" duty to uphold reason itself as a white creation, even as this meant the decimation and genocide of nonwhites through brutal colonial logics. So, as one white student reaches for Hume's text, there is the smooth performance of white normativity without a hint of spilled blood. Her reach is weightless. She has all of the support that she needs. White history is her scaffold. And running through her white body—her eyes, her arms, her legs—is acquired white privilege, ready-made for her. Something as mundane as reaching for a philosophical text constitutes a confluence of white power, the historical accretion of white embodied habits, falsehoods, and lies. Her act of reaching is a ceremonial gesture "in honor of white supremacy."[16]

The brief reflections in this foreword mirror the conceptual framework of this important book, *The Logic of Racial Practice*. Philosopher Brock Bahler, the editor, is clear about the guiding theme that runs throughout the text: race and racism are not natural kinds that cut at the joints of reality. Race is not an ahistorical phenomenon, and racism is not some deep metaphysical teleological unfolding. Race and racism are historically and socially dynamic processes that presuppose embodied sociality, calcified social practices, performative stylizations, iterations, and repetitions, habituated modes of being, institutional structures, semiotic and material forces. These assumptions are radically important as they point to the metastable reality of race and racism, pointing to their contingency, but never forgetting about their lived reality, their *social ontological* weight. As Bahler writes in his introduction, the essays in this book "explore how white supremacy produces a racialized modality by which we live as embodied beings. Stated simply, race (and racism) is performative, habituated, enacted." This framing of the text is consistent with what I have called elsewhere, "the *lived* density of race."[17] Stressing our current historical context, Bahler clearly marks the urgency of our collective *now*, our shared moment in human history, that is plagued by the unabashed emergence (or reemergence) of pervasive and toxic national and global forms of racialized xenophobia and violence predicated on white supremacy. To address the urgency of our collective now is not about us gaining conceptual clarity regarding the *ontic* nature of race (though this is an indispensable philosophical investigation), but of undoing, un-suturing the lived or phenomenologically embodied performances that perpetuate or suture white supremacy. It is a question of embodied *practice*; indeed, embodied *Sarx*, not disembodied *Logos*. This is an important text that is a clarion call to action, and to mutually embodied, loving, kenotic practices. It is a text that envisions modes of being-embodied-in-the-world *otherwise*, a text that bespeaks our mutually dependent porosity and embodied vulnerability. In keeping with the emphasis on the organizing philosophical, political, and somatic motif of practice, ours is to change the world and not simply to interpret it differently.

George Yancy
The Samuel Candler Dobbs Professor of Philosophy
Emory University

NOTES

1. Fanon, *Black Skin, White Masks*, 114–15.
2. Editor's Note: During the Jim Crow era, signs with this warning were posted at the city limits of towns not only in the Deep South but throughout the United States. For extensive information on this history see Loewen, *Sundown Towns*.
3. Baldwin, *The Fire Next Time*, 4.
4. Regarding the concept of opacity and the problematics of giving an account of oneself, see Butler, *Giving an Account of Oneself*.
5. Johnson, "A Phenomenology of the Black Body," 258.
6. Editor's Note: The "curse of Ham" is one of several ways in which Christian white supremacists read the social construct of race back into the Bible in order to justify colonialism and slavery. The theory, based on a literalistic reading of the Bible claims that of Noah's three sons, people of African descent can trace their genealogy

back to Ham who was cursed for seeing his father's nakedness (Genesis 9:20–24; 10:6—though the attentive reader of the text will note that it is only *one* line of Ham's family, his son Canaan, that is actually cursed). Further, it was claimed that Black skin was evidence of this curse, a kind of damnation that could never be removed, and thus a justification for lifelong enslavement. It is difficult to trace it's exact origins, though discussion of it in reference to American chattel slavery can be found as early as the Puritan Cotton Mather's, *The Negro Christianized* (1706), which, despite doubting the Ham genealogy, defended lifelong enslavement; however, scholar David Goldenberg has traced interpretations of the curse of Ham much further back in time than that (see Goldenberg, *The Curse of Ham*, esp. chapter 12).

7. Butler, 'Endangered/Endangering," 15–16.
8. Smith, *Killers of the Dream*, 96.
9. Ibid., 96.
10. Ibid., 83.
11. Ibid., 84.
12. Ibid., 27.
13. Sullivan, *Revealing Whiteness*, 188.
14. Smith, *Killers of the Dream*, 96.
15. Editor's Note: It was Hume who wrote: "I am apt to suspect the negroes to be naturally inferior to the whites. There scarcely ever was a civilized nation of that complexion, nor even any individual eminent either in action or speculation. No ingenious manufactures amongst them, no arts, no sciences" (Hume, "Of National Characters," note 10).
16. Smith, *Killers of the Dream*, 96.
17. Yancy, *Look, a White!*, especially chapter one.

BIBLIOGRAPHY

Baldwin, James. *The Fire Next Time*. New York: Modern Library, 1962/1995.
Butler Judith. "Endangered/Endangering: Schematic Racism and White Paranoia." In *Reading Rodney King/Reading Urban Uprising*. Edited by Robert Gooding-Williams, 15–22. New York: Routledge, 1993.
———. *Giving an Account of Oneself*. New York: Fordham University Press, 2015.
Fanon, Frantz. *Black Skin, White Masks*. Translated by Charles Lam Markman. New York: Grove Press, 1967.
Goldenberg, David. *The Curse of Ham: Race and Slavery in Early Judaism, Christianity, and Islam*. Princeton: Princeton University Press, 2003.
Hume, David. "Of National Characters." Essay XXI. In *Essays Moral, Political, Literary*, Edited by Eugene F. Miller, with an appendix of variant readings from the 1889 edition by T. H. Green and T. H. Grose. Indianapolis: Liberty Fund, 1987. Accessed at: https://oll.libertyfund.org/titles/704.
Johnson, Charles. "A Phenomenology of the Black Body." In *America and the Black Body: Identity Politics in Print and Visual Culture*. Edited by Carol E. Henderson, 252–65. Madison, NJ: Fairleigh Dickerson University Press, 2009.
Loewen, William. *Sundown Towns: A Hidden Dimension of American Racism*. New York: The New Press, 2018.
Mather, Cotton. "The Negro Christianized. An Essay to Excite and Assist that Good Work, the Instruction of Negro-Servants in Christianity (1706)." Edited by Paul Royster. *Electronic Texts in American Studies* 28. Accessed at https://digitalcommons.unl.edu/etas/28.
Smith, Lillian. *Killers of the Dream*. With a new introduction by Margaret Rose Gladney. New York: W. W. Norton, 1949.

Sullivan, Shannon. *Revealing Whiteness: The Unconscious Habits of Racial Privilege.* Bloomington, IN: Indiana University Press, 2006.
Yancy, George. *Look, a White! Philosophical Essays on Whiteness.* Philadelphia, Pennsylvania: Temple University Press, 2012.

Acknowledgments

Essay collections are a communal effort that take substantial time and energy from many people in order to bring them to fruition. Numerous people had a hand in this project—a process that took nearly three years to complete. I am thankful for the other contributors who willingly offered their expertise and scholarly efforts to be included in this collection. I have been challenged by their insight and have become better informed as a result of reading their work. In addition to the contributors and the books cited throughout our essays, some of these essays were especially informed and shaped by discussions with fellow colleagues who read and commented on earlier versions. Special thanks to Joy James, Michael Brownstein, Lacey Davidson, Keota Fields, Janine Jones, Dan Kelly, Céline Leboeuf, Terrance MacMullan, David Mills, Will Penman, and Gabby Yearwood. We are also appreciative of the work of Nicolette Amstutz, Holly Buchanan, and Jana Hodges-Kluck from Lexington Books, who believed in this manuscript and helped to bring it to publication. And we are especially grateful for Dr. George Yancy, who not only wanted to include this anthology in his Philosophy of Race book series, but whose scholarship has also deeply influenced the work of the contributors who are included in this collection. In his introduction to *Christology & Whiteness,* George defined philosophy as "asking of us nothing less than to face both who we are and the world with as much honesty as we can manage, to grieve that world and to grieve our own mistakes within that world, and, yet, to be moved and transformed by the love of wisdom and the wisdom of love." It is that vision for philosophical work that has guided this collection. Finally, I want to personally thank my wife, Amber, and children, Emerson and Olivia, who have not only put up with living with an academic, but who have also profoundly shaped my life and my processing of the issue of race as we have lived life together and talked openly about white privilege, racism, and social justice.

Introduction

Brock Bahler

I write this introduction in the wake of the lynching of Ahmaud Arbery, an unarmed Black man murdered while jogging near Brunswick, Georgia, the victim of a vigilante extrajudicial killing. Two men decided to take the law in their own hands; another filmed the event. For weeks, the killers were free, protected by the DA and their whiteness, arrested only after the video was made public. The event was reminiscent of Trayvon Martin, who in 2012 was killed while walking with a bag of Skittles and some iced tea, reminiscent of so many people of color profiled as criminal simply for being in assumed-to-be white spaces.

I write in the midst of a global pandemic that has disproportionately traumatized historically marginalized populations in the United States, particularly Black, Brown, and Native American communities, where decades of institutionalized racism has made quality healthcare inaccessible to them and has left them more likely to have preexisting conditions, and thus, more likely to die from COVID-19. At this moment, African-Americans have died from COVID-19 at a rate that is three times higher than the white population.[1]

I write in the wake of the killing of Breonna Taylor in Louisville, Kentucky. She was shot eight times by the police. While sleeping in her home. The police were issuing a search warrant in the middle of the night. To the wrong house. They barely identified themselves. Upon hearing the news, I was reminded of not only Atatiana Jefferson and Botham Jean, murdered in their homes by police, but of the homicide of Black Panther party leader Fred Hampton in 1969, shot in the head at point-blank range in his sleep in a raid by the Chicago Police Department.

I write in the wake of the public execution of George Floyd by a Minneapolis police officer. It was the same city where Philando Castile was shot and killed by the police four years earlier, despite legally having the right to own a gun, despite slowly complying with the officer's orders. It is the same city where in 1931, a mob of over 3,000 white people surrounded the home of Edith and Arthur Lee, threatening the African-American family to move for weeks as police officers looked on.[2] For nearly ten agonizing minutes George Floyd was suffocated to death. In his dying moments, the gentle giant said he couldn't breathe numerous times, asked for water, said his body hurt, and cried out for his mother. Civilians pleaded on behalf of Floyd, as three other police officers watched. We had seen this one before too. In 2014, Eric Garner was strangled to death by a New York police officer. While in the chokehold, eleven times Garner whispered, "I can't breathe," before he died. Across the world, people protested Floyd's death, many of them hit with tear gas by the police, cruelly preventing them from breathing while protesting a man who couldn't breathe, compounding cruelty upon the cruelty of a coronavirus that is more likely to kill those with a respiratory disease.

I write this introduction in the wake of the releasing of the viral video of Amy Cooper who willfully falsified a 911 call while exploiting her white privilege and the institutionalized racism at her disposal because a Black man told her to leash her dog. It too was reminiscent of white people calling the cops on Black people for having a barbeque, selling lemonade, talking loudly, or just being in public, reminiscent of so many *white* lies by white women that have gotten Black people killed like Emmett Till and the victims of the bombing of Black Wall Street in Tulsa.

PURPOSE

Within this historical context, the purpose of this collection of essays is to explore how white supremacy produces a racialized modality by which we live as embodied beings. Stated simply, race (and racism) is performative, habituated, enacted. Rather than privileging theory, which reduces race to a (socially constructed) theoretical concept and defines one's racism/antiracism based on mental assent to a list of propositions, these essays seek to describe how race is primarily a *praxis* before it is articulated as an epistemological claim. Race and racism are embodied habits that have become sedimented into our ways of being-in-the-world, instilling within us racialized (and racist) dispositions, postures, and bodily comportments that inform how we interact with others.

This claim itself is not necessarily novel, as it is situated within a growing body of literature in philosophy of race.[3] What is unique, however, is the current scholarly milieu in which this claim is being made that allows us to imagine the extensive interdisciplinary possibilities of such a framework. For across the disciplines, a renewed emphasis on embodiment has illuminated embodied practices into sharper relief that not only seeks to undo the damage that has been done through centuries of Cartesian dualistic thinking that separates the mind from the body but also highlights the many implicit and unconscious ways in which we live and move and have our being.

For example, numerous scholars in anthropology and religious studies have highlighted the meaningfulness and significance of religious rituals and practices over mental assent and propositional thought, suggesting that what drives religious communities is not primarily doctrinal agreement, but rather, shared practices.[4] Scholarship in neuroscience known as embodied cognition has challenged Cartesian dualism, arguing that bodily movements, emotions, and habits not only profoundly shape cognition and brain activity but that *thinking itself* extends throughout the body and is scaffolded upon a material and social world.[5] Trauma specialists have shown that traumatic experiences are not just memories in the brain but are physically imprinted on the body.[6] Child psychologists are pointing out the myriad of ways in which the cognitive, social, emotional, and physical development of infants is conditioned on their bodily engagement with others and the world.[7] And social psychologists are arguing that the *majority* of our actions and behaviors operate from a bodily system that functions "automatically and quickly, with little or no effort and no sense of voluntary control"—as Daniel Kahneman summarizes: "Cognition is embodied; you think with your body, not only with your brain.[8] As philosopher Maurice Merleau-Ponty stressed throughout his career, we do not merely *have* bodies; we *are* our bodies.

Within this context, the title of this collection, *The Logic of Racial Practice*, pays special tribute to the work of Pierre Bourdieu. Bourdieu, who coined the term "social capital" (which has also been utilized to think about race),[9] also coined the term *habitus*. Bourdieu writes, "*Habitus*, then, is shorthand to refer to those 'dispositions' we have to constitute the world in certain ways—the habitual way that we construct our world. And those dispositions and habits are not primarily intellectual or rational; they are certainly not something we 'think about.'"[10] Particularly in the context of religious practices and symbols—which is relevant to this issue and I discus below—Bourdieu observes that they carry a deeply meaningful significance without them having to be verbally articulated or conceptually constructed: "A *habitus* is a kind of embodied tradition, not as some external 'deposit' or data or content but as a handed-down way of being. It is in this sense that a *habitus* is a 'structured' structure—it is something that comes *to* me, from outside me, conditioning and enabling my constitution of the world."[11] I am shaped by my cultural and social situation, shaped to viscerally respond to images, words, activities, and events that occur on the level of the body and without any self-reflective conceptualization. Yet I am also held responsible for my unique individual actions and agency within this social milieu. The unique benefit of the language of *habit* is that it takes into account *both* the passivity and activity that constitute our lived experience: we are simultaneously conditioned by our social environments in ways we don't even notice, yet we also *choose* to enact our habits and can change them.

Collectively, then, what these essays uniquely seek to demonstrate is that the language of *habit, embodiment,* and *praxis* are necessary tools for explaining how we enact racial stereotyping or respond based on racist assumptions—what is often called unconscious or implicit bias. We don't have to "think" about race; race is performed as an embodied response to a social milieu that has habitually trained us to perceive the world in a racialized way—and that we perpetuate throughout our day-to-day choices. This framework provides an especially useful explanation for observing how individuals who *say* they are not racist or assent to antiracist ideals often still *perform* racist actions. For her part, Robin DiAngelo has utilized Bourdieu's work to suggest that "white fragility" is a habitus, a kind of comporting in the world that is the result of being socialized to take up a set of "unconscious dispositions. . . . White Fragility may be conceptualized as a product of the habitus, a response or 'condition' produced and reproduced by the continual social and material advantages of the white structural position."[12]

The image on the cover of this book serves as a clarifying example of how we are primed to be habituated about race in banal ways without being consciously told to do so. Religious art is a powerful mechanism for not merely transmitting ideas but also for producing a particular affective response and bringing about bodily spiritual formation. Religious art is a salient example of how change is produced through ritual, habituation, praxis. Yet another kind of habituation simultaneously occurs. In Christian religious art, Jesus and other characters of the Bible are *regularly* depicted as white Europeans, whereas, people of color are rarely depicted at all—and are often reduced to the peripheral, the outsider, even the demonic.[13] For example, in the summer of 2019, I traveled through Spain visiting several cathedrals. In the thousands of images I viewed, I observed people of color as only two possible characters: either as representatives of the Magi visiting baby Jesus (see cover) or as beheaded victims of Christian Crusaders.

The tacit messages of such images—especially given their ubiquity—are clear though not explicitly stated. What is unspoken yet perceived is that whiteness is normative; in fact, whiteness grants one *insider status* in Christianity. Whiteness is divine, godlike, a better (or the only) depiction of the *imago Deo*. The Black body, in contrast, is an outsider, a foreigner, perhaps not entirely excluded, but only granted provisional status in the Kingdom of God. The Black body must bow before the white Jesus in order to receive salvation. Whiteness is privileged as primary in the Christian tradition and Black bodies are treated as ancillary—even though Africa figures quite prominently in the Bible and the Early Church Fathers, while Europe as we know it does not yet exist.[14]

AMY COOPER AND THE HABITS OF RACIAL PRACTICE

The scene of Amy Cooper threatening to call the cops on an African-American man, Christian Cooper, offers a particularly salient example of how racism can be articulated as habituated and performative rather than merely epistemic. In our culture, still shaped by modern Enlightenment sensibilities, we tend to allow someone to determine who they are or what values they have based on a list of epistemic claims they say they hold. This is most clearly evident in creedal-based religions like Christianity where the requirements for baptism, church membership, or successful completion of confirmation is mental approval to a set of doctrines (e.g., Do you believe in one God in three persons? Do you believe in Jesus Christ the Son of God? Do you believe the Bible to be the authoritative Word of God?, etc.). The propositional statements serve as a litmus test, an entrance exam, that are almost entirely detached from an evaluation of how one *lives*.

Likewise, with regard to whether one is "racist" or antiracist, in American culture, we often let people off the hook for perpetuating racist assumptions or performing white supremacist behaviors because we tend to reduce racism and antiracism to mental assent to propositional claims. Yet the Amy Cooper video reveals the incredible cognitive dissonance that can be sustained between one's stated beliefs and one's lived practices. If we go by entrance exams, then Amy Cooper is not a racist. By her admission to CNN, "I'm not a racist. I did not mean to harm that man in any way."[15] Like a good Kantian, she points out her well-meaning intentions in theory but pays no heed to the actual flesh and blood repercussions of her actions. She gave money to Barack Obama's campaign.[16] She's a progressive liberal (though contrary to popular belief, liberals consciously and unconsciously perpetuate racist beliefs and practices too).[17] Amy Cooper does not identify as a racist, she does not ascribe to racism as one of her deeply held beliefs; and therefore, we are obliged by our white values of being nice and trusting someone's intentions to believe her. But her actions speak otherwise. As the scene[18] plays out, Amy quite effortlessly takes up a *persona* that reveals how quickly one can *dramatize* white supremacy:

Scene: The Ramble
The houselights fade, the curtain abruptly lifts. We feel disjointed, interrupting an encounter that is already proceeding. Dogwalker Amy Cooper has just unleashed her Cocker Spaniel to run through the clearing within the park. Avid birdwatcher Christian Cooper kindly requests the woman to obey the posted laws regarding dogs being leashed. Christian is recording.

Amy: Stop, sir. I'm asking you to stop.

Christian: Please don't come close to me.

Amy [approaching]: Sir, I'm asking you to stop recording me.

Christian: Please don't come close to me.

Amy [approaching]: Sir, I'm asking you to stop recording me. Please take your phone off.

Christian: Please don't come close to me.

Amy: Then I'm taking pictures and calling the cops.

Christian: Please call the cops. Please call the cops.

Amy: [Pause] I'm going to tell them there's an African-American man threatening my life.

Christian: Tell them whatever you like.

[*Amy backs away from Christian. Pausing while calling, she lifts the dog onto its hind legs by the collar, choking it. The dog squirms vigorously to catch some air.*]

Amy: [*To 911 dispatcher*] I'm sorry, I'm in the Ramble. And there is a man, an African-American man, with a bicycle helmet. And he is recording me and *threatening me and my dog.* . . . [*With emotion*] There is an *African-American* man. I am in Central Park. He is recording me and threatening myself and my dog.

[*The dog at this moment flails to the ground, trying to be let loose so it can breathe. Christian has not moved.*]

Amy: I'm sorry, I can't hear you either. [*Switching to higher vocal register, speaking in a frantic, terrified vocal pitch*] I'm being threatened by a man in the Ramble. Please send the cops immediately. . . . I'm in Central Park, I don't know.

[*Amy leashes the dog.*]

Christian: Thank you.

I reimagined this encounter as a scene from a play, not to minimize the implications of Amy's actions (it is *not* fiction), but to highlight how she puts on an *act*. Racism and racist behavior are not an objective seeing-the-world-as-it-really-is, but constitute a *performance* developed out of the white supremacist imagination. The ways in which Amy attempts to weaponize Christian's black skin against him and exploit her own white privilege appear to the observer as almost *rehearsed*, even *scripted*. Her whiteness is not a mere idea, but rather, is a modality that is *enacted* within space and time. As Andre Henry puts it, her capacity to enact her whiteness was achieved not as a result of distress, but with an adept facilitation that we can only describe as a kind of "practical wisdom" or *skillfulness*.[19] Upon seeing the kind of *ease* at which she displayed her skillfulness, the Greeks would have concluded she had a well-rounded *paideia* in white ways of being-in-the-world, achieved through training and rigor. Christian Cooper's reflections of the event are worth considering in light of this point. To the *LA Times* he said, "There is something deeper she tapped into that she was consciously or unconsciously trying to deploy, which is this fear of African-American males, the presumption that we are automatically guilty."[20] Similarly, to CNN he responded: "We live in an era with things like Ahmaud Arbery, where black men are seen as targets. This woman thought she could exploit that to her advantage, and I wasn't having it."[21]

What do we make of this *skillful* racist performance? How do we describe and explain it? What conceptual tools can helpfully unpack Christian Cooper's reflection on the event? How was it that she was able to so effortlessly play the part of a helpless white women being attacked by an allegedly threatening *African-American man*—with a bicycle helmet—as if we were watching a digitally remastered scene from *Birth of a Nation*?

Within the backdrop of Bourdieu's notion of *habitus*, which I have already described, I propose that a useful term for conceptualizing Amy Cooper's actions is that of *affordances*,[22] a neologism coined by psychologist James Gibson in 1979 and which has become popularized in phenomenology and cognitive neuroscience literature regarding the role of the body in how we "think."[23] For Gibson, the term illuminates the intertwined "complementarity of the animal [or human] and the environment," namely that the bodily possibilities of an individual is informed by the makeup of the environment, and yet simultaneously, the make-up of the environment is conditionally perceived by how the individual has been trained to comport themself to the environment.[24] In other words, humans do not simply encounter environments as blank slates, but rather, interpret them through a meaningful *gestalt* that assigns to the contours of the environment different *values* insofar as they might help one achieve various *purposes*.[25] Hence, humans encounter objects and situations with an intuitive know-how, but one that is conditioned by their previous experiences, which follow along in the wake of the present moment.

So then, the same environment, and the objects therein, may solicit different possibilities to different people. A sandy beach might solicit various possibilities, but they will be remarkably different between my daughter, the beach volleyball great Kerri Walsh Jennings, or a professional sand sculptor. Sewing needles speak differently to me—I can clumsily sew on a loose button if I need to—than they to do my mother-in-law who has an entire room devoted to sewing materials. What's key is that this familiarity or *attunement* to a given environment or object can produce actions that don't require premeditated, self-reflective consideration—just watch a video of LeBron James perform a no-look pass threaded between multiple defenders or a professional musician performing an improvisational solo.

Bringing this notion of *affordances*, then, into the scenario between dog owner Amy Cooper and birdwatcher Christian Cooper, I argue that white supremacy has been so habituated into our social environment that it solicits *racialized* affordances, a kind of intuitive logic of racial practice. In considering the scenario, three points appear salient: (1) Affordances—whether of a racial nature or not—are not only perceived in a given situation due to conscious, intentional preparation (e.g., the musician or athlete) but also through implicit societal messaging. (2) Due to the long history of white supremacy, *race* informs how a given environment or intersubjective encounter solicits us. We are not colorblind, but rather the category of race imbues a situation with a certain meaning and solicits certain possibilities. (3) Depending on how we are situated within that white supremacist milieu, the environment will solicit us differently.

(1) The phrase "consciously or unconsciously" in Christian Cooper's reflection is particularly poignant. At times in the video, Amy pauses before she speaks, as if she is thoughtfully composing how she might structure the lie she is about to fabricate. At other moments, her actions are automated, performed immediately yet informed by assumptions about reality that have been habituated into her body and that were available to her in that moment.

Again, importantly, if asked point-blank (with Christian Cooper's comments in mind), "Should one assume Black people are criminals, thugs up to no good? Should we assume them to be targets?" I highly doubt Amy Cooper would answer in the affirmative. Further, I highly doubt anyone ever sat her down and said, "Now remember, when you see a Black man, always perceive them as a threat." Amy was able to produce her skilled whiteness *without having ever been in this situation*. We have reason to believe that Amy had never *practiced* calling the cops on a Black man (remember, she's "not racist"). She had never *rehearsed* those lines. She had never read a manual or taken a course titled, "Three Easy Steps to Maximize One's White Privilege." She had never been given a reverse corollary to "The Talk" by her white parents that explained to her what to do when she encountered a Black birdwatcher in the park.

But she didn't need to, for she would have no difficulty picking up this tacit understanding of how our white supremacist society perceives the Black body through a vast array of implicit messages that become internalized into our way of being-in-the-world. And indeed, what makes humans uniquely different from AI is that the vast majority of how we learn about our situatedness in the world, of how we construct an understanding of our milieu, is by what we learn implicitly and indirectly from others. Implicit learning is itself a kind of training that allows us to instantaneously perceive our possibilities in a given situation.

(2) Next, consider Christian's observation of the "presumption that [Black people] are already guilty." By the time the third edition of the *Encyclopaedia Britannica* was published in 1798, the "Negro," as a whole race, had become defined as being "most notorious" for "idleness, treachery, revenge, cruelty, impudence, stealing, lying, profanity, debauchery, nastiness, intemperance. . . . They are strangers to every sentiment of compassion, and are an awful example of the corruption of man when left to himself."[26] Importantly, Black people have not defined *themselves* in this way but are perceived as such by the all-seeing white gaze. George Yancy describes this as "a process of interpellation, a process of hailing," whereby the Black body is perceived "as a problem body. It is a process of racist ascription through a visual technology that 'knows' the Black body well in advance."[27] This centuries-long construction of the Black body was imagined into existence by white Europeans who then wielded it as a justification for their financial self-interests and whatever violent actions they felt were necessary to preserve and protect that accumulation of wealth: slavery, colonial imperialism, genocide, Black Laws, convict leasing, Jim Crow segregation, lynchings, redlining, dog-whistling political slogans, drug legislation against "super-predators," "stop and frisk" policing, a for-profit prison–industrial complex, and stand-your-ground laws (just to name a few). Hence, the Black body, as Trevor Noah has put it, is always already *born a crime*.

This history informs our present-day actions, informs the meaning of the words we use, as they are contextualized not only by the present moment but by the historical weight that follows along in their wake. The words we use carry a conceptual baggage to them; they are loaded with meaning and power that cannot simply be untethered from their past history, for that history is precisely what empowers (and weaponizes) them. This is most clearly evident when Amy pauses and then replies, "I'm going to tell [the cops] there's an *African-American man* threatening my life." When Amy says this, she is not referring only to the singular event of the encounter between *this* white woman (herself) and *this* African-American (Christian Cooper). Rather, the comment is a threat—and a threat on Christian's life—precisely because she seeks to tap into the centuries-long legacy of perceiving the (male) Black body *as a* threat, an evil brute. It is an act of violence because she desires to employ a long history of state-sanctioned police violence against Black bodies to her advantage.

The very location of the encounter and the objects at hand are endowed with a racialized meaning, as the events that led to the false accusations, forced confessions, and wrongful convictions of the Central Park Five in 1989 reverberate in the background of her threat. These connections are not just accidental or coincidental but are layers of meaning to Amy's comment that are (unconsciously?) intended precisely so that Christian Cooper will feel intimidated and dehumanized. And the reference to Christian having a bicycle helmet is laughable in isolation; and yet it isn't humorous precisely for the painful fact that police have killed unarmed Black men because they "perceived" them to be a threat while holding nonviolent objects on countless occasions—a toy, a cell phone, a wallet, a cigarette, a vape pen. Within the racialized milieu it takes on a particular meaning, one that has been utilized to justify homicide.

(3) Finally, we can consider the unique possibilities that our situatedness affords us within an environment that is endowed with a racialized meaning. Consider that in her interview with CNN, Amy claimed that Christian's comments (which were about giving the dog a treat) were "absolutely terrifying,"[28] but terrified people do not typically approach the person they are terrified of—during a contagious pandemic—or pause to develop an effective threat. At the outset of the video, Amy approaches Christian, her hand defiantly raised, pointing at his cellphone, demanding him to turn it off. There seems to be an unstated assumption about the affordances of the space that is at work in this moment. Amy assumes all space is white space, so it appears, that the white body has permission to freely move about as she wishes, can do whatever she wants: the laws of leashing her dog don't apply to her, the Ramble is hers to utilize however she pleases, Christian's Black body and his personal space can be encroached upon at liberty, and even as she takes offense to Christian recording her she threatens to take pictures of him. One component of white privilege is precisely this freedom to move about in one's own body, to assume space as one's own. It is as if the legacy of the Doctrine of Discovery is so embedded in American society, so ingrained in our bodies, that Amy feels at liberty to colonize this space.

The different racialized affordances that are solicited by the environment come in stark relief if we try to imagine for a moment the situation in reverse. Had Amy been a birdwatcher recording Christian for unleashing his dog, it would have been beyond the realm of imaginable possibilities for him to have called the police and say, "A white woman is threatening me and my dog in the park, and she has a bicycle helmet." Granted, part of the absurdity of this imagined statement is shaped by the realities of misogyny and sexual assault that also plague our society; it is well documented that men are statistically far more likely to be the abuser in cases of domestic violence or sexual assault. Yet in certain respects, Amy's gender *as a white woman* reveals how comparing the situation in reverse leads to a false equivalence, for there is no history of American policing whereby white women have been perceived as a threat. On the contrary, white women have for centuries been perceived as a vessel of purity that must be protected from the advances of the "Black brute." As a result, Amy perceives that the phrase "*African-*

American man" will *hasten* the arrival of the police; such a possibility would have never occurred to Christian had the situation been reversed. Further, mentioning the bicycle helmet in the hand of a white woman would have not evoked anything of the sort of threat that it had in connection with an *African-American man*. To add, "and she has a bicycle helmet," to "a white woman is threatening me and my dog in the park" is to include an inconsequential fact, a red herring. However, in Amy's original statement, it is meant to imply that Christian is *armed and dangerous*. Finally, for such a small offense, it likely would not have been in the realm of imagined possibilities for Christian to even call the police. While white children are socialized to call the police in the event of virtually *any* perceived danger, African-American communities are deeply aware of the potential perils of calling the police, even when it is a call for help. They remember the stories of how often Black people who call for help in a moment of distress are likely to be shot and killed rather than given aid—just ask the families of Keith Lamont Scott, Renisha McBride, Corey Jones, Kaldrick Donald, Terrence Crutcher, or Charles Kinsey. Indeed, less than a month after Amy Cooper's viral video, sixty-one-year-old African-American man Leon McCray was verbally and physically threatened in Edinburg, Virginia, by five white people who hurled racial epithets at him and threatened to kill him. He called 911 for the police to come, while brandishing his legally owned handgun in an effort to stave off the mob. When the police arrived, they arrested McCray, not the white mob. The fact McCray was elderly, a pastor, a military veteran of 24 years, and had no criminal record did not prevent the officers' rush to judgment.[29]

SUMMARY OF ESSAYS

The collection begins with three essays that investigate white supremacy and the construction of race within the personal lives and interpersonal encounters of members of historically marginalized communities. These essays are phenomenological and qualitative in scope, describing some of the unique ways in which people of color must respond to a racialized social milieu in order to establish a sense of self, protect themselves, and procure meaningful relationships. In "'The Talk': The Transference of Black Body Memory," Autumn Redcross traces the bodily contours of a Black mother's conversation with her son regarding how to behave when encountering the police. The Talk is not merely a rhetorical device, but a conversation that habituates Black participants into a particular racialized body memory that reveals not only how Black bodies are defined by the white gaze but how Black sons are inscribed with an embodied orientation for successfully navigating a violent world.

In a similar vein, Sarah Adeyinka-Skold's "Searching for Love in the Age of Trumpism: The Impact of Race and Political Ideology in Partner Preferences among Ethno-Racial Minorities" offers a sociological examination of the ways in which heterosexual Black, Latina, and Asian women must navigate online dating apps in search for intimate romantic relationships during an age of deep racial unrest and political division. Providing both quantitative data and qualitative research, she illuminates how race and racism significantly effect the dating process of ethno-racial minorities who must develop dating strategies that will allow them to survive, flourish, and protect their humanity.

In "The Asian-American Experience and the White Gaze: On the Potentiality of Naming Oneself from Nowhere," Nora Tsou examines the peculiar double (or triple?)-consciousness of being Asian-American, of trying to establish one's identity while actively resisting the caricatures that are assigned to oneself by the white gaze. As she narrates, those who identify as Asian-American are often overdetermined: the term itself is a broad generalization for dozens of nationalities and ethnic backgrounds who must simultaneously navigate between the implications of being labeled as a "model minority" and as never quite fully being considered "American." This process of self-identity is further layered by an assimilation process whereby the Asian-American experience is often interwoven with a sense of solidarity with the Latinx community and its culture.

The second trilogy of essays explore some of the more subtle approaches to discussions about race—tone management, colorblindness, and abstraction—which are commonly employed that, while often well-meaning, are deeply problematic and often create further harm and compound the oppression of historically marginalized communities. Alison Bailey's "Anger, Silence, and Epistemic Injustice" explores how silencing, tone policing, and tone management function as forms of epistemic and psychological oppression enacted by those in power to prevent historically marginalized voices from being heard, and how anger is a justified response to such racist acts. Focusing particularly on the scholarship of women of color, Bailey observes how this "anger-silencing spiral" not only creates a situation in which women of color are perceived to lose their credibility for becoming angry at being silenced but are also expected to take up the greater amount of emotional labor in caring for the feelings of the white person who has silenced them. Bailey then considers how we might better explore the various textures of this "knowing resistant anger" and creatively utilize it as a resource to address epistemic injustice.

In "The 'What,' 'How,' and 'Why' of Racialized Seeing," Katie Tullmann explores some of the problems with the liberal solution of advocating colorblindness as a response to racism. She argues that even if we advocate colorblindness, we nevertheless develop "evaluative" racialized ways of seeing the world, perceptual habits, and attitudes that are not likely to be value neutral given our societal setting. She advocates that we seek to *unlearn* this form of racialized seeing, and rather than pursue colorblindness, develop a kind of "nonevaluative racialized seeing" of others.

In "Embodiment and Oppression: Reflections on Haslanger, Gender, and Race," Erin Beeghly critiques the theory of social oppression outlined by American philosopher Sally Haslanger. While Beeghly believes there is much that is provocative and worthwhile in Haslanger's use of the concept of "mindshaping" to explain how we are socially conditioned to perpetuate oppressive thought patterns, Beeghly argues that Haslanger's account is overly one-sided and detached from everyday experience due to its privileging of a structural theory of oppression. Such abstraction not only renders it inaccessible for political action but also remains detached from our lived, embodied experiences and sense of personal, moral agency.

The next three essays consider spaces and institutions where white supremacy and the construction of race are firmly, systemically, built into the fabric of the United States: education, immigration courts, and Hollywood film. In my essay, "The Embodied Practices of Whiteness: Unpacking One's White Supremacist Education," I elaborate on both the explicit and tacit messages about race and racism that are communicated in American K–12 education. Drawing on reflections from my own educational experiences as well as revealing conversations with my children, I argue that as white people, we take up "white ways of being-in-the-world" as a result of imitating models and habituated ritualization, both of which profoundly shape us on the embodied, prereflective, and narratival levels of human existing. Hence racialized perceptions and social cues can be internalized and enacted without having been self-reflectively articulated. While considering the present and futural effects of being habituated into whiteness, I consider steps we might take to unlearn a white supremacist education through the cultivation of alternative habits.

Jessie Finch's "Racialized Habitus in Criminal Immigration Defense Attorneys" investigates the structural racism at work on the criminalization of migrants and immigrants to the United States, which disproportionately marginalizes and oppresses Latinx people or those who identify as of Hispanic origin. Finch explores how seemingly abstract, institutionalized racism in the criminal immigration system produces racialized embodied practices in the attorneys who work in these court proceedings. Through her sociological lens, she provides an analysis of how participants within a racialized institution are habituated into racist practices and normalize racist assumptions about their clients.

In "Three Kinds of Racialized Disgust in Film," Dan Flory considers how race is portrayed in Hollywood film, particularly clarifying how films compel us to feel a certain way when the topic arises. Such films especially provoke audiences to feel a powerful sense of disgust, a sensation that philosophers have long understood to produce an immediate visceral reaction to stimuli that is often interwoven with assumptions about morality. Flory explores three ways that race and disgust intersect in film in order to help us better cultivate antiracist strategies to how we respond to cinema.

The final essay of this collection uniquely stands alone yet functions perfectly for conceptualizing how we might imagine race in the future, or futuristically. In "Disappearance, or, the Neat Punctuation of an Invisible Sentence," James B. Haile offers an essay framed within the genre of Black speculative fiction/science fiction (e.g., Sheree R. Thomas, Octavia Butler), and informed by existentialist thought, that explores how we "see" Black bodies. Haile fictionalizes an investigative reporter who is looking into accounts that Black people have disappeared. Drawing off of previous discussions of the theme by Ray Bradbury, Richard Wright, Ralph Ellison, Fred Moten, and others, Haile wonders what a "disappearance" of Black bodies would mean in a white cultural world. Would white people even notice the absence of Black bodies? Given the hegemony that white culture creates, do "Black" people even "exist" if they cannot be approximated by the stereotypes and boundaries by which white society perceives them? And is speculative fiction, while having the power to distort the real in order to better see *reality* and expose race as "tragically fictive," well equipped to theorize race given that the language and concepts we have may already be subsumed within the ethos of hegemonic whiteness?

While no collection can be all-encompassing or describe the full extent of race and racism, together these essays elucidate a spectrum of the effects that white supremacy and the social construction of race continue to have on human existence—both in their institutionalized forms and in their imprint on somatic selves living and moving in the world. No silver bullet exists that will magically overturn the long legacy of racism and eradicate its effects. No book will single-handedly change society. However, the collective effort of this anthology is to dramatize how the ubiquitous power of race to divide, marginalize, and oppress cannot be undermined by mere theories, laws, or public statements alone. Rather, we must take seriously the logic of racial *practice*, examining our existence as *bodily* beings, naming the racialized rituals and symbols that we both actively and passively habituate ourselves into, and imagining new practices that can help us simultaneously unlearn racist assumptions while appreciating and valuing human difference.

NOTES

1. Pilkington, "Black Americans Dying of COVID-19 at Three Times the Rate of White People." The statistic was noted by numerous news agencies, including the BBC, *Time Magazine*, NPR, and *The Atlantic*.

2. Welter, "Angry White Mob Surrounds Minneapolis Home."
3. See, for example, Sullivan, *Revealing Whiteness*; Ahmed, "A Phenomenology of Whiteness"; Yancy, *Black Bodies, White Gazes*; MacMullan, *Habits of Whiteness*; Ngo, *The Habits of Racism*.
4. See Csordas, *Embodiment and Experience*; Stoller, *Sensuous Scholarship*; Asad, *Formations of the Secular*; McGuire, *Lived Religion*; Vásquez, *More than Belief*; Smith, *Imagining the Kingdom*.
5. Damasio, *Descartes's Error*; Gallagher, *How the Body Shapes the Mind*; Gallagher and Zahavi, *The Phenomenological Mind*; Rowlands, *The New Science of the Mind*; Shapiro, *The Routledge Handbook of Embodied Cognition*; Zahavi, *Self and Other*; Bahler, "Merleau-Ponty on Embodied Cognition."
6. Van der Kolk, *The Body Keeps the Score*.
7. Gopnik, Meltzoff, and Kuhl, *The Scientist in the Crib*; Field, "Neonatal Perception of People"; Meltzoff, "The Roots of Social and Cognitive Development"; Sheets-Johnstone, "Embodied Minds or Mindful Bodies?"; Decety and Meltzoff, "Empathy, Imitation, and the Social Brain"; Bahler, *Childlike Peace in Merleau-Ponty and Levinas*.
8. Kahneman, *Thinking, Fast and Slow*, 20, 51.
9. Yosso, "Whose Culture Has Capital?"
10. Bourdieu, *The Logic of Practice*, 81.
11. Ibid., 81.
12. DiAngelo, "White Fragility," 57—58.
13. Black bodies are also sometimes associated with the demonic. For instance, St. Teresa of Avila writes, "On another occasion I was tormented for five hours with such terrible pains and such inward and outward disquiet that I do not believe I could have stood it any longer. . . . The Lord plainly wished me to understand that this was the devil's work; for I saw close beside me a most hideous little Negro gnashing his teeth. . . . He made me thresh about with my body, head, and arms, and I was powerless to prevent him" (Teresa, *Interior Castle*, 222).
14. As church historian C. Eric Lincoln writes, "Africa knew the Hebrew nation in its infancy, from Abraham even; and the civilizations of Africa were ancient even then. Still, it is sometimes necessary to remind Christians in the West that Egypt is in Africa, and that Egyptians are Africans, despite the desperate efforts of our race-conscious latter-day historians to deny Africa a place of significance in the history of civilization" (Lincoln, "The Racial Factor in the Shaping of Religion in America," 158).
15. Vera and Ly, "White woman who called police on a black man."
16. Burton, "It looks like Amy Cooper, the white woman in the viral Central Park video, is a liberal."
17. A sobering percentage of Americans still hold explicitly racist stereotypes about Black people. In a 2016 survey, Reuters found that Republican Trump supporters believed Black people to be more criminal (50 percent), more violent (50 percent), more rude (44 percent), more lazy (40 percent), and less intelligent (30 percent) than white people. And yet many Democrat Clinton supporters also held explicitly racist views, believing Black people to be more criminal (33.2 percent), more violent (30 percent), more rude (30 percent), more lazy (25 percent), and less intelligent (22.5 percent) than white people (see Voorhees, "New Poll Finds That Hillary Supporters Are Pretty Racist Too"; Flitter and Kahn, "Exclusive"). And in a 2017 PRRI survey, 80 percent of Republicans and 40 percent of Democrats said that they didn't think Confederate monuments were racist (Vandermaas-Peeler et. al., "One Nation, Divided Under Trump").
18. The video is available all over the internet. See here: https://www.youtube.com/watch?v=iUQWd4q3tjA.
19. Henry, "Amy Cooper's Anti-Black Wisdom."
20. Kaleem, "A birdwatcher, a dog and Amy Cooper."
21. North, "Amy Cooper's 991 call."

22. See for example, Dings, "Understanding Phenomenological Differences in How Affordances Solicit Action," 681; Dawson, "Embedded and Situated Cognition," 62; Dijkstra and Zwaan, "Memory and Action," 301.

23. I place "think" in scare quotes for the fact that given our penchant for Cartesian (and Platonic) dualism, we tend to faultily reduce thinking to something that occurs solely in a very specific part of the brain, namely the prefrontal cortex, which is what largely distinguishes human brains from other animal brains and is the site of self-reflective, conceptual forms of thinking. By doing so we already eliminate the possibility of evaluating how our brains are embodied and material, how our bodies are holistically interconnected, and how our bodies interact with the world in a myriad of informed and intuitive ways without any premeditated, self-reflective conceptual thinking.

24. Gibson, *The Ecological Approach to Visual Perception*, 127. See all of chapter 8.

25. In my view, long before Gibson established this theory of affordances, Edmund Husserl, Martin Heidegger, Maurice Merleau-Ponty, and other phenomenologists were already describing this phenomenon through a variety of terms. We can observe similar theories about language and how it is facilitated with an embedded meaningfulness and utilized for a purpose in thinkers like Wittgenstein and Gadamer.

26. Ishay, *The History of Human Rights*, 113.

27. Yancy, *Black Bodies, White Gazes*, 4. Yancy argues that the "white body" is *habituated* into the capacity of interpellating the Black body "through the larger white social imaginary" that is "linked to larger forms of white historical power" (ibid., xxxvii).

28. Vera and Ly, "White woman who called police on a black man."

29. Associated Press, "Sheriff Apologizes to Black Pastor."

BIBLIOGRAPHY

Ahmed, Sarah. "A Phenomenology of Whiteness." *Feminist Theory* 8, no. 2 (2007): 149–68.

Asad, Talal. *Formations of the Secular: Christianity, Islam, Modernity*. Stanford: Stanford University Press, 2003.

Associated Press. "Sheriff Apologizes to Black Pastor in Virginia for His Arrest Following Alleged Racial Attack." *Time*. June 15, 2020. Accessed June 16, 2020 at https://time.com/5853679/pastor-virginia-arrested-attack/.

Bahler, Brock. *Childlike Peace in Levinas and Merleau-Ponty: Intersubjectivity as Dialectical Spiral*. Lanham, MD: Lexington Books, 2016.

———. "Merleau-Ponty on Embodied Cognition: A Phenomenological Interpretation of Spinal Cord Epidural Stimulation and Paralysis." *Essays in Philosophy* 17, no. 2 (July 2016): 69–93.

Bourdieu, Pierre. *The Logic of Practice*. Translated by Richard Nice. Stanford: Stanford University Press, 1990.

Burton, Nylah. "It Looks Like Amy Cooper, the White Woman in the Viral Central Park Video, Is a Liberal. That's Important." *The Independent*. May 26, 2020. Accessed June 8, 2020 at https://www.independent.co.uk/voices/amy-cooper-central-park-racist-dog-walker-trump-a9533581.html.

Csordas, Thomas J., ed. *Embodiment and Experience: The Existential Ground of Culture and Self*. Cambridge: Cambridge University Press, 1994.

Damasio, Antonio. *Descartes's Error: Emotion, Reason, and the Human Brain*. New York: Penguin, 1994.

Dawson, Michael. "Embedded and Situated Cognition." *The Routledge Handbook of Embodied Cognition*. Edited by Lawrence Shapiro, 59–67. London: Routledge, 2014.

Decety, Jean and Andrew N. Meltzoff. "Empathy, Imitation, and the Social Brain." In *Empathy: Philosophical and Psychological Perspectives*. Edited by Amy Coplan and Peter Goldie, 58–81. Oxford: Oxford University Press, 2011.

DiAngelo, Robin. "White Fragility." *International Journal of Critical Pedagogy* 3, no. 3 (2011): 54–70.
Dings, Roy. "Understanding Phenomenological Differences in How Affordances Solicit Action. An Exploration." *Phenomenology of Cognitive Science* 17 (2018): 681–99.
Dijkstra, Katina and Rolf A. Zwaan. "Memory and Action." *The Routledge Handbook of Embodied Cognition*. Edited by Lawrence Shapiro, 296–305. London: Routledge, 2014.
Field, Tiffany. "Neonatal Perception of People: Maturational and Individual Differences." In *Social Perception in Infants*. Edited by Tiffany M. Field and Nathan A. Fox, 31–52. Norwood, NJ: Ablex Publishing, 1985.
Flitter, Emily and Chris Kahn. "Exclusive: Trump Supporters More Likely to View Blacks Negatively—Reuters/Ipsos Poll." *Reuters*. June 28, 2016. Accessed June 1, 2020 at https://www.reuters.com/article/us-usa-election-race-idUSKCN0ZE2SW?feedType=RSS&feedName=topNews&utm_source=twitter&utm_medium=Social.
Gallagher, Shaun. *How the Body Shapes the Mind*. Oxford: Clarendon Press, 2005.
Gallagher, Shaun and Dan Zahavi. *The Phenomenological Mind*. 2nd Edition. Abingdon: Routledge, 2008.
Gibson, James. *The Ecological Approach to Visual Perception*. Boston: Houghton Mifflin, 1979.
Gopnik, Alison, Andrew N. Meltzoff, and Patricia K. Kuhl. *The Scientist in the Crib: What Early Learning Tells Us about the Mind*. New York: Perennial, 1999.
Henry, Andre. "Amy Cooper's Anti-Black Wisdom." *Medium.com*. May 26, 2020. Accessed on June 12, 2020 at https://medium.com/@andrehenry/amy-cooper-isnt-innocent-e9e4dc24a879.
Ishay, Micheline. *The History of Human Rights: From Ancient Times to the Globalization Era*. Berkeley: University of California Press, 2008.
Kahneman, Daniel. *Thinking, Fast and Slow*. New York: Farrar, Straus and Giroux, 2011.
Kaleem, Jaweed. "A Birdwatcher, a Dog and Amy Cooper. Another Viral Racial Incident in America. *Los Angeles Times,* May 26, 2020. Accessed June 8, 2020 at https://www.latimes.com/world-nation/story/2020-05-26/amy-cooper-george-floyd-ahmaud-arbury.
Lincoln, C. Eric. "The Racial Factor in the Shaping of Religion in America." In *African-American Religious Thought: An Anthology*. Edited by Cornel West and Eddie S. Glaude Jr., 156–86. Louisville: Westminster John Knox Press, 2003.
MacMullan, Terrance. *Habits of Whiteness*. Bloomington: Indiana University Press, 2009.
McGuire, Meredith. *Lived Religion: Faith and Practice in Everyday Life*. Oxford: Oxford University Press, 2008.
Meltzoff, Andrew. "The Roots of Social and Cognitive Development: Models of Man's Original Nature." In *Social Perception in Infants*. Edited by Tiffany M. Field and Nathan A. Fox, 1–30. Norwood, NJ: Ablex Publishing, 1985.
Ngo, Helen. *The Habits of Racism: A Phenomenology of Racism and Racialized Embodiment*. Lanham, MD: Lexington Books, 2012.
North, Anna. "Amy Cooper's 911 Call is Part of an All-Too-Familiar Pattern." *Vox*. May 26, 2020. Accessed at https://www.vox.com/2020/5/26/21270699/amy-cooper-franklin-templeton-christian-central-park.
Pilkington, Ed. "Black Americans Dying of COVID-19 at Three Times the Rate of White People." *The Guardian*. May 20, 2020. Accessed at https://www.theguardian.com/world/2020/may/20/black-americans-death-rate-covid-19-coronavirus.
Rowlands, Mark. *The New Science of the Mind: From Extended Mind to Embodied Phenomenology*. Cambridge, MA: MIT Press, 2010.
Shapiro, Lawrence, ed. *The Routledge Handbook of Embodied Cognition*. London: Routledge, 2014.

Sheets-Johnstone, Maxine. "Embodied Minds or Mindful Bodies? A Question of Fundamental, Inherently Inter-Related Aspects of Animation." *Subjectivity* 4 (2011): 451–66.

Smith, James K. A. *Imagining the Kingdom: How Worship Works*. Grand Rapids: Baker Academic, 2013.

Stoller, Paul. *Sensuous Scholarship*. Philadelphia: University of Pennsylvania Press, 1997.

Sullivan, Shannon. *Revealing Whiteness: The Unconscious Habits of Racial Privilege*. Bloomington: Indiana University Press, 2006.

Theresa of Avila, *Interior Castle*. Translated by E. Allison Peers. Mineola: Dover Publications, 2007.

Vandermaas-Peeler, Alex, Daniel Cox, Molly Fisch-Friedman, and Robert P. Jones. "One Nation, Divided, Under Trump: Findings from the 2017 American Values Survey." *PRRI*. Dec. 5, 2017. Accessed June 1, 2020 at https://www.prri.org/research/american-values-survey-2017/.

van der Kolk, Bessel A. *The Body Keeps the Score: Brain, Mind, and Body in the Healing of Trauma*. New York: Viking, 2014.

Vásquez, Manuel A. *More than Belief: A Materialist Theory of Religion*. Oxford: Oxford University Press, 2011.

Vera, Amir and Laura Ly. "White Woman Who Called Police on a Black Man Bird-Watching in Central Park has been Fired." *CNN*. May 26, 2020. Accessed at https://www.cnn.com/2020/05/26/us/central-park-video-dog-video-african-american-trnd/index.html.

Voorhees, Josh. "New Poll Finds That Hillary Supporters Are Pretty Racist Too." *Slate*. June 29, 2016. Accessed June 1, 2020 at https://slate.com/news-and-politics/2016/06/reuters-hillary-clinton-supporters-are-pretty-racist-too.html.

Yancy, George. *Black Bodies, White Gazes: The Continuing Significance of Race*. 2nd Edition. Lanham, MD: Rowman & Littlefield, 2017.

Yosso, Tara J. "Whose Culture Has Capital? A Critical Race Theory Discussion of Community Cultural Wealth." *Race, Ethnicity and Education* 8, no. 1 (March 2005): 69–91.

ONE
"The Talk"

The Transference of Black Body Memory

Autumn Redcross

I learned about "the talk" in a room full of public educators. Engaged in an exercise on responsible conversations about race, participants were asked to share aloud what they teach their children to do when stopped by the police. The respondents were divided by the line of color. In fact, only the Black participants had a ready answer. What they said often sounded like this: "Address the officer as 'Sir.' Do not look at the officer in the eye, as doing so may be regarded as a sign of disrespect. Keep your hands on the steering wheel where they can be seen. Ask permission before reaching for your identification, registration, or insurance information which might be stored in the glove compartment. Move slowly. And do not get out of the car."

"The talk," as it has come to be known, is one had between parents and their Black children. It is a conversation made popular with the notoriety of the ubiquitous public display of police harassment and violence against Black bodies. Not that such violence is new. A history of Africans in America follows a timeline fraught by violence and oppression. However, in this moment of social media fervor, police and self-deputized shootings of unarmed Black bodies have been given a wide platform and the consequences of being Black in America are now in public view. The talk is a warning intended to prevent undue harm. Thus, the talk described here is a list of directives on how to conduct oneself—that is, one's Black self—when pulled over by police.

Not limited to vehicular police confrontation, the talk takes on various scenarios and is reciprocal as well as ongoing, however. The talk manifests itself as a giving over or a sharing of Black body memory. Black body memory is an amalgamation of a phenomenological Black body, and the notion of body memory. Black body memory is what grounds the notion of the raced body. While popular belief considers race to be a social construct, there remains a *something* to Blackness that we cannot get beyond.

I do not suggest that Black people have a monolithic narrative; however, some common experiences are shared by raced bodies in racist social settings.[1] Black body memory enveloped by the talk is a demonstration of what is common. The talk imbues habituated understandings of race both through its process and goal. This conversation begs holders of the Black body to realize how they are seen and interpellated according to a world of others, to act accordingly, and to commit those actions to memory. With the talk as a rhetorical artifact that perpetuates Black body memory, in the following I will elaborate on what I mean by Black body memory, first by recourse to the phenomenological Black body as described by Frantz Fanon, Charles Johnson, and George Yancy, and second, with an account of body memory according to Edward Casey and Michael Fuchs. I offer Black body memory as a metaphor for the existential disposition of Black people in today's social economy in America. Hence, the talk emerges as a vehicle by which Black body memory is revealed and reproduced.

THE BLACK BODY

Phenomenology, generally speaking, seeks to arrive at truth and reality of the life-world, outside of a taken-for-granted, *natural attitude* of one's daily experiences. While empirically based natural sciences may consider the Black body only at the biological, genetic level, debating whether these anthropological markers provide scientific evidence of Blackness, phenomenology seeks meaning and understanding derived from the everyday in and with the world. As David Smith puts it, "Phenomenology inspects more closely what it sees in order to see better what it sees."[2] Moreover, "the essential task of phenomenology is to . . . uncover and restore to everyday light the true nature of our human world."[3] To that end, Husserlian phenomenology is an analysis of seeing more clearly what often goes unnoticed in the everyday.

Our world is impregnated with meanings and phenomenology is concerned with human meaning. Smith continues, "Human life and behaviors are social and communal in a profound sense."[4] Human behavior is inheritably intersubjective, yet experiences, consciousness and intended meanings of others are accessible and "out in the open before my eyes."[5]

Compared to the methodology of empirically based natural science, which is a secondary discipline, reality is grasped in and through our first-person experiencing of the world and others.[6] In achieving this, we are attentive to the structure of consciousness.

The structure of consciousness and experience in phenomenology is *bipolar*.[7] For phenomenology, "consciousness is not just one thing among other things in the world . . . but it is intending."[8] "A rule for phenomenology," as Johnson articulates, "is that there is never an object without a corresponding subject."[9] Moreover, "what is essential to all experience—the correlate of consciousness and its content, *noesis-noema*, or subject and object."[10] As Husserl is famous for stressing, consciousness is always conscious *of* something.

In this vein, perception is not a static mechanical concern with brute things of *fevered, naturalistic objectivity*.[11] Instead, phenomenology is concerned with our bodily *existence* in the world. For only in and through our lived/living bodies are we engaged with the world. One experiences the world through his or her body. Therefore, "our experience properly described must acknowledge that it presents itself as the experience of engaging directly with the world."[12] Moreover, the lived body of Merleau-Ponty emerges as that by which and from which all natural objects are experienced.

As one's most "basic mode of being in the world,"[13] the lived body is the "center from which everything else is observed."[14] Stewart and Mickunas write, "One can never view his lived-body as another object due to the fact that the lived-body is the necessary condition for any experience whatsoever."[15] In other words, we both have and are our bodies. "Everything in the world is seen from the perspective and situatedness of one's own body; the lived body thus constitutes an irreducible standpoint for any natural experience."[16] The body embodies consciousness. As such, the body and consciousness are unequivocally linked. Moreover, the body is the consciousness incarnate. We are bodily. Thus, through the phenomenological (and existentialist) tradition, one may take up questions of race and embodiment as points of philosophical interest, given its concern with "the concrete situated experience of human beings."[17]

In "A Phenomenology of the Black Body," Charles Johnson seeks to articulate his raced experience as one variation among others, and to depict "the ambiguity of his situation and describe the harrowing constraints" by which the Black body operates.[18] There are cultural assumptions which interrogate the Black body as symbolic. Western philosophy and literature traditionally overlook the diversity of experiences as articulated by Johnson, George Yancy, and other scholars. Within the discipline of philosophy, for example, as Yancy notes, "the white philosopher/author presumes to speak for all of 'us' without the slightest mention of his or her 'raced' identity."[19] As a result, Yancy writes, "the embodied self is bracketed and deemed irrelevant to theory, superfluous and cumbersome in one's search for the truth."[20] In this way, whiteness becomes a transcendental signifier; Blackness must *announce* its coming.

The Black body is a raced body. Theories on *racial formation* frame race as a "way of making people up" as well as a "process of 'othering.'"[21] Unintended consequences of race have positioned the Black body as the point of radix for interpreting racial experiences. As a raced body, the Black body is steeped in stereotypes and preconceived ideas rising from an *epidermal logic*. The complexion of Black people is just one anthropological marker which gave rise to the notion of race in the first place. Anthropological markers, including skin color, hair, and physical features, "have long been associated with the Negro."[22] Attention to such physical markers gave way to racial distinction, race thinking, and ultimately, racism. "Racism is the given, historically constituted and lying in wait for black consciousness, concealing the ethical dualism which has—over long centuries of Western cultural development—made white 'good' and black 'evil.'"[23] What began with legal, racial slavery, the legacy of anti-Black racism in America persists through this day. Moreover, the Black body has a distinct phenomenological presence which informs shared experiences.

The question persists: "What is to be understood by *Black suffering*?"[24] Martinique native Frantz Fanon became a psychiatrist working in response to a European ethnopsychiatrist's model, which at that time sought to understand the psychology of non-European people. Fanon looked at the effects of colonial racism as perpetrated during and following the time of the Algerian war. His writings surround the existential effects of colonialism to the point of the colonization of the Black body. For Fanon, a self-reflective brutal awareness of the reality of an economic and social disalienation of the Black body results from an "internalization or rather epidermalization" of inferiority.[25] Fanon develops a conviction that "what is called the Black soul is a construction by white folks."[26] Beginning with language, the Black body exists, in part, in a dimension of being-for-others. For example, as a colonized body made to take on a new language, Fanon explains that *"to speak* is to exist absolutely for the other."[27] Moreover, Fanon remarks, "Not only must the black man be black; he must be black in relation to the white man."[28] The lived experience of the Black person is one which not only involves a confrontation with oneself as a raced body but also determines how the Black body *compares* to the white other.

As a student of psychology in the 1970s, Charles Johnson hoped to "examine the Black male body as a cultural object and to inquire how it has been interpreted, manipulated, and given to us, particularly in popular culture."[29] Early in the essay, Johnson details how cultural assumptions, folklore, and myth lock Black people into their bodies.[30] His assertion highlights the notion of the constitution of the lived body as object.[31] Epidermalization is what objectifies the "Black-as-body"; it is how one is given to the world through his or her Black body. Citing Fanon, he writes, "My world is epidermalized, collapsed like a house of cards into the stained casement of my skin. My subjectivity is turned inside out like a shirtcuff. 'And so it is not I who make a meaning for myself, but it is the meaning that was already there, pre-existing, waiting for me,' much like a mugger at a boardwalk's end."[32]

Writing after Johnson, George Yancy notes that the lived experience as a Black man requires a consideration of more than merely his Blackness. Yancy writes that his Blackness precedes his coming. "Hence," Yancy writes, "my emergence upon the historical scene requires that I engage in a battle that is not only iconographic and semiotic but is also existential."[33] The meaning of the Black body cannot be determined merely by his internal reflection alone, for his Blackness has been taken captive, already named, by an aforementioned history. This precarious state informs his sense of agency: "The Black body has been historically marked, disciplined, and scripted and materially, psychologically, and morally invested in to ensure both white supremacy and the illusory construction of the white subject as a self-contained substance whose existence does not depend upon the construction of the Black qua 'inferior.'"[34] The Black body constitutes *a different* reality. As a raced body, Blackness helps to determine my identity. I am locked into my body, seen and treated according to my epidermalized situation. According to Yancy, "the Black body has been confiscated." He explains, "This confiscation occurred in the form of the past brutal enslavement of Black bodies, the cruel and sadistic lynching of Black bodies, the sexual molestation of Black bodies on Southern plantations, the literal breeding of Black bodies for white exploitation, and the unethical experimentation on Black bodies."[35] One could go on. In the historic timeline that provides evidence to how the Black body has been confiscated, Yancy mentions mass incarceration, the construction of sexuality, and quotidian interactions on the social level as well.

Phenomenological existentialism accounts for the experience of the body. Drawing on this tradition, Lewis Gordon writes, "The body can be understood in three dimensions: the body as one's perspective on the world. The other two are the body as seen by others, and the body's (consciousness) realization as it is seen by others."[36] Essentially, we are more than what we think of ourselves, for we are also deeply shaped by what others think about us. This takes on a unique character in the lived experience of the Black body. "The meaning of my Blackness is not intrinsic to my natural pigment, but has become a value-laden 'given,' an object presumed untouched and unmediated by various contingent discursive practices, history, time, and context."[37] I can neither move beyond nor ignore the perspective through and by which I am interwoven to the world.[38] Moreover, "one can never view his lived-body as another object due to the fact that the lived-body is the necessary condition for any experience whatsoever."[39] As George Yancy writes, "It is this existential standpoint, this past inheritance, that informs my sense of agency."[40] For the Black person in truth does not possess an ability to peel the mind from the body, nor the body from its Blackness, for one cannot talk about things outside of one's experience with them. Blackness cannot be overlooked. From the subjective body that we have, and we are, we experience the world and everything in it. The world that receives us objectifies us and defines the body in a way that we, ourselves, cannot. It is within this exclusive paradigm that we live, we recall, and we remember.

BODY MEMORY

With this phenomenological account of the Black body in mind, I now turn to a phenomenological account of body memory. Body memory is the never-forgetting *how-to* one manifests, as with riding a bike or driving a stick-shift vehicle, tapping the melody on a piano or typing on a keyboard. Body memory may reenact pain and trauma, or it may draw on episodes of pleasure and eroticism. Yet, body memory is not to be confused with memory of the body. Whereas memory of the body is a derivative act of self-reflection where we are "recollecting our body as in a given situation—representing ourselves as engaged bodily in that situation," body memory concerns "*being* in the situation and feeling it through our bodies."[41] As Casey writes, "Body memory alludes to memory that is intrinsic to the body, to its own ways of remembering: how we remember in and by and through the body. Memory *of* the body refers to those manifold manners whereby we remember the body as the accusative object of our awareness, whether in reminiscence or recognition, in reminding or recollection, or in still other ways."[42] However, a memory of the body arises as a chronotropic snapshot.[43] In counter distinction, body memory takes us to where we had been when the event first arose.

Casey's body memory is drawn from both the lived body of Merleau-Ponty, and the habit memory of Henri Bergson. Through the lived body, one is interwoven with the world. Body memory makes up "the connective tissue that ties us to the world in the first place."[44] As Casey explains, the lived body "anchors perception and thought, imagination and memory—*and habit*."[45] Habit results from repetition of an action. Further, habit is a product of familiarity. Body memory born of habit provokes the notion "of being 'on tap,' or being ready to activate: so ready that conscious deliberation or decision is not called for and would even act to inhibit the action to be undertaken."[46] Habitual memory presents a *holding-in-readiness*. Therefore, what is habitual is also a part of the subconscious and may be understood as preconsciousness.

Habitual memory of the lived body oversteps active recollection. Movement is instigated in a manner that is almost timeless. Through body memory, the past is given in and through the body. Citing Merleau-Ponty, Casey notes, "The body is the 'general medium' for habit and the past."[47] He argues there is "no habit or past without body; no body without habit or past."[48] In short, one's lived body serves as an anchor to "our temporal being." We are grounded by the past, which "subtends a hectic present and projected future" through our lived body; habit memory achieves a co-immance with the past, where "the past is fully immanent in the present."[49]

The lived body is marked with the characteristic of *sedimentation,* which is implied by the very nature of being in the world.[50] For Casey, sedimentation must not be understood as an accumulation of experiences, per se, but as an active precipitation of the past into the present, always in action. Sedimentation is a necessary complement to spontaneity and accounts for the capacity of acquiring worlds. The actualization of sedimentation works to "develop those patterns of behavior that identify us as a continuous person over time and make meaning possible in our lives."[51] Sedimentation works in tandem with the concept of habitualization, connoting passivity whereas one's animation is "locked-in formation."[52]

Casey's notion of "activity in passivity" is integral to habit memory as a means of effecting sedimentation. Yet the habitual ought not to be understood as a locking in of a routine or routinized behavior. Instead, the active, sedimented behavior is accomplished through an *active habituation.* Casey writes, "Habituation here takes its most concrete form in the body's inhabitation of the world, its active insertion into space and time."[53] The lived body inhabits space and time. Habituation involves a dialectic involving the body's enclosure in space and time and one's ability to navigate the same field. As Casey writes, "I, therefore 'belong to [space and time]' and that in turn 'my body combines with them and includes them."[54] For Casey, "Inhabiting taken as a paradigm of the bodily expression of habit memory, is at once 'wholly active and wholly passive,' with the world and *of* it. It is made possible by *sedimentation* even as it carries *sedimentation* itself to new depths."[55] The lived body actualizes as effectuation of active *sedimentation* while both in the world and of the world. Its representation of memory is bodily, as the lived body is the material by and through which what is past makes connection to the present, and what is present reaches for the future. Through my body, I belong to my past and anticipate future bodily behaviors and responses.[56]

Memory is also constructed and carried through by a living body. Habit provides a clue to the nature of the living body. Moreover, habitual activity of the body enforces habitual body memory.[57] Body memory is pivotal and presupposed.[58] Body memory constitutes the "central most concern in any adequate assessment of the range of remembering powers."[59] As such, body memory is a privileged point of view from which "other memorial points of view can be regarded and by which they can be illuminated."[60] Body memory underscores how remembering is continually at work in our daily experience, in how our body *knows* how to interact with and respond to various stimuli.

Thomas Fuchs has written on the notion of body memory with the use of the terms "embodied knowledge" and "embodied memory." Fuchs considers that an investigation of implicit memory is what has given embodied knowledge a larger stake in the field of knowing. Fuchs writes, "This kind of memory is formed in the course of the interaction of organism and environment."[61] Body memory becomes a form of implicit knowledge as one interacts with the world through and in one's own body.

Fuchs's approach to implicit memory illuminates the difference between knowing *how* and knowing *that*. Knowing how is acquired through direct interactions; however, knowing that is obtained in a less direct manner—"namely based in propositional language, for example through description or explanation."[62] He continues: "Recurring patterns of interaction are sedimented in the form of sensorimotor, but also affect-motor schemes. We may speak of an implicit "body memory" that underlies our habits and skills, connecting body and environment through cycles of perception and action. This embodied knowledge is actualized by suitable situations or by overarching volitional acts, without necessarily being made explicit."[63] Recall is therefore not necessary for the actualization of body memory. Embodied knowledge is a function of knowing which "may in principle not be completely converted into declarative or symbol-based knowledge."[64] Believing that "we always know more than we can tell," Fuchs taps into a notion of tacit knowledge.[65]

As Fuchs explains it, embodied knowledge/embodied memory proceeds out from a space of familiarity and everyday relation to the world. What becomes of us is a "skillfulness acquired [through] early infancy before the development of symbolically and verbally mediated knowledge." In one's early life stages, knowing *how* precedes knowing *that*. In this way, knowledge is embodied. Knowing is fundamentally prereflective. For Fuchs, perception and action are inherently connected through the medium of the body where the representational mind and the external world are linked. Embodied knowledge is a training based in implicit knowing how that cannot be reduced to a set of propositions.[66]

Implicit knowledge and embodied memory do not manifest as a property of the body. Instead, body memory is developing and in flux throughout one's lifetime. Without a need to remember, body memory results from the acquisition of practices and skills developed throughout one's lifetime. Body memory is represented through the medium of the lived body. Body memory resides in the unconscious, "not in the form of an explicit memory, but as a 'style of existence.'"[67] Body memory is manifested in "habits formed through repetition and practice," which then are activated of their own accord.[68]

There are two ways in which body memory is acquired. The first is by way of a synthesis of perception and movement with deliberate training. The second means of gaining body memory is in learning by doing with repeated practice like the first. However, the second way of gaining body memory is unintentional and free of deliberate training. Overall, body memory is based on a habitual structure of the lived body.[69] As Fuchs writes, "Indeed, the most fundamental skills which have disclosed the world for us and upon which our everyday practices are based have sedimented into our body memory" without our even knowing.[70] In other words, "most of what we have experienced and learned is not made accessible to us in retrospect but is reenacted through the practices of everyday life.[71] It is through the medium of the lived body that an entirety of nuances, behaviors, and skills are animated daily without the need of conscious recollection. "Body memory is thus the ensemble of all habits and capacities at our disposal."[72]

Fuchs summarizes body memory as "the totality of implicit dispositions of perception and behavior mediated by the body and sedimented in the course of earlier experiences."[73] As a "corporeal and intercorporeal unconsciousness," body memory is manifested through patterns of repeated behavior. "The unconscious of body memory is thus characterized by the absence of forgotten or repressed experiences, and at the same time by their corporeal and intercorporeal presence in the lived space and in the day-to-day life of a person."[74] Body memory is the paramount location for all remembering. Body memory supersedes a mental confinement that recognition, reminding, and reminiscing imply.[75] Events and images stored away among the mental recesses and capacity of my mind hide as impressions on the body as well. According to Casey, one's memory is intrinsic to the body; it is pivotal and presupposed. Body memory is the paramount location for all remembering and the conduit for all memory functions. Body memory is enduring and "comes home to us most vividly precisely when [other] memory fails us."[76] Put poetically, body memory is in one's bones. Moreover, there is "no memory without body memory."[77] As such, body memory grounds one's world.

BLACK BODY MEMORY

Black body memory is an amalgam of the phenomenological Black body and body memory. The lived body allows for a conception of the body, presupposing an empirical description of the body. The lived body constitutes one's perception of the world. I both have and am my body. Hence, a phenomenological Black body is a raced body, which emerges among others. As an object that anchors me to this world, everything I experience is had from the perspective of my body. The possibility of Black as body awaits to inform, and further determine, the world I experience. My identity informs my sense of agency. Body memory lives at the foreground of all remembering powers. Memory is constructed and carried through by a living body. Habit animates the living body. Its gait, its composure, its rituals are dependent upon body memory. Therefore, it is the habitual body that directs my actions. Such is Black body memory.

Compelled by the notion that the social construction of race is not a fully sufficient explanation to describe the state of race and racism in America today, this essay offers Black body memory as language to describe the phenomenological disposition of Black people in America. Black body memory provides an opening through which we can view and understand racial identity, particularly in response to those who cling to the hope of a postracial society. However, there remains a *stuckness* when it comes to the idea of race, which cannot easily be denied.

Black body memory serves as a rhetorical description for the ways in which race is sustained. It reveals the anthropological markers which were used to designate racial categories. Contemporary science has nearly called into question the legitimacy of racial assignments, and yet a postracial society eludes us. Race remains a major factor of identity. For Black people, our stories go with us. It's a story forged in slavery and wrought by oppression and violence. Black body memory is a metaphor for our stories.

We can speak of the weight of body memory with regard to its marginality, density and depth, and co-immanence of past and future. Regarding marginality, body memory is both peripheral and centrally significant. However, because our existence is painted by the terms of a constructed race, which has so influenced our embodiment, the Black body is subjected to and defined by the dispensation of others. Yet, it does its best when out of the forefront of the mind. Instead of latent and at rest, Black body memory is available to be called upon on command. With the pleasurable and imagined, Black body memory bears what is possible rather than actual. Concerning the traumatic, Black body memory regresses to afford the body respite from pain. With the habitual, Black body memory is "so deeply ingrained in our behavior as not to need explicit recalling."[78] Instead, repetition is an effortless function.

Density and depth reflect a "high specific gravity" of the memory otherwise ingrained. "It is as if the density of body memories, their rootedness in the heft, the thick palpability of the lived body, rendered them mute."[79] The Black body discloses the world to us in a certain way. As George Yancy writes, "The fact of the matter is that from the perspective of an oppressed and marginalized social position, Blacks do in fact possess a level of heightened sensitivity to recognizable and repeated occurrences that might very well slip beneath the radar of others."[80] Spanning the poles of density and depth at varying degrees "represents a mode of self-transcendence out of and into depths which the mind in contemplation or recollection can neither fathom nor abide."[81]

Regarding the co-immanence of past and present, there are two possibilities. Either the present is co-opted by the past, driven by the repetition that is in habitual memory, or the past exists to become the present. In either case, the two take up partnership in the moment. It can be argued that raced memories of my Black body are of a "bygone past, trapped in a Fanonian time loop, that America is different now, and that one's abundance of melanin is irrelevant."[82] However, progress does not negate current realities, or how the past still shapes the present. Rather than emerge as a focal point of intersection, "the co-immanence verges on an identity of the past and present."[83] These three aspects, marginality, density, and depth, along with co-immanence, draw together the functional effect of the body's weighted memory as Black.

These features are all critically important qualifiers to Casey's body memory, which work to bring palpable language of the transference of body memory from mother to son. Though Casey's marginality speaks about the periphery, his wider explanation, however, supports that body memory is central to the bodily experience. Marginality, rather, becomes a misnomer and the Black body is objectified by the gaze of the other and a symbol of *negrophobia*. Density and depth afford weight to the reflection of greater signs and symbols surrounding intentions, circumstances, and an event's unfolding. Finally, the notion of co-imminence of past and present links the value of previous experience as valuable for the present and even for future outcomes. It's nothing new. I embody these experiences as embodied knowledge and prepare to share with others with whom I share a Black body like mine.

The Black body is the phenomenological juxtaposition which I claim, and from which I interact with the world. Black body memory is that which is found in the members of the body. It is orienting, habituated, effortless, performative, and necessary for the successful navigation of the world. It is this Black body memory that is harkened by the talk with my son. As a Black mother of Black sons, this historical moment is one marked by perpetual threat and fear. In response, I caution my sons with words of remembrance of what they are in their bodies, and what it may mean for others. The talk is one way in which I am compelled to encourage their behavior. Just as the body is said to be consciousness incarnate, language is the manifestation of thoughts. The talk becomes a prayer for my sons to do what is best.

THE TALK AND ITS CONSTITUENTS

There's a saying that death passes around your bed twice when you're in labor. My mother shared this adage with me. The logic in the narrative hints at the nature of the gravity of actual life in the balance that giving birth involves. Death, as a ghost, circles the bed, first taunting to take the mother and a second time for the soul of the baby. Babies are born every day with no consequence; however, during delivery sometimes infants—and sometimes mothers—are lost. My first living birth was a girl.

Disappointed as I was by what I perceived as a misstep in ideal birth order, my mother encouraged me, "You'll be glad that you had a girl first." And I am. Two years later, I got my boy. Shortly after that, my third was born, another male. Three babies! I count my lucky stars. As if by prophecy, my mother was right about having my girl first, because of how well she takes care of her brothers. Truly maternal, she looks out for us all. However, I cannot help but reflect on the act of giving birth—and birth to Black boys further augments the illustration of a two-fold brush with death.

Contorted during the pains of the labor and bearing down hard to deliver, I give birth to this being—this image of God, this child of my own body's making. However, flesh of my flesh, this child is not simply a baby, he is a Black baby. His epidermal encasing precedes his being. He can never experience otherwise. Because our identity is dictated by the world of others, we are left to navigate from this unyielding cast.

For my sons, the implications of their Black bodies were not self-evident. However, as bodily beings with language, we are rhetorically defined; self-identity comes from others. These others carry with them generational memories and cultural wisdom in their bodies that objectify our own. We are left to defend our lifeline against what has become commonsensical. The death passing around the bed twice is further exacerbated to symbolize death as a dehumanizing of the Black body; Blackness augments its potentiality. The second passing could be in the loss of a naïve hope of what a mother of a privileged race could afford.

Fear of the symbolic Black body emerges from a precarious history. Blackness "is a signifier of negative values grounded within a racist social and historical matrix that predates" its existential emergence.[84] Originally forced into racial slavery, the Black body's traversing through the birth of America was one of inferiority and oppression. As history records, the amendments to the Constitution and later Civil Rights legislation freed the Black body to a state of equality within the law—at least on paper. Yet, societal memory has not been so forgiving. Black people continue to suffer discrimination, racism, and violence for reasons acquainted with their raced body. It is therefore within this milieu where the memory of the peculiar situatedness of the Black body emerges. I recall my eldest son's early confrontations with race.

He was the only Black boy in the sweet little preschool in the suburbs where we lived. He came home after a day of learning and play to tell me that his friend, Colin, had called his locs (hair) "black snakes." I was immediately taken aback. I told my son that his hair was not at all like black snakes. He was no Medusa. His hair was beautiful. It was locked and taking on the form similar to the double-helix strand of DNA. It was natural—natural and black. My response was of one who feared my body's—and his body's—shaming. In that comment, years of struggle of Black people to reach stature and respect in this American society was being threatened. Thirty-five million Black bodies were displaced from their homeland in Africa for the purposes of enslaved labor. Four million Black bodies were released from racial slavery in America upon the close of the Civil War, with the Fourteenth Amendment promising citizenship and the Fifteenth promising Black men participation in the democratic process.

The Civil Rights Act demanded this nation to make available for Black bodies the same freedoms and rights that were had by others. Our parents and grandparents grew up with a much harsher reality of disenfranchisement surrounding an epidermal logic. Our hair, one telling product of our ethnicity, was being challenged—and by the words of a blonde four-year-old. But my son thought the image of "black snakes" was cool. At age four, he had no idea of its harsh and racial potentiality, the image held with his friend as its messenger. Despite the indications that even babies show racial preferences, in my son's four-year-old mind, he liked the correlation. It captured his imagination.

During my son's elementary school years, the class was tasked with memorizing historical characters. There were wooden casts of famous figures with nose and hand cut-outs for the small students to step behind and press their noses and hands through. The class had to guess who the historic figures were, and who was hiding behind them. My son did not have a chance to be so mysterious. The only Black boy in his class, not to mention the entire school, in that moment his nose peered through the wooden cutout, he felt the consequence of being Black. Easily visible and in complete contrast to all the figures represented, my son's dark skin gave him away. The distinguishing mark of the Black body alone makes it precariously identifiable. Yet our identity is not our own making. Instead, we rely on the will of others to determine what our body is and therefore, who we are.

It is not intrinsically understood to perceive bodily differences on account of how we will be viewed and treated. The Black body encountered in the mirror is different from that subjected to the gaze of others. Stereotypes are folklore often made up under the gaze of the other. My son recounts the experience of being stereotyped as a confirmation to his Blackness.

As part of a musical production summer camp, my son met with the largely white group every day of the early summer through the production of the final shows. One afternoon during their break, my son was walking through the halls of the private building where the camp met. He encountered the aroma of fried chicken. Though he could see no one, he stopped in his tracks. "I smell fried chicken," he announced loudly. An individual emerged from their hiding place and said, while laughing, "I didn't think you were really Black. But now it's confirmed! I was hiding because I did not want to share my food. But since you smelled me out, you may have some of my fried chicken! You're definitely Black." I have never made fried chicken at home. In fact, we were vegetarian, and are now vegan. Yet my son's Facebook page served to let the world know of his newly discovered, raced status: "Blackness confirmed," he posted.

What it means for my son to find his Blackness confirmed by others, is that his Black body takes on the form of something similar to myth or superhero legend. Instead of realizing the vulnerability that his Black body succumbs to, he is led to think instead that his Black body yields affirmation to a larger-than-life, stereotypical image painted by the others who define us. He is a peacock in all his glory; he is negrophied—in a good way. The symbol of the Black body when interrogated discloses "a racial experience wrought mythically" which "must be carefully unpacked if we wish to wrench self-understanding from it."[85]

Their perception is disorienting for my son. My son wears the painted veil of a Black body as a shield of protection rather than as a cloak of mystery draping him in vulnerability. Blackness confirmed by others distracts him from "turning to the body as radix for interpreting racial experience."[86] He thus is given over to the objectifying mythical realities of others. He is that guy. He is superman. A mother knows her son.

Later in his high school years, I knew that he was not sleeping through the night. What I did not know was that he was hopping on his bike at 1:00 am, 2:00 am, or 3:00 am and going for a ride. When I confronted him, he tried to negate my concerns saying, "Mom, I'm a Black guy with dread locs. No one is going to mess with me!" "No one may, but the police might," I would respond. The Black body can be stopped, detained, harassed, maimed, and unduly subjected to various violence for doing in your body what is normal. I forbade my son to go out in the middle of the night to ride his bike for lack of sleepiness.

In this historical moment, the young, Black male's life is subject to a perpetual threat of violence. Not that there has been a lull of both legal and unlawful violence against Blacks. Rather, the ubiquitous use of cell phones and social media have brought more awareness to the problem. Though not new, what is perpetually seen is of great concern. Similar to the indiscriminate whippings and killings of the enslaved; the lynching of the free Black bodies between the World Wars; the hosing, gas bombings, and use of attack dogs during the modern Civil Rights era; up through the beating of Rodney King and many more recent events, perpetrators have proven to be armed public servants, charged to serve and protect. The self-deputized and the police are the scary ones.

Giving birth to Black sons extends my responsibilities in motherhood into another dimension; it is a skewed context. It echoes the sentiment of

W. E. B. Du Bois in his term, "double-consciousness," which acknowledges the dualism of living in America with the veil of Blackness. Likewise, Black motherhood in America magnifies the notions denoted in critical race theory, largely enveloped through the teachings of Derek Bell, which bring attention to race biases in the law.

The Black mother in me whispers *Sankofa*, (the West African Adrinka symbol of a bird letting an egg fall from its beak), meaning, "to go back and get it . . . *lest we forget."* I insist that my Black children not deny from where they have come. I urge them to use that past to build on their future. But in order for this to be a possibility, they must know their past. Their past is my past and the past of those who have come before me. I reach into my memories of the past and hand them over as a prized and pleasing gift. What is not only in my mind is found stored in my body—it is in my bones. As with every mother, we do our best with what we have. In my case, my best includes an intentional fracture of their original consciousness. Thus, I have the talk.

Not limited to vehicular police confrontation, but as ongoing and reciprocal, the talk emerges as a (pre)cautionary tale to our youth to understand their raced disposition in America. Ta-Nehisi Coates dedicates an entire book, *Between the World and Me*, as a letter to his son concerning what it is like to inhabit a Black body. His articulation struggles with the idea that despite a false reality that race exists, one must discern how to live with, and "honestly reckon" with a racist history.[87] Coates esteems America's position as Empire as something built on the ideas of race, and that the race idea has subjected the Black body to exploitation through slavery and segregation and is today threatened to be locked up and or murdered "out of all proportion."

He begins, "Last Sunday the host of a popular news show asked me what it meant to lose my body."[88] Coates then reflects on the history of America and the notion of personhood as something not obtained by those Black bodies living prior to 1863 as the Gettysburg Address delivered by then (Republican) President Abraham Lincoln.[89] Coates then reels back further in history to the Middle Passage and a discussion of an "othering" that occurred to justify that people were made to be enslaved. "But race is the child of racism, not the father,"[90] the father says to his Black son.

For Coates, to talk about hope (in response to the talk show host) is to fail. Coates is resolved not to hope for his son, but rather, through a telling of his own stories, to inform his son how to live—through his body—amidst it all. To his son, Coates issues truth. Coates shares "that this is your country, that this is your world, that this is your body, and you must find some way to live within it all."[91] The title of his book, Coates's letter to his son, is taken from the words from James Baldwin's *The Fire Next Time*.

Baldwin's *The Fire Next Time* is comprised of two essays. The first is written to his nephew. Having lived long enough and having gained a "strange perspective on time and human pain and effort,"[92] he writes this letter in the first person, "to try to tell [his nephew] about how to handle [his countrymen], for most of them do not yet really know that [his nephew] exists."[93] Baldwin accuses his countrymen "for which neither I nor time nor history will ever forgive them, that they have destroyed and are destroying hundreds of thousands of lives and do not know it and do not want to know it."[94]

Baldwin's countrymen at that time were not only those of his nephew in the 1950s, but also ours in the twenty-first century as well. All have inherited habits of racism into which we have been born. Living among them, Baldwin advises his nephew that he should proceed in life with an attitude of love. Love will "force our brothers to see themselves as they are, to cease fleeing from reality and begin to change it."[95] The crimes of even the innocent among these countrymen manifest an inability to acknowledge their sins that oppress Black people. Baldwin continues, "For this is your home, my friend, do not be driven from it; great men have done great things here, and will again, and we can make America what America must become."[96] Baldwin's "talk" advises his nephew about what he needs to understand. His words reproduce a reality of the past social conditions that have occurred, and now precede the Black body's coming.

Kelly Brown Douglas revisits the writings of Baldwin, describing them as a process of "negotiating the reality of being Black and male in a world where Blackness was not valued."[97] Douglas sought insight from Baldwin's wisdom "in order to equip her son to be a proud and healthy Black man in America," despite the notion that his body is not valued nor cherished among the tirade of violence against the young Black body.[98] She describes the talk as an act to "raise our Black sons to be aware of their surroundings and to know how they are being perceived—whether they are shopping in a store or walking down the street with a group of friends, or even wearing a hoodie over their heads."[99]

Recalling the deaths of Trayvon Martin and Jordan Davis, Douglas contends that "none of our children deserve to be collateral damage," as if their young Black bodies are in the middle of war.[100] But as they are a battleground, we instinctively seek to speak a fortress to surround them. Repeating the same words, she had spoken to her son before, she says, "I am your mother, and like Trayvon [Martin] and Jordan [Davis]'s mother I will defend you until my death. But I don't want to have to defend you in death. So, be safe because the world is not safe for a Black male body."[101] For even in death Trayvon and Jordan were criminalized while being victims of murder. Their young Black bodies were put on trial, leading to greater grief and despair.

It is a painful position to rebuke a child for their naïve assumptions of fairness and freedom. Yet parents like me still believe the talk to be the clear and necessary course of action. For what other way can we keep our children well? Even Black enslaved parents who had no rights and often owned nothing—neither their bodies nor their own offspring—wanted survival, protection, and a peaceful existence for their children.[102] Sanders-Lawson and Lawson write, "Accordingly, [the enslaved] knew that children must be taught to believe that they can succeed in their chosen life plan if they developed their abilities. And yet, they knew that their children must be aware that race and racism can impact their life-chances."[103] That need continues: "Nearly one hundred and fifty years after slavery, Black parents must still teach their children to believe in their own abilities, but at the same time must acknowledge that, in the United States, ability often is not enough. The specter of racism in the lived experience of Black children still presents problems for Black parents. This is and has always been the dilemma of Black parenting."[104]

The moral dilemma presented in the talk is the desire not to impress fear onto my Black children to the point that it damages their self-esteem, but at the same time to acknowledge the reality of the legacy their body holds.[105]

The history of raising Black children in the United States has consistently presented Black parents with a moral dilemma. The elders of my family recount the days when to look a white man in the eye was criminal. Their Black bodies had to move into the street to let a white person past. For, not doing so one could be arrested or worse, they said. They carried themselves appropriately—eyes cast down. "Hold your head up high," says grandma Alma because she knows a time when her father, her husband, her children, even herself could not. People say this was a long time ago, but no, it's here in my memory, my Black body memory.

I become a broken record to my children. I walk into their room, interrupting their lives. The younger one was not yet driving age. However, my older son had his permit. "If you are ever stopped by the police, you have to be careful," I begin. The younger one looks wide-eyed. The elder takes my words in stride. I am not so sure that he's convinced. I remember him saying, "When they see the way I'm dressed, and when I begin to speak, they won't treat me badly." Now, I'm the one who's not convinced. I respond, "First of all, it doesn't matter what you wear, or how you talk, son. And second, you might not get that far." We have to make them aware that other people exhibit a "tendency to see you first as 'here comes a black man.'"[106] The perception of the world weighs on the whole of our being, and so we teach our Black children how to handle *other people's* problems."[107] Other people's racism can quickly become our worst nightmare.

In the formative years during my son's engagement with me and with the talk, we grieve those who have died at the hands of uniformed police officers who had sworn an oath to protect and serve. The long list includes, but is not limited to, Tarika Wilson who died holding her fourteen-month-old son—who was also shot, but survived—Oscar Grant III who was shot while prostrate with his hands cuffed behind his back, and Eric Garner wrestled to the ground in a choke hold while pleading "I can't breathe" to the police who sequestered him for selling cigarettes. It includes Renisha McBride who was shot to death for seeking help; John Crawford, shot in the aisle of a department store while he shopped; and twelve-year-old Tamir Rice who was shot and killed while playing in a park. There's also Walter Scott, shot in the back five times after a police stop for a nonfunctioning brake light; Freddie Gray, who slipped into a coma and died after he sustained injury to his spinal cord in a police van after they found that he carried a knife; and Sandra Bland, whose death in jail had been ruled a suicide (while the police withheld video evidence of her arrest); Philando Castile, who notified the officer he was a registered gun owner but was still shot and killed in his car while his girlfriend and four-year-old daughter looked on; Omarian Banks, who was killed after knocking on the wrong door at the apartment complex he shared with his girlfriend; Stephon Clark, who was shot in his grandmother's back yard when his cell phone was mistaken for a gun; and the seventeen-year-old Antwon Rose II, who was shot in the back and killed, while unarmed, after fleeing a vehicle stopped by the police.

The talk is a pleading that my Black children consider and know themselves as raced Black bodies. This orientation is gleaned from the view of the other whom throughout history incites whatever proclivity that epidermal logic may entail. Identity is subject to the other; it is interpellated. Were it not for systemic racism, which has coded the current social order, reality might be different. The critical race studies of Du Bois and Bell would long be deemed irrelevant as would phenomenological accounts of the Black body. However, as long as such undue harm continues to occur to our Black bodies, the narrative remains. The story is one of the Black body. What happens when a mother like me is determined to corrupt her sons with a memory so haunting is an act of transference of Black body memory.

In the course of my writing and editing this essay, my son was pulled over for having an expired sticker on his license plate. It was after midnight. Although his vehicle was registered and in order, six officers in three police cars surrounded his car. He was alone. As if to protect me from my own worry and fear, my son waited several days before he told me. "Were you polite?" I asked. "Yes" was his answer. "Did you keep your hands where they could be seen," I asked. "Yes, mom," he responded. Did you ask permission to reach for your insurance card and registration?" Again, it was yes. But he was aggravated. "I know what to do when I'm stopped," he insisted. His physical response had become habitual and ingrained in his body memory. The procedure had overtaken his recall. Ironically, my son no longer remembers that he had been told those idiosyncrasies by me during our talk. They have ingrained themselves into his body.

CONCLUSION

The Black body as an entity of racial construction contends with the mysteriousness afforded by its maker and is confirmed by others. Downgraded by some from relecting the image of God, Blackness and the social construction of race was the result of pseudo-scientific inquiry to support belief systems of the inferiority of peoples of African descent. Still race matters. Although the smartest people can see holes in the theory that seeks to separate humanity, there are both myths and truths in developed cultures, motions, and memories within Black lives. And they cannot be easily separated.

It is our bodies that define us and account for the lives that we will experience. We are disclosed to the world in a certain way through our bodies. This lived body that is Black carries with it a symbolic meaning and memory. Recall and reenactment of the past may well be cause for undue repetition, but in this historical moment, it is also cause for protection. We live in a "larger epistemic, ontological—and thoroughly racist — semiotic field in which the Black male is criminalized before his appearing."[108] With the amount of violence enacted in the Black community and particularly against its male members, many Black parents have independently, and in unison, developed a tradition of having a "talk" with our children. As the body is an incarnation of consciousness, speech is an incarnation of thought, thereby making speech an expression of the body and body memory. The talk accounts for a particular expression of Black body memory.

NOTES

1. As Harvey Young puts it, "Not that all Black people have the same experience; ... rather ... a remarkable similarity, a repetition with a difference, exists among embodied Black experiences" (Young, *Embodying Black Experience*, 5).
2. Smith, *Born to See*, 6.
3. Ibid., 11.
4. Ibid., 10.
5. Ibid., 6.
6. Ibid., 6.
7. Ibid., 10.
8. Ibid., 10.
9. Johnson, "A Phenomenology of the Black Body," 600.
10. Ibid., 600.
11. Smith, *Born to See*, 8.
12. Ibid., 19.
13. Steward and Mickunas, *Exploring Phenomenology*, 65.

14. Ibid., 97.
15. Ibid., 97.
16. Ibid., 65.
17. Johnson, "A Phenomenology of the Black Body," 600.
18. Ibid., 599.
19. Yancy, "Whiteness and the Return of the Black Body," 215.
20. Ibid., 215.
21. Omi and Winant, *Racial Formation in the United States*, 105.
22. Du Bois, "The Conservation of Races," 53.
23. Johnson, "A Phenomenology of the Black Body," 600.
24. Gordon, "Introduction," 1.
25. Fanon, *Black Skin, White Masks*, xv.
26. Ibid., 1.
27. Ibid., 1; my emphasis.
28. Fanon, "The Fact of Blackness," 257.
29. Johnson, "A Phenomenology of the Black Body," 611.
30. Ibid., 599.
31. Ibid., 604.
32. Ibid., 606.
33. Yancy, *Black Bodies, White Gazes*, 17.
34. Ibid., 17.
35. Ibid., 17–18.
36. Gordon, *Existentia Africana*, 120.
37. Yancy, *Black Bodies, White Gazes*, 19.
38. Gordon, *Existentia Africana*, 120.
39. Ibid., 120.
40. Yancy, *Black Bodies, White Gazes*, 17.
41. Casey, *Remembering*, 147.
42. Ibid., 147.
43. Bakhtin, *Speech Genres and Other Late Essays*, 42.
44. Casey, *Remembering*, 149.
45. Casey, "Habitual Body and Memory in Merleau-Ponty," 44.
46. Casey, *Remembering*, 143.
47. Casey, "Habitual Body and Memory in Merleau-Ponty," 44.
48. Ibid., 44.
49. Ibid., 44, 45.
50. Ibid., 44.
51. Ibid., 44–45.
52. Ibid., 45.
53. Ibid., 45.
54. Casey, "Habitual Body and Memory in Merleau-Ponty," 45.
55. Ibid., 45.
56. Ibid., 50.
57. Ibid., 51.
58. Casey, *Remembering*, 146.
59. Ibid., 147.
60. Ibid., 147.
61. Fuchs, "Embodied Knowledge—Embodied Memory," 215.
62. Ibid., 215.
63. Ibid., 215.
64. Ibid., 216.
65. Polanyi, *The Tacit Dimension*.
66. Ibid., 218.
67. Fuchs, "Body Memory and the Unconscious," 86.
68. Fuchs, "Embodied Knowledge—Embodied Memory," 221.
69. Fuchs, "The Phenomenology of Body Memory," 9.

70. Fuchs, "Embodied Knowledge—Embodied Memory," 222.
71. Fuchs, *Collective Body Memories*, 335.
72. Ibid., 335.
73. Fuchs, "Body Memory and the Unconscious," 86.
74. Ibid., 86.
75. Casey, "Habitual Body and Memory in Merleau-Ponty," 147.
76. Ibid., 147.
77. Casey, *Remembering*, 148.
78. Ibid., 163.
79. Ibid., 165.
80. Yancy, *Black Bodies, White Gazes*, 6.
81. Casey, *Remembering*, 167.
82. Yancy, *Black Bodies, White Gazes*, 9.
83. Casey, *Remembering*, 168.
84. Johnson, "A Phenomenology of the Black Body," 600.
85. Ibid., 600.
86. Ibid., 600.
87. Coates, *Between the World and Me*, 7.
88. Ibid., 5.
89. Ibid., 6.
90. Ibid., 7.
91. Ibid., 11–12.
92. Baldwin, *The Fire Next Time*, 4.
93. Ibid., 6.
94. Ibid., 5.
95. Ibid., 7.
96. Ibid., 7.
97. Douglas, *Stand Your Ground*, 45.
98. Ibid., xi.
99. Ibid., xi.
100. Ibid., 89.
101. Ibid., 89.
102. Sanders-Lawson and Lawson, "Trayvon Martin, Racism, and the Dilemma of the African American Parent," 184.
103. Ibid., 184.
104. Ibid., 184.
105. Ibid., 184.
106. Lewis, "A Mother's Pain," 156.
107. Ibid., 156.
108. Golden, "Two Forms of Transcendence," 74.

BIBLIOGRAPHY

Bakhtin, M. M. *Speech Genres and Other Late Essays*. 2nd Edition. Edited by Caryl Emerson and Michael Holquist. Translated by Vern W. McGee. Austin: University of Texas Press, 1986.

Baldwin, James. *The Fire Next Time*. Reissue Edition. New York: Vintage, 1992.

Casey, Edward S. "Habitual Body and Memory in Merleau-Ponty." In *Phenomenology and the Human Sciences*. Edited by J. N. Mohanty, 39–57. Dordrecht, Netherlands: Springer, 1985.

———. *Remembering: A Phenomenological Study*. Second Edition. Bloomington: Indiana University Press, 2000.

Coates, Ta-Nehisi. *Between the World and Me*. New York: Spiegel & Grau, 2015.

Douglas, Kelly Brown. *Stand Your Ground: Black Bodies and the Justice of God*. Maryknoll, NY: Orbis, 2015.

Du Bois, W. E. B. "The Conservation of Races." In *The Problem of the Color Line at the Turn of the Twentieth Century: The Essential Early Essays*. Edited by Nahum Dimitri Chandler, 51–67. New York: Fordham University Press, 2015.

———. *The Souls of Black Folk*. CreateSpace Independent Publishing Platform, 2017.

Fanon, Frantz. *Black Skin, White Masks*. Translated by Richard Philcox. New York : Grove Press, 2008.

———. "The Fact of Blackness." In *Theories of Race and Racism: A Reader*. Edited by Les Back and John Solomos, 326–36. New York: Routledge, 2000.

Fuchs, Thomas. "Body Memory and the Unconscious." In *Founding Psychoanalysis Phenomenologically*. Edited by Dieter Lohmar and Jagna Brudzinska, 69–82. Dordrecht, Netherlands: Springer, 2012.

———. "Collective Body Memories." In *Embodiment, Enaction, and Culture: Investigating the Constitution of the Shared World*. Edited by Christoph Durt, Thomas Fuchs, and Christian Tewes, 333–52. Cambridge: MIT Press, 2018.

———. "Embodied Knowledge—Embodied Memory." In *Analytic and Continental Philosophy: Methods and Perspectives*. Edited by Sonja Rinofner-Kreidl and Harald A. Wiltsche, 215–30. Berlin, Boston: De Gruyter, 2016.

———. "The Phenomenology of Body Memory." In *Advances in Consciousness Research*. Edited by Sabine C. Koch, Thomas Fuchs, Michela Summa, and Cornelia Müller, 9–22. Amsterdam: John Benjamins Publishing Company, 2012.

Golden, Timothy Joseph. "Two Forms of Transcendence: Justice and the Problem of Knowledge." In *Pursuing Trayvon Martin: Historical Contexts and Contemporary Manifestations of Racial Dynamics*. Edited by George Yancy and Janine Jones, 73–84. Lanham, MD: Lexington Books, 2013.

Gordon, Lewis. *Existentia Africana: Understanding Africana Existential Thought*. New York: Routledge, 2000.

———. "Introduction: Black Existential Philosophy," In *Existence in Black: An Anthology of Black Existential Philosophy*. Edited by Lewis R. Gordon, 1–10. New York: Routledge, 1996.

Johnson, Charles. *I Call Myself an Artist*. Edited by Rudolph P. Byrd. Bloomington: Indiana University Press, 1999.

———. "A Phenomenology of the Black Body." *Michigan Quarterly Review* 32, no. 4 (1981): 599–614.

Lewis, Tracey McCants. "A Mother's Pain: The Toxicity of the Systemic Disease of Devaluation Transferred from the Black Mother to the Black Male Child. In *Pursuing Trayvon Martin: Historical Contexts and Contemporary Manifestations of Racial Dynamics*. Edited by George Yancy and Janine Jones, 155–72. Lanham, MD: Lexington Books, 2013.

Merleau-Ponty, Maurice. *Phenomenology of Perception*. Translated by Donald Landes. New York: Routledge, 2013.

Omi, Michael and Howard Winant. *Racial Formation in the United States*. New York: Routledge, 2015.

Polanyi, Michael. *The Tacit Dimension*. Chicago: University of Chicago Press, 2009.

Smith, David L. *Born to See, Bound to Behold: The History of the Simon Silverman Phenomenology Center*. Pittsburgh: Simon Silverman Center, 2007.

Stewart, David and Algis Mickunas. *Exploring Phenomenology: A Guide To The Field and Its Literature*. 2nd Edition. Athens: Ohio University Press, 1990.

Wright, Regina Sims. "A Letter to CJ." In *Our Black Sons Matter: Mothers Talk about Fears, Sorrows, and Hopes*. Edited by George Yancy, Maria del Guadalupe Davidson, and Susan Hadley, 163–66. Lanham, MD: Rowman & Littlefield, 2016.

Yancy, George. *Black Bodies, White Gazes: The Continued Significance of Race*. Second edition. Lanham, MD: Rowman & Littlefield, 2016.

———. "Trayvon Martin: When Effortless Grace is Sacrificed on the Altar of the Image." In *Pursuing Trayvon Martin: Historical Contexts and Contemporary Manifestations of Racial Dynamics*. Edited by George Yancy and Janine Jones, 237–50. Lanham, MD: Lexington Books, 2013.

———. "Whiteness and the Return of the Black Body." *The Journal of Speculative Philosophy* 19, no. 4 (2005): 215–41.
Young, Harvey. *Embodying Black Experience: Stillness, Critical Memory, and the Black Body.* Ann Arbor: University of Michigan Press, 2010.

TWO

Searching for Romance in the Age of Trumpism

The Impact of Race and Political Ideology in Partner Preferences among Ethno-Racial Minorities

Sarah Adeyinka-Skold

In the United States, individuals' ethno-racial background influences their life experience, their life opportunities and outcomes, and their practices that they utilize to overcome the consequences of systemic racism and racial abuse. Numerous studies additionally show that ethno-racial background influences the romantic partner search, variation in intimate romantic relationship formation, and who partners with whom.[1] In this chapter I will analyze how experiences of racial/ethnic marginalization and being an ethno-racial minority informs the partner preferences of heterosexual Asian, Black, and Latina women. Specifically, I argue that their desires for and selection of partners who are also ethno-racial minorities and who embrace a liberal political ideology reveal how race and racism shape their intersubjective encounters as they seek a romantic partner. This is significant given that intimate romantic relationships are a crucial part of the human experience.[2]

This exploration of how experiences of race and racism inform partner preferences among women of color is important for three reasons. First, ethno-racial homogamy[3] and political ideology homophily[4] are observed in intimate romantic relationships. However, there has been little examination about what motivates individuals' desires for and selection of partners who are similar to them in these ways. Family formation scholarship also rarely explores how living in a racially stratified society informs the decision to partner with people who share the same ethno-racial background and political ideologies as oneself.[5] I maintain that examining these questions can demonstrate how partnering along ethno-racial lines and political ideologies are strategies among ethno-racial minorities for surviving, thriving, and safeguarding their humanity, as it is often under threat within a system of racial oppression. These actions are necessary because the consequences of the social construction of race are real.[6] They have concrete and practical implications for how individuals and entire communities make important life decisions, including choosing romantic partners.

Second, with the rise of the Tea Party and the 2016 election of now former President Donald Trump, appeals to white nationalism and other racist ideologies have become mainstay, and even applauded, aspects of conservative political ideology. With Trump's presidency, white nationalism enjoyed the kind of positive attention from the executive branch that has been absent since the beginning of the Civil Rights Era.[7] Trump's election actually amplified racism as a tenet of conservative ideology,[8] including a rise of anti-Black and anti-immigrant rhetoric.[9] There is a palpable recognition among ethno-racial minorities that race and racism remain not only a significant aspect of their lived experiences, but that under Trumpism they may have even greater consequences for their outcomes and life opportunities in the future.

Lastly, nearing the end of Trump's presidency, racial abuse against ethno-racial minorities from the former president, police and extrajudicial killings of unarmed Black people such as Breonna Taylor, Ahmaud Arbery, George Floyd, and Rayshard Brooks; the global pandemic of COVID-19 that disproportionately killed Black and Latino people; and national and global protests decrying these events, characterized the realities of Black and Brown people under this administration. Given this political climate, what does it mean for women of color to select partners who share the same ethno-racial background and/or political ideology? And what does it reveal about the embodied significance of race?

RACIAL/ETHNIC HOMOGAMY

Most heterosexual marriages in the United States are ethno-racially homogamous. That is, the majority of marriage partners share the same ethno-racial background.[10] In 2016, 83 percent of newlyweds married someone of the same racial/ethnic background as themselves. Among those who had been married for more than one year, 90 percent of those marriages were ethno-racially homogamous.[11] This persistence of ethno-racial homogamy in intimate romantic relationships is despite the increase in and acceptance of interracial marriage since anti-miscegenation laws became illegal with the Supreme Court ruling in *Loving vs. Virginia* (1967). Data also shows that even before getting married, heterosexual men and women, regardless of ethno-racial background, desire and overwhelmingly select romantic partners of the same race and/or ethnicity as themselves.[12] Research on intimate romantic relationships provides three compelling explanations for the persistence for the desire and selection of ethno-racial homogamy in heterosexual romantic relationships. Marriage market explanations maintain that individuals search for romantic partners within a local marriage market. Marriage markets can be examined at the neighborhood level as measured by census tracts;[13] metropolitan areas;[14] or at the level of organizations such as churches, schools, or workplaces. Marriage market proponents argue that marriage markets structure opportunities for individuals to meet and interact with other potential partners. Therefore, the demographic composition of local marriage markets can constrain or expand individuals' chances to meet people who match their partner preferences. Given that most local marriage markets are shaped by a long legacy of de jure and de facto segregation,[15] marriage markets may then facilitate ethno-racial homogamy in intimate romantic relationships. While marriage market explanations show how structural factors such as residential segregation or integration can facilitate homogamy, they do not explain *why* individuals choose partners of the same ethno-racial background other than their availability. Also, what explains desires for same race partners when women are not searching for partners in marriage markets with men who share their ethno-racial background? This is often the case for college-educated Black women.[16]

Marriage market explanations for the persistence of ethno-racial homogamy may also be limited given the expansion of dating technology. Dating technology, otherwise known as app or online dating, has replaced local marriage markets and social networks as the most common way of searching for and finding romantic partners.[17] Additionally, sociological research on dating technology demonstrates that preferences for and selection of ethno-racial homogamy remain relatively unchanged.[18] Individuals still prefer and choose partners who share the same ethno-racial background even when a larger (essentially boundaryless) marriage market offers them the opportunity to choose partners outside of their preferences.

Another explanation that social psychologists have put forward is the preference for marrying someone who shares a similar culture as oneself. This similarity includes cultural similarities that arise from ethno-racial background such as language, food, and traditions, but also include similarities in tastes, values, and opinions. These similarities ultimately allow for "mutual understanding" in the intimate romantic relationship.[19] Beyond cultural similarities as a basis for mutual understanding, this explanation does not examine what constitutes cultural similarities for ethno-racial minorities within a racialized social structure. If race and racism matter for people's experiences and life opportunities in the United States, how does this shape what people of color characterize as cultural similarities? I argue that partner preferences are deeply connected to experiences of racial/ethnic marginalization due to the embodiment of a particular ethno-racial status in the Unite States; hence, those experiences inform the desire and selection of partners who share a similar ethno-racial background. This examination goes beyond the availability of those partners in a marriage market and examines what cultural similarities mean to women of color in order to demonstrate that a preference for ethno-racial homogamy is an act of resistance and a way to continually ensure the recognition of ethno-racial minorities' humanity.

The last explanation for the persistence of ethno-racial homogamy focuses on how third parties, particularly among Latinos and Asians, utilize same race/ethnicity marriage to retain their place in the racial hierarchy and to reproduce racial/ethnic inequality. Jessica Vazquez shows that via "disciplined preferences," Latinos are encouraged by third parties—families, friends, and community members—to shun intimate romantic relationships with individuals who occupy a lower ethno-racial status in the racial order.[20] Individuals are instead encouraged to search for relationships that demonstrate ethno-racial homogamy or elevate Latinos' position in the racialized structure. Asians and Asian-Americans report similar experiences in their search for romantic partners.[21] This research demonstrates racial/ethnic homogamy is both influenced by racial hierarchies and perpetuates them. I also show, however, that desires for and selecting partners of the same ethno-racial background can also be a form of ethno-racial solidarity and/or resistance against the harms of white racial oppression.

POLITICAL IDEOLOGY HOMOPHILY

Research on political ideology homophily also shows that married couples tend to partner with individuals who share the same political views and opinions as themselves. Alford and colleagues examined a variety of political measures and found that married couples tend to share the same political beliefs.[22] Dating technology has not changed individuals' desires for political ideology homophily in intimate romantic relationships. For instance, Huber and Maholtra found that individuals who used dating technology in their romantic partner search were more likely to reach out to and engage with people who shared similar political viewpoints as themselves.[23] In fact, desires for political ideology homophily was as important a preference for individuals as educational homogamy.

Scholarship on political homophily among dating and married couples has also examined the intersection of race/ethnicity and political ideology on preferences for partners who share the similarities in both areas. One study found that white conservatives were more likely to choose whites as romantic partners compared to white liberals.[24] Other research explored how political ideology influences desires for ethno-racial homogamy. Another study demonstrated that while conservatives were more likely to state preferences for same-race romantic relationships than liberals, both liberals and conservatives *chose* same-race partners.[25] Thus, partner selection among conservatives and liberals revealed a desire for ethno-racial homogamy. Moreover, Huber and Maholtra also found that preferences for racial homogamy were more important for individuals than preferences for similarities in political ideology.[26] These findings suggest that preferences for partners who share the same ethno-racial background trump preferences for partners who share the same political ideology. This is not surprising as ethno-racial status in the United States has implications for inequality that political ideology does not have. Given Donald Trump's 2016 election, however, it is important to explore if desire for homophily in political ideology has become a more significant desire for those searching for romantic relationships.

Research on political ideology homophily is less focused on explaining why people desire and choose partners of the same political ideology as themselves. The scholarship is even less concerned with how race/ethnicity may factor into these desires and choices. However, marriage market and cultural similarities explanations may shed light on these trends and their persistence. In terms of marriage market explanations, political beliefs, views, and values do cluster regionally (e.g., blue and red states and/or cities) and may also inform or be a proxy for other deeply held core values on issues such as child-rearing, religion, or interracial marriage.[27] As with ethno-racial homogamy, these explanations do not explore what political ideology homophily in intimate romantic relationships means for individuals who desire and choose it and how race and racism inform these partner preferences. Indeed, much of the literature about political ideology homophily tends to separate race/ethnicity from the choice for a partner who shares the same political ideology. Historical research, however, shows that for both ethno-racial minorities and whites, race is intertwined with political ideology.[28] Therefore, it is important to examine how racialized experiences shape desires not only for ethno-racial homogamy, but also political ideology homophily in intimate romantic relationships.

FINDING LOVE IN THE TRUMP ERA

When the former president Donald Trump was elected in 2016, many Brown and Black voters were rightfully horrified given Trump's racist history and current bigotry.[29] Alas, Trump's only term as president was filled with the kind of racial abuse and violence that people of color and their white allies feared would become a reality with his election. Within this context, individuals searching for romantic partners have become more vocal and particular about their partner preferences in terms of political ideology. For example, on June 21, 2020, a woman who goes by the Twitter handle @Ordinary1World submitted to social media the following question: "Is supporting Trump a dating deal-breaker?" Her Tweet was retweeted over 30,000 times and "liked" over 170,000 times.[30] Trump's presidency was also a catalyst for taking political views more seriously in the search for a romantic partner. For example, a man who goes by @makk1123 similarly posted on Twitter on July 12, 2020: "I joined a dating site. My profile says no Trumpers. Got this message. 'The only problem is I'm a Trump fan. Is that a dealbreaker? I do not agree with his personality but I do believe he has done great things for our country. If that is a dealbreaker' etc. Advice?????" The Tweet evoked nearly 10,000 comments by users who weighed in on the question.[31]

Such anecdotal evidence is confirmed by data from popular online dating apps. OkCupid found a "64% increase in political terms appearing in users' dating profiles shortly after the 2016 election."[32] Tinder noted that 71 percent of their users refuse to date Trump supporters. "Trump voters, swipe left" was a popular blurb on Tinder profiles.[33] Trump supporters were also somewhat adamant about not dating people who do not support Trump. In total, 59 percent stated that they would not date anyone who did not like the president.[34] These supporters could use dating sites such as Conservatives Only, Donald Daters, Patrio, or TrumpSingles to find individuals who more closely aligned with their political views.[35] With the exception of Conservatives Only, these niche[36] dating platforms were created soon after the Trump election, as many conservatives and Trump supporters suddenly found themselves unable to get a first or second date using mainstream platforms such as Tinder, Bumble, or OkCupid.[37] Post–2016 election scholarship on the demographic characteristics of couples who met online additionally suggested that being in a relationship with a person who shares the same political beliefs may be as important as having a partner of the same ethno-racial background as oneself. Thomas found that while couples who met online were more likely to be interracial, they are not more or less likely to partner across political boundaries.[38] This finding was not surprising given that the political climate has become more polarized since Trump's election in 2016. Additionally, issues that were once seen as "political," such as police brutality, systemic racism, rights for LGBTQ+ individuals, and poverty, are generally now seen as nonpartisan, basic human rights issues.

While interesting, much of the reporting on love in the Trump era does not explore whether liberals or progressive people of color or whites are most likely to exclude conservatives and/or Trump supporters as potential romantic partners, or how experiences of race and racism among ethno-racial minorities impact these partner preferences. This consideration is crucial given Trump's racist rhetoric and its adverse impact on people of color. Since Trump's election, we have witnessed both a rise in the visible presence of alt-right groups, sometimes intimidating and harassing people of color,[39] as well as a spike in hate crimes in counties where he won by a large margin.[40] Given this present reality, compounded by past experiences with race and racism, how do these experiences impact ethno-racial minorities' decisions to exclude conservatives and/or Trump supporters as romantic partners? Using interview data from Asian, Black, and Latina women about their dating and nondating experiences of ethno-racial marginalization, I show that women of color see Trump's rhetoric, and conservative enabling of it, as an affront to their humanity. Therefore, not including conservatives in their partner preferences, much like their desires for ethno-racial homogamy, is about safeguarding their humanity, which is continuously under threat in this particular political context.

LEARNING ABOUT THE ROMANTIC PARTNER SEARCH

Between 2017 and 2018, I interviewed 111 college-educated women who self-identified by ethno-racial categories that were mutually exclusive. The breakdown of respondents by self-identified ethno-racial background were as follows: Asian (28 respondents), Black (29), Latina (25), and white (29). None of my Latina respondents identified as Black or white, but strictly as Latino.

I confined the scope of the study to women between the ages of twenty-five and thirty-three to increase the likelihood of recruiting women who are college graduates and to capture the population of women most likely to be actively searching for a partner given the culture-wide increase in age at first marriage.[41] Additionally, the women all identified as heterosexual, had no children, and were currently single or had been in an exclusive dating relationship for a year or less at the time of interview. The sample was also a very educated one, with slightly more than half of the respondents possessing a postcollege degree. It is important to note that this research sample is not a nationally representative sample.

I recruited respondents using snowball sampling, Facebook, Meetup.com groups, affinity groups at a university campus in Philadelphia, and college alumni Facebook groups. The recruitment blurb included a link to an online survey that asked interested participants about their college education, sexual orientation, race/ethnicity, current relationship status, and children to determine eligibility. The interviews were semistructured and ranged from 60 to 120 minutes. I inquired about respondents' partner preferences, frustrations in their search, and experiences with online dating. I performed face-to-face interviews at cafes, offices, conference rooms, and in respondents' homes with women who were in my geographic area (e.g., Philadelphia and central and southern New Jersey). I conducted all other interviews by Skype, Google Hangouts, and telephone.

The last phase of this project included a year of monthly follow-up interviews with 10 women from the original sample from 2018 to 2019. These interviews were intended to gather more detailed, qualitative data about the larger patterns that appeared in the original data set, to provide greater context and continuity from the original interviews, and to address any issues of recall bias. In the follow-up interviews, I asked about dates, men in whom they were interested, on- and offline interactions, and frustrations and joys of the romantic partner search. Initial and follow up interviews were transcribed. I used a grounded theory approach to analyze the data.[42]

DESIRES FOR ETHNO-RACIAL HOMOGAMY IN INTIMATE ROMANTIC RELATIONSHIPS

The women in my study responded to survey questions I asked about their ethno-racial preferences for potential romantic partners. I used Survey Monkey to generate and disperse the survey. I additionally used their suggested ethno-racial categories as the options for respondents to choose from when selecting their partner preferences (see table 2.1).

These suggested categories separate men who are racially white from potential white-passing men (Middle Eastern and Multiracial) and who may have cultural differences from whites, which could impact a dating relationship. I asked respondents, "What race/ethnicity would you prefer that he [potential romantic partner] be? Check all that apply." There was

Table 2.1. Table 2.1 Respondents' Ethno-Racial Partner Preferences

Ethno-Racial Background of Potential Partners (in percentages)	Asian	Black	Latina	White	Total
White/Caucasian	26%	6%	26%	41%	34
Black	6%	59%	28%	6%	32
Asian (Korean, Japanese, Indian, etc.)	61%	13%	13%	13%	23
Latino	7%	29%	61%	4%	28
Middle Eastern	23%	23%	46%	8%	13
Multiracial	33%	13%	53%	0%	15
Any Race/Ethnicity	30%	21%	15%	34%	47

a 93 percent response rate. That is, 108 out of 111 women completed this part of the survey. Table 2.1 shows the rates at which women in each ethno-racial group included men of a particular race/ethnicity in their partner preference. For example, 15 women desired to date men with a Multiracial background. Latinas were the most likely to include men of this ethno-racial background in their preference. There are some notable results, and they align well with US Census data and sociological research that examines who partners with whom. First, Latina and Asian women outside of white women, were most likely to desire white men as potential romantic partners. This supports data that demonstrated that Asian and Latina women were the most likely to be intermarried to white men.[43] Second, Latinas in this study were the most likely to include Middle Eastern and Multiracial men in their ethno-racial partner preferences. Census data showed that Latinos were the mostly likely to be in an interracial marriage with other ethno-racial minorities and Multiracial individuals.[44] The results from this may also suggest that Latina women, as Vazquez argues, may also desire Middle-Eastern and Multiracial men because they could be potentially white-passing. This ethno-racial status may help Latinas secure their place in the racial hierarchy, and in doing so, also perpetuate racism. It could also suggest that because Latinos are much more used to race mixing than other ethno-racial groups in the United States, a desire for Middle Eastern and Multiracial men among Latinas may not be unusual. The last finding and most important for this paper, is that regardless of racial/ethnic background, the women interviewed overwhelmingly desired partners who shared the same race/ethnicity as themselves. In speaking with them about these preferences, Asian, Black, and Latina women often mentioned how their dating and nondating experiences of ethno-racial marginalization contributed to their decision to seek and select partners who were either men of color or shared the same ethno-racial background as themselves.

Dating-Related Experiences of Ethno-Racial Marginalization

Women of color explained that they frequently experienced fetishization as a form of ethno-racial marginalization—both on- and offline—as they searched for romantic partners. They typically endured it as a condition of being included as romantic partners, especially among white men. Fetishization, otherwise known as being seen as exotic, is the sexual objectification of women of color—due specifically to their ethno-racial status—as a "preferential lust object."[45] Because this objectification is rooted in white sexual conquest of nonwhite women, fetishization reveals conscious and unconscious white supremacist perspectives.[46] Serena, a twenty-nine-year-old Latina, recalled how white men she met online wanted her to call them "Papi or asked if I would speak to them in Spanish." One white man not only asked Serena if she would call him

"Papi," but also, "if I would let him spend all day down on me." Serena stated frankly, "I tend to stay away from white men because of that," and thereby connected her dating experiences with white men directly to seeking out men of color exclusively as romantic partners. Jada, a twenty-six-year-old Black woman, also recounted instances of being fetishized by white men, both on- and offline. She explained how it impacted her decision to exclude white men as romantic partners:

> I had this one dude on Hinge [dating application] who I was, in the beginning, very open to hanging out with him. . . . We had been talking back and forth, and he had mentioned that he was a cop. Cops make me nervous, for a lot of reasons, and we didn't share the same racial background. I wasn't going to rule him out, but then he started talking about using his handcuffs and whether I wanted a massage. He went and ruined it. I didn't want to hang out with him because I felt it was going to be physical. I've definitely been involved with a lot of people in their fetish situations. I'm over doing that. I think that may also be why I may be steering away from white men. Because that's been a lot of the dynamic.
>
> Also, I'm just on a journey right now. I'm not saying I'm against dating white males. I'm very well-known in the circles as being like—I mean some of my sorority sisters have given me nicknames like "Ghost Buster" and "Vanilla Killa," trying to be funny. Because I'm the one that's known to date white guys, while they're not necessarily open to it. But, given the current situation in the country, I feel like I'm looking more for Black men just because having that common connection would be really helpful.

Similar to Serena and other women in this study, Jada decided to date Black men due to her own personal experiences with fetishization. She additionally links this decision to the recent "current situation in the country," Donald Trump's 2016 election to be exact. Due to the political climate, "having that common connection" to Blackness was important to her. Jada's desire for a Black partner is not only a response to being fetishized, but also about racial solidarity via a romantic relationship in a climate that threatens Black people's ability to survive and thrive. This connection to Blackness that she craves is about being in a romantic partnership with a man that can be identified phenotypically as Black. It is also importantly about a connection to Black culture and its insistence on the affirmation of Black humanity and Black liberation from white supremacy.

Furthermore, Jada's desire for Black love, both phenotypically and in a cultural sense,[47] is representative of a historical legacy of romantic relationships between Black people as a form of resistance to white supremacy.[48] From slavery, where Black people were often denied the agency of selecting their own romantic partners or to remain with them for life, where "Black women gave birth to the capital that helped forge the nation's wealth, typically under the duress of coerced sex with the very men who sired biracial progeny and turned them into commodities,"[49] to modern-day stereotypes of Black men as incompetent partners and deadbeat dads,[50] and to the alleged inability of Black people to form long-term relationships and healthy families as outlined in the Moynihan Report,[51] Black love has been defined by oppression and inequality. Thus, Jada's decision to seek a Black partner as a way to mitigate racial oppression during the Trump era is both powerful because of the agency that it demonstrates, and it is an affront to beliefs and ideologies that attempt to dehumanize Blackness.

Nacine, a twenty-seven-year-old Black woman, also sees Black love as resistance. She describes why she exclusively dates Black men:

> I just want to have a Black family, not just for me, but to kind of show the world. There are people who do believe that Black men overall aren't good fathers, aren't good husbands, and aren't good providers. I want my family to be an example to challenge people's mindset in that respect.

Sol, a twenty-five-year-old Asian woman, started exclusively dating men of color after hitting "cultural roadblocks" with white men and upon interrogation of her attraction to them:

> I went on this decolonization of my personal tastes. I was like, "I have a problem, and it's internalized racism. Why is it that I don't see an attractive man of color and think, Yeah, I'm totally down for that?" When I'm looking at these mediocre white boys and being like, "Oh, yeah, that looks great." I'm like, "There's a really hot, you know, Black, brown, Asian fellow right there," and I'm still swiping on these mediocre white guys.
>
> In my experience of dating white guys, it would always sort of hit this cultural roadblock where I was like, "You are not understanding where I'm coming from," or "You're making these kind of racial, racist assumptions, and I'm having a really hard time making you realize why that statement you made offends me." There are so many "-isms" that I couldn't break down without having that person be offended. Or they would be so entrenched in, "But I'm so woke. I'm so self-aware." And I'm like, "You're still a racist." Once I started dating nonwhite guys, I realized that was a much lesser factor.

Jane, a twenty-five-year-old Latina, similar to Sol, also described the assumptions white men had about her. With dating technology, these assumptions often led them to ignore the descriptions of herself and what kind of partner she desired as she described in her profile:

> I feel like a lot of people have assumptions about my race, and assumptions about women of my race. I feel like people just stick to those assumptions. In terms of online, they don't read the profile. In person, they don't ask the right questions or make the right conversation. Peo-

ple are sometimes surprised that I have a degree in what I have a degree in and graduated, which feels a little insulting. You can tell there was an assumption of "You're brown and"—you know. Which, to me is really upsetting, because I was under the impression that those stereotypical conversations didn't exist; but I guess they do.

In speaking about these assumptions, Jane astutely observes the reduction of herself to a caricature of a particular ethno-racial category. This is in spite of her efforts to humanize herself as a person with real achievements and real desires in her profile description. The assumptions and generalizations of white men reveal an important mechanism of racism: to separate what white people believe being a Latina is from how Latinas may define themselves. There is a refusal to acknowledge and embrace the self-definitions that ethno-racial minorities make, but rather to make perceptual assumptions due to one's embodiment of a minority ethno-racial status and act on those preconceptions.

Nondating Related Experiences of Ethno-Racial Marginalization

Racialized experiences that were not connected to searching for a romantic partner also informed Black, Latina, and Asian women's desires for ethno-racial homogamy in their romantic relationships. Cadence, a twenty-seven-year-old Black woman, discussed both past and present racialized moments that informed her decision to seek out and choose Black men exclusively as romantic partners:

> The comments that my [white] friends would say, and their parents would say about Black people, especially as it relates to dating. . . . I remember there was the star football player. Great, super nice guy. So humble, really well put together. Families loved him. I mean, even my mom loved him. She questioned why I never dated him. So anyway, he was loved and beloved as this star football player, and of course, got along with his teammates. One of his particular teammates, his sister started dating him [the football star]. It was fine going to the house when he was on the team, but when he started dating the daughter, the family got very upset about that and told her that she could not be with him. It was because he was Black. So, there's those kinds of things that I think about.
>
> Or even now, if there is a Black guy in particular, I want to date, my [white] friends would say, "Oh, Black guys are nasty." It's like, "Wait, what? You know I'm Black, right?" Or how many of them had interests in Black men and we're friends, so they would share comments that their parents would say about, you know, Black boys and things of that nature, in derogatory ways. It's just like, "Okay, they may be fine to be friends, but they're going to cuss you out and call you the N-word." I think those things are really real in terms of thinking what that means in a dating relationship.

Cadence's experiences with white people in her life demonstrate how racialized experiences have a global affect on other choices. First, she witnessed the denigration of Black men which made her wonder if a white man's family and friends would denigrate her too in their romantic relationship. She was not sure that she could trust him or his family to deride her via her exclusion or racial abuse either in her presence or behind her back. Second, her white friends appeared to treat her as different from other Black people—an exception to all other Black folks—which in turn made them feel comfortable about saying "derogatory" things about Black men in front of her. This is another issue she could potentially have with a white romantic partner. Would he see her as an "exceptional Negro"[52] and feel free to speak badly about Black people in her presence? These racialized experiences made an important impression on Cadence: to avoid racial abuse and trauma and to keep her humanity from denigration, romantic partnerships with white men were simply not an option.

Leona, a thirty-two-year-old Black woman, wanted to date men of color because of whites' history of oppression of ethno-racial minorities in the United States. Similar to Cadence, she harbors a mistrust of white Americans. Leona explained that she could not "trust white people" because they came from a line of people for whom subjugating others seemed to be second nature. She stated:

> I don't feel like I necessarily have to be with a Black man, but I definitely don't want to be with somebody who is 100 percent white, either. I have dated an Indian guy before. In the back of my mind, I feel like I can't 100 percent trust white people just because of the history of slavery and all of the evil segregation and mistreatment of African-Americans in this country. I just feel that some of the things that went on in the past and even currently with the shootings of Black men by police officers and things of that nature. . . . I know that God loves everybody, and people are individuals, definitely, but in the back of my mind I am thinking, "Is something really evil deep-seated in these people's nature?" I don't know. I kind of feel like that. So, I kind of keep a little bit of a distance.

For Black women specifically, ethno-racial marginalization was also connected to feeling invisible.[53] They described this invisibility in two ways: not being physically seen or noticed as potential romantic partners by non-Black men, and thereby overlooked as such. Or being viewed through the lens of a stereotype which had the similar effect of not being fully visible to potential romantic partners. On the other hand, Black women repeatedly discussed how they felt seen by Black men and how this visibility made them feel special and desired. Kassian, a twenty-seven-year-old Black woman, explained that Black men noticed and recognized her as a potential romantic partner. She stated, "I prefer Black men. I go out and they see me. It makes you more visible." My exchange below with Leona highlights how being visible to Black men made her feel special and desirable:

LEONA: I think guys can recognize me as a queen.

INTERVIEWER: When you say "recognize you as a queen," what does that mean?

LEONA: [Laughs] I don't know. Just a beautiful Black woman.

INTERVIEWER: It sounds like what you are saying is that other Black men may recognize you as someone who has a lot to offer. Is that what you are saying?

LEONA: Yes.

INTERVIEWER: So, if Black men are looking for Black women, they can say, "Oh, Leona is a great Black woman?"

LEONA: Yes.

Although she was also open to dating other men of color, Leona clearly felt that Black men recognized her as a "queen" and a "beautiful Black woman." These words point specifically to being seen as a whole human being who is worth having as a romantic partner. This situation stood in stark contrast to being seen through the lens of a stereotype or caricature. Twenty-five-year-old Yolanda described being seen in this way versus how Black men saw her: "I just happen to have dated more Black men because it's usually mutual when it comes to attraction. It just doesn't seem mutual when it comes to another race. And I feel like maybe there's some stereotype—before they even hear me talk or even get to know me—it just seems like there's some stereotype that they're clinging onto." In this case, non-Black men saw Yolanda as a potential romantic partner because she fit a particular stereotype of Black womanhood, not because of who Yolanda was as a person. She felt, however, that this was not the case with Black men.

The invisibility of Black women is a tenet of white supremacy and racism. When Black people were deemed subhuman via slavery and the declaration of them as being three-fifths of a person, their invisibility became entrenched in American institutions.[54] Laws that deemed children born to Black women as perpetual slaves, whether they were fathered by Black men or white slaveowners, secured the invisibility of Black women. The absence of laws that protected enslaved and free Black women from being raped by white men further codified Black women's invisibility. This invisibility lives on in the twenty-first century as tropes such as the Black matriarch, Jezebel, the welfare queen, and the angry

Black woman. These tropes make Black women, and the consequences of racism on their lives, invisible to a country that depends on their physical and emotional labor to thrive economically, socially, and politically.[55] Consequently, for Black women, the preference for ethno-racial homogamy in their romantic relationships, is significant as it illustrates a desire for visibility via cultural similarities that are forged from a lived experience of past and present ethno-racial oppression. The dating and nondating racialized experiences that they endured impacted how they viewed potential romantic relationships with non-Black men, especially white men, and what these relationships could mean for their humanity as Black women.

*The Subconscious Nature of Desires for
and Selection of Ethno-Racial Homogamy*

The preference for men who shared the same ethno-racial background as respondents of color or were men of color was often conscious, as seen above. Sometimes, however, it was also subconscious—something that women of color did not always realize they preferred or consciously sought out in their search for a romantic partner. This finding in particular reveals how the experience of race and racism become embodied and habituated for people of color. Octavia, a twenty-six-year-old Black woman, described her subconscious preference to date only Black men and other men of color:

> I think, subconsciously, I want to give African-American men more benefit of the doubt. . . . Because already I'm assuming that you and I have a culture and something else, a history right, a heritage in common that we can connect with. And that's a different connection that you—I mean it depends. But on the onset, you probably won't get that with all white men. You could, but you would have to dig and see what their background is and what they've been exposed to and you would probably be doing a lot of that exposing. . . . With Black men, or other people of color, I think we can connect in our mutual adversities.

Liora, a thirty-three-year-old Asian woman, discovered during our interview that she indeed had a preference for Asian men and men of color. This desire was more subconscious for her than she had realized. She explained:

> I think the bigger sort of insight from this [interview] is probably the fact that you know while I [checked off that] I don't have an ethnic preference, I think that actually maybe I do have an ethnic preference. I think my preference stems from just feeling like I'll just have more in common. For example, certain Asian belief systems like having respect for elders. I know it's not strictly an Asian thing, but there is that sort of extra level of consideration like just generally respecting elders. Or being more communal in terms of thinking like "How do we do this for

the group?" or "How do we elevate ourselves as a group?" I think it's a very non-American thing . . . when I was seriously dating someone from Ghana, he and I got along very well because he has that belief system in place. His mom actually preferred that he date me than an American [white] woman. Even though I am American, but you know me being an Asian American, she preferred that he date me actually. But again, it's just so much easier to check Asian than say, "Oh please send me someone who has these belief systems in place." I think it's just who I am. I'm constantly thinking about ways to improve like efficiency, and it just comes out. It comes out at work. It comes out in my personal life. It's like the way I actually do things, so subconsciously like I wasn't even thinking like, "Let's be as efficient as possible." Subconsciously, it just ends up happening. It's weird, because now that I'm talking to you about it, I'm like, "Oh wow. I can't believe that I'm doing all this without even realizing it."

In examining these quotes from Octavia and Liora, one thing stands out about their subconscious preference for men who share their ethno-racial background or who are also ethno-racial minorities: the *labor* or *work* associated with searching for or being with a white partner. This was not work they would have to do with men of color. Octavia describes this work as "digging" to find out if white men have been "exposed" to some knowledge or understanding of race and racism. Liora conceptualizes not having to do this work as being "efficient" in her romantic partner search. Both women had an expectation or assumption of shared history, experiences, or values with men of color precisely because ethno-racial minorities are touched in one way or another by racial/ethnic marginalization that shapes their experiences in the United States and thereby creates a point of commonality for them. Octavia explains that she can safely assume that "with Black men or other people of color, I think we can connect in our mutual adversities," and get on with exploring romantic interest. This is not something she can assume with white men. In Liora's case, it was "efficient" to desire and select Asian men or other men of color because she assumed that with this ethno-racial social location also came certain shared values such as respect for elders and a belief in the communal, not only individual, well-being. She states, "It's just so much easier to check Asian than say, 'Oh please send me someone who has these belief systems in place.'" Why spend her energy and time hoping that a white man would have these same beliefs when her experience has shown her that they typically do not?

This theme of doing labor as a consequence of including white men as potential romantic partners was a constant among my Asian, Black, and Latina respondents. They explained that part of the search and dating process with white men involved educating them about racism, both personal and structural, being unable to connect with them emotionally because of their lack of understanding, and in some cases, having to "prove" why a particular incident was racist. They found this work "exhausting." Research on interracial relationships also support this finding. Frankenburg interviewed white women in interracial marriages and romantic relationships and learned that many of them were oblivious to racism prior to being in their interracial relationship.[56] Steinbugler also found that Black partners in white-Black interracial couplings often did labor, which she called "race work," that was often invisible to white people, including their own partners, to maintain the interracial relationship within a racialized structure.[57] It is not surprising then that for Octavia, Liora, and other women of color in my study, partner preferences for men who shared the same ethno-racial background as themselves or were also ethno-racial minorities became habituated and subconscious. This habituation helped them to avoid doing unnecessary and unrecognized emotional labor in their romantic partner search that they would not need to do if they were white women.

Desires for Political Ideology Homophily in Intimate Romantic Relationships

To determine desires for political ideology homophily among my respondents, I asked them to identify their own political ideology and which political ideologies they wanted their romantic partner to embrace. Again, 93 percent of the sample answered this portion of this survey. Survey Monkey suggested the following options for political ideologies: Extremely liberal, Liberal, Slightly Liberal, Moderate (Middle of the Road), Slightly Conservative, Conservative, Extremely Conservative, and No Specific Political Leanings/Views/Opinions. I chose these categorizations because they were comprehensive and gave respondents a variety of options. Respondents were only allowed to choose one political ideology for themselves. Table 2.2 shows the percentage of women in each ethno-racial category that identified with a particular political ideology. Note that regardless of ethno-racial background, women in this study were most likely to identify with a liberal political ideology. This finding is similar to other studies that show that individuals with a college education are most likely to identify with liberal political ideology.[58]

I also asked respondents, "What political ideology would you prefer that he [potential romantic partner] have? Check all that apply." They were given the same options to choose from as they had for their own political ideology. However, they could select more than one political ideology for their partner preference. Table 2.3 demonstrates a desire for political ideology homophily among the women in this study. Respondents were most likely to identify as liberal and were also most likely to include men who identified with a liberal ideology in their partner preferences. The total in the table represents how many women chose that particular political ideology and the percentages represent the rate of

Table 2.2. Table 2.2 Respondents' Political Ideology by Ethno-Racial Background

Political Ideology (in percentages)	Asian	Black	Latina	White	Total
Extremely Liberal	25%	4%	8%	15%	14
Liberal	36%	46%	44%	41%	45
Slightly Liberal	14%	14%	28%	15%	19
Moderate (Middle of the Road)	11%	11%	12%	7%	12
Slightly Conservative	11%	4%	4%	11%	8
Conservative	0	0	0	11%	3
Extremely Conservative	0	0	0	0	0
No specific political leanings/views/opinions	4%	21%	0	0	7
Sample Total	28	28	25	27	108

women per ethno-racial category that included that political ideology they wanted a potential partner to embrace.

In speaking with them, both the white women and women of color I interviewed generally did not agree with or endorse conservative ideology, especially as it pertained to Trumpism. However, women of color's experience with being an ethno-racial minority, the former presidency of Donald Trump, and dates with Republicans and/or Trump voters further motivated their preference for and selection of men who embraced liberal ideologies.

Life as an Ethno-Racial Minority and Political Ideology Homophily

Respondents' experiences of living in a racialized structure was a strong factor in their desire for and selection of partners who aligned themselves with liberal ideologies. These lived experiences were especially influential for the partner preferences of Black and Latina women. Giselle, a twenty-five-year-old Latina, discussed how her ethno-racial identity, her status as an immigrant, and her gender were continuously politicized and maligned in American life. She also felt strongly that giving government aid to immigrants, people of color, and those in poverty was not an issue of politics, but of human rights. Consequently, she explained that she could not be in an intimate romantic relationship with men who downplayed these realities and/or did not share her views. She stated frankly:

> I'm a woman of color ... I'm an immigrant. Too much of my identity is politicized for someone to not agree with me politically. . . . All these centuries, they don't realize that for other people who have been literal-

Table 2.3. Table 2.3 Respondents' Partner Preferences for Political Ideology

Political Ideology of Potential Romantic Partners (in percentages)	Asian	Black	Latina	White	Total
Extremely Liberal	31%	23%	20%	26%	35
Liberal	30%	21%	21%	29%	73
Slightly Liberal	40%	18%	21%	21%	57
Moderate (Middle of the Road)	26%	24%	24%	26%	54
Slightly Conservative	24%	24%	16%	36%	25
Conservative	38%	13%	0	50%	8
Extremely Conservative	0	0	0	100%	1
No specific political leanings/ views/opinions	0	67%	38%	8%	12

ly chained, it's not that easy to just wake up one day, have money, wealth, be of high education levels. So, I think when people are conservative, they don't take that into consideration, and that leads them to political parties that think in that same sphere of supporting people being fiscally conservative, not creating programs that give aid. As a woman—birth control. Conservatives don't really want that to happen, but as a woman, I want it to happen. . . . Things of that nature. I couldn't deal with someone who thinks that my people are lower—achieve lower levels of education just because we're lazy or don't want to. If they don't recognize there are so many social barriers to the success of my people, I can't get along with them, because they are so blind to real life.

As a Black woman, Cadence's liberal ideology was one that highlighted the political importance of racial hierarchies for ethno-racial inequality in the United States. She wanted a partner who understood and embraced this reality of being Black in America:

I think that what it means to be Black in society really sees a sense of understanding of inequities. I think it allows you to understand and relate to people in your unique ways, just in terms of thinking how racial hierarchies function in a US context. Well, really in a global context . . . I think there's a level of being able to understand people for what they are, but also what they've been through.

Cadence had also witnessed first-hand how being with someone who did not hold the same political views could be toxic for a romantic relationship. She described an incident between her aunt and uncle shortly after Trump's 2016 election that further solidified her desire to exclusively date men who identified with liberal political ideologies. She explained:

> After Trump was elected, there was a lot of these stories coming out of, you know, these interracial, specifically Black women dating white men. Articles about how just from the election and post the election, instances of hatred coming out from their partners that they didn't see before, which I personally know is really true, because my aunt was in a similar situation. . . . I don't know [the details of] what happened in the incident, but he just became very angry with her. That spilled out towards my family, and in his sense of rage, he used very racially derogatory terms directed to her and the larger family. I think those are all things that I'm very cautious of. I think prejudice happens. I think it's that we all have a challenge daily, but I think in terms of racial prejudice, I think there are certain things that come out in people in anger, and I don't know if that's something I necessarily want to deal with.

What this story also reveals, along with the survey data, is that race/ethnicity and political ideology are closely linked in the United States. This is no surprise given the general racial demographics of the Republican and Democratic parties and their respective historical treatment of people of color, along with the increasing association between conservativism and white nationalism. For many of my respondents of color, especially Black women, a desire for ethno-racial homogamy was also a proxy for liberal political ideology homophily in their romantic relationships. Dating white men without finding out about their political leanings could be troublesome down the road as Cadence shows with her story.

Dates with Republicans and/or Trump Supporters

Offline, women could not always tell where men stood politically until the first date. With dating technology, some men were open about being Republicans, conservatives, and/or Trump supporters on their profiles. Others did not always make it so obvious. Unless respondents asked about specific views on issues such as birth control, immigration, Black Lives Matter, and so forth, they could unwittingly find themselves on a date with someone who did not embrace liberal political ideologies. As marriage market theory proposes, if respondents resided in urban city centers where individuals are known to generally hold more liberal views and "vote blue," it may be easy to assume that if a man does not state his beliefs up front, then he identifies with liberal ideologies. This is what happened to Maia, a twenty-five-year-old Asian woman who lived in Philadelphia. She described how she found herself on a date with a Republican:

> My default is that I assume because I am in Philly, if we don't talk about politics, you either don't care or you are moderately liberal. That is my baseline. One time I accidentally went on a date with a Republican, and I was mortified. We were both like, "Oh, this is really awk-

ward." But, on paper he was great. But then, in real life, he was every Republican stereotype that doesn't exist for real people. My family in Texas is Republican and they are not these stereotypes. But, he actually was . . . hitting every ridiculous bullet. He was like, "So, do you think Obama's American?" I was like, "Alright." . . . And he thinks reverse racism is real. . . . I was like, "Alright." Then, he was super pro-Israel. I was like, "No. You can't do that." It was just all these things that I was like, "Okay. You are Republican. It is fine. I can try." But then, it was just, unintentionally, it was all the wrong stances on everything. And I am so engrossed in politics and stuff that if it is something where we are not aligned, I feel like it would be an issue at least down the line, if not immediately.

After this date, Maia was more proactive about sussing out men's political beliefs even if "on paper" they were "great." This became especially important for her after Trump's election in 2016.

Vicki, a thirty-year-old Black woman, was initially reluctant to exclude men as romantic partners because of their political beliefs. She felt that she did not necessarily have to be romantically involved with men who held the same political ideology as herself. This changed for her after a date with a Trump supporter:

> To be honest, our first date was really cool. We met up. I was working on my thesis back then. I remember he had to read it for me. So, we met at a coffee shop the first time and I was like, "Oh, my god, we were talking forever. I didn't even realize." He was so cool, and we met again. But then, you know, there are certain things you don't notice about people when they meet you. For instance, he doesn't open the door. The day that really was bad [the second date], we went to this sushi spot. It was cool and we had a good time and then some way, somehow, we just started talking about our dear President. . . . He made a joke about, "Yeah, Black people should just shut up and just honor the flag like the President said." You know what, it's okay for you to vote for Trump, for you to be a Republican. Yet if you're going to make a statement like this to me, that shows you don't look at this thing [Colin Kaepernick's protest] with enough depth. No, you're just silly because you don't see the whole picture. Whether you're white, Black, or purple, this whole issue is a problem. It's not acceptable. That's why, whichever one you are [race/ethnicity], I don't care. But to me, that was just more a human issue than a political issue. . . . I told him [on the second date], "I don't find it funny. Don't make the joke again." And then we were fine [for the rest of the date]. And then after that, maybe the next day or two days later, we were talking on the phone, and he remakes the joke purposely. He knows he's pissing me off. He knows certain things I don't like laughing about. He shouldn't even be laughing about it. Then, I just told him never to call me again.

As Vicki alluded to, the biggest issue she had with this man was that his joke about kneeling to protest police brutality revealed to her that he did not see or care about Black people as humans. The fact that he repeated the joke to her, even after she told him not to, further confirmed for her what she felt was an inability to understand that the protest was "more a human issue than a political issue." Moreover, and perhaps more importantly, it demonstrated that he did not care about her feelings regarding this issue, and neither did he respect her requests not to joke about it. One could argue that his lack of caring and disrespect were a dehumanization of Vicki's Blackness.

The Election of Donald Trump

The election of Donald Trump in 2016 was also a significant catalyst for women of color who had not considered, prior to his election, the importance of being partnered with someone who shared the same or similar political ideology as themselves. These women reported that the election of a man who openly supported white supremacists, who called Mexicans "rapists," and who stated during the debates that he had no solution for racial reconciliation, created an opportunity to reexamine their partner preferences. This was particularly the case for Asian and Latina women. Shani, a twenty-seven-year-old Asian woman explained:

> I never used to be someone who thought about political leanings very much. I think especially after this past presidential election that actually bumped up, what I thought about my preferences in terms of political leanings. . . . I think for me I tend to be a little bit more liberal on social issues because I have a social justice background. That's why I went to policy school and the area of work that I pursue. A lot of why I care about social justice issues also stems from my faith, in my understanding of my faith. I had met a couple of guys who I remember talking to them about the [presidential] primaries and the lead up to the election. They said some things that were very, I think, socially conservative. You know as someone who cares a lot about immigration, diversity, and race, it was really hurtful to hear. The first time, it clicked that, "Wow, I wouldn't be able to date someone like that." Whereas, I think prior to the election cycle, it wasn't anything I had ever really thought about.

Twenty-seven-year-old Adamina, a Latina, stated frankly that due to the 2016 election, she was no longer open to dating men who held any extreme political views, including conservative views. She explained, "I think that's mostly because of the last election. I think I probably would have answered this differently before that."

Genevieve, a twenty-five-year-old Black woman who grew up in the South and in predominantly white neighborhoods, found herself struggling with her attraction to white men after Trump was elected. This was because many of the white men she had dated often held Republican or conservative views. She explained:

Politically, I've been on dates with men that I didn't realize, like didn't align with me politically. I keep saying these days, but since the election that it's much harder to date someone that is not aligned with me politically. I'm from the South, and I'm usually around white Republican men. That's how I grew up. My preference in my life, not even preference, but I guess preference has been white men, because that's what I saw, that's what I was growing up with. Now it's much harder though to not—because I'm still very attracted to white men—but it's harder to consider like a Republican man. Or it's unlikely to happen, because what that means now is such a divisive thing, right? I see it as more of a character trait, than I see it as a political thing. As soon as I find out on a date that a guy's Republican, or specifically voted for Trump and doesn't really know why he did it, I'm out. I can no longer be present. Basically, my humanity is not seen the same way in a Republican person's eyes. And so, it's hard for me to think of like, "Yeah, I can date a Republican man if he also believes that Muslims should be banned."

Similar to Vicki, Genevieve felt that Trump's politics, and as an extension, Republican politics, were a politics of dehumanization of Black people and other ethno-racial minorities. As a Black woman, it made little sense to her to be with someone whose political beliefs demeaned her as less than human, even if the men who held these beliefs did not always understand this reality about the political ideology they embraced.

For women of color in this study, conservative ideologies were not simply about how big or small government should be. Conservative ideologies threatened their very personhood. In at least one case, an embrace of these ideologies manifested itself in actions that implied the dehumanization of a respondent. When Trump reduces Mexicans to "rapists and murderers," refers to Black people as "the Blacks" or "my Blacks," or insists on calling the novel coronavirus the "Chinese virus," and conservatives remain silent, or worse, repeat this rhetoric, women of color are reminded that their personhood is precarious within this political climate. They are reminded that conservative ideologies do not acknowledge or recognize their full humanity. Therefore, not dating a Trump supporter or men who hold conservative views becomes a part of their political activism. Excluding men who embrace these political ideologies additionally becomes resistance to a political system that seeks to dehumanize them.

CONCLUSION

Individuals' ethno-racial background, including lived experiences of race and racism, continue to inform how they live their lives in a racially stratified society. This is especially significant for ethno-racial minorities living in the Trump era. This chapter demonstrates that for even something as personal such as preferences for romantic partners, experiences of race and racism are important for informing and shaping these preferences. Specifically, I found that heterosexual women of color desire and tend to select either partners of the same ethno-racial background as themselves or men of color. These preferences are influenced by dating-related experiences of ethno-racial marginalization such as fetishism and nondating-related experiences of racism. Within the context of Trump's former presidency and increasing blatant racial/ethnic abuse toward ethno-racial minorities, these experiences ultimately revealed to participants the importance of being in racial/ethnic solidarity via romantic relationships as a way to survive and thrive in this political climate.

While ethno-racial homogamy among racial/ethnic minorities may be a way to solidify their place within the racial hierarchy in the United States, I found no evidence of this in my study. This may be because in Trumpism, all ethno-racial minorities are equal targets for racial abuse and no group is exempt from being viewed as less than human. Furthermore, the pitting of ethno-racial minority groups against each other for political gain and the maintenance of white supremacy[59] appeared to be missing under the Trump administration. The elevation of whiteness and white people was the main priority of Trump and his enablers. Thus, within this political climate, securing one's place in the racial order as a racial/ethnic minority may be far less important than forming ethno-racial solidarity via romantic partnerships to overcome an oppressive racial structure.

Respondents also desired and selected partners, who like themselves, embraced a liberal political ideology. This preference was informed by the lived experience of being an ethno-racial minority in a racially stratified society, going on dates with Republicans and/or Trump supporters, and Trump's former presidency as a catalyst for greater pondering of what it means to be in a romantic relationship with someone whose political views did not align with theirs. Women of color, especially Black women, saw issues that involved ethno-racial minorities and inequality less as political issues and more as human rights issues. Consequently, it was difficult for them to include or accept men who identified with conservative political ideologies as partners. Given Trump's racial rhetoric and the Republican's open embrace of white nationalism, these issues are less about how the government must address them, and more about if the government should address them at all, because ethno-racial minorities are perceived as less than human under Trumpism.

While marriage market, social psychology, and maintenance of one's racial status within the racial hierarchy are all compelling reasons for the persistence of ethno-racial homogamy, and to some extent, political ideology homophily, it is important to understand how individuals' experiences of race and racism can also influence the persistence of these trends. In a racialized social structure, but especially within a climate of

Trumpism, ethno-racial minorities must find ways to safeguard their humanity against white supremacy. Desires for and selection of ethno-racial homogamy and political ideology homophily are two strategies they can use to do so.

NOTES

1. Choi and Tienda, "Marriage-Market Constraints," 302; Hwang, "Who are People Willing to Date?" 36; Clarke, *Inequalities of Love*; 116; Lin and Lundquist, "Mate Selection in Cyberspace," 202; Lichter, et al., "Race and the Retreat from Marriage," 784.
2. Musick and Bumpass, "Reexamining the Case for Marriage," 9; Braithwaite, Delevi, and Fincham, "Romantic Relationships and the Physical and Mental Health of College Students," 8.
3. I use the word "homogamy" instead of "endogamy" to describe marital relationships where partners share the same ethno-racial background. Sociological research shows that different ethno-racial backgrounds occupy different statuses in the United States' racial hierarchy; thus, homogamy denotes the importance of ethno-racial background as a consequential status in the United States.
4. As political ideology is not a status and therefore has no consequence for inequality, I use the word "homophily" to describe a romantic relationship where partners share the same political ideology.
5. For an exception, see Muro and Martinez, "Constrained Desires," 184.
6. Bonilla-Silva, "Rethinking Racism," 472.
7. Bump, "Trump Didn't Introduce Racism to Conservative Politics," 1.
8. Ibid., 1.
9. Williamson and Gelfand, "Trump and Racism," 1; Flores and Schachter, "Who Are the 'Illegals'?" 844.
10. Geiger and Livingston, "8 Facts About Love and Marriage in America," 2; Wu, "Homogamy in U.S. Marriages," 157; Kalmijn, "Intermarriage and Homogamy," 396.
11. Wu, "Homogamy in U.S. Marriages," 157.
12. Hwang, "Who are People Willing to Date?" 36; Schwartz, "Trends and Variation in Assortative Mating," 452.
13. South and Crowder, "Neighborhood Effects on Family Formation," 118.
14. Choi and Tienda, "Marriage Market Constraints," 305; Cohen and Pepin, "Unequal Marriage Markets," 4.
15. Massey and Denton, *American Apartheid*, 17; Squires and Kubrin, *Privileged Places*, 4.
16. Cohen and Pepin, "Unequal Marriage Markets," 6.
17. Rosenfeld, Thomas, and Hausen, "Disintermediating Your Friends," 17753; Moira, *Labor of Love*, 6.
18. Hwang, "Who are People Willing to Date?" 36; Lin and Lundquist, "Mate Selection in Cyberspace," 207.
19. Kalmijn, "Intermarriage and Homogamy," 399; Byrne, *The Attraction Paradigm*, 5.
20. Vazquez, "Disciplined Preferences," 456.
21. Chou, *Asian American Sexual Politics*, 82; Nemoto, *Racing Romance*, 27; Chow, "The Significance of Race in the Public Sphere," 4.
22. Alford et al., "The Politics of Mate Choice," 376.
23. Huber and Maholtra, "Political Homophily," 275.
24. Eastwick et al., "Is Love Colorblind," 1262.
25. Anderson et al., "Political Ideology and Racial Preferences," 38.
26. Huber and Maholtra, "Political Homophily," 276.
27. Anderson et al., "Political Ideology and Racial Preferences," 28.

28. Mangum, "The Racial Underpinnings of Party Identification," 1224; Bump, 1.
29. Graham et al., "An Oral History of Trump's Bigotry," 1, 7.
30. See https://twitter.com/search?q=%40ordinary1world%20trump%20deal-breaker&src=typed_query.
31. See https://twitter.com/search?q=%40makk1123%20trump%20deal-breaker&src=typed_query.
32. Cox, Clemence, and O'Neil, "Partisan Attachment," 1; Spira, "Love Vs. Trump," 3.
33. Bonos, "Strong Views on Trump," 1; Del Valle, "For Conservatives, By Conservatives," 1–3.
34. Bonos, "Strong Views on Trump," 1.
35. Del Valle, "For Conservatives, By Conservatives," 1–3.
36. Mainstream apps and websites are those that are well-known and do not cater to any particular demographic or user group. Niche apps and websites are those that cater to individuals in specific demographic groups which include race/ethnicity, nationality, religion, hobbies, lifestyles, etc.; Del Valle, "For Conservatives, By Conservatives," 1–3.
37. Del Valle, "For Conservatives, By Conservatives," 2.
38. Thomas, "Online Exogamy Reconsidered," 1281.
39. splcenter.org, "Alt-Right," 1.
40. Williamson and Gelfand, "Trump and Racism," 2.
41. Geiger and Livingston, "8 Facts About Love and Marriage in America," 1; Meltzer et al., "Men Still Value Physical Attractiveness," 435.
42. Charmaz, *Constructing Grounded Theory*, 191. In the following statements from the women who were interviewed, the names of participants have been changed and kept anonymous.
43. Livingston and Brown, "Intermarriage in the U.S." 9; Lee and Bean, *The Diversity Paradox*, 85.
44. Livingston and Brown, "Intermarriage in the U.S." 9.
45. Serna, "She's Not Your African Goddess," 1.
46. Nagel, *Race, Ethnicity, and Sexuality*, 255.
47. Mills, *The Racial Contract*, 131.
48. Moore, "Black Radical Love," 325.
49. Hunter, *Bound in Wedlock*, 4.
50. Edin and Nelson, *Doing the Best I Can*, 65.
51. Moynihan, "The Negro Family," 10.
52. O'Neal, *The Exceptional Negro*, 4.
53. Mills, *The Racial Contract*, 97.
54. Ibid.
55. Collins, *Black Feminist Thought*, 76.
56. Frankenberg, *White Women, Race Matters*, 70.
57. Steinbugler, *Beyond Loving*, 74.
58. Schoon et al., "Social Status, Cognitive Ability, and Educational Attainment as Predictors of Liberal Social Attitudes," 149; Kozloski, "Homosexual Moral Acceptance," 1379–80.
59. Kim, "The Racial Triangulation of Asian Americans," 107–8.

BIBLIOGRAPHY

Alford, John R., Peter K. Hatemi, John Hibbing, Nicolas G. Martin, and Lindon J. Eaves. "The Politics of Mate Choice." *Journal of Politics* 73, no. 2 (April 2011): 362–79.

Anderson, Ashton, Sharad Goel, Gregory Huber, Neil Maholtra, Duncan J. Watts. "Political Ideology and Racial Preferences in Online Dating." *Sociological Science* 1 (February 2014): 28–40.

Bonilla-Silva, Eduardo. "Rethinking Racism: Toward a Structural Interpretation." *American Sociological Review* 62, no. 3 (1997): 465–80.
Bonos, Lisa. "Strong Views on Trump Can Be a Big Dating Dealbreaker, and Other Takeaways from a Survey on Love and Politics." *Washington Post*. February 7, 2020. https://www.washingtonpost.com/lifestyle/2020/02/07/strong-views-trump-can-be-big-dating-deal-breaker-other-takeaways-survey-love-politics.
Braithwaite, Scott R., Raquel Delevi, and Frank D. Fincham. "Romantic Relationships and the Physical and Mental Health of College Students." *Personal Relationships* 17, no. 1 (2010): 1–12.
Bump, Phillip. "Trump Didn't Introduce Racism to Conservative Politics—But He Cultivated and Amplified It." *Washington Post*. July 18, 2019. Accessed at https://www.washingtonpost.com/politics/2019/07/18/trump-didnt-introduce-racism-conservative-politics-hes-cultivated-amplified-it/.
Byrne, Donn Erwin. *The Attraction Paradigm*. New York: Academic, 1971.
Charmaz, Kathy. *Constructing Grounded Theory*. 2nd Edition. Thousand Oaks: Sage Publications, 2014.
Choi, Kate H., and Marta Tienda. "Marriage-Market Constraints and Mate-Selection Behavior: Racial, Ethnic, and Gender Differences in Intermarriage." *Journal of Marriage and Family* 79, no. 2 (2016): 301–17.
Chou, Rosalind S. *Asian American Sexual Politics: The Construction of Race, Gender, and Sexuality*. Lanham, MD: Rowman and Littlefield, 2012.
Chow, Sue. "The Significance of Race in the Private Sphere: Asian Americans and Spousal Preferences." *Sociological Inquiry* 70, no. 1 (Winter 2000): 1–29.
Clarke, Averil Y. *Inequalities of Love: College-educated Black Women and the Barriers to Romance and Family*. Durham: Duke University Press, 2011.
Cohen, Philip, and Joanna Pepin. "Unequal Marriage Markets: Sex Ratios and First Marriage Among Black and White Women." *Socius: Sociological Research for a Dynamic World* 4 (2018): 1–10.
Collins, Patricia Hill. *Black Feminist Thought: Knowledge, Consciousness, and the Politics of Empowerment*. New York: Routledge, 2009.
Conway, Madeline. "How Donald Trump Changed the Dating World." *Politico*. October 30, 2016. Accessed at https://www.politico.com/story/2016/10/donald-trump-dating-world-singles-230493.
Cox, Daniel A., Jacqueline Clemence, and Eleanor O'Neil. "Partisan Attachment: How Politics is Changing Dating and Relationships in the Trump Era." American Enterprise Institute. February 6, 2020. Accessed at https://www.aei.org/research-products/report/partisan-attachment-how-politics-is-changing-dating-and-relationships-in-the-trump-era/.
Del Valle, Gaby. "'For Conservatives, by Conservatives': The Rise of Right-Wing Dating Apps." *Vox*. December 26, 2018. Accessed at https://www.vox.com/the-goods/2018/12/26/18150322/righter-donald-daters-patrio-conservative-dating-apps.
Eastwick, Paul W., Jennifer A. Richeson, Deborah Son, and Eli Finkel. "Is Love Colorblind? Political Orientation and Interracial Romantic Desire." *Personality and Social Psychology Bulletin* 35, no. 9 (September 2009): 1258–68.
Edin, Kathryn, and Timothy J. Nelson. *Doing the Best I Can: Fatherhood in the Innercity*. Berkeley: University of California Press, 2013.
Frankenberg, Ruth. *White Women, Race Matters: The Social Construction of Whiteness*. Minneapolis: The University of Minnesota Press, 1993.
Flores, René D., and Ariela Schachter. "Who Are the 'Illegals'?: The Social Construction of Illegality in the United States." *American Sociological Review* 83, no. 5 (2018): 839–68.
Geiger, A.W. and Gretchen Livingston. 2019. "8 Facts About Love and Marriage in America." *Pew Research Center*. Retrieved February 10th, 2020. Accessed at https://www.pewresearch.org/fact-tank/2019/02/13/8-facts-about-love-and-marriage/.

Graham, David A., Adrienne Green, Cullen Murphy, and Parker Richards. "An Oral History of Trump's Bigotry." *The Atlantic.* June 1, 2019. Accessed at https://www.theatlantic.com/magazine/archive/2019/06/trump-racism-comments/588067/

Huber, Gregory A., and Neil Maholtra. "Political Homophily in Social Relationships: Evidence from Online Dating Behavior." *Journal of Politics* 79, no. 1 (October 2016): 269–83.

Hunter, Tera W. *Bound in Wedlock: Slave and Free Black Marriage in the Nineteenth Century.* Cambridge: The Belknap Press of Harvard University Press, 2017.

Hwang, Wei-Chin. "Who are People Willing to Date? Ethnic and Gender Patterns in Online Dating." *Race and Social Problems* 5, no. 1 (2013): 28–40.

Kalmijn, Matthijs. "Intermarriage and Homogamy: Causes, Patterns, and Trends." *Annual Review of Sociology* 24 (1998): 395–421.

Kim, Claire Jean. "The Racial Triangulation of Asian Americans." *Politics and Society* 25, no. 1 (1999): 105–38.

Kozloski, Michael. "Homosexual Moral Acceptance and Social Tolerance: Are the Effects of Education Changing?" *Journal of Homosexuality* 57, no. 10 (2010): 1370–83.

Lee, Jennifer, and Frank D. Bean. *The Diversity Paradox: Immigration and the Color Line in Twenty-First-Century America.* New York: Russell Sage Foundation, 2010.

Lichter, Daniel T., Diane K. McLauglin, George Kephart, and David J. Landry. "Race and the Retreat from Marriage: A Shortage of Marriageable Men?" *American Sociological Review* 57, no. 6 (1992): 781–99.

Lin, Ken-Hou, and Jennifer H. Lundquist. "Mate Selection in Cyberspace: The Intersection of Race, Gender, and Education." *American Journal of Sociology* 119, no. 1 (2013):183–215.

Livingston, Gretchen, and Anna Brown. "Intermarriage in the U.S. 50 Years After Loving v. Virginia." *Pew Research Center.* Retrieved July 6, 2020. Accessed at https://www.pewsocialtrends.org/2017/05/18/intermarriage-in-the-u-s-50-years-after-loving-v-virginia/.

Mangum, Maurice. "The Racial Underpinnings of Party Identification and Political Ideology." *Social Science Quarterly* 94, no. 5 (December 2013): 1222–44.

Massey, Douglas S., and Nancy A. Denton. *American Apartheid: Segregation and the Making of the Underclass.* Cambridge: Harvard University Press, 1993.

Meltzer, Andrea L., James K. McNulty, Grace L. Jackson, and Benjamin R. Karney. "Men Still Value Physical Attractiveness in a Long-Term Mate More Than Women: Rejoinder to Eastwick, Neff, Finkel, Luchies, and Hunt." *Journal of Personality and Social Psychology* 106, no. 3 (2014): 418–28.

Mills, Charles W. *The Racial Contract.* Ithaca: Cornell University Press, 1997.

Moore, Darnell L. "Black Radical Love: A Practice." *Public Integrity* 20, no. 4 (2018): 325–28.

Moynihan, Daniel P. "The Negro Family: The Case for National Action." Office of Policy Planning and Research. United States Department of Labor, 1965.

Muro, Jazmin A., and Lisa M. Martinez. "Constrained Desires: The Romantic Preferences of College-Educated Latinas." *Latino Studies* 14, no. 2 (2016): 172–91.

Musick, Kelly, and Larry Bumpass. "Reexamining the Case for Marriage: Union Formation and Changes in Well-Being." *Journal of Marriage and Family* 74, no. 1 (2012): 1–18.

Nagel, Joane. *Race, Ethnicity, and Sexuality: Intimate Intersections, Forbidden Frontiers.* New York: Oxford University Press, 2003.

Nemoto, Kumiko. *Racing Romance: Love, Power, and Desire among Asian American/White Couples.* New Brunswick: Rutgers University Press, 2009.

O'Neal, Traci D. *The Exceptional Negro: Racism, White Privilege and the Lie of Respectability Politics.* Atlanta: iCart Media LLC, 2018.

Rosenfeld, Michael J., Reuben J. Thomas, and Sonia Hausen. "Disintermediating Your Friends: How Online Dating in the United States Displaces Other Ways of Meeting." *PNAS* 116, no. 36 (2019): 17753–58.

Schoon, Ingrid, Helen Cheng, Catharine R. Gale, G. David Batty, and Ian J. Deary. "Social Status, Cognitive Ability, and Educational Attainment as Predictors of Liberal Social Attitudes and Political Trust." *Intelligence* 38 (2010): 144–50.

Schwartz, Christine R. "Trends and Variation in Assortative Mating: Causes and Consequences." *Annual Review of Sociology* 39, no. 1 (2013): 451–70.

Serna, A., Jr. "She's Not Your African Goddess, Spicy Latina, or Jade Princess—She's a Fucking Person." *Substance* Blog. January 10, 2017. Retrieved February 2, 2020. Accessed at https://substance.media/shes-not-your-african-goddess-spicy-latina-or-jade-princess-she-s-a-fucking-person-1c4e1ecaab6b.

South, Scott J., and Kyle D. Crowder. "Neighborhood Effects on Family Formation: Concentrated Poverty and Beyond." *American Sociological Review* 64, no. 1 (1999): 113–32.

Spira, Julie. "Love Vs. Trump: Is Politics Polarizing Relationships?" *Cyber-dating Expert*. 2017. Accessed at https://cyberdatingexpert.com/love-vs-trump-politics-relationships/.

Squires, Gregory D., and Charles E. Kubrin. *Privileged Places: Race, Residence, and the Structure of Opportunity*. Boulder: Lynne Rienner Publishers, 2006.

Steinbugler, Amy C. *Beyond Loving: Intimate Racework in Lesbian, Gay, and Straight Interracial Relationships*. New York: Oxford University Press, 2012.

Thomas, Reuben J. "Online Exogamy Reconsidered: Estimating the Internet's Effects on Racial, Educational, Religious, Political and Age Assortative Mating." *Social Forces* 98, no. 3 (2019): 1257–86.

Vazquez, Jessica M. "Disciplined Preferences: Explaining the (Re)production of Latino Endogamy." *Social Problems* 62 (2015): 455–75.

Williamson, Vanessa, and Isabella Gelfand. "Trump and Racism: What Do the Data Say." Brookings. Wednesday, August 14, 2019. Accessed at https://www.brookings.edu/blog/fixgov/2019/08/14/trump-and-racism-what-do-the-data-say/.

Wu, Huijing. "FP-18-18 Homogamy in U.S. Marriages, 2016" National Center for Family and Marriage Research Family Profiles, 2018. Accessed at https://scholarworks.bgsu.edu/ncfmr_family_profiles/157.

THREE

The Asian-American Experience and the White Gaze

On the Potentiality of Naming Oneself from Nowhere

Nora Tsou

I did not foresee my arrival to this place I have yet to name. Within this vicinity of no name, I sense a belonging and a pressure that uplifts me and demands great responsibility. I am an Asian-American despite never considering myself Asian-American; and yet, I have no other name to call myself. I have no present space, no readily available ancestral home; as an Asian-American I am always outside of my identity. I know myself through what I am not, and never claim who I am or who I ought to be. In my identity diaspora, I want my Asian-hood, but I find myself passing into alterity.

To hold onto and let go of identity in the same motion, moving within contradiction yet not wanting a way out, I watch as my identity is transfigured, interpellated, by persons outside of my body. I watch as layers of history and culture press down on me and tell me to stay put. They call it power, the power to name, to press and oppress. But there exists another power, the power to liberate, to call into question the constructs and their weight without being weighed down.

As a marginalized woman of color, I have not had the same authority to speak as do white men emboldened by centuries of Eurocentric, patriarchal views of truth. Before they speak, their voice is always already endorsed with a social capital that my voice does not have. Before I can join in the conversation about the Beautiful with Plato, there are steps I must take to fight for the recognition of my personhood and position simply so that I can be included and heard. Hence, before I speak about the white gaze and the Asian-American experience, I first reflect on what it means to acquire a voice. Without the same social capital that white people inherit, I, like other people of color, am prompted to ask myself a question that people who identify as white often naturally assume: Do I have my own agency, and if so, what does it look like to lay claim to and restore my positionality as an "I"?

Put simply, the Asian-American is a person of Asian decent living in America. Those of us who fall under this identification may share this, but realistically, our narratives are radically widespread. What we do share in common is how the white gaze limits the Asian-American to a particular vision of the self. As we come to a racial understanding of ourselves in the context of America—to see how we are seen by others—there is a kind of emptiness that is created, an abyss, for potential narratives to be lived and heard. Our possibility for authenticity is stifled under the white gaze. The white gaze both upholds and coincides with the denial and perpetuation of institutionalized racism. It not only penetrates the world by fixing people of color in a status upheld by both myth and stereotype via mass media and education, but it also denies the existence of its gaze and interprets the world it created by assuming whiteness as normative, natural. As it continuously affirms itself, it denies people of color an ontology of potential. And so, the "Asian-American" does not identify with the caricature that is presented to her; as a result, she often begins to identify with the lived experience and cultures of her marginalized counterparts. Here she finds a feeling of belonging that coincides with an understanding she does not belong, throwing her into an identity diaspora.

Concurrently, she cycles through an ongoing contemplative process of what it means to be raced, or Asian-American, or woman, or constructed, or oppressed in America. Although this essay does not encompass each identity category in its entirety, or each individual lived experience in its uniqueness, I hope that it may give voice to the Asian-American experience, as one who is raced and fighting for agency and personhood. Oppressed and marginalized people are always under a veil;[1] we are never fully seen, for we become extensions of the white imagination. Eurocentric colonialist thought attempts to colonize the mind of people of color so that we remain forever veiled. To decolonize the mind[2] is to understand that oppressive power opposes love. To write out of love and to undergo love in order to write is a necessary responsibility in order to speak truth to power.

THE ACQUISITION OF THE I

Marginalized groups are regularly subjected to a reinforced miseducation.[3] Hence, when one does not question the system, one does not learn to reveal the depths of her own oppression.

Who am I? A woman, an Asian woman, a raced woman. Resilient in nature, but constructed as weaker, passive, silent; I opened my mouth and only felt the butterflies in my gut. A colonialist history hanging over me tried to reach inside of me; it ordered me to be subservient and scolded me for questioning the status quo.

Given a racialized name and a role, I was told not to look for more. If I accepted things for how they were, disruption would not occur, and peace would be maintained. Alas, it is a false peace, predicated on a deep despair coursing from generation to generation, that is oppressed by the interpellated vision of others, by their Manifest Destiny, their Make America Great Again. It is a false peace grounded in the "imperialist, White supremacist, capitalist, patriarchy" system.[4]

I rise to speak, but before I can, the white gaze has layered me, overdetermined me, with biases that veil me from being heard or seen. I become covered and altered, for their perception of me overrules what I have yet to say so that what I have yet to say is misconfigured and muffled. My intention, my purpose is no longer clear nor mine; it is projected onto me from another's mind as he misinterprets my intention. Regardless, whether the white gaze's misinterpretation of me is the result of overt intention or by an implicit confirmation bias, the miseducation and circulating language around "who raced woman are" has been shaping the social milieu long before my birth.

How can my disguised personhood, my voice that is veiled, speak honestly in a place yet to be named, in a room with no listeners? But I must speak. A voice becomes a voice when it is listened to by another. But that other could be the same self, re-absorbing and taking seriously the message, taking it in compassionately and in its full value.[5] But the self longs to be heard by the other. She wants welcome and acknowledgement, understanding and dialogue. To speak is to acquire the *I*. To listen is to heed the other. We both need to acquire understanding. Acquiring the *I* needs the other; I am *I* when you see me as *you*, or as Buber famously put it, as *Thou*. But as long as the Asian woman is a construction, she is not truly seen as a "you." Rather, she is seen as a category: "an Asian," a "girl," referred to as a "she" without a name.[6]

When a voice is silenced, her personhood is masked; she fades out of memory, rendered invisible.[7] With no memory of her voice, her testimony, her witness, she is almost not there, but she was! She cried in streams and echoes and the people heard, but did not listen. Without the I, one is grouped into a category, rendered abstract. She is subsumed within a monochromatic crew of people, the *They*, constricted, each marching alike, each in melody with the other. She has no self-autonomy, no self-sovereignty, she is relegated to the herd of the oppressed. Never does she walk without the group in her shadow; she walks for all.[8]

The space she lives in shrinks her down and minimizes her being, her potential. She moves and it contracts. Her expansiveness is limited without the I to expand into. What can she question if first not her I? Hence, the I is imperative in order to inquire further into life. As Du Bois writes, "And yet he saw in himself some faint revelation of his power, of his mission. He began to have a dim feeling that, to attain his place in the world, he must be himself, and not another."[9] It seems obvious to be a self, but the self has been denied to people of color. A person of color has been referred to as inferior to the self of a white person, as incapable of self-reflection. So how can we claim our *I* when we have for centuries been told we have no consciousness of an *I*?

It is first described as lived experience, as narrative and story. I affirm as true the life I have faced and the life that exists through me. I affirm the empirical reality of my life; I affirm my memories, these reflections of my lived experience. I affirm the temporality of my existence—of past oppression that persists into the future, that I wish not to pass on to future generations. I affirm the capacity for imagination: I can reimagine the racialized constructions. I can imagine things beautiful—love, laughter, and tears. Even if muffled, these affirmations will disrupt the veil.

This process takes effort; it is a fight, an act of resistance. The one without voice battles the internalization of a colonized mind. She battles her counterparts that have yet to question the herd. The dominant system of power grants her no room to rise up, but she must surge forth to the point of her own rupture.

WHO IS THE ASIAN-AMERICAN?

The term "Asian-American" was birthed from the necessity of needing a name, a space, and a voice in America. In order to participate in American political dialogue and the internal layers of culture, people of Asian descent desired to step into the arena with a name. At the time I was born, the term was already circulating, thus it was "externally imposed" onto me.[10] Rather than creating a name, I was told what my name should be, similar to the name one is given by their parents at birth. There is always a weight and a history that goes along with a name.

The name "Asian-American" creates a space, even if the very contours of that space challenge the adequacy of the term itself. The term conflates the vast array of ethnic groups and experiences within the Asian community and their intragroup relations.[11] Compressed into this one term are Asian people of different cultures, skin tones,[12] and languages; of varying socio-economic levels or social classes; American-born or immigrant, first generation or several generations in; those residing on the West Coast, in the South, in large urban areas with a designated "Chinatown" (NY, San Francisco, Chicago, etc.), or scattered throughout the country. These various groups of Asian-Americans do not have the same lived experience. Further, we may individually trace ourselves to Asian countries of ancestral origin, but we may (or may not) know about that place and feel displaced from our ancestral context.

"Asian" and "American" each carry a tradition and history that maintain a distance from each other. For the term to merge into a new historical context, the joining of the two histories asks us what must shift or be erased as a result of this combination. Its hyphenation illustrates the conjoining of two separate entities; each word on its own is insufficient to describe the reality of the Asian living in America. "To claim a hyphenate identity is to assert a subject position while simultaneously asserting the impossibility of stable positioning."[13] The hyphen, a metaphorical gap, bridges and also distances the two. The gap, as it were, an absence, a null-space, is a site of incompletion. The two spaces cannot be fused and morphed into one, but they can press on each other and stand in relation.

Within the community of Asian-Americans are people that identify as multiracial. As Asian people are already a minority in America, so the multiracial Asian-American is a marginalized subset of the overarching (yet already marginalized) Asian-American group. To be a multiracial Asian-American means to be the combination of one or more Asian ethnicities and one or more ethnicities exterior to the Asian population. Because multiracial Asians can come from many backgrounds, there is no one face or one look that can truly represent a multiracial Asian person.[14] Thus, it is difficult for the multiracial person to feel reflected in family, popular culture, or the academic classroom. In my family, I do not look like my Chinese side or my Irish side, for I am a mixture of both ethnicities. In American culture, I may see parts of my multiracial identity represented in only monoracial ways. Hence I never see myself, my full multiracial experience, represented and mirrored before my eyes.

To be multiracial is to be raced, for the question of race is always relevant to the lived experience of the multiracial Asian-American. It is something she must contemplate, must work through, must doubt and transfigure. As Asian-Americans search for the meaning of their identity in terms of language, multiracial-ness and situated history, they undergo a process of becoming. Asian-Americans go into the unknown with an opportunity to create a new identity.

Although we know the terms "Asian-American" or "multiracial Asian-American" do not gather in them our full realities, we are compelled to use them in order to speak from an identity and form a community. But instead of clinging to the term as fixed and stagnant, Asian-Americans grant these terms space to change in interpretation and meaning. For we may move away from them, as language and its word genealogy has stood testimony to this type of evolution. Instead of *being* Asian-American, we use that word as beginning a process of *becoming* what is not yet named. Our evolution travels into what is unknown, for our very experience of this world has not yet been lived and our language must support that new experience.

THE WHITE GAZE

America is a white supremacist space not only due to its fundamentally assumed racist hierarchy, one that is intended to keep "minorities in a subordinated position,"[15] but also due to the perpetuation of racist institutions and laws. Racism as a political, economical, and cultural system remains intact through processes of denial and perpetuation. The white gaze is the way in which whiteness penetrates and perceives the world, shaping a collective understanding of the world and a status quo that supports white supremacy. It operates with a fallacious epistemology, "linked to various raced and racist myths [and] white discursive practices," in order to look upon the world from a position of superiority.[16]

The white gaze operates with a three-fold denial: it denies the white supremacist system, it denies the white self as complicit with the system, and it denies the ontological personhood of people of color. White people find themselves the inheritors of America's white supremacy, but they are often unable to understand the effects both on themselves and society as a whole. From their positionality as the ones who holds the gaze and the truth, they have in turn created a "structured blindness"[17] that damages their ability to see. This blindness reinforces that America holds equal opportunity for people across all races, all the while denying the ways in which the system and our collective psyche are influenced by slavery, generational wealth, redlining, inequitable distribution of education and resources, and mass media representation. When white people do not understand institutionalized racism and how their white bodies perpetuate the system, it is not difficult for them to then claim that they are not racist. Because they have limited racism to discrete intentional personal actions—a vocalized hatred for people of color or open support for white supremacy—they think they are not racist. However, as Yancy points out, "racist actions are also habits of the body and not simply cognitively false beliefs . . . constructed ignorance is *cultural*, and not just an individual act."[18] Through a historical and generational miseducation, white people absorb racist propaganda that they perform mundanely and implicitly when they encounter racialized bodies. This performance has nothing to do with the person of color with who they are standing before, face-to-face, but instead with the imagined and constructed person of color they are trained to see. Thus, the person of color is denied, for the white gaze renders invisible the people and the process by which the people are turned invisible. On a mundane subconscious level and on a structural level, the system perpetuates in its ability to obscure its performance of whiteness.

When something is denied, it tries to avoid question. In fact, it relies on not being questioned, so that it will not be exposed as something that exists. While it is denied, it insidiously perpetuates and creates an operative intentionality within the world. "Operative intentionality depicts an intentionality always already present in the world because we occupy a specific spatial and historical location within a community."[19] Other than our autonomous intentionality, operative intentionality is the intentionality that keeps the status quo, that keeps white supremacy as the normative system. As our bodily movement inhabits space and time, we have a responsibility for the situation and the history we are born into, and not only our autonomous intentionality. Additionally, our bodily movement reflects and responds to the social situation at the same time that it perpetuates the social situation. Hence, if our bodily movement coincides with the white supremacist operative intentionality, then we are complicit in the injustice of inequality. In this line of argument, the white woman born in America who reaps the benefits of her whiteness that comes at the expense of prejudice against people of color, even without intending to, is still held responsible for her situation. Although the status quo perpetuates without our consent, as we live in America without question or fight, white people—and even people of color—can unintentionally (and intentionally) perpetuate white supremacy.

White people in America inherit "the privileged status of being the 'lookers' and gazers, with all the power that this entailed."[20] As the one who sees, she is the one who knows: "her perspective, her subjectivity, is deemed the only important perspective, the one that makes a difference, the one that has historically reaped the benefit of recognition within the context of white North America."[21] Through the white gaze, his judgment is truth so that he is the gatekeeper of our cultural canon, from deeming what laws are in place to what political matters are most valuable, to who may get hired for a job, or to what counts as beautiful. Thus, when a white person comes into contact with a racialized body—and it is almost always a nonwhite body that is racialized—her cultural gaze has already informed herself how to categorize this person of color. Yancy continues: "The White woman thinks that her act of 'seeing' me is an act of 'knowing' who I am, of knowing what I will do next, that is, hers is believed to be simply a process of unmediated or uninterpreted perception. However, her coming to 'see' me as she does is actually a cultural achievement, a racist sociohistorical schematization, indeed, an act of epistemic violence."[22] The white woman does not question how her country's history and its perpetuation of white supremacy has shaped her gaze. She believes her perceiving is objective and coincides with what is natural, but fails to recognize how generations of white supremacist propaganda have influenced and *trained* her to see the world in a certain way. Again, this is another way in which whiteness denies itself—it tries to pass itself off as natural, as normative, instead of a construction of truth.

In knowing people of color, the white woman fixes her state of knowing, which in fact limits her potential for knowledge and her potential to broaden her own horizon of being. Such a hegemonic act of comprehensive knowing is really totalitarianism by another name. As Levinas writes, "If one could possess, grasp, and know the other, it would not be other. Possessing, knowing, and grasping are synonyms of power."[23] When the white woman encounters a racialized body, she possesses it as it becomes an extension and formulation of the white mind. The knowledge gathered from the white gaze is truly a form of power. It has the liberty to call itself knowledge and to control the image of another human while denying the perspective and forms of knowledge of that other person. Under the power of the white gaze, my uniqueness and my alterity is subsumed, for I am seen only as a constructed image. These constructions, often called stereotypes, saturate images of people of color. This fabricated image begins to take place and precedence over all people of color and their autonomy. Thus, their personhood and autonomy is erased. The white gazer, (sometimes) unaware of her asymmetrical positionality as one who holds the only valued truth, but always already having that power over the person of color, does not see her perception of me as a construction: the Asian woman. She does not see this process of constructing me, and thus misses the opportunity to encounter me as I see myself.

In turn, the person of color may not know to what extent she is not seen. Likewise, she may not know the depths of her own oppression. However, she is accustomed to receiving certain habits and patterns of white behavior so that she acquires a "heightened sensitivity" to racial interactions.[24] In the approach of a white person, who I know myself to be is disrupted. Du Bois calls this double consciousness. He defined double consciousness as a way in which one sees herself, at the site of her body, through the eyes of the other, who interprets her as being different than who she knows herself to be. Yancy writes "Du Bois was forced into a state of doubleness, *seeing* himself as other (the inferior Black) through the gaze of the young girl as the one (the superior white)."[25] Through the years of coming in contact with repeated and habitual responses to my racialized body, I come to understand what I am to the white man (or woman). I understand his perception of me, but I also understand my perception of myself. However, his perception of me holds a heightened historical and cultural power in the American context. Before I understood myself apart from the white gaze, I grew up seeing images and listening to rhetoric about my race and gender that we were supposed to accept as normal. Thus, the white gaze is internalized by people of color and must be unsown and deconstructed. Again, it is difficult to know the depth of my oppression because I was raised to see myself inauthentically.

As we uncover an understanding of our oppression, we also try to decipher and rationalize the white gaze. One way to survive oppression is to make sense of the oppressor, to understand that his actions are a reflection of his psyche and not merely a fair response to the oppressed. If not, we may believe we are to blame for good reason and internalize a form of self-hate. According to Anzaldúa, the white gaze locks us into a role of us-versus-them antagonism, where white vulnerabilities and fears are projected onto the raced minority group. Anzaldúa, speaking from her brown experience, addresses the white audience and states: "To say you've split yourself from minority groups, that you disown us, that your dual consciousness splits off parts of yourself, transferring the 'negative' parts onto us. (Where there is persecution of minorities, there is shadow projection. Where there is violence and war, there is repression of shadow)."[26]

To maintain whiteness as something intrinsically good and pure, the white gaze scapegoats minorities and defines them as intrinsically bad. To separate from and "disown" the minority population is a denial of responsibility for the role white people have in the struggle people of color face. Furthermore, under a white supremacy that operates through denial, the white person denying the system, in turn, denies his complete self. Instead of seeing himself, he projects what he does not want to face about himself onto people of color. Thus, he removes parts of the self and removes the responsibility to face those parts.

The white gaze, grounded in denial, results in a self-inflicted trauma. The white person lives in fear of people of color, but this fear is predicated upon self-created myths and constructions of people of color. If not for these constructions, white people would save themselves from embodying fear whenever they encounter a "criminalized" person of color—a young Black teen carrying iced tea and Skittles is perceived as a threat, as "up to no good" and "on drugs or something," worthy of being followed and attacked.[27] It seems as if America is stuck in the stage of denial. It would be such a painful process to grieve and reconcile the America that white supremacy has created, that it is easier for white America to stay in denial.

Although we must challenge the white gaze and expose its operation, an us-against-them dynamic limits us as reactionary, always in a mode of defense and challenge. Anzaldúa continues:

> A counterstance locks one into a duel of oppressor and oppressed; locked in mortal combat, like the cop and the criminal, both are reduced to a common denominator of violence. The counterstance refutes the dominant culture's views and beliefs, and, for this, it is proudly

defiant. . . . Because the counterstance stems from a problem of authority—outer as well as inner—it's a step towards liberation from cultural domination. But it is not a way of life.[28]

Anzaldúa argues that the act of resistance is necessary. Her book *Borderlands* would not have been written if it were not for the need to serve as an active form of resistance to white supremacy. However, remaining in this counterstance limits the minority population to a reactive sense of identity. Like two billiard balls in a constant motion of swinging back and forth only to hit each other, this perpetuation of reactionary motion leads to no growth. The reaction of defiance against the white gaze is a means to liberation, but it is not liberation itself.

Greg Carr writes, "There's a political nature to all scholarship. . . . This is a conversation you could only have in a black space . . . because if you don't have it in a black space, you're challenging the white space."[29] While Carr is speaking in particular about Hip-Hop and the Black experience, for my purpose it speaks to the importance of supplementing acts of resistance to white supremacy with positive forms of identity construction that occur within one's own space or community. Writing an essay on race already assumes a white space, assumes a process of negotiating what can or cannot be said, assumes an act of resistance. People of color cannot remove the white gaze, but we can situate ourselves in borderlands or liminal spaces where we have the freedom of conversation to explore our authentic selves.

A PHENOMENOLOGY OF THE LATINIZED ASIAN AND HER SECONDARY CULTURE

Inflections sound like rain, rain with semantics, a comfort never understood, foreign inside the home, myself, a foreigner as home. From the voice of my grandmother I hear Mandarin. I hear short syllables, but the meaning slips away as something I cannot capture. ¿Cómo se dices yes in Mandarin? She loved me I knew, she talked to me through laughter and smiles. My first definition of love, laughter, and smiles in the midst of incomprehension, of language barriers, of grandmother distanced from granddaughter, a severed bond. Love in a place of disconnect, laughter as an instrument of love.

I found comfort in the dialogue I could not understand. My grandparents and my father spoke around me and I was invited to join in, but the language was not in my mind as meaningful. Rather, it registered in my mind affectively, as a safe haven for not needing semantic meaning. Though I did not understand, I listened to this otherness that was dear to my heart that signified I was home. It was soothing to hear rhythms as opposed to comprehension.

I listened as words poured into the air. Mandarin was intended for me; one line of my ancestors believed that I would carry on the language. But I was stripped of my heritage, *Americanized*. My Chinese father discontinued his native tongue, doing what he thought was best for his children. My roots pushed further down. If I wanted them, I'd have to dig. I'd have to search in the soil for parts of me, lost parts, severed parts, erased. Living in search of broken pieces, my hand shooting blindly into the soil, sometimes retrieving thorns, sometimes roses. These were parts of me that were unknown to myself, dormant; yet I still call them mine. I needed to begin from a broken place. "I will keep broken things. I will keep you: Pilgrim of sorrow. I will keep myself."[30]

I left home and found home in the same form, but in a shifted context, in a different language. Spanish was like the soul of my counterpart twin, the bordering tongue of Mexico to California, California once Mexico. *Yo soy China, pero todavía aprendiendo español. Quiero saber español.* At first, I enjoyed the comfort of not knowing this language well. I enjoyed listening without understanding and it sounded beautiful to me. But it started to enter me; I began to learn. And once I learned a little, I yearned to learn more. It isn't just discrete words; it's the way dialogue is exchanged that reflects a culture, a language. *¿Verdad que si? Si, es verdad.* It's true yes? Yes, it's true. Spanish is rhythmic in its reflection, reflection in the other before embarking on independent thought. The dialogue is marked by connection before separation. I was ruptured once more by a third tongue. I found refuge in it, its idiosyncrasies, but it is still outside of me, where I cannot go. Where I can sense, but not live.

I did not attend Chinese school to learn the language, to be with my people in the space of my people. I did not have the community, the culture, the home, the cousins, aunts or uncles. I longed for my Asian reflection, but I could not manifest it in my circumstances. And while I had no home for my relationship to my community, I had the geographical place of the Bay Area and California that cultured me. Marked as other, I searched for my others. I looked in the faces of my Latina friends, the closest mirror I could find, and in return, I augmented my Asian identity in the struggle of not having, not having community, not having reflection nor home. Out of need came this authentic augmentation, a way out and a way in, a development of character I could not separate from, for I have no memory of another version of me.

I work at a taqueria, a borderland, where Spanish music moves through the rooms and Spanish language can be heard in the kitchen and be read on the menu. For Hispanic people, this is a place of home, a place of familiarity in a country where dominant spaces are white spaces created for white people. Because of my multiracial heritage, I am often mistaken as Latina, by both Hispanic people and by white people. While working at the taqueria, I was assumed to be Latina by the customers, and this led me to a deeper solidarity with Hispanic people; at the same time I felt the pain of undergoing the micro-aggressions Hispanic people face that result from the white gaze. Hispanic customers would speak to me in Spanish, and I would hold my own in the Spanish conversation. They would ask me ¿de donde eres? Because they noticed the difference in my accent. I would explain that I was actually Chinese and they would often not believe me and tell me I look Mexican or Salvadorian. Even before working at the taqueria, I experienced people thinking I was Latina, but the taqueria increased the frequency of such an event.

My ethnic heritage and my cultural upbringing do not reflect either the biological or lived experience of my Latina counterparts. My oppression is subsequently different because the structural barriers for Asian-Americans are different. When I fill out applications, my last name, Tsou, reads Asian. However, when I am face-to-face with many people, my face reads Latina. On paper, I am the beneficiary of the so-called 'model minority' created by the white gaze; in person I experience the micro-aggressions and implicit biases that Latina people face.

For example, at the taqueria a white man calls, "Excuse me" and indicates through body language that he has a question. "Can I have a box to go?" His hands form the shape of a box. "Yes, would you like a smaller one or a larger one?" "No. Can I have a box?" Suddenly, I realize my words are erased and I am not heard. My English words, which I intentionally used to tend to him more specifically, do not constitute his reality of our joint experience. The harsh "No" signals that there is no question of *both* of us being misunderstood. It is I that is at fault for our, per se, lack of communication. The white man performs his whiteness by acting as a knower. Before he walks into the taqueria, he has assumptions of the type of people that work there. Before he hears me speak, he *knows* I do not speak English, or I do not speak English well. He assumes I cannot understand nor be understood and manifests his experience to that degree. He erases my language from his ears. He erases his chance to have dialogue with me. Precisely because I am *not* really seen by this white man, I am seen as merely a caricature of a Latina. With his performance of whiteness, I lose my English language; I become un-intellectual.

It is through these lived experiences where my empiricism overlaps with the lived experiences of Hispanic people. We share a solidarity insofar as I am taken as Mexican, and thus treated as such, treated as if I were one and the same and a part of the community. Treated as other, the white gaze sees me as Latina, in a modality that tears at my personhood. Between the features of my face and my dark hair, the geographical location I live in that situates me around Hispanic culture, and my performance of language and labor at a taqueria contributes to my Latinization when I am interpellated and perceived by others.

In East Los Angeles, poet Carol Lem lived, wrote, and taught among Chicano people and came to know herself culturally as Chicano, although she is of Chinese descent. She writes, "I survived the border mentality that comes with living in an urban environment such as Los Angeles all my life. . . . [That] living on the borderlands is both a geographical and psychological reality for the majority of students, has given me a shared identity with the Chicano population there."[31]

Lem's ancestral line reduces her to Chinese, but her cultural environment enlivened her experience of self and influenced her identity. This is not a case of disowning her Chinese roots, but she finds that "home comes out of this imagined place in the heart, something I create for myself each day."[32] Lem found that home was an emotive connection and a willingness to find what a home should be rather than what a home is. She realized that identity is closely tied to geography, for the geography of a place and the space and time created there fills one's memory of what it means to live. In her creation of home, Lem found solidarity with a racialized group in America that did not reflect her biology, but rather, reflected her lived experience and performance of race.

In order to understand the process in which Asian-Americans re-identify and feel more fully authentic by relating to another racialized culture, I turn to the 2019 film *Always Be My Maybe*. This film was directed by Nahnatchka Khan, written by Ali Wong, Randall Park, and Michael Golamco, and stars Ali Wong and Randall Park, all of whom are of Asian descent. Hence, this movie is an Asian-American narrative played and told by Asian-Americans themselves. The film takes place in San Francisco; I am from the Bay Area as well and have grown up in the culture. A monumental piece of Bay Area culture is its music, specifically its hip-hop. Music is a form of cultural expression and identity, for the music one plays reflects the person who chooses to listen. In *Always Be My Maybe*, hip-hop music is used to illustrate an Asian-American reality.

The movie opens to the song "93 'Til Infinity" by Souls of Mischief, a hip-hop group based out of Oakland. This song is a hallmark in the film, as it repeats throughout and Marcus (Randall Park) is shown listening to it in his room. Our introduction to the film through rap already situates the film as embedded within cultural and racial dimensions. The film directors do not whitewash the film; rather, they expose the strong connection some Asian-Americans have to hip-hop that comes from their community. Later in the film, it is revealed that Marcus is a rapper in a hip-hop band called Hello Peril. Although his sound does not replicate Souls of Mischief or mainstream Bay Area rap, his art form is one of rhythmic hip-hop. Marcus performing hip-hop is a reflection of his culture and an expression of his identity, an Asian-American identity connected to the African-American experience.

Unlike African-American or Latin-American cultures, Asian-Americans do not have a mainstream form of music that is regularly recognized in American pop culture. Nor is there a well represented group of Asian-American artists with a platform that speak on behalf of the Asian-American experience, although this movie may show there are some underrepresented groups that are trying to do so. Due to the lack of Asian-American representation in mainstream American culture, Asian-Americans growing up in places like San Francisco often identity with African-American culture in order to understand their own culture.

Carol Lem's biographical narrative and the film *Always Be My Maybe* reveal an Asian-American self-identification diaspora. These stories expose how Asians relate to a culture that is not intended for them because they have no other place to see their reality reflected among their own people within American life. Part of Asian-American culture becomes finding connections with other minority cultures, including Latin-American and African-American culture. The lack of representation on a mainstream scale leads Asian-Americans to forfeit their Asian identity in hopes to, like Carol Lem said, find home.

When we speak of an Asian-American, African-American, Latin-American and Native-American, we refer to a person's race in relation to their American nationality. However, when we refer to someone as American, we assume they are Euro-American; hence, the term "American" is synonymous with whiteness. When I utter "Asian-American," it feels somehow unfitting, not only because it involves attaching "Asian" to a nationality, but because I am also attaching "Asian" to whiteness. In attaching my Asian-hood to white America, I centralize whiteness as the base of my being-in-the-world. I am off-white, Asian-American, off-American, Asian-white. If it is the linguistic basis of my being, I am never fully accepted in my being-in-the-world, because I am never fully American.

America as a place of yellow, black, brown, red, and white[33] cultures allows one to assimilate not only into white-American culture, but into marginalized culture as well. The Asian-American performance of African-American and Latin-American culture as ritual and habitual becomes intrinsic to Asian-Americans' identity. While we experience distance from our Asian-hood, whether that be due to rarely seeing Asian visuals in popular culture, or because the images we do see fail to reflect our individual identity (for example, the caricature images of Asian-Americans with harsh accents as humor to the white gaze or numerous ethnic populations subsumed under the heading "Asian"), whether our Asian community or the lack thereof does not foster our personhood, we find ourselves searching for a place yet to be named. We identify ourselves through our relation with other cultures, but we have yet to create a space for our own culture.

WHAT AROSE FROM INDIGNATION

The oppressed person feels a righteous anger, but she may be unaware of the causes for that anger. This anger may become manifested as misdirected, one that fails to target the cause. Nonetheless there is a turmoil that builds as a result of a denied liberation. Instead of flourishing, there is contracting and a stifling of a potentially thriving authentic voice in the world. As a result, her spirit pushes back. This indignation is a feeling that is unfulfilling in itself and not something one wants to live in. For it gives one the opportunity to turn in to one's self and reflect on this sentiment. Intuitively, she feels a resistance against a system or people she does not want to assimilate into. She says, "No" to imitating her surroundings. As Frantz Fanon writes, "It is easy to understand why the first reaction of the black man is to say *no* to those who endeavor to define him. It is understandable that the black man's first action is a *reaction*."[34] It is from a place of indignation that brings her to her consciousness of what she has experienced. It is from this passion that she thinks there must be a better way. She can no longer remain silent about her condition, but must ask herself for change.

In this desire for change, the person of color approaches the other in a modality of already decided intention, in hopes that the gazer will perceive this intention in its truth. Adjacently, the one who gazes, who receives the person of color's action, is the interpreter of such intention of act, and has the responsibility to see its truth and react accordingly. This interpreting may be less noticeable in bodily appearance, but it is not a passive act. As the person of color approaches, the gazer's being and her knowledge of the situation yet to take place is suspended, is called into question. As Merold Westphal writes, "My gazing is *aufgehoben* or teleologically suspended in my being addressed" by the other.[35] However, the white gaze distorts this process of receiving and reading when the white person fails to suspend herself, when she thwarts, bypasses, or prematurely puts a stop to this reversal of intentionality. In privileging an assumed construction of the person of color, she has already dictated who this person is and how she will act. With no suspension of the self, she has no room to interpret the person of color's intentions truthfully.

In a public talk, George Yancy asked what it would look like for a white person to perform the question, "Who art thou? . . . without a speech act."[36] With this question, the white person suspends her being and suspends her knowledge. In order to recognize the other as one who is "I"—or as a *Thou*—the white gazer's "identity is placed in abeyance" so that both the person of color and the white person "become after the question is answered."[37] For example, an Asian woman may approach the space of a white man. If the white man assumes she embodies the China doll stereotype,[38] she becomes the China doll and he becomes a man who exerts power over the woman through the sexualized stereotype of the woman. However, the question, "Who art thou?" halts the process of assumption, and the act without speech informs the person of color that she is not being misconstrued. This act of questioning disrupts the assumptions and constructions of knowledge that have been indoctrinated in the minds of many white Americans. With this act, the white person has the chance to become different as well.

When the person of color is, in fact, unknown, she regains her agency and has the power to make herself known through her actions. She is received, not as a construction, not as preimagined and therefore predestined, but with autonomous personhood. As Gloria Anzaldúa writes, "I seek an exoneration, a seeing through the fictions of white supremacy, a seeing of ourselves in our true guises and not as the false racial personality that has been given to us and that we have given to ourselves."[39] If this is to be achieved, there must be a process of white self-reflection that attempts to perform the "Who art thou?" question, which is ultimately not an interrogation of the other, but an interrogation of the self. Whiteness must learn about itself in ways that do not include denial and "epistemic dishonesty."[40] Presently, social relations between races are unhinged and disconnected through constructions of the white gaze. We must learn about this process of disconnect before we start the process toward reconnection. We must peel back the mask of whiteness, for this simultaneously begins the process of removing our veil.

As the person of color exposes whiteness, she must tend carefully to her own self-reflection. When she is not in the process of healing the hurt and strife that is inflicted upon her by white supremacy, she risks projecting her unreconciled anger in the form of resentment or revenge, most often manifesting itself in self-sabotaging ways. It can easily be projected onto others. Frantz Fanon describes one example of projection as such: "Since I was abandoned, I shall make the other suffer, and abandoning the other will be the direct expression of my need for revenge."[41] As mimetic beings, we are inclined to imitate the behavior of those around us. This becomes troublesome when we mimic "the master." The master could very well be the white gaze, or the trauma that has a hold on our present state of mind. When we imitate the master, we experience the pain we felt reflected in someone else's eyes and revenge becomes our salvation, or so we think. But this perpetuation of trauma spreads most commonly within the veil, to our beloveds. When we are not self-aware of when we are reliving our trauma, either through projection or reaction, we risk horizontally spreading hurt among the community as well as vertically cycling our grief through generational trauma. Our indignation may be quite necessary in order to awaken reform or revolution. However, the emotional baggage of this awakening cannot be left unsettled, for it will simmer in destructive ways. When we work through a lens of healing, we can also suspend our being before we react. A suspension and self-reflection familiarizes the self with an ontology of potential and a longing to grow.

WHAT AROSE FROM HOPE

She must speak. She must speak with courage, with a willingness to empty truth in the face of suppression. Her speech as testimony is a great act of resistance, for many people remain silent, and this silence is compliant and in accord with systemic oppression. The voice in itself leads back to one's agency and personhood. The questioning "troublemaker" voice is *the* philosophical task, the Socratic gadfly.[42] She performs an act of freedom when her voice is released from her body. As Anzaldúa writes, "The struggle is inner: Chicano, *indio*, American Indian, *mojado*, *mexicano*, immigrant Latino, Anglo in power, working class Anglo, Black, Asian—our psyches resemble the bordertowns and are populated by the same people."[43]

However, when her intention for justice is extended outside of herself, her voice no longer solely impacts her, but it impacts the consciousness of those around her. When the woman is within a place she has yet to name, she searches for a home, a feeling of deep belonging in the search for wisdom and commitment to others that is deeper than any set place. When this deep belonging is found, she feels a sense of return, a re-membering, more than a sense of discovery. The voice that speaks is always accompanied with a hope. "Through all the sorrow of the Sorrow Songs there breathes a hope—a faith in the ultimate justice of things."[44] Philosophy is performed as an act of great hope in the interrogation of the world and what the world may become as a result.

I find myself in this place I have yet to name. It is a place larger than myself, for it includes the experiences of others—other women, other Asian traditions, other oppressed people—that cannot be fully represented in this one life. To echo Feng, the Asian-American experience is one of becoming. We navigate the experience as we live through it; our embodied experiences become clearer as our lives go on. Because Asian-Americans draw from a multiplicity of narratives, of countries of origin and cultures, our experiences truly form a web, which is then situated within the web of positionality of race in America. A web is not rigid, but allows movement and augmented shape; this evolution is necessary in order to reflect the reality of Asian-American experience.

Since my philosophical studies at the institutions I have attended never named nor taught the views of an Asian-American philosopher, the discovery of this place I have yet to name was a discourse I had to find outside the classroom and curriculum. I knew I was not the white man of whom I was reading, but I did not know who I was in the context of philosophy. Yet my love for philosophy pushed me to keep studying and find racialized experiences to which I could relate, landing me first within the Black experience and the Latinx experience. Now I realize the furtherance of my Asian-American philosophical studies is one that must also include African-American, Latin-American, and Native-American philosophical studies. There is a liberation in finding epistemologies that do not support my oppression. These traditions are positioned from an epistemology that grows out of struggle for our truths to be heard and to be taken as serious endeavors.

As we come to understand the implications of whiteness, we see the ways in which it has shaped our understanding of ourselves. Latinized Asian-Americans and Asian-Americans that feel as if they can only relate to culture secondarily, reflect the ways in which we interpret stereotypical images of ourselves in popular culture. Thus, we do not feel Asian because we do not fit these stereotypes, and yet we implicitly think that is what being Asian means. In feeling displaced from our race or ethnic backgrounds, we assimilate into other racially lived experiences in order to encounter a reflection of our reality. This participation in cultural borderlands becomes a site of freedom and an opportunity to begin to see ourselves without the veil that comes from the white gaze.

NOTES

1. The veil is a metaphor created by W. E. B. Du Bois to describe how Black people experience the world. "Leaving, then, the world of the White man, I have stepped within the Veil" (Du Bois, *The Souls of Black Folk*, 3). "Then it dawned upon me with a certain suddenness that I was different from the others; or like, mayhap, in heart and life and longing, but shut out from their world by a vast veil" (ibid., 8). Regarding Du Bois's notion of the veil, Yancy writes, "Whether interpreted as symbolic of systemic racism/structural segregation or as that which 'indicates, rhetorically, a knowledge of difference that is itself discursively based,' the veil is fundamentally linked to the hegemonic performances of whiteness, performances that can lead to deep societal fissures or to profound levels of existential phenomenological fracture" (Yancy, *Black Bodies, White Gazes*, 79).

2. In a presentation, bell hooks discusses the process of decolonization of the mind in order to become whole. As she puts it, "Decolonization is a centering process" (hooks, "Moving from Pain" 1:04:35). People of color decolonize their minds from a hegemonic Eurocentric thought in order to find the self; it shifts racial, gender, and class identity.

3. Here, I am alluding to the book *The Mis-Education of the Negro* by Carter G. Woodson and the album *The Miseducation of Lauryn Hill* by Lauryn Hill. This term speaks to the whitewashed miseducation we are taught from grammar school and onward, that passes off slavery and the oppression of people of color in America as a means to "our" progress. It speaks to the miseducation we receive in the media and the news that criminalizes people of color. It speaks to the miseducation people of color are taught through Eurocentric thought.

4. hooks, "A Public Dialogue," 14:03.
5. See, for example, Ricoeur, *Oneself as Another*.
6. See Buber, *I and Thou*, 17.
7. See Ellison, *Invisible Man*.
8. As Peggy McIntosh famously described it, some of the marks of white privilege include how "I can do well in a challenging situation without being called a credit to my race" and "I am never asked to speak for all the people of my racial group" (McIntosh, "White Privilege").
9. Du Bois, *The Souls of Black Folk*, 12.
10. Feng, "Being Chinese American," 190.

11. LaBlance et al., "The Burden of Being 'Model,'" 255. See also, Chow, "Model Minority."
12. This conflation often perpetuates the racial hierarchy system of Carl Linnaeus in his *Systema Naturae*, fueled by white supremacy and biological essentialism, that typed all people of Asian descent as "yellow" (Marks, "Long Shadow of Linnaeus's Human Taxonomy," 28).
13. Feng, "Being Chinese American," 190.
14. Nishime, "Mixed Race Matters," 150. See also Nishime, *Undercover Asian*.
15. Kawai, "Stereotyping Asian Americans," 114.
16. Yancy, *Black Bodies, White Gazes*, xxxii.
17. Ibid., 39.
18. Ibid.
19. Lee and Yancy, "Asian, American, Woman, Philosopher."
20. Yancy, *Black Bodies, White Gazes*, xxxiii.
21. Ibid., 22.
22. Ibid., 34.
23. Levinas, *Time and the Other*, 90.
24. Yancy, *Black Bodies, White Gazes*, 23.
25. Ibid., 79.
26. Anzaldúa, *Borderlands*, 108.
27. These are the words of George Zimmerman during his 911 phone call before he killed Trayvon Martin on Feb. 26, 2012.
28. Anzaldúa, *Borderlands*, 100.
29. Carr, "HipHop in the Academy @HBCUs" (video), 19:55.
30. Walker, "I Will Keep Broken Things."
31. Lem, "Carol Lem," 188.
32. Ibid.
33. These, of course, stem from the four color codings for race that were codified in Carl Linnaeus's 1735 work, *Systema Naturae* (red, yellow, black, white), which continues to shape how we socially construct race today.
34. Fanon, *Black Skin, White Masks*, 19.
35. Westphal, "Transfigurations as Saturated Phenomenon," 5.
36. Yancy, "A Letter of Love."
37. Ibid.
38. The China doll stereotype constructs the Asian woman as domesticated, submissive, and docile. She is in need of the white knight to save her from the men in her own culture.
39. Anzaldúa, *Borderlands*, 109.
40. Yancy, "A Letter of Love."
41. Fanon, *Black Skin, White Masks*, 56.
42. Yancy, "Introduction: No Philosophical Oracle Voices," 1.
43. Anzaldúa, *Borderlands*, 109.
44. Du Bois, *The Souls of Black Folk*, 186.

BIBLIOGRAPHY

Anzaldúa, Gloria. *Borderlands La Frontera: The New Mestiza*. San Francisco: Aute Lute Books, 2007.
Buber, Martin. *I and Thou*. Translated by Ronald Gregor Smith. New York: Collier Books, 1958.
Carr, Greg. "HipHop in the Academy @HBCUs." *YouTube*. Uploaded by Center for African Studies at Howard University. 9 Apr. 2018. Accessed at https://www.youtube.com/watch?v=qNg71R-l2Jc&t=2277s.

Chow, Kat. "'Model Minority' Myth Again Used as a Racial Wedge between Asian and Blacks." *NPR.* 19 April 2017. Accessed at https://www.npr.org/sections/codeswitch/2017/04/19/524571669/model-minority-myth-again-used-as-a-racial-wedge-between-asians-and-blacks.

Du Bois, W. E. B. *The Souls of Black Folk.* New York: Barnes and Noble Classics, 2003.

Ellison, Ralph. *Invisible Man.* New York: Vintage Books, 1995.

Fanon, Frantz. *Black Skin, White Masks.* New York: Grove Press, 2008.

Feng, Peter X. "Being Chinese American, Becoming Asian American: Chan Is Missing." *Screening Asian Americans.* Edited by Peter X. Feng, 185–216. New Brunswick: Rutgers University Press, 2002.

hooks, bell. "A Public Dialogue Between bell hooks and Cornel West." *YouTube.* Uploaded by The New School. 10 Oct 2014. Accessed at https://www.youtube.com/watch?v=_LL0k6_pPKw&t=862s.

———. "bell hooks: Moving from Pain to Power | The New School." *YouTube.* Uploaded by The New School. 12 Oct. 2015. Accessed at https://www.youtube.com/watch?v=cpKuLl-GC0M&t=4234s.

Kawai, Yuko. "Stereotyping Asian Americans: The Dialectic of the Model Minority and the Yellow Peril." *The Howard Journal of Communications* 16, no. 2 (2005): 109–30.

LaBlance, Sandra S., Ebony O. McGee, and Bhoomi K. Thakore. "The Burden of Being 'Model': Racialized Experiences of Asian STEM College Students." *Journal of Diversity in Higher Education* 10, no. 3 (2017): 253–70.

Lee, Emily S. and George Yancy. "Asian, American, Woman, Philosopher." *The New York Times.* 6 April, 2015. Accessed at https://opinionator.blogs.nytimes.com/2015/04/06/asian-american-woman-philosopher/.

Lem, Carol. "Carol Lem." *The Geography of Home: California's Poetry of Place.* Edited by Christopher Buckley and Gary Young, 188. Berkeley: Heyday Books, 1999.

Levinas, Emmanuel. *Time and the Other.* Translated by Richard A. Cohen. Pittsburgh: Duquesne University Press, 2015.

Marks, Jonathan. "Long Shadow of Linnaeus's Human Taxonomy." *Nature* 447 (May 2007): 28.

McIntosh, Peggy. "White Privilege: Unpacking the Invisible Knapsack." Orig. pub. Winter 1990. Accessed online at https://www.racialequitytools.org/resourcefiles/mcintosh.pdf.

Menzel, Christopher. "Possible Worlds." *Stanford Encyclopedia of Philosophy.* Edited by Edward N. Zalta, 2017. Accessed at https://plato.stanford.edu/entries/possible-worlds/.

Nishime, LeiLani. "Mixed Race Matters: What Emma Stone and Bruno Mars Can Tell Us about the Future of Asian American Media." *Cinema Journal,* 56, no. 3 (2017): 148–52.

———. *Undercover Asian: Multiracial Asian Americans in Visual Culture.* Urbana: University of Illinois Press, 2014.

Ricoeur, Paul. *Oneself as Another.* Translated by Kathleen Blamey. Chicago: University of Chicago Press, 1995.

Smith, Tara D., and Maton, Kenneth I. "Perceptions and Experience in Higher Education: A National Study of Multiracial Asian American and Latino/a Students in Psychology." *Cultural Diversity and Ethnic Minority Psychology,* 21, no. 1 (2015): 97–104.

Walker, Alice. "I Will Keep Broken Things." Words for the Year, 8 Apr 2014, https://wordsfortheyear.com/2014/04/08/i-will-keep-broken-things-alice-walker/.

Westphal, Merold. "Transfigurations as Saturated Phenomenon." *Journal of Philosophy and Scripture* 1, no. 1 (2003): 1–10.

Yancy, George. "A Letter of Love: An Encounter with White Backlash." The Logic of Racial Practice: Embodiment, *Habitus,* and Implicit Bias. 13 April 2018, University of Pittsburgh, PA. Keynote Speech.

———. *Black Bodies, White Gazes: The Continuing Significance of Race*. 2nd Edition. Lanham, MD: Rowman & Littlefield, 2017.
———. "Introduction: No Philosophical Oracle Voices." *Philosophy in Multiple Voices*. Edited by George Yancy, 1–20. Lanham, MD: Rowman & Littlefield Publishers, 2007.

FOUR
Anger, Silence, and Epistemic Injustice

Alison Bailey

Anger is the emotion of injustice.[1] Historically, members of subordinated groups have defended our anger as a morally and politically appropriate response to daily injustices. Our anger surfaces quickly, pulling us back into our bodies. This is how injustice feels. Those of us who live in epistemic twilight zones—that is, in worlds where testimony about our lived experiences is repeatedly silenced, dismissed, distorted, or gaslighted— are familiar with the ever-present anger these constant erasures trigger.[2] Historically, discussions of anger and injustice have focused on the political uses of anger, but, as Kristie Dotson once remarked, "All injustices are epistemic at root."[3] So, I am curious: if anger is the emotion of injustice, and if injustices have prominent epistemic dimensions, then where is the anger in epistemic injustice? Despite the question, my project is not to explain the lack of attention to anger in the epistemic injustice literature. Instead I argue that a particular texture of anger—*a knowing resistant anger*—offers marginalized knowers a powerful resource for countering epistemic injustices. I begin by making visible the anger that saturates the complex silences that epistemic injustices repeatedly manufacture. I outline four silencing practices to illustrate the obvious point that social practices of silencing produce angry experiences. Next, I introduce two additional silencing practices—*tone policing* and *tone vigilance*—because they best illustrate the intimate relationship between silencing and angry knowledge management. My third section uses María Lugones's pluralist account of anger to bring out the epistemic dimensions of knowing resistant anger in a way that also calls attention to the histories and textures of this anger. Anger is a powerful resource for resisting epistemic injustice. Anger does things. Anger can be a claim to respect. It offers us clarity. And, it is useful for mapping epistemic terrains. Anger calls attention to bad epistemic habits. It prompts us to seek out resistant epistemic communities and new worlds of sense where our epistemic confidence can be restored.

ANGER IS A JUSTIFIED RESPONSE TO SOCIAL PRACTICES OF SILENCING

Social practices of silencing produce angry experiences. So, my first task is to make visible the overlooked and undertheorized resistant anger present in the silences that epistemic injustice repeatedly manufactures. All testimonial exchanges take place on an *unlevel knowing field*—that is, "on contested terrains where knowledge and ignorance circulate with equal vigor, and where dominant groups have a deep and abiding interest in maintaining their epistemic home turf advantage."[4] Dominant groups use silencing practices to defend their epistemic home terrain. Silencing does epistemic violence to marginalized epistemic communities not only by undermining speakers' epistemic credibility, but also by causing them to doubt their ability to make judgments about their moral worth.[5] Effective silencing practices make it difficult for marginalized knowers to hold their epistemic ground.

The epistemic injustice scholarship identifies a variety of silencing practices. Knowers can be silenced preemptively, when they are excluded in advance from participating in a testimonial exchange. Miranda Fricker describes this as "a tendency for some groups simply not to be asked for information in the first place."[6] Consider, for example, how women have been accidently on purpose excluded from US government committees on reproductive healthcare policy. Silencing practices also treat knowers as *epistemic objects, or as truncated subjects*.[7] Here, knowers are treated as (re)sources from whom so-called "legitimate inquirers" glean information to produce proper knowledge. Here, speakers *are* asked for information, but their knowledge is coopted in support of the asker's project, undermining their capacity as givers of that knowledge.[8] Think about how universities coopt the resistant work done by gender studies programs and use it to market their commitment to diversity in ways that do not threaten institutional comfort. Kristie Dotson's scholarship on epistemic violence identifies two additional silencing practices, *testimonial quieting* and *testimonial smothering*.[9] Testimonial quieting happens when an audience fails to recognize the speaker as a knower whose testimony is worth hearing. The speaker does not just suffer a credibility deficit, because that would presuppose her ability to make a credibility judgment. The speaker's credibility deficit is so severe that her words are not heard at all. It's as if she never spoke. Consider the court scene in *To Kill a Mockingbird*. Tom Robinson does not simply suffer a credibility deficit because he's a Black man. His testimony is "worth nothing to the jury. As if he did not testify at all."[10] Finally, testimonial smothering is a coerced self-silencing that happens when "the speaker perceives her immediate audience as *unwilling or unable to gain the appropriate uptake of proffered testimony.*" The speaker's knowledge from previous conversations teaches her to shape or truncate her testimony to "insure that [it] contains only content for which [her] audience demonstrates testimonial competence."[11] People of color, for example, tactically limit the conversations they are willing to have with white people about race, knowing that white audiences typically lack the epistemic competence to judge those experiences accurately.

So where is the anger in social practices of silencing? It's *everywhere*. Silence is a condition of oppression, and part of resisting oppression is finding a voice that effectively pushes back against the weight of imposed silences. Silence is saturated with anger because injustice is painful. Anger is an audible expression of resistance to the sufferings of injustice. Our anger pushes back against the complex silences that injustice repeatedly manufactures. When Audre Lorde says: "My response to racism is anger," she means that her anger is a justified response to the social and cultural habits, ideologies, institutions, and laws that dehumanize, erase, and do violence to her.[12] Anger is a justified response to all subordination injuries, even epistemic ones. When a speaker's testimony is smothered, silenced, or rendered inaudible, her anger is smothered, silenced, or rendered inaudible. Silencing anger exacerbates the harms of epistemic injustices because silencing neutralizes or renders invisible the knowledge speakers have of the injury their anger communicates. To be angry is to make a claim on respect.[13] Silencing is disrespectful precisely because it communicates to the speaker that her testimony is not worth hearing, that she is incapable of making accurate judgments about how she has been wronged, or that the emotional injuries she sustains during a testimonial exchange are unworthy of consideration. The audience's failure to give the speaker's testimony and anger uptake illustrates a failure to respect the speaker as a credible knower; and, like all discredited knowers, she is denied the right to social participation.[14]

TONE MANAGEMENT AS ANGRY KNOWLEDGE MANAGEMENT

My task so far has been to make visible the resistant anger that saturates social practices of silencing. The fact that silencing practices produce angry experiences should now be evident. This section suggests that resistant angry experiences have epistemic content and that the aim of silencing is to manage resistant anger's epistemic content. To illustrate this, I examine two anger-silencing practices—*tone policing* and *tone vigilance*—which are aimed at directly managing subordinate groups' angry knowledge. My discussion highlights the epistemic and psychological harms that tone-managing practices produce when subordinate groups are caught in *anger-silencing spirals.*

Tone policing has a prominent epistemic function. The clearest example comes from Audre Lorde's account of a moment during an academic conference when she spoke out of direct and particular anger to a white woman who replied, "Tell me how you feel but don't say it too harshly or I cannot hear you." Lorde comments, "But is it my manner that keeps you from hearing, or the threat of a message that [your] life may change?"[15] Anger is a response to injury; but, for subordinated knowers, it is treated as something to be managed. In general, tone management weakens epistemic credibility by targeting, isolating, and attempting to manage the affective content (the speaker's *manner* of speaking) and the epistemic content (the *message*) in testimony. At its core is the expectation that subordinated knowers, if they want to be heard, must calibrate the timbre of their message in order to fall within the audience's comfort zone. The connections between anger and tone management are so predictable that I have come to understand them as anger/knowledge management tactics. In fact, anger's epistemic strength can be measured in direct proportion to the amount of energy used to contain it.[16] But anger-silencing practices are not just about quieting uncomfortable tones as a parent hushes a child at a movie. There is power in the hush. The hush reasserts dominance: it restores the audience's own epistemic and psychological comfort. There are at least two patterns of managing this angry knowledge.

In cases of *direct angry knowledge management,* tone policing may trigger an exhausting and familiar anger-silencing spiral.[17] Lorde's anger at racial injustices prompts the white woman to make a request for psychological and epistemic comfort. Angry demands for justice are prone to escalation. Suppose that following this exchange, sensing that she's not been heard, Lorde reasserts her message in a hotter tone. The white woman may understand the amplified tone as further evidence against Lorde's epistemic credibility and more firmly ask Lorde to soften her voice. These exchanges fuel *anger-silencing spirals*: closed hermeneutical systems in which the speaker suffers a double epistemic injury—neither her testimony nor her anger get uptake, and she is left with a dense, hot, swelling rage in her chest.

Lorde's story illustrates a form of tone policing that focuses directly on the audible anger in a speaker's voice, but anger need not be heard to be managed. There is a second, more insidious, form of tone management that happens when an audience attributes anger to a speaker's testimony (independently of her tone) simply because the speaker belongs to a group that is culturally characterized as angry. Roxane Gay's description of how race complicates anger gets at the heart of attributive anger. She writes,

> I AM an opinionated woman so I am often accused of being angry. This accusation is made because a woman, a black woman who is angry, is making trouble. She is daring to be dissatisfied with the status quo. She is daring to be heard. When women are angry, we are wanting too much or complaining or wasting time or focusing on the wrong things or we are petty or shrill or strident or unbalanced or crazy or overly emotional. Race complicates anger. Black women are often characterized as angry simply for existing, as if anger is woven into our breath and our skin.[18]

Here, anger is attributed to a speaker even when her tone is well within the listener's comfort zone. Listeners implicitly assign anger to speakers' words based on their social identity. Attributive anger sparks a prescient form of tone policing that I call *tone vigilance*. Tone vigilance prompts an audience either to listen for anger in a speaker's testimony, or to fold a perceived or imagined anger into the testimony because they assume that Black women always speak from an angry place. As if, recalling Gay's words, anger was "woven into [her] breath and skin." Attributing anger to marginalized knowers presilences them. It triggers an insidious anger-silencing spiral, where reasonable judgments and observations are reduced to the angry nature of a particular group. Sara Ahmed explains, "The figure of the angry black woman is also a fantasy figure that produces its own effects. Reasonable thoughtful arguments are dismissed as anger (which of course empties anger of its own reason), which makes you angry, such that your response becomes read as confirmation of evidence that you are not only angry, but also unreasonable!"[19]

When anger is attributed to a speaker based on group membership, the causal relationship between reasonable claims about injustice and the speaker's anger is reversed. It's not that her anger makes the claim unreasonable, it's that the perceived or imagined unreasonableness of the claim is attributed to an angry essence at the core of one's group identity. Ahmed continues,

> You might be angry *about* how racism and sexism diminish life choices for women of color. Your anger is a judgement that something is wrong. But in being heard as angry, your speech is read as motivated by anger. Your anger is read as unattributed, as if you are against x because you are angry rather than being angry because you are against x. You become angry at the injustice of being heard as motivated by anger, which makes it harder to separate yourself from the object of anger. You become entangled with what you are angry about because you are angry about how they have entangled you in your anger. In becoming angry about that entanglement, you confirm their commitment to your anger as the truth "behind" your speech, which is what blocks your anger, stops it getting through.[20]

Tone-managing practices are epistemically and psychologically harmful. Anger-silencing spirals have different consequences for marginalized speakers than they do for dominant hearers. From the perspective of dominators, tone management serves to restore their psychological and epistemic comfort. The white woman's request that Lorde not speak too harshly is a demand to accommodate her unmet psychological need for racial comfort. Tone management is a defense against "white fragility"—"a state in which even a minimum amount of racial stress becomes intolerable, triggering a range of defensive moves. These moves include the outward display of emotions such as anger, fear, or guilt, and behaviors such as argumentation, silence, or the desire to flee a stress-inducing situation. These responses, in turn, function to reinstate white racial equilibrium."[21] The white woman is requesting not to have her epistemic confidence—that is, the sense she has of herself as a good white woman who is knowledgeable about race matters—called into question. It's easier to mark Lorde as an angry Black woman than it is for Lorde's interlocutor to mark her own white ignorance. It is easier to shut down the conversation than to linger in the uncomfortable silences these conversations create. When white people choose their comfort over listening to the testimonies of people of color, we deny ourselves the opportunity to know something important about the world—a strain of knowledge that is rarely visible to us from where we sit or stand.

However, from the perspective of those silenced, anger-silencing spirals are epistemically and psychologically damaging. Silenced anger faces what José Medina calls a "wrongful interpretive obstacle."[22] When anger is misinterpreted it is emptied of knowledge. Instead of being taken as evidence of lived injury, trauma, or harm, the speaker's anger is used to confirm a character flaw or personality disorder. Women's anger is bitchy, crazy, or hysterical rather than civil or righteous. We are too thin skinned. People of color's rage is uncivil(ized), uppity, or aggressive. They have attitude. These tropes pathologize anger, robbing it of its energy, force, and epistemic content. Our anger is weaponized against us. It is isolated from our testimonies, neutralized, and thrown back at us in limp unrecognizable forms.

Tone management tactics also have a damaging *gaslighting* effect, making speakers feel psychologically insecure and epistemically underconfident. Gaslighting, as Rachel McKinnon explains, "is when a hearer tells a speaker that the speaker's claim isn't that serious or they're overreacting, or they're being too sensitive, or they're not interpreting events properly. This is used to discount the speaker's testimony."[23] Gaslighting is part and parcel of most anger-silencing spirals. Telling a woman that she is "overreacting" or "being too sensitive" is code for she'd better "dial it back." It diffuses angry knowledge by quietly planting seeds of doubt that cause speakers to second-guess the legitimacy of their anger. As Saba Fatima explains, when anger is present, the demands for civility are almost always placed on white women and people of color. The 2018 Blasey-Kavanaugh Senate Judiciary hearing offers a jaw-dropping illustration of the radically different expectations for anger and civility. After admitting to being terrified, Dr. Blasey Ford offered testimony in support of her earlier allegation that Kavanaugh sexually assaulted her at a high school party in the 1980s. She narrated her story with grace, clarity, and humility, knowing full well that any sign of anger or fear would render her "hysterical" and weaken her credibility. She understood the unwritten rules about the appropriate demeanor and tone needed for a white woman's testimony to be taken seriously. Those rules did not apply to Judge Brett Kavanaugh. Within less than a minute of his opening remarks Kavanaugh's performance slid into what can be best described as an entitled-adolescent-white-boy tantrum. He shook with anger, crunched his face, and stuffed his tears. He drank water compulsively and turned the pages of his written remarks with prepubescent fervor. He was rude, arrogant, and disrespectful, but his appointment was confirmed.[24] This social double standard leads to paranoia for women. You begin to doubt your own experience and your own ability to judge that experience. You can never be certain if your emotional responses are on target. You begin to feel depressed, guilty, or ashamed. You wonder if you have read too much into the situation, or if you are making a big deal out of nothing, or if you are too thin skinned.[25] Here, angry knowers are not simply mistaken about their emotions. Their very ability to judge whether the injuries that their anger signals are real is called into question. Under the gaslighting effect, a woman might say to herself, "I don't know why I'm so angry!" Gaslighting works against the gaslighted because gaslighters are fragile beings who rabidly defend their epistemic home turf. They cannot tolerate interpretations of events that challenge their worldview. So, if their worldview reads women's anger as irrational, or as an oversensitive response to trivial matters, then all explanations that point to anger as evidence of unjust harm must be extinguished. The disorienting nature of gaslighting neutralizes the knowledge that is disclosed through anger, thus trapping angry knowers in a hermeneutically closed system where epistemic traction is rarely possible.

But, the effects that tone management has on resistant anger concerns me for another reason. Tone management may prompt speakers to trade our anger for the chance to either be heard or to restore our epistemic confidence. Hoping to be heard we may consciously soften our voices or swallow our anger halfway. Testimonial smothering has an affective dimension that I call *affective smothering*, which is a form of self–tone policing that happens when the speaker recognizes that her audience lacks either the empathy or the affective competence to make sense of her anger as she experiences it.[26] Thinking, *"They can't understand how this anger feels,"* she swallows her anger half way and repeats herself in a "more appropriate tone." I know this feeling intimately. There are times when my own resistant anger has injured my epistemic credibility. In a panic, I circled back to restore my audience's comfort. I softened my anger. Sometimes I apologize and repeat my testimony in honey-toned restatements. But these retreats come at a cost. The terms of exchange require trading the chance to voice injury and to consider the transformative possibilities of my anger, for the outside chance that restoring my audience's comfort will also restore my epistemic credibility. I almost always lose this wager. And, when I do, I become an accomplice in the dominator's anger management project. I assume that my audience's comfort, and not my anger, will restore my epistemic confidence. I convince myself that this is the only way to get epistemic traction. But I lose ground, and my anger is carried forward into the next conversation where there are more wagers to lose. I have, in Martia Golden's words, paralyzed my anger and "brilliantly shaped it into the soft armor of survival."[27]

My task in this section has been to make visible the resistant anger that saturates the social practices of silencing. I have argued that tone policing and tone vigilance are forms of angry knowledge management that injure knowers. Speakers suffer a double epistemic injury—neither their testimony nor their anger get uptake. The next section focuses more intimately on the texture and distinct epistemic features of this resistant anger and sets the stage for my final discussion of anger's transformative power.

THE TEXTURE AND AFFECTIVE ANCESTRY OF KNOWING RESISTANT ANGER

The silences that tone management produces are never empty, still, or mute. Angry tones are not affective embellishments that run alongside knowledge; they are woven tightly into it. Silence is not the voice of submission. Silencing pushes down, but resistant anger pushes back against the normalizing abuse of silencing practices. Resistant anger then, is not a raw unfocused energy. It is a *knowing resistant anger*. "Knowing" because, in Lorde's words, it "is loaded with energy and information" and "resistant" because its vibrancy endures repeated silencing.[28] This anger is not an automatic response to silencing; it must be cultivated in the same ways that those working for social justice must cultivate a practical knowledge of how systemic barriers shape their experiences. We must understand the structural origins of our anger. Without an understanding of how an oppressed group's anger is *systemically* silenced, resistant anger feels muddy-headed. So, it's not that some angers have knowledge and others are empty of it, only that anger's knowledge may not yet be intelligible to the subject because anger's resistant possibilities are not yet apparent.

I want to argue that knowing resistant anger is a source of epistemic traction. This requires that I reject the closed hermeneutical framework of the anger-silencing spiral, which is inattentive to the plurality of angry experiences. María Lugones's pluralist account of anger offers a useful vocabulary for making visible the anger that saturates the silences that epistemic injustice repeatedly manufactures. Before making this case, I need to give readers unfamiliar with Lugones's work the basic gist of her pluralist view of the self and explain how this view shapes her account of angry selves.

In "Playfulness, 'World' Traveling, and Loving Perception," Lugones develops a pluralistic feminism, "one that affirms the plurality in each of us and among us as richness and as central to feminist ontology and epistemology."[29] Her pluralist view of the self is revealed through the practice of playful, loving, "world" travel. The basic idea here is that outsiders to dominant cultures have acquired a flexibility in moving from mainstream constructions of life, where they are constructed as outsiders, to constructions of life where they are more or less at home. For example, people of color must learn to navigate safely white worlds where they feel ill at ease and are constructed as outsiders. So, their senses of self are plural because they shift across worlds. Lugones uses the term "world" in a way that is purposely ambiguous and unfixed. Worlds are purposely incomplete. Worlds are not utopias. They are filled with flesh and blood people. Worlds need not be constructions of a whole society, they may be niches (e.g., a gay bar, a barrio, or a college campus). Lugones is interested in how the shift from one world (i.e., a barrio) to another (i.e., a predominantly white campus) reveals the plurality of one's self. In some worlds our sense of self is intelligible, in other worlds it is distorted. In the barrio, a Chicana might be at ease, outgoing, funny, or generous. On campus she might be shy, reserved, and cautious. Lugones explains, "Those of us who are 'world'-travelers have the distinct experience of being different selves in different 'worlds' and of having the capacity to remember other 'worlds' and ourselves in them."[30] "Travel" is how she names this shift from being one self in one world to being another self in another world.

Lugones's account of anger reflects her pluralism. If social selves are plural, then angry selves are plural. Our anger is not always intelligible across worlds. In some worlds, knowing resistant anger is a clear righteous anger against injustice. In other worlds, anger is interpreted as hostile, threatening, uncivil, inappropriately timed, or crazy. Worlds have distinct epistemic terrains. So, angry experiences are world-dependent in the sense that worlds shape the *affective textures* of our angry experiences. This means that knowing resistant anger has particular textures and features that will only be intelligible in particular resistant worlds where its use and value are clear. I am particularly interested in cultivating an understanding of how different angers *feel* so I can quickly identify those particular angry experiences that offer resources for resisting epistemic injustice. To do this, I need to spell out the specific texture of knowing resistant anger.

In "Hard-to-Handle Anger," Lugones claims that she can "make more sense of anger if [she] captures it in its specificity."[31] Her term, "hard-to-handle anger," is purposely ambiguous: it contains the plurality of ways angry experiences are "hard." If selves are plural, then marginalized knowers are at once oppressed⇔resisting. As Lugones remarks, "One eye sees that oppressed reality, the other sees the resistant one."[32] Plurality saturates the hardness of oppressed/silenced⇔resisting/angry subjects' responses to injustice. These are angry pluralist selves. In one sense, hard-to-handle anger has a *hard/heavy* texture that is burdensome, exhausting, laborious, strenuous, and fatiguing.[33] It has a heaviness born of frustration with the exhausting process of directing our anger at dominators in dominant worlds of sense where our anger gets no uptake. For example, when women experience a hard/heavy anger in response to campus sexual violence, the heaviness comes from trying to be heard in worlds of sense shaped by campus rape culture—worlds that construct our anger as unintelligible on the assumed grounds that *women's* anger about sexual violence is overexaggerated or irrelevant. In these worlds our resistant anger pushes back: it "has communicative *intent* but it does not always succeed in getting uptake from the oppressor in the official world of sense."[34] Women's anger about sexual violence can only be hysteria or a delayed reaction to having sex she now regrets. This is, for Lugones, a self-controlled anger "attentive to the official interpretation of her movements, voice, message, asking for respectability, judging those who have wronged her."[35]

But there is a plurality in these angry experiences. They are at once shaped by the one eye that understands oppressed reality and the other eye that pushes back against the oppression from which angry knowers must separate. Hard-to-handle anger also has a *hard/rebellious* texture that presupposes or establishes the need to speak "from within separate [non-dominant] worlds of sense. Separate, that is, from worlds of sense that deny intelligibility to the anger."[36] This anger is hard in the sense that it is messy, disorderly, complex, and difficult to manage. It resists being well-ordered, controlled, disciplined, and tidy. Consider how spaces that affirm women's testimony around sexual violence create resistant worlds where our anger is validated. Women experience a hard/rebellious anger about sexual violence when we seek out or create worlds where our angry experiences are intelligible. I have in mind worlds such as sexual assault survivors' support groups or social media spaces like the #MeToo movement where our safe, sound, collective anger gets uptake and where rape myths are dim artifacts of worlds where our voices have been silenced.

Following Lugones, I ask that readers hold both anger's hard and rebellious textures in mind. Angry selves have the capacity to remember those worlds where our anger is intelligible and those worlds where it is not. And, as I will argue in the next section, resisting silencing practices requires that, when we are in dominant worlds, we never forget those worlds where our anger at injustice makes perfect sense. So, we must consider questions related to angry selves and the worlds they occupy. We must ask: which self is angry? Is the angry self the subordinate self? Or the resisting self? Is the subordinate self's anger intelligible to dominators when it is expressed in dominate worlds of sense? Or, is it the subordinate angry self pushing back against dominant worlds of sense in an attempt to be heard? Or, is it the fully resistant angry self, whose anger is fully intelligible in nondominant worlds of sense? In which worlds is her anger epistemically productive? In which worlds is it neutralized?

My account of knowing resistant anger mirrors Lugones's pluralist view of anger. Knowing resistant anger is a *hard/heavy/rebellious anger* attentive to the epistemic terrains where it is and is not intelligible. It recognizes the hostile worlds that make it heavy but retains the memory of worlds where its rebelliousness is intelligible. It expands on Lugones's pluralist account by highlighting the epistemic dimensions of anger, acknowledging anger's affective ancestry, and attending to anger's felt experiences. So, I will describe this expanded notion of plural angry selves as parts of oppressed/silenced⇔resisting/angry communities.

Our anger is never fully our own. It is partially formed by the world-dependent *affective ancestries* of marginalized social groups. The anger of the ages is always with us in our collective memory. I believe that some types of anger are inherited along with the historical traumas of colonized and oppressed peoples and the worlds that gave rise to that ancestral anger. As Lorde observes, "Every Black woman in America lives her life somewhere along a wide curve of ancient and unexpressed angers."[37] Members of oppressed/silenced⇔resisting/angry communities have collective memories of their suffering, and that historical trauma and pain shapes the contours of their collective anger. U.S. Black anger's coherent genealogy begins with trafficking African bodies in the Middle Passage and continues through colonizers' use of enslaved labor, the convict-leasing system, Jim Crow, lynching, the rape of Black women and girls, police violence, mass incarceration, and the school-to-prison pipeline. I cannot help but believe that the memories of past injustices remain alive in these communities today, because these injustices continue under different names. Ta-Nehisi Coates's memoir offers a glimpse of Black ancestral anger. He describes the moment when a white woman came up behind him in a crowded movie theater and yelled "Come on!" as she pushed his son out of her way. He writes, "I turned and spoke to this woman and my words were hot with all of the moment and all of my history."[38] Anger's abiding historical nature suggests that the differences between and among our lived identities are as affective as they are social and cultural, and that "various historically coherent groups 'feel differently' and navigate the material world on a different emotional register."[39]

However, hard-to-handle anger's affective ancestry does not mean that its angry energy is oriented exclusively toward the past. Ancestral anger resonates in both backward- and forward-looking ways. Sometimes our anger requires that we dwell on the past. Sometimes our anger reorients itself toward the creation and maintenance of new worlds. So, one texture of anger *feels* the oppressed reality and history, and the other *feels* the resistant reality and possible futures. The feminist literature on anger is filled with references to the visionary and transformative dimensions of anger. Lorde's visionary anger is marked by its ability to move people to act in the service of their collective vision.[40] Sara Ahmed acknowledges anger's bidirectional perspective when she remarks that "anger is not simply defined in relationship to a past, but as opening up the future. In other words, being against something does not end with 'that which one is against.' Anger does not necessarily become 'stuck' on its object, although that object may remain sticky and compelling. Being against something is also being for something, something that has yet to be articulated or is not yet."[41] Lugones describes anger's transformative power as "cognitively rich, cut from the same tonality and cloth as metamorphosis." It's an anger "driven by the weight of resistance and fully inspiring."[42] So, these hard/heavy/rebellious angers flicker back and forth. They hold the felt memories of communities of angry selves and their histories along with the transformative visions of future angry resistant communities.

Finally, knowing resistant angry experiences just feel differently. They do not feel like the angry experiences you have when you are so angry that you *can't* think straight—that is, when your anger moves in unfocused, wasteful, useless, and destructive ways. Unfocused anger moves in ways that diminish its energy, like water moving through the "shower" or "mist" settings of a garden hose nozzle. Knowing resistant anger is "a lucid, clearly focused, and orchestrated anger that is articulated with precision."[43] It moves with the force and energy of water that flows through the "jet stream" setting of that garden hose. You are so angry that you *can* see straight. As Lorde explains, "None of its energy is wasted, for it knows its object and all of its energy is focused on that object in hopes that this anger will be heard and things will change."[44] It is a "safe and sound anger," a clear-headed anger with the power to destroy and construct, and to inspire courageous action.[45] Knowing resistant anger is dangerous not because it muddies reason, but because it pushes back against the forces that repeatedly try to rob it of its energy, clarity, and knowledge.

Readers should now have a sense of knowing resistant anger's plurality, texture, ancestry, and feel. Attention to felt experiences is important. I find it easier to name my anger by attending to how it feels than thinking about how it fits into a predetermined taxonomy. I start from the body and work out. This requires attending to which self is angry, in which world, the anger's felt texture, and its ancestry. My final section explains the ways that knowing resistant anger offers oppressed/silenced⇔resisting/angry groups a resource for resisting epistemic injustice.

KNOWING RESISTANT ANGER AS A RESOURCE AGAINST EPISTEMIC INJUSTICE

Feminists have long acknowledged the vital role emotions play in knowledge construction. As Jen McWeeeny observes, feminist analyses are grounded in "the radical idea that *angry experience is a kind of knowing experience.*"[46] This is not news. Resistant epistemic communities have long recognized the transformative energy of anger that the literature on epistemic injustice curiously overlooks.[47] Despite the epistemic wear and tear that hermeneutically closed systems place on disenfranchised knowers, anger-silencing spirals are epistemically rich spaces. The strength of Lugones's pluralism is that it points at once to the ways hard/heavy anger is neutralized and to the ways hard/rebellious anger is a resource that pushes back against dominant worlds of sense. So, where is the knowing resistant anger in epistemic injustice? It's everywhere, but it often escapes our notice because nonpluralist views of anger train knowers to focus exclusively on how anger gets silenced, and not on how anger pushes back. If we shift our attention to the world-breaking hard/rebellious angry experiences (while also keeping hard/heavy anger in mind) we can better understand knowing resistant anger as a transformative creative epistemic resource.

Anger-silencing spirals are epistemically rich spaces. They are as paralyzing as they are transformative—paralyzing because our anger fails to get uptake, and transformative because this failure obliges us to sit with our anger and in Lorde's words, "listen to its rhythms."[48] Sitting mindfully with our anger is transformative because it grounds us, reorients us, and prompts us to move and to seek out alternative epistemic terrains where our anger is intelligible. It brings us "back to our bodies, to the gut-level, signaling that we are in a situation that is unjust, damaging, cruel, or dangerous."[49] Lorde's image of anger's rhythm highlights both the meter of our angry tones and the intelligibility of the unjust patterns that repeatedly evoke our anger—the silences that epistemic injustices repeatedly manufacture. Rhythms are patterns. Patterns reveal structures. When we sit with anger's rhythms we are made aware of the epistemically damaging effects practices of silencing have on us. In a recent interview with Access Hollywood, Uma Thurman was asked to comment on the prevalence of the abuse of power and sexual violence in the Hollywood film industry. Speaking slowly and deliberately, through gritted teeth, she responded, "I don't have a tidy soundbite for you, because I've learned—I'm not a child—and I have learned that when I've spoken in anger I usually regret the way I express myself. So, I've been waiting to feel less angry. And when I'm ready, I'll say what I have to say."[50] She sat with these rhythms and four months later spoke clearly and directly to the patterns of abuse she endured on and off the Hollywood set.

Here's the general idea. When we shift our attention from the hard/heavy texture of knowing resistant anger toward the hard/resistant texture of our anger, its epistemic resources become visible. Knowing resistant anger is transformative because it reorients us. This shift restores our courage and confidence: It prompts us to seek out new epistemic terrains where our anger is alive and intelligible. This intelligibility comes from the epistemic confidence of collectives of oppressed/silenced⇔resisting/angry selves and is an essential ingredient in the creation and sustenance of resistant communities. This last point requires some unpacking.

For starters, knowing resistant anger reorients knowers by alerting us to the fact that the dominator's interpretations of our anger are not the only means of making sense of that anger. The nonpluralist interpretation of women's anger as "bitchy" or "uppity," is simply a privilege-protecting bad epistemic habit. Becoming mindful of anger-silencing patterns creates a space in which to reorient our angry energy toward creating and sustaining worlds where that anger is intelligible. In Medina's words, it offers us "a lucidity, to see things afresh and redirect our perceptual habits, to find a way out of or an alternative to an epistemic blind alley."[51] Reorienting angry knowledge requires resisting the socialized urges to make our anger heard in hermeneutically closed systems and to resist epistemic bad habits like falling back into making sense of our anger on the dominator's terms. Instead, we must challenge the urge to restore our audience's comfort. Our anger will never be at home in the dominator's anger-silencing spirals. Our anger needs a new home. It must move. But, for anger to move it needs traction, and traction requires that we ground ourselves in a particular kind of angry self—*a knowing resistant angry self*. Returning to Lugones's pluralist view of angry selves we can now ask: which self is angry? The subordinate hard/heavy angry self or the resistant hard/rebellious angry self? On whose epistemic terrain is she angry? Where does her anger get traction? Where does it get silenced?

Knowing resistant anger helps us to move because it is a useful instrument of cartography.[52] It helps us to "see" structure because we continually traverse epistemic terrains where our anger may or may not be intelligible. This is why Uma Thurman waits to tell her story. She knows that she needs to be less angry to be heard in the context of a live television interview. Knowing where, when, and with whom our anger gets traction offers us spatial information about the worlds where we are most vulnerable and the worlds where we are most intelligible. I have a particular image for this practice. Think about how dogs come to know the boundaries of the invisible fences that confine them by repeatedly testing the limits of their movements in any direction. A cartography eventually emerges from this exercise that identifies fissures in the fencing. If there are regions of the unlevel knowing field where injustice robs anger of its epistemic friction, then we must reorient ourselves, look for fissures, and move toward rougher terrain. We must gather on new ground where our knowing resistant anger is validated and its energy can be redirected productively toward justice-restoring projects. We must seek out new epistemic home terrains where oppressed/silenced⇔resisting/angry selves can gather collectively to restore our epistemic confidence. There we can affirm how practices of silencing are harmful, as if to say, "You *should* be angry! I'm angry too. Together we will pool our anger in a place where it gets uptake, and we will hold firm to its intelligibility even when we are sucked back into anger-silencing spirals. We will keep alive the memory of epistemic terrains where our anger is heard, even when we are on the dominator's terrain. Together, we will not be silenced!"

Next, seeking out or creating resistant epistemic worlds where our anger is intelligible fills our bodies with confidence and courage. On hospitable epistemic terrains, knowing resistant anger can be a creative force for change. From the standpoint of epistemic injustice hard/rebellious anger is an epistemic confidence booster in the sense that it can restore a knower's self-respect. As Frye notes, "To get angry is to claim implicitly that one is a certain sort of being. . . . One claims that one is in certain ways and dimensions *respectable*. One makes a claim upon respect."[53] On resistant epistemic home terrains, our anger is heard, it gets traction, and we are made newly aware of our power, agency, and self-worth. Anger brings courage.

When we are angry enough to be brave, we take risks. These acts of resistance are also acts of creation. Consider how those of us who work for social justice continue to weather the anger-silencing spirals we find ourselves in during university diversity committees, city council meetings, or community forums on policing. One occasion stands out for me. I was at a semester-long series of meetings where department chairs were asked to respond to the campus climate report. At some point, I became aware that I was repeating myself. I realized that my claim that there are no safe spaces for students of color on campus was unintelligible to the committee. I gave up and sat with my anger. I listened to its rhythms. In that stillness I realized, *Ohhhhhh! It's not that my argument is incoherent. It's not that I'm not being clear. It's not that I've not given enough evidence. Either they cannot hear what I'm saying, or it makes no sense to them, or they just don't want to hear it.* The committee could not make sense of diversity initiatives outside of the possible ways they could use them to rebrand our campus as welcoming. No traction was possible in that space. Once I realized this I walked out. I no longer yearned to make myself heard in these spaces or to restore the comfort of my audience. I looked for a new home for my anger. I approached allies after the meeting and asked them, "Am I right about this? Is this your experience too?" They assured me it was. We shared our angry experiences and from our conversations emerged alternative epistemic communities and projects that focused directly on creating safe spaces where students of color could be heard.

Knowing resistant anger, then, not only restores the collective epistemic confidence of angry selves, it is also an essential ingredient in the creation and sustenance of resistant epistemic communities. It offers us beneficial epistemic friction because we can collectively direct that anger toward change. Projects in feminist epistemology and epistemologies of ignorance have argued that when marginalized knowers encounter hermeneutical sink holes (i.e., anger-silencing spirals) we would do well to remember that the unlevel knowing field contains alternative interpretive resources and resistant practices.[54] Yet, in academic philosophy, little attention is paid to knowing resistant anger as an alternative resource. This is tragic, because anger is central to the formation and maintenance of resistant communities. Anger has a bonding effect—it provides the affective fuel that brings us together and helps us to form cohesive social networks and organized movements. Anger at injustice unites us because, in our moving, we come to realize that we are not alone in our anger. What first feels like an isolated subordinated anger is really part of a larger collective resistant angry experience. There are terrains where our anger feels at home, where it is supported by coalitions of oppressed/silenced⇔resisting/angry selves. Resistant epistemic communities must treat our collective knowing resistant anger (and its affective ancestry) as an epistemic resource because collaboratively it offers us epistemic traction. For this resource to be effective, however, it must be sustainable—that is, our knowing resistant anger must not exhaust itself. It must maintain the single-pointed "jet stream" focus on the objects of injustice. We need not be angry all the time, but oppressed/silenced⇔resistant/angry communities need to keep our collective anger hot and oriented toward transformative projects. Our anger must remain alive and accessible, even if it only simmers gently below the surface. In Lorde's words, this anger "expressed and translated into action in the service of our vision and our future is a liberating and strengthening act of clarification, for it is in the painful process of this translation that we identify who are our allies with whom we have grave differences, and who are our genuine enemies."[55]

Knowing resistant anger, then, counters the effects of tone/anger/knowledge management. The purpose of tone policing is to tame, discipline, and extinguish angry knowledge. The purpose of resistant epistemic and political communities is to affirm, nurture, and cultivate that angry knowledge as a resource. Resistant communities are worlds where we practice inoculating our anger against silencing practices. You can't silence anger in an epistemic ecosystem that is designed to keep knowing resistant anger vibrant and visible. The trick here is to keep the communal memory and feeling of knowing resistant anger fresh within us when we find ourselves trapped in anger-silencing spirals. Resistant communities keep anger hot by maintaining cultures where tone management and other silencing practices are ineffective. In this way, they can collectively take action based on their knowledge of epistemic injustice. It is difficult to silence anger in communities that come together around injustices that are transparent to them. Think about how resistant movements in the United States, such as Black Lives Matter, Standing Rock Sioux water protectors, or national student walk-outs in response to gun violence have made their knowing resistant knowledge of police violence, water rights, and the impact of gun violence available to their communities to the point where that knowledge is so widespread and obvious that it has become woven into the very fabric of their epistemic home terrain. As if to say: We've had enough! We can't be silenced! This stops NOW! Don't you dare tone manage us and spin our stories! There is no doubt that the collective anger of these communities is justified and real.

The purpose of this discussion has been to excavate the resistant uses of anger that circulate in anger-silencing spirals and to suggest that Lugones's pluralist account of anger offers a way of making knowing resistant anger visible as an epistemic resource. On a closing note, I want to circle back to the concern I raised in the introduction. I am worried that accounts of epistemic injustice that fail to recognize anger's plurality and power will continue the work of silencing, dismissing, and erasing angry knowledge as a resource for resisting epistemic injustice. I worry that we have failed to heed Kristie Dotson's cautionary tale that "when addressing and identifying forms of epistemic oppression one needs to endeavor not to perpetuate epistemic oppression."[56] The failure to engage knowing resistant anger is not a simple oversight. As Gaile Pohlhaus's work suggests, ignoring knowing resistant anger's transformative power is itself an act of willful hermeneutical ignorance that occurs "when dominantly situated knowers refuse to acknowledge epistemic tools [e.g., Lorde's transformative anger and Lugones's pluralism] developed from the experienced world of those situated marginally."[57] I fear that such oversights leave too many of us to wallow in *epistemic despair*, a condition that happens when epistemic communities swallow their anger, surrender to silence, and lose hope of ever being heard. Epistemic despair drains off knowers' resistant energies and consigns us to a world where epistemic traction is a matter of chance.

NOTES

1. As Aristotle says, "Anger is a response to apparent injustice" (*Nicomachean Ethics*, V.8 1135b30).
2. Bailey, "The Unlevel Knowing Field," 62–68. "Epistemic twilight zones" are undefined or intermediate conceptual areas where there are insufficient or inadequate epistemic resources. Here, epistemic resources are not shared as much as people think.
3. Dotson, in conversation. Dotson's claim is intentionally strong. Unpacking the "all" is beyond the scope of this project. I ask readers to feel the weight of the *all* in Dotson's claim by considering how the epistemological dimensions of violence are integral to the process of dehumanization: Reducing knowing subjects to dehumanized subjects or objects (i.e., noncitizens, property, animals, savages, criminals, etc.) is the first step toward doing violence to them. Charles W. Mills makes a weaker claim: the historical production of the racial contract has *prominent* epistemic dimensions, in *The Racial Contract*.
4. Bailey, "The Unlevel Knowing Field," 63.
5. Dotson distinguishes between episodic, nonrepetitive *instances of silencing* and deeper systemic and socially functional *practices of silencing* that concern "a repetitive *reliable* occurrence of an audience failing to meet the dependencies of a speaker that finds its origins in a more pervasive ignorance." I focus on Dotson's repetitive reliable occurrences. See Dotson, "Tracking Epistemic Violence," 236–57.
6. Fricker, *Epistemic Injustice*, 130.
7. "Epistemic objectification" is Fricker's term (Fricker, *Epistemic Injustice*, 133). "Truncated subjects" comes from Pohlhaus Jr., "Discerning the Primary Epistemic Harm in Cases of Testimonial Injustice," 99–114.
8. Fricker, *Epistemic Injustice*, 133.
9. Dotson, "Tracking Epistemic Violence," 242–45.
10. McKinnon "Epistemic Injustice" 240.
11. Dotson, "Tracking Epistemic Violence," 244.
12. Lorde, "On the Uses of Anger," 124.
13. Frye, "A Note on Anger."
14. Lyman, "The Politics of Anger," 71–72.
15. Lorde, "On the Uses of Anger," 125.
16. Cooper, *Eloquent Rage*, 167.
17. This is McKinnon's "epistemic injustice circle of hell" (McKinnon, "Allies Behaving Badly," 169; McKinnon, "Epistemic Injustice," 240). See also Ahmed, *Living a Feminist Life*, 38.
18. Gay, "Who Gets to Be Angry?"
19. Ahmed, *The Promise of Happiness*, 68.
20. Ibid., 68.
21. DiAngelo, "White Fragility," 54.
22. Medina, *The Epistemology of Resistance*, 91.
23. McKinnon, "Allies Behaving Badly, 167.
24. For a concise summary of key moments in the hearing see "Key Moments: The Blasey-Kavanaugh Hearing," *New York Times*, September 28, 2018. Web.
25. Fatima, "Being Brown and Epistemic Insecurity.'" See also Fatima, "On the Edge of Knowing," 147–54.
26. Fatima treats this as testimonial smothering in "On the Edge of Knowing."
27. Golden, *Migrations of the Heart*, 21. Cited in Collins, *Black Feminist Thought*, 97.
28. Lorde, "On the Uses of Anger," 127.
29. Lugones, *Pilgrimages/Peregrinajes*, 85.
30. Ibid., 86.
31. Ibid., 103.
32. Ibid., 78.
33. To reduce both the conceptual clutter for those unfamiliar with Lugones's pluralism, and to focus on the textures of anger. I've substituted *hard/heavy* anger for first-

order anger and *hard/rebellious* anger for second-order anger. First-order anger sees the oppressed reality and second-order anger resists.
  34. Ibid., 107.
  35. Ibid., 104.
  36. Ibid., 104–5.
  37. Lorde, "Eye to Eye," 145.
  38. Coates, *Between the World and Me*, 94.
  39. Muñoz, "Feeling Brown," 70.
  40. Lorde, "The Uses of Anger," 127.
  41. Ahmed, *The Promise of Happiness*, 175.
  42. Lugones, *Pilgrimages/Peregrinajes*, 103, 112.
  43. Lorde, "The Uses of Anger," 131.
  44. Ibid., 129.
  45. Frye, "A Note on Anger," 85.
  46. McWeeney, "Liberating Anger, Embodying Knowledge," 295.
  47. Consider how Fricker drains anger from her paradigm example of testimonial injustice. She selects the anger-free hotel room conversation between Marge and Herbert in *The Talented Mr. Ripley* rather than the water taxi conversation where Marge's clearly-focused anger is resistant and alive. Anger is also drained from the courtroom testimonial exchanges in her *To Kill a Mockingbird* examples, even though it's clear that Tom Robinson, a Black man, must swallow his anger to be heard, and that Mayella, a young white woman, uses anger to bolster her false rape charge against Tom.
  48. Lorde, "Uses of Anger," 130.
  49. Jaggar, "Love and Knowledge," 167.
  50. West, "Brave Enough to be Angry."
  51. Medina, *The Epistemology of Resistance*, 45.
  52. Lugones, *Pilgrimages/Peregrinajes*, 107–8. See Frye, "A Note on Anger," 94–95.
  53. Frye, "A Note on Anger," 90.
  54. For examples see Spillers, "Mama's Baby, Papa's Maybe," 64–81; Lugones, *Pilgrimages/Peregrinajes*; Collins, *Black Feminist Thought*; Medina, *Epistemologies of Resistance*.
  55. Lorde, "Uses of Anger," 127.
  56. Doston, "A Cautionary Tale," 24.
  57. Pohlhaus Jr., "Relational Knowing and Epistemic Injustice," 715.

BIBLIOGRAPHY

Ahmed, Sara. *Living a Feminist Life*. Durham: Duke University Press, 2017.
———. *The Promise of Happiness*. Durham: Duke University Press, 2010.
Aristotle. *Nicomachean Ethics*. Second Edition. Translated by Terence Irwin. Indianapolis: Hackett, 1999.
Bailey, Alison. "The Unlevel Knowing Field: An Engagement with Dotson's Third-Order Epistemic Oppression." *Social Epistemology Review and Reply Collective* 3:10 (2014): 62–68.
Coates, Ta-Nehisi. *Between the World and Me*. New York: Random House, 2015.
Collins, Patricia Hill. *Black Feminist Thought: Knowledge, Consciousness, and the Politics of Empowerment*. Boston: Unwin Hyman, 1991.
Cooper, Brittney. *Eloquent Rage: A Black Feminist Discovers Her Superpower*. New York: St. Martin's Press, 2018.
DiAngelo, Robin. "White Fragility." *International Journal of Critical Pedagogy* 3:3 (2011): 54–70.
Dotson, Kristie. "A Cautionary Tale: On Limiting Epistemic Oppression." *Frontiers: A Journal of Women's Studies* 33:1 (2012): 24–47.
———. "Tracking Epistemic Violence, Tracking Practices of Silencing." *Hypatia* 26:2 (2011): 236–57.

Fatima, Saba. "Being Brown and Epistemic Insecurity." Hypatia Conference. Villanova University. May 29, 2015.
———. "On the Edge of Knowing: Microaggression and Epistemic Uncertainty as a Woman of Color." In *Surviving Sexism in Academia: Feminist Strategies for Leadership*. Edited by Kirsti Cole and Holly Hassel, 147–54. New York: Routledge, 2017.
Fricker, Miranda. *Epistemic Injustice: Power and the Ethics of Knowing*. New York and Oxford: Oxford University Press, 2007.
Frye, Marilyn. "A Note on Anger." In *The Politics of Reality: Essays in Feminist Theory*, 84–94. Trumansburg, NY: The Crossing Press, 1983.
Gay, Roxane. "Who Gets to Be Angry?" *New York Times*. 10 June 2016. Web.
Jaggar, Alison. "Love and Knowledge: Emotion in Feminist Epistemology." *Inquiry* 32:2 (1989): 151–76.
Lorde, Audre. "Eye to Eye: Black Women, Hatred, and Anger." In *Sister Outsider: Essays and Speeches by Audre Lorde*, 145–75. Trumansburg, NY: The Crossing Press, 1984.
———. "On the Uses of Anger: Women Responding to Racism." In *Sister Outsider: Essays and Speeches by Audre Lorde*, 124–33. Trumansburg, NY: The Crossing Press, 1984.
Lugones, María. *Pilgrimages/Peregrinajes: Theorizing Coalition against Multiple Oppressions*. Lanham, MD: Roman and Littlefield Publishers, 2007.
Lyman, Peter. "The Politics of Anger: On Silence, Resentment, and Political Speech." *Socialist Review* 11:3 (1984): 55–74.
McKinnon, Rachel. "Allies Behaving Badly: Gaslighting as Epistemic Injustice." In *The Routledge Handbook to Epistemic Injustice*. Edited by Ian James Kidd, José Medina, and Gaile Pohlhaus, Jr., 167–75. New York: Routledge, 2017.
———. "Epistemic Injustice." *Philosophy Compass* 11, no. 8 (2016): 437–46.
McWeeney, Jen. "Liberating Anger, Embodying Knowledge: A Comparative Study of María Lugones and Zen Master Hakuin." *Hypatia* 25, no. 2 (Spring 2010): 295–315.
Medina, José. *The Epistemology of Resistance: Gender and Racial Oppressions, Epistemic Injustice, and Resistant Imaginations*. New York: Oxford University Press, 2013.
Mills, Charles. *The Racial Contract*. Ithaca, New York: Cornell University Press, 1997.
Muñoz, José Estaban. "Feeling Brown: Ethnicity and Affect in Ricardo Bracho's *The Sweetest Hangover* (and other STDs)." *Theatre Journal* 52 (2000): 67–97.
Pohlhaus, Gaile, Jr. "Discerning the Primary Epistemic Harm in Cases of Testimonial Injustice." *Social Epistemology* 28, no. 2 (2013): 99–114.
———. "Relational Knowing and Epistemic Injustice: Toward a Theory of 'Willful Hermeneutical Ignorance.'" *Hypatia* 27, no. 4 (Fall 2012): 715–35.
Scott, James C. *Domination and the Arts of Resistance: Hidden Transcripts*. New Haven: Yale University Press, 1990.
Spillers, Hortense. "Mama's Baby, Papa's Maybe: An American Grammar Book." *Diacritics*, 17:2 (Summer 1987): 64–81.
West, Lindy. "Brave Enough to be Angry." *New York Times*. 8 November, 2017. Web.

FIVE

The "What," "How," and "Why" of Racialized Seeing

Katie Tullmann

RACIAL COLORBLINDNESS

A recent edition of *National Geographic* features an article on "biracial" twins, eleven-year-old Marcia and Millie Biggs.[1] Marcia, who has white skin, blue eyes, and blonde hair, takes after her English mother. Millie has darker skin, brown eyes, and black hair that favors her Jamaican father. The twins say that many people assume that they are best friends and are surprised to learn that they are actually fraternal twins. The article suggests that surprise over Marcia and Millie's relationship captures something interesting about the way people understand race: that race is scientifically significant, genetically determined, and results in determined sets of visible markers (skin color, eye color, hair color and texture, face shape, etc.) that are reliable indicators of different races. The Biggs twins upend these assumptions precisely because they do not *appear* to us the way we may assume they ought to.

Perhaps what the Biggs twins should teach us is that we should not see race at all—that, in fact, we should see the inherent value and merit of an individual and not his or her skin color. That tactic reveals a commitment to racial *colorblindness*, the perspective that one does not, or should not, see race and, moreover, that a person's racial identity should not play a role in his or her social value or individual worth. The problem with colorblindness is that it often hides a new form of racism that is both covert and institutionalized; it allows whites to plead innocence of overt racism while still benefiting from racial privilege and perpetuating racial biases.[2] Philosopher Linda Martín Alcoff warns her readers, "[Some] white folks have declared, no doubt prematurely, that they have already reached utopia. While the rest of us continue to see in color, they declare themselves to be color-blind, to not notice whether people are 'black, white, green or purple.'"[3] Colorblindness implies that by ignoring a person's visible racial markers, I will thereby treat her according to her merit and not based on unwarranted racial stereotypes. However, it's possible that claims of colorblindness actually perpetuate systemic racism. Sociologist Jenni Mueller states that

> colorblindness resolves the tension of endorsing racial equality in a social structure still designed to preserve white advantage, and is thus central to the persistence of white supremacy in the post-civil rights era. Colorblindness rationalizes white supremacy in everyday thought and discourse, supporting whites' ability to ignore the significance of racial discrimination and white privilege, as well as engage in (or remain passive or apathetic bystanders to) everyday racism, even when they are well-meaning and intend to be non-racist.[4]

Similarly, legal scholar Patricia Williams contends that colorblind statements, such as "I just see people; I don't see color" reflect "a deeply hidden effect of racism. This statement reduces socially significant human differences to invisibleness and meaningless hype whereby one does not have to acknowledge what one does not see."[5] Denying race ignores existing social problems, dressing them up in seemingly permissible practices.

Building on these worries, we can see that racial colorblindness is at best a flawed perspective, and at worst a deeply misguided one. Yet, if colorblindness—not seeing race—is not a moral ideal, then what is? What, ultimately, is the goal concerning racial categorization and treatment? It is difficult to articulate an answer to this question. Still, we can spell out some reasons why it is so hard to make any real progress in eliminating racist practices. A primary reason is the pervasiveness and history of white privilege and ignorance.[6] Colorblind racism suggests another: individuals possess *implicit* racist attitudes—including racist beliefs, intentions, desires, and so on—of which a subject might be unaware, but which nevertheless play a role in her behavior.[7]

Implicit racial attitudes and colorblindness are the launching point for my present project. I will discuss implicit perceptual attitudes—the ways in which one's visual experiences reflect and reinforce unconscious attitudes concerning a target's racial identity, the ways in which race seems to us to be embodied, and the ways in which we cultivate racial perceptual habits. I call this *racialized seeing*: the capacity to "see" another person's race.[8] Conceptually—though, unlikely in practice—racialized seeing can be either bare or value-laden. *Bare racialized seeing* is the act of visually categorizing a target into a particular racial group on the basis of allegedly relevant visible racial markers (whatever those may be). It portends to be value neutral; it is the visible act of racial categorization without assigning social significance to those categories.[9] *Evaluative racialized seeing*, in contrast, goes beyond bare racialized seeing in assigning or associating value-laden concepts to different races. For instance, when a prejudiced white subject visually confronts a person of color, she may see that the perceptual target is Black (bare racialized seeing) and also visually experience the target as dangerous, aggressive, or ignorant. Conversely, the same subject could see a white man (bare racialized seeing) and also see that he is powerful, educated, and wealthy. Evaluative racialized seeing depends on the adopted social values and beliefs associated with people of different races. Whether evaluative racialized seeing is a strictly perceptual process, or rather a cognitive one, is a question I will explore in the following sections.

My goal in this essay is to explore the ways in which racialized seeing develops within an individual and how both types of racialized seeing contribute to harmful racial practices. I argue that even if humans cannot directly perceive a person's race, we nevertheless have the conscious experience of doing so. It *seems* to us that we see race. Furthermore, I argue that bare racialized seeing is a type of visual error: we claim to have the experience of perceiving something that, strictly speaking, is imperceptible. I will also elaborate on the wrongness of racialized seeing—the reasons why we should strive to develop a nonevaluative racialized seeing, even if genuine colorblindness is impossible and, indeed, undesirable. As I see it, racialized seeing is a learned practice. If so, it may be possible to *unlearn*.

I will begin by elaborating on the nature of racialized seeing. I draw upon recent work in both analytic philosophy of perception and critical race and intersectional feminist theory to show that racialized seeing is a social practice that depends on cultural norms and values. I will then turn to a discussion of the moral and epistemic harm caused by racialized seeing. I will conclude with some brief comments on the implications of racialized seeing for moral responsibility.

PERCEPTION AND THE ONTOLOGY OF RACE

I begin with two assumptions about racialized seeing. First, I think that it is a genuine phenomenon. Many people do, in fact, seem to *just see* other peoples' race. This is a descriptive, rather than a normative, claim. And yet, it could be that we *should* eliminate racialized seeing (both bare and evaluative). I will attempt to elucidate the practice as it happens in our society and suggest some reasons why we should amend these practices. My second assumption is that racialized seeing is generally uncontrollable. It happens automatically and without conscious intent. We generally do not choose to see race; rather, it is something that we learn to do over time. Thus, it would be very difficult to *unlearn*.

Consider the following example of racialized seeing from George Yancy:

> Well-dressed, I enter an elevator where a white woman waits to reach her floor. She "sees" my Black body, though not the same one I have seen reflected back to me from the mirror on any number of occasions. Buying into the myth that one's dress says something about the person, one might think that the markers of my dress (suit and tie) should ease her tension. What is it that makes the markers of my dress inoperative? . . .
>
> Her body language signifies, "Look, *the* Black!" On this score, though short of a performative locution, her body language functions as an insult. Over and above how my body is clothed, she "sees" a criminal, she sees me as a threat. Independently of any threatening action on my part, my Black body, my existence in Black, poses a threat. It is not necessary that I first perform a threatening action. The question of *deeds* is irrelevant. . . . My dark body occludes the presumption of innocence. It is as if one's Blackness is a congenital defect, one that burdens the body with tremendous inherited guilt.[10]

Yancy's elevator example highlights the harm of both types of racialized seeing: the assumptions and stereotypes inherent to seeing race and the unconscious behaviors and denials of individuality that occur as a result. Yancy captures his own experiences as a Black man in a white supremacist America, but we can imagine similar anecdotes surrounding the experiences for all persons of color, simply because they appear to match some culturally indoctrinated stereotype. My point is that racialized seeing is both indicative of and perpetuates these harmful stereotypes.

I will return to this example throughout the essay in order to explain the effects of bare and evaluative racialized seeing. For now, I wish to introduce several key questions about racialized seeing. We can organize these questions into three different clusters, covering the "how," the "why," and the "what" of racialized seeing:

1. *How* do we see race? What are the cognitive mechanisms involved? Is visual racial categorization learned or the result of an innate capacity, similar to the ability to perceive faces and colors? Relatedly, is racialized seeing strictly perceptual, or does it involve further cognitive judgments?
2. *Why* do we see race in the ways that we do? In general, why are certain races seen in particular ways, and what social practices and beliefs are implicated?
3. *What* are the social implications of racialized seeing? In what way does racialized seeing help to explain actual social behaviors, in-

cluding the racist practices that we encounter in the media and everyday life?

I will address the how, why, and what of racialized seeing in what follows. Before doing so, it is worth considering the "race" part of racialized seeing. What is that property that we supposedly experience? This question depends on the metaphysics of race. Perhaps race is a social construct—whatever that means. Perhaps race is biological. One's position on the metaphysics of race will help to answer the how/what/why of racialized seeing. Alcoff distinguishes three different positions on race categories:

- *Nominalism* (eliminativism): "Race is not real, meaning that racial terms do not refer to anything 'really real,' principally because recent science has invalidated race as a salient or even meaningful biological category."
- *Essentialism*: "Race is an elemental category of identity with explanatory power. Members of racial groups share a set of characteristics, a set of political interests, and a historical destiny."
- *Contextualism*: "Race is socially constructed, historically malleable, culturally contextual, and reproduced through learned perceptual practices."[11]

Alcoff rejects both nominalism and essentialism. The former incorrectly posits that race is purely biological. It assumes that, if race is not a biological concept, then it is meaningless. This is false; not all socially and scientifically significant concepts are biological (e.g., theories and abstracta). Nominalism also seems to underlie colorblindness: eliminating meaningless racist concepts will also eliminate racist practices. Essentialism fails to capture the "fluidity and open-endedness" of racial meanings. To say that there exist essential racial characteristics—for instance, that all whites share a Western European history, or that all Black people have dark brown skin—assumes that all racial categories are homogenous, when they are not. Essentialism ignores "global hybridization," the melding of racial beliefs and practices over time.

Alcoff favors contextualism. It allows us to "acknowledge the current devastating reality of race while holding open the possibility that present-day racial formations may change significantly or perhaps wither away."[12] I agree with Alcoff and will maintain a contextualist position in this essay. I believe that race depends on a subject's beliefs and assumptions on race, which, in turn, depend on that subject's social context. Moreover, contextualist approaches recognize the role of *learned perceptual practices* in maintaining racial categories. Perceptual recognition and categorization reinforce and shape racial concepts. In my terms, both bare and evaluative racialized seeing sustain racial beliefs: the idea that we can categorize people in terms of race at all, and that people of particular races possess certain value-laden characteristics.

The catch is that contextualism does not obviously explain racialized seeing. In fact, if contextualism is correct, then it is a mistake to formulate racial categories on the basis of visual experience alone. We should not determine a target's race solely on her physical appearance. Taking this point further, I think that most people are visual racial *essentialists*. We tend to see people as belonging to a particular racial category because they have certain visual features—face shape, skin color, hair color and texture, dress, and so on—and not because of their social experiences and history. This is what allows subjects to enter a busy conference room (for example) and quickly determine who is white, Black, Eastern Asian, Latinx, and so forth. We do this on the basis of how those people appear to us, not based on knowledge of their historical and cultural beliefs and practices. That information may influence racial judgments later on, to update one's beliefs about a target's racial category. However, the initial categorization is often strictly perceptual.

It could be that many people tend to think of racial categories as *natural kinds*.[13] Gold is a noncontroversial example of a natural kind. We can formulate many scientifically relevant generalizations about it: gold has the atomic number 79, it dissolves in mercury to form liquid alloys, its standard atomic weight is 196.966 570(4), its melting point is 1337.33 K, and so on.[14] These are necessary conditions that define gold. Edouard Machery describes natural kinds in two ways. First, the *essentialist* view posits "a set of intrinsic, causally explanatory properties that are necessary and jointly sufficient for belonging to the kind."[15] Second, a *causal* notion of natural kinds states that "a natural kind is a class about which many generalizations can be formulated: its members tend to have many properties in common. These generalizations are not accidental: there is at least one causal mechanism that explains why its members tend to have those properties."[16] Each of these ways of understanding natural kinds is at work in racial essentialism. Natural kind essentialism states that to belong to the natural kind of whiteness (for instance), one must have some set of necessary characteristics, some of which may be visible markers (fair skin, hair texture, face shape, but also cultural characteristics, such as ancestral background and ethnic history). The causal view of natural kinds would likely state that genetic markers or some other biological feature is causally significant for determining race; if a person has this genetic makeup, then she is Black, white, or Latinx.

Many people may *see* race through an essentialist lens, but ideally, we can formulate better judgments about racial categories rather than rely primarily on our limited perceptual experiences. However, it turns out that we need more information than biology and physical appearance to determine racial categories.

PERCEIVING VALUE

So far, I have discussed bare racialized seeing and evaluative racialized seeing as separate mental actions. A subject categorizes others into a race according to observed visible markers. Subjects may also visually evaluate others on the basis of that recognition. It's time to muddy those waters. Perhaps *all* racialized seeing is evaluative, in which case there is no such thing as bare racialized seeing. Many philosophers have argued that there is no such thing as an "innocent eye," that our perceptual experiences are always clouded by our beliefs and values. Ultimately, I think that this is an empirical question that is worthy of debate; nevertheless, I think that it certainly feels like perceptual experiences are influenced by thoughts, beliefs, and emotions. Importantly, the lack of an innocent *racialized* seeing follows from a contextualist theory of race: if racial concepts depend on social beliefs and practices, which are themselves subject to evaluation, then race is also an inherently evaluative concept.

There are two ways to understand the capacity to see value. Option 1: evaluative concepts may be perceptible. This means that a subject's visual system can recognize and process evaluative concepts, and, further, that the subject has the conscious experience of seeing them. For instance, some philosophers argue that moral qualities such as "goodness," "badness," "right," or "wrong" can be seen by a sensitive moral agent.[17] I *see* that an action is wrong; I just *see* what the right decision is. Many adults can see emotional properties on another's face or associated with particular objects. I see a friend's happiness or that a snake is dangerous. Perhaps the same applies to racial properties. We can just see "whiteness," or "Blackness" in the same way that we are able to just see a morally right action.

Option 2: humans can literally *perceive* only simple properties such as colors, shapes, and some objects and *then* associate those simple properties with (or judge them to be associated with) evaluative concepts. For example, we may perceive a person and collection of objects, then *judge* that the action is morally right; we see a facial expression and *associate* that expression with sorrow. We do not see sorrow, danger, or moral wrongness. We see (visually process, experience) shapes and colors, then cognitively judge that evaluative concepts are associated with those properties. Perhaps racialized seeing is like this: we perceive skin color, associate that skin color with a particular race, and also associate that skin color/race with further evaluative properties (moral goodness, thick properties such as safety or danger, etc.). This is, for instance, how implicit attitude tests purport to work: they measure the ease and speed in which we associate different colored faces with evaluative concepts, such as danger or aggression.[18] In my terms, option 1 blends bare and evaluative seeing; indeed, in this view bare racialized seeing is impossible because race itself is a thick evaluative concept. Option 2 suggests that, even though it *seems* to us that both bare and evaluative racialized seeing are possible, we do not actually perceive race at all. Instead, we very quickly and unconsciously associate value-neutral perceptible properties with value-laden racial properties.

Deciding between option 1 and option 2 depends in large part on one's position on the rich/thin, cognitive penetration, and perceptual learning debates. The rich/thin debate concerns what types of properties can be perceived—what is processed by the visual system (see Jerry Fodor), or what properties we have the conscious experience of seeing (see Susanna Siegel).[19] Some philosophers and cognitive scientists believe that only "thin" properties are perceptible. This means that only color, shape, size, illumination, movement, and perhaps objecthood are technically perceived. Only they are processed by neural visual systems.[20] This corresponds with option 2 of racialized seeing: we do not perceive race, even if it seems to us that we do. Alternatively, the "rich" view of perceptual content states that some high-level properties are perceptible. We can perceive causation (A causes B), emotion properties (happiness, sadness), natural kinds (tigers, gold), and even some artificial properties (teacup, table) in addition to mere color, shape, and size.[21] This corresponds with option 1.

I do not wish to adjudicate between the rich and thin views of perceptual content. Race is a rich property because it is not merely a matter of a simple property, such as color. It would seem, then, that a theory of racialized seeing should embrace a rich content view of perceptual content. I think that the *experience* of racialized seeing is possible in both views. In either view it may seem to us that we have conscious visual experiences of a target's race and related evaluative properties (seeing a white person as bigoted, for instance). I disagree with scholars such as Tim Bayne and Siegel that our own conscious experiences can help us determine which view is correct.[22]

There is a further question concerning the cognitive processes involved in racialized seeing or in any kind of value-laden perceptual experience. *How* do evaluative concepts show up in our visual experiences? One theory is that cognitive states may permeate our perceptual processing. This is the *cognitive penetration of perception thesis*. Fiona MacPherson defines cognitive penetration as follows:

> If it is possible for two subjects in these conditions to have different perceptual experiences (different in respect of phenomenal character and content) on account of the differing states of their cognitive systems, or if it is possible for one subject at different times in these conditions to have different experiences on account of the difference between the states of their cognitive systems at those times, then cognitive penetration is possible.[23]

A subject's cognitive mental states—her beliefs, desires, intentions, and emotions—directly influence how she sees objects in her environment. Thus, two subjects with different beliefs will see the same object in a different way. Siegel, an advocate of the rich content view, gives the following example:

> Suppose you have never seen a pine tree before, and are hired to cut down all the pine trees in a grove containing trees of many different sorts. Someone points out to you which trees are pine trees. Some weeks pass, and your disposition to distinguish the pine trees from the others improves. Eventually, you can spot the pine trees immediately: they become visually salient to you. Like the recognitional disposition you gain, the salience of the trees emerges gradually. Gaining this recognitional disposition is reflected in a phenomenological difference between the visual experience had before and after the recognitional disposition was fully developed.[24]

In this case, your acquired beliefs about the key characteristics of pine trees influence how you experience the trees in the forest. The trees appear to you once you know that they are pine trees. This is an example of *diachronic* cognitive penetration: it is the capacity for cognitive states, such as beliefs and intentions, to influence one's perceptual experience over time. Diachronic penetration could also explain why wine tastes different to an experienced taster as opposed to a novice, or why the Spanish language sounds different to a Spanish speaker and an English only speaker.

Siegel also suggests that *synchronic* cognitive penetration is possible: the capacity for a cognitive state to influence one's perceptual experience at a particular time. Consider an example. Suppose that Mary and Martin attend an exhibit of Rothko's colored square paintings. Suppose that they have virtually identical perceptual input from one blue and yellow painting: the lighting is the same for each viewer, they visually attend to the same features of the work, and they stand in roughly the same location relative to the canvas. The only difference between them is that Mary is an artist, and so possesses many relevant beliefs about the painting's history and construction (not to mention a deeper understanding of the rules and styles of painting that may contribute to her capacity to evaluate the painting's quality), while Martin is an artistic novice, and so lacks those beliefs. On the cognitive penetration thesis, Mary would have a different perceptual experience of the Rothko painting because of her beliefs about his work. This would be true even if we hold all of Mary and Martin's physical perceptual processing the same. Perhaps Mary experiences the bright blue of the painting as more saturated than Martin does, because she is familiar with Rothko's layering technique.[25]

We can imagine a scenario in which Martin and Mary have a similar perceptual encounter concerning race. Let's suppose that Martin is an "expert" on racial categories: he possesses relevant beliefs about racial visible markers, different races' culture and history, and present social circumstances. On the other hand, Mary was raised in such a way that she is a "novice" about race. She is only familiar with her racial group and has no perceptual experience with persons of other racial groups. Martin and Mary encounter a visual representation of a person of a different race than their own while watching a TV program. Their encounter is roughly similar to that of the Rothko painting. Mary and Martin's perceptual landscape and attention are the same, but their perceptual experience is different. Martin sees the person on TV as raced. Mary only sees the person as having a certain skin tone.

On the rich content view of perceptual content, paired with a positive thesis of the cognitive penetration of perception, our beliefs and recognitional habits allow us to see race. Over time, our beliefs that people of a particular racial group look a certain way trains us to quickly and unconsciously visually recognize and categorize people according to those groups. This accounts for bare racialized seeing. Cognitive penetration of perception can also explain evaluative racialized seeing. Suppose that Martin also possesses generalizing stereotypes about Latinx persons: that they enjoy certain foods, that they enter Martin's country illegally, and that they are lazy. These are all evaluative racial judgments—they each propose normative claims about Latinx people. We can even suppose that Martin doesn't endorse these beliefs. He simply knows that these are common stereotypes about Latinx people in his own country. On the cognitive penetration view, Martin's evaluative judgments of Latinx people influence his perceptual experience of them. He doesn't just see Latinx people—he sees them as "illegals" or as lazy. We will consider the ethical and epistemic implications of evaluative racialized seeing later on.

Importantly, even the thin perceptual content view can explain the ways in which subjects have the conscious experience (stated here as "phenomenal character") of seeing value-laden properties such as race without appealing to cognitive penetration. The perceptual experience depends on the way in which perceptual properties are processed. MacPherson states:

> [In this view there is no] difference in the phenomenal character of the experiences in a given case—there is merely a difference (or change) in the *judgments* made on the basis of the experiences with the same phenomenal character. Another strategy is to claim that, while the experiences differ in phenomenal character, this change hasn't come about because a state of the cognitive system has penetrated experience, but on account of *a change in perceptual processing*—such as a change in perceptual attention or in eye movement.[26]

Consider again Mary and Martin's encounters with the Rothko painting and TV racial representations in terms of the thin content view. Mary's expert knowledge on Rothko's work does not directly influence her perceptual experience of the painting. The phenomenal character of her experience is different from Martin's, but not because of cognitive penetration. Instead, her expertise serves as a *selection filter*.[27] She attends to and visually processes the painting in a slightly different way than Martin does because of her expert knowledge. Mary judges that the painting is beautiful, rich, or artistic. These are not properties that she perceives—they are properties that she unconsciously and very quickly judges to be part of the painting.

We can tell a similar story for racialized seeing. Mary and Martin have isomorphic perceptual experiences of the raced individual on the TV screen, but their unconscious judgments about his racial category and character are different. We can apply this idea to bare and evaluative racialized seeing more generally. On the thin content view, Martin only *perceives* a person's skin color—that's all brains visually process. However, he may *see* race due to fast, unconscious judgments of race and evaluative properties. Martin's knowledge about racial categories acts as perceptual selection filters. He *attends* to different visible markers—the target's body shape, facial features, clothing, hair, and so on. Thus, Martin's cognitive states indirectly influence his experiences. The phenomenal character of Martin's experience is the same as Mary's if all else is equal, but the judgments he makes concerning race and racialized properties are different.

There is some common ground between the different positions in philosophy of perception. Proponents of both the rich and thin views of perceptual content and pro and anticognitive penetration thesis typically accept some kind of *perceptual learning*. Perceptual learning is similar to diachronic penetration: the capacity for the phenomenal character of one's perceptual experiences to change over time due to repeated encounters with stimuli. The mechanisms involved in perceptual learning might differ (penetration on the rich view, attention on the thin view), but even "mad dog nativists" such as Fodor accept that some perceptual learning occurs that can impact our visual experiences.[28] The cognitive scientists Joshua Gold and Takeo Watanabe define perceptual learning as the "experience-dependent enhancement of our ability to make sense of what we see, hear, feel, taste or smell. These changes are permanent or semi-permanent as distinct from shorter-term mechanisms like sensory adaptation or habituation."[29] Perceptual learning helps the brain's visual processing systems to streamline the plethora of visual input they receive. Brains learn to prioritize different features of a perceived stimulus to be relevant to its categorization. Perceptual learning takes place through an extended process of acquiring concepts and skills to recognize or gain increased sensitivity to particular stimuli.

I propose that we must perceptually learn to see race. Arguably, we do not have an innate ability to have bare experiences of race even if we have an innate ability to see different colors, given the contextualist theory of racial categories. It seems especially clear that evaluative racialized seeing must be learned through some process of perceptual learning or diachronic penetration. Average people grow up exposed to persons of different races in their everyday lives, in the media, or through testimony from others. Over time, we acquire beliefs about racial categories and learn to see them in the way that we can learn to see pine trees or learn to hear Spanish.

We now have several different conceptions of the cognitive mechanisms involved in racialized seeing work—and how evaluative concepts associated with different races can be smuggled into one's phenomenal experience. The next two sections will explore the potential harm of both bare and racialized seeing.

THE WRONGNESS OF RACIALIZED SEEING

It may seem obvious that racialized seeing can be harmful. It's less obvious what that harm amounts to given the perceptual nature of racialized seeing. I will divide the potential harm of racialized seeing into four categories: epistemic harm to the seen individual (what I have been referring to as the *target*), epistemic harm to the seer (the *subject*), moral harm to the target, and moral harm to the subject. This categorization is largely methodological in order to elucidate the variety of ways in which racialized seeing can be wrong. I doubt that we can separate epistemic and ethical harm on any but the most arbitrary of lines.[30] Moreover, we can consider the potential moral or epistemic harm of either *bare* or *evaluative* racialized seeing for both subjects and targets. I argue that racialized seeing may commit a subject to irrational judgments and denies the target full epistemic agency. The moral harm of racialized seeing is related; it stems from not *treating* a target as a fully rational individual. This form of harm is related to the wrongness of stereotyping and bias in general.[31]

Epistemic Harm

It may seem strange to discuss epistemic harm done to the person who does the racialized seeing. Why discuss the harm done to a biased seer? Why focus on the negative effects of racism for the racist, as opposed to the victims of racism? Mainly, I think that it is important to be clear on what is going wrong in the mind of the subject when she engages in racialized seeing in order to help explain the wrongness done to the target as a result of that seeing. Moreover, people with false beliefs about race are not the only people who engage in racialized seeing. If my discussion above was correct, then all (or almost all) people see race in some respect. So it is worth considering when and why racialized seeing can be an epistemic problem to the subject.

To begin, I understand the epistemic harm of racialized seeing as a detriment to a subject's cognitive capacities—her ability to appropriately and reliably think, judge, form and maintain consistent beliefs, understand and formulate rational arguments, or in other ways process information—as the result of biased or unwarranted racial categorization. There are multiple ways that epistemic harm to the subject can be interpreted. First, the subject's beliefs about race may be flawed. Thus, whether the subject's beliefs directly (through cognitive penetration) or indirectly (through selection filters) influence her perceptual experience, the racial categorization and evaluation may be incorrect because the beliefs that influence the experience are flawed. This is an error in cognitive *content*. Second, something may go wrong in a subject's perceptual *processing*. The subject misidentifies a person's race or makes invalid assumptions about a target's race based on limited or stereotypical visual information. Errors in both content and in processing may cause a subject to acquire or perpetuate false beliefs about a target's racial identity, and racial categories in general.

The epistemic harm of racialized seeing is a subset of what Siegel calls hijacked perception. A subject's perceptual experience is hijacked when her cognitive states influence her perceptual judgments. Siegel offers the following example to illuminate hijacked perception:

> Before seeing Jack, Jill fears that Jack is angry at her. When she sees him, her fear causes her to perceive Jack as angry, and this perception strengthens her fear. If Jill's fear affects only her perception only at the level of perceptual belief, leaving her perceptual experience untouched, there is little temptation to say that the resulting judgment is formed epistemically well.[32]

Siegel argues that Jill's belief that Jack is angry is hijacked because her previously held cognitive state (fear that Jack is angry) unduly influences that belief. Jill has not properly formulated a belief that Jack is angry. She performed an act of perceptual confirmation bias: Jill was (perhaps unconsciously) looking for evidence that Jack was angry, and so interpreted neutral input as evidence in favor of this belief. Thus, Jill has an irrational mental framework concerning Jack.

We can generalize from this case to other instances of hijacked perception. Hijacked perception is epistemically harmful when a cognitive state inappropriately influences the subject's perceptual experience, thereby rendering her mental framework irrational. Racialized seeing may be hijacked when the process by which the subject sees a target's race is irrational; she makes a perceptual judgment about a target's race due to the unwarranted influence of her cognitive states or when the content of her cognitive states is flawed. Let's return to Martin and Mary. Martin's beliefs about different racial groups influence how he recognizes and categorizes individuals he encounters. One day at work, Martin passes a stranger in the hallway. Unconsciously, Martin racially categorizes this person according to the beliefs he possesses about Black people in his culture. Martin sees that the target is Black. But suppose that Martin's information about this particular target is incomplete. He only possesses visual racial markers and should not jump to any conclusions when making a perceptual judgment. The point is that even if Martin is right—the person he passes in the hallway is Black—Martin's perceptual judgment was brought about by irrational processes. Martin's epistemic framework concerning this individual is thus irrational. His bare racialized seeing has caused him epistemic harm. This becomes clearer in instances of evaluative racialized seeing: Martin does not simply see that the target is Black, but also sees the target as aggressive *because* the target is Black. This, too, is a case of irrational perceptual judgment: Martin's belief that Black people are aggressive has influenced how he sees the target even if the person in question gives no visual indication of being so.

Sometimes epistemic harm affects well-meaning, good-intentioned people (as I am supposing Martin to be). Perhaps Martin would not *consciously endorse* the claim that Black people are aggressive, but this is a racist stereotype within Martin's society with which he is familiar. These kinds of evaluative associations may be brought to bear in implicit bias and racialized seeing.[33] However, there are other instances of hijacked racialized seeing that cause more obviously pernicious forms of epistemic harm. This occurs when the subject's racial beliefs are prejudicial, incomplete, or misguided. Indeed, Kwame Appiah suggests that extrinsic racism—the idea that there are moral distinctions between members of different races based on different racial essences—is a cognitive incapacity for the racist.[34] This is a matter of both flawed cognitive content and poor cognitive processing.

Racist beliefs—particularly held by white folk who are in positions of relative social power—may negatively influence the subject's perceptual experiences of others. As Charles Mills states, "At all levels, interests may shape cognition, influencing what and how we see, what we and society choose to remember, whose testimony is solicited and whose is not, and which facts and frameworks are sought out and accepted."[35] Imagine a white subject who possesses false beliefs about the moral and cognitive superiority of his own race. It is in this subject's interests (personal, financial, social) to maintain his white identity and social privilege. We can even imagine that these interests are unconscious. He does not explicitly endorse racist beliefs and would never openly avow them. If I am right about racialized seeing, the subject's beliefs in white superiority and the relative inferiority of other races may influence how he sees people in terms of their race. He sees white people as more morally upstanding, intelligent, and successful than persons of color. Perhaps he visually attends to different features of persons of color, which in turn, confirms his belief in their inferiority. This is analogous to the Jack and Jill example, in which Jill's belief that Jack is mad at her influences how she visually interprets his facial expression. This, in turn, bolsters Jill's belief that Jack is angry. There is a vicious circularity at play here: if a subject expects to see particular properties she will be more likely to find them. In Mills's terms, white ignorance can produce "self-deception, bad faith, evasion, and misrepresentation,"[36] each of which may plague the seer if her beliefs hijack her perceptual experiences.

I have focused so far on the epistemic harm of racialized seeing to the seer. This discussion also makes it clear how racialized seeing is epistemically harmful for the target: she is subject to visual stereotyping and associations based on the seer's biased or generalized beliefs. Following the literature on epistemic injustice, I contend that racialized seeing can be a form of epistemic oppression.

One could argue that the very act of visual racial categorization is oppressive because it relies on incomplete information about the target. I am unsure about this. It seems, to me, that there is something of value in racial identification: personal pride, history, and community. Bare racialized seeing may reflect and reinforce these positive feelings of racial identification. Moreover, I think that the question of whether racialized seeing should be eliminated depends on whether we can change our evaluation of different races. In what follows, then, I will focus on the epistemic harm from *evaluative* racialized seeing.

Kristie Dotson defines epistemic oppression as the "hindering of one's contribution to knowledge production; [the] unwarranted infringement on the epistemic agency of knowers."[37] For example, a person of color may not be considered a reliable source of knowledge[38] or her perspective may lack credibility.[39] In my view, evaluative racialized seeing is a significant contributor to epistemic oppression in two ways. First, it is possible that the very act of associating generalizing or stereotypical properties to an individual lowers her epistemic standing, especially when the attributed property concerns the target's epistemic abilities. This kind of epistemic oppression would clearly be at play in evaluative seeing—for instance, when a subject sees a person of color as unintelligent or unreliable. Overall, this first view claims that the very act of evaluative racialized seeing is epistemically oppressive.

Another view is that evaluative racialized seeing is epistemically oppressive only when it plays a necessary role in motivating oppressive behavior.[40] Consider a real case of (what I consider to be) epistemic oppression: the reactions to Rachel Jeantel's testimony on the George Zimmerman trial in 2013. There was quite a bit of commentary about Jeantel's testimony: that she referred to Zimmerman as a "creepy ass cracker," that her diction was difficult to understand (one lawyer asked her if she had difficulty with English), and that she was often unresponsive or curt in her answers. Jeantel's testimony drew a great deal of negative attention; some media outlets simply dismissed her report of the events offhand because of her courtroom demeanor. She stated after the trial that she was mad at the way the lawyers and society at large judged her. Indeed, an article in the *Washington Post* states that Jeantel's testimony "became a proxy for pitched cultural debate, a stand-in for projections about race, class and especially all the things Americans—Black and white—want, don't want, and can't tolerate seeing in young Black women."[41]

The last point—that there are "things" that we want, don't want, or cannot tolerate "seeing" in young Black woman—can be understood both literally and figuratively. Figuratively, many racially biased Americans do not wish to "see" a young Black woman as a reliable source of information. In this view, young Black women, perhaps, shouldn't be seen or heard in socially important contexts. Jeantel's inappropriate (in their minds) courtroom behavior may reinforce this belief. Beliefs about the untrustworthiness of young Black women could influence how viewers evaluatively see Rachel. It could be that their perceptual experience of Jeantel was colored by fear, anger, or disdain. This, in turn, can cause subjects to disregard her testimony.

Rachel Jeantel was a victim of epistemic oppression: her voice was silenced and her perspective wasn't deemed significant in Zimmerman's trial. We can extrapolate from this case: evaluative racialized seeing may play a role in how we treat others as rational agents. If a subject's perceptual experience of a target is negatively hijacked by biased racial beliefs, then any further interactions may be tainted by that initial impression.

Moral Wrongness

Consider again Yancy's elevator example. Is there something inherently morally wrong about the white woman's perceptual judgments? Yancy thinks that there is: "[It] is against my will to have my body transformed, to have it reshaped and thrown back to me as something I am supposed to *own*, as a meaning I am supposed to accept."[42] This quote shows how the epistemic and moral wrongness of racialized seeing go hand in hand: it is morally wrong to oppress others on the basis of irrationally formed perceptual judgments, especially when those irrational judgments undermine a target's epistemic worth. Ultimately, the specific type of moral wrongness involved in racialized seeing depends on one's normative ethical view. In a roughly Kantian sense, we can say that racialized seeing denies the target—and, perhaps, the subject—full subjectivity and agency. This is a matter of the target's worth as an epistemic agent and also in her inherent value as an autonomous person. A virtue theorist could contend that racialized seeing erodes the subject's moral character. A consequentialist could focus on the overall emotional, physical, and social pain that racialized seeing causes.

I turn now to discussing the moral wrongness of evaluative racialized seeing itself, without its playing a causal role in further actions. Can perceptual experiences—the way I see the world around me—be immoral? Consider Martin, who possesses a belief that some other racial group is dangerous. This belief leads him to see an individual member of that group as being dangerous (evaluative racialized seeing). Suppose that the perceptual experience does not affect Martin's actions or judgments concerning that individual. Perhaps it is causally inert or he recognizes the biased experience and actively works to override it. Arguably, the harm of Martin's perceptual experience is *epistemic* because it undermines his own rationality. Martin's biased racialized seeing may not even be morally harmful to anyone other than himself—one may say that it erodes his character—if he never acts on the experience and it doesn't play a causal role in his decisions.

Of course, the worry remains that if Martin truly is unaware of his biased belief then that belief *could* and *would* impact his judgments and actions. It is almost commonplace to recognize that biased perceptual experiences play a causal role in morally harmful actions. I have in mind cases such as police shootings and weapons bias.[43] Consider, for instance, the tragic case of Amadou Diallo: a Guinean Black immigrant who was stopped by four Bronx police officers in 1999 because he matched the description of a wanted criminal. The police officers approached Diallo on his property and requested him to raise his hands. Instead, Diallo reached in his pocket (most likely for his wallet). One of the officers shouted: "Gun!" and the officers opened fire, shooting Diallo 41 times. Diallo died and the four officers were acquitted of charges of second-degree murder and reckless endangerment.[44]

The innumerable cases like Diallo's seem to indicate that there exists a perceptual (that is, nondeliberate, unconscious, nonrational) bias against Black men amongst some Americans. This is *perceptual* in the sense that one must only see the target in order for the bias to be activated. In my terms, the police officers in the Diallo case engaged in evaluative racialized seeing: their beliefs about the supposed aggression and danger of Black men influenced how they saw Diallo, leading them to interpret his actions as potentially harmful. In turn, the officers' perceptual judgment caused them to act in morally wrong ways.

Various implicit attitude tests and weapons/shooter tests strive to measure this perceptual bias. For example, Keith Payne's weapon bias test on split-second decision making indicates that participants are faster and more likely to perceptually judge that an ambiguous object is a gun if they are primed with a stereotypical Black face than a white face.[45] As Payne notes, "Snap judgments didn't change people's stereotypes. Snap judgments allowed those stereotypes to spill out into overt behavioral errors."[46] Correll and associates found similar results in their article designed to recreate the experience of a police officer who must decide whether or not to shoot when confronted with a potentially dangerous target.[47] Participants were presented with a video game-like scenario and shown either a Black or white male target, each holding either a gun or a nonthreatening object. They were instructed to shoot only armed targets. The subjects fired on armed targets more quickly when the target was Black rather than white and decided not to shoot unarmed targets more quickly when he was white rather than Black. Error rates increased under forced pressure when the participants were asked to decide to shoot very quickly and with little reflection. The authors conclude that "shooter bias is a result of distorted interpretations of an ambiguous target" and that there are multiple stages in the shooting process wherein stereotyping may be activated: in the perception of the target, the object interpretation, and the decision to shoot.[48] The first two stages—perception of the target and object interpretation—are clearly perceptual, and indicate where evaluative concepts can creep into a subject's visual experience.

The shooter and weapon bias examples are extreme cases of harmful racialized seeing. More everyday instances could include various microaggressions: a subject will only sit next to someone of her own race in a classroom, she will cross the street in order to avoid a person of color that she sees as dangerous, or she feels entitled to touch a person of color's hair because she sees the target as exotic. Cases like these all rely on some form of evaluative seeing; the unconscious perceptual experience of a racial property and some other value-laden property that influence further actions.

Overall, the danger of racialized seeing is that it results in perceptual judgments about a person that is stereotypical and unfounded, in the sense that perceptual experiences cannot adequately capture the individuality and racial experiences of a particular person. To some degree, we cannot help but categorize and associate in our perceptual experiences; this happens unconsciously, automatically, and outside of our cognitive control. But that does not make the resulting actions any less harmful.

UNLEARNING RACIALIZED SEEING

My goal in this essay was to better understand the sense in which a subject can see race. I have brought to bear the concepts of perceptual learning and the cognitive penetration of perception to help explain the sense in which a target's race might be seen. Whether or not race is perceptible depends on the metaphysics of race. In contextualist views, for instance, race is not strictly speaking a perceptible property, even if we tend to make racial categorizations on the basis of visual markers. Nevertheless, we can capture some sense in which it *seems* to a subject that racial categories are perceptible.

I have also investigated the potential harm of both types of racialized seeing. Racialized seeing can be both morally and epistemically harmful. Racialized seeing can be unjust, lead to bad social practices and pain, and undermine the target's autonomy and rational standing. This is especially true for evaluative racialized seeing: when a subject associates a particular racial category with some value-laden property, and then, in turn, associates that property with an individual belonging to the category. Thus, we may not simply see someone as Black, white, or Latinx, but also as being lazy, aggressive, or dangerous.

In the background of my discussion were questions concerning colorblindness and the desire to eliminate racist bias. I think that an adequate understanding of racialized seeing also helps us to respond to claims about colorblindness, both as it is currently practiced and as an ideal. Given that bare racialized seeing is automatic and uncontrolled, genuine colorblindness is impossible. Evaluative racialized seeing may also be impossible to avoid; perhaps human subjects cannot help but visually associate particular races with evaluative properties. If I'm right, then evaluative racialized seeing is a learned, habitualized behavior. Humans learn to associate different racial categories with normative concepts from a very young age, and are bombarded with similar messages in their communities and in the media. However, that might be all the better for genuinely changing racial prejudice. As Alcoff states, "An effective antiracism cannot be rooted in avoiding race but in an awareness and acknowledgement of its power."[49]

I will conclude my discussion of racialized seeing by briefly highlighting a lingering question that may arise from considering the wrongness of racialized seeing: can we hold racial seers morally responsible, either for the seeing itself or for the actions that it causes? One might think that knowledge and control are necessary conditions for moral responsibility, in which case a subject must be aware of her biased racialized seeing and be able to stop it.[50] Some further questions naturally arise: can we judge mental attitudes (e.g., percepts and beliefs) or only actions? How *implicit* are implicitly biased perceptual experiences? Can we unlearn or control our perceptual experience?

I can only gesture at responses to these questions here. One important point is that we seem to want to hold people responsible for their racist beliefs. As Angela Smith points out, we blame people for their mental attitudes all of the time.[51] We contend that humans *should not* adopt prejudicial beliefs or, if they already possess them, then they should do whatever they must to eliminate them. The same may hold for visual experiences: perhaps we should be aware of perceptual bias and do everything we can to eradicate it — which, in turn, depends on reshaping our beliefs.

I have argued that racialized seeing — especially evaluative racialized seeing — is a learned capacity. If we learn to see race, then perhaps the harmful aspects of racialized seeing can be *unlearned*, or at least modified. Moreover, we may have a moral obligation to unlearn bad practices involved in racialized seeing and should be held morally responsible if we do not. Consider a final point from Alcoff:

> Yet, if racism is learned, we can try to teach a different lesson. And if the racial unconscious can be opened up for inspection and accountability, the human capacity for reflection might alter the specific constellation of sedimented practices of relationality, empathic identification, and general comportment with others that exists in a particular social context. . . . If racism is unstable, then neither a permanent fatalism nor a relaxed optimism is warranted. If it is not natural, then it is not inevitable but rather contingent and learned. But it remains a powerful ideological response that can be mobilized anew, transformed, and redeployed in a new more palatable guise.[52]

It may seem that eliminating implicit racialized seeing is impossible to avoid and hopeless to eradicate. But I think that Alcoff's statement, and my claims, leave some room for hope. Once we understand the cognitive mechanisms involved in racialized seeing, then we can take some steps to change them. We don't need racial colorblindness; we need better ways of seeing.

NOTES

1. Edmonds, "These Twins, One Black and One White."
2. Mueller, "Producing Colorblindness," 219–38.
3. Alcoff, *Visible Identities*, 199.
4. Mueller, "Producing Colorblindness," 221.
5. Williams, *Seeing a Color-Blind Future*, 46. Quoted in Alcoff, *Visible Identites*, 199.
6. Mills, "White Ignorance," 13–25.
7. See, for instance, Brownstein, "Implicit Bias and Race," 261–76.
8. I will discuss the ontology of race and visible markers in a later section. Ultimately, I disagree with the claim that race is a perceptible property of individuals. Rather, subjects visually experience physical markers of race (skin color, face shape, etc.).
9. Beeghly, "What is a Stereotype?" 675–91.
10. Yancy, "Elevators, Social Spaces, and Racism: A Philosophical Analysis," 846–47.
11. Alcoff, *Visible Identites*, 182.
12. Ibid., 182.
13. See Al-Saji, "A Phenomenology of Hesitation: Interrupting Racializing Habits of Seeing," 137.
14. Machery, *Doing without Concepts*, 231.
15. Ibid., 231.
16. Ibid., 232.
17. See McDowell, "Are Moral Requirements Hypothetical Imperatives?" 77–94; Audi, *Moral Perception*.
18. Payne, "Weapon Bias," 287–91; Correll et al., "The Police Officer's Dilemma," 1314–29; Brownstein, "Implicit Bias and Race."
19. Fodor, "Observation Reconsidered," 23–43; Siegel, *The Contents of Visual Experience*.

20. See Fodor, "Observation Reconsidered"; Brogaard, "Do We Perceive Natural Kind Properties?"; Clark, *A Theory of Sentience*; Fodor & Pylyshyn, "How Direct is Visual Perception?"; O'Shaunessy, Consciousness and the World.
21. See Bayne, "Perception and the Reach of Phenomenal Content"; Siegel, *The Contents of Visual Experience*.
22. Ibid.
23. MacPherson, "Cognitive Penetration of Color Experience."
24. Siegel, *The Contents of Visual Experience*, 100.
25. Zoe Jenkin proposed this example during the NEH Summer Institute on Perception in 2016.
26. MacPherson, "Cognitive Penetration of Color Experience," 25. Emphasis added.
27. See Siegel, *The Rationality of Perception*.
28. Fodor, "Observation Reconsidered."
29. Gold and Watanabe, "Perceptual Learning."
30. Many thanks to Erin Beeghly for raising this point.
31. Beeghly "What is a Stereotype?"
32. Siegel, *The Rationality of Perception*, 6.
33. Brownstein, "Implicit Bias and Race"; Beeghly, "What is a Stereotype?"
34. Appiah, "Racisms."
35. Mills, "White Ignorance," 24.
36. Ibid., 17.
37. Dotson, "Conceptualizing Epistemic Oppression," 115.
38. Fricker, "Epistemic Injustice and a Role for Virtue in the Politics of Knowing," 169.
39. Medina, "Hermeneutical Injustice and Polyphonic Contextualism," 205.
40. Erin Beeghly's work on the wrongness of stereotyping has greatly influenced my distinction between the different types of harm involved in racialized seeing. See Beeghly, "What is a Stereotype?"
41. Thompson and Parker, "For Trayvon Martin's Friend Rachel Jeantel, a 'Village' of Mentors Trying to Keep Her on Track."
42. Yancy "Elevators, Social Spaces, and Racism: A Philosophical Analysis," 852.
43. Cooper, "Officers in the Bronx Fire 41 Shots, and an Unarmed Man Is Killed."
44. Ibid.
45. Payne, "Weapon Bias," 287.
46. Ibid., 289.
47. Correll et al, "The Police Officer's Dilemma."
48. Ibid., 1326.
49. Alcoff, *The Future of Whiteness*, 129.
50. Brownstein, "Implicit Bias and Race."
51. Smith, "Responsibility for Attitudes."
52. Alcoff, *The Future of Whiteness*, 126–27.

BIBLIOGRAPHY

Alcoff, Linda Martín. *The Future of Whiteness*. New York: Oxford University Press, 2015.

———. *Visible Identities: Race, Gender, and the Self*. New York: Oxford University Press, 2006.

Al-Saji, Alia "A Phenomenology of Hesitation: Interrupting Racializing Habits of Seeing." In *Living Alterities: Phenomenology, Embodiment, and Race*. Edited by Emily S. Lee. State University of New York Press, 2014. 133–72.

Appiah, Kwame A. "Racisms." In *Anatomy of Racism*. Edited by David Goldberg, 3–17. Minneapolis: University of Minnesota Press, 1990.

Audi, Robert. *Moral Perception*. Princeton: Princeton University Press, 2013.

Bayne, Timothy. "Perception and the Reach of Phenomenal Content." *Philosophical Quarterly* 59 (2009): 385–404.
Beeghly, Erin. "What is a Stereotype? What is Stereotyping?" *Hypatia* 30 (2015): 675–91.
Brogaard, Berit. "Do We Perceive Natural Kind Properties?" *Philosophical Studies* 162 (2013): 35–42.
Brownstein, Michael. "Implicit Bias and Race." In *Routledge Companion to the Philosophy of Race*. Edited by Paul C. Taylor, Linda Martín Alcoff, and Luvell Anderson. London: Routledge, 2018. 261–76.
Clark, Austin. *A Theory of Sentience*. Oxford: Oxford University Press, 2000.
Cooper, Michael. "Officers in the Bronx Fire 41 Shots, and an Unarmed Man Is Killed." *New York Times*, February 5, 1999. Accessed at http://www.nytimes.com/1999/02/05/nyregion/officers-in-bronx-fire-41-shots-and-an-unarmed-man-is-killed.html.
Corell, Joshua, Bernadette Park, Charles M. Judd, and Bernd Wittenbrink. "The Police Officer's Dilemma: Using Ethnicity to Disambiguate Potentially Threatening Individuals." *Journal of Personality and Social Psychology* 83 no.6 (2002): 1314–29.
Dotson, Kristie. "Conceptualizing Epistemic Oppression." *Social Philosophy* 28, no. 2 (2014): 115–38.
Edmonds, Patricia. "These Twins, One Black and One White, Will Make You Rethink Race." *National Geographic, The Race Issue*. April 2018. Accessed at https://www.nationalgeographic.com/magazine/2018/04/race-twins-black-white-biggs/.
Fodor, Jerry. "Observation Reconsidered." *Philosophy of Science* 51 (1984): 23–43.
Fodor, Jerry and Zenon Pylyshyn. "How Direct is Visual Perception? Some Reflections on Gibson's 'Ecological Approach'." *Cognition* 9 (1981): 139–96.
Fricker, Miranda. "Epistemic Injustice and a Role for Virtue in the Politics of Knowing." *Metaphilosophy* 34 (2003): 154–73.
Gold, Joshua and Takeo Watanabe. "Perceptual Learning." *Current Biology* 20, no. 2 (2010): 46–48.
Machery, Edouard. *Doing without Concepts*. Oxford: Oxford University Press, 2011.
MacPherson, Fiona. "Cognitive Penetration of Color Experience: Rethinking the Issue in Light of an Indirect Mechanism." *Philosophy and Phenomenological Research* 84 (2012): 24–62.
McDowell, John. "Are Moral Requirements Hypothetical Imperatives?" In *Mind, Value, and Reality*. Cambridge, MA: Harvard University Press, 1998. 77–94.
Medina, José. "Hermeneutical Injustice and Polyphonic Contextualism: Social Sciences and Shared Hermeneutical Responsibilities." *Social Epistemology* 26, no. 2 (2012): 201–20.
Mills, Charles. "White Ignorance." In *Race and Epistemologies of Ignorance*. Edited by Shannon Sullivan and Nancy Tuana. Albany: State University of New Yok Press, 2007. 13–25.
Mueller, Jenni. "Producing Colorblindness: Everyday Mechanisms of White Ignorance." *Social Problems* 64 (2017): 219–38.
O'Shaunessy, Brian. *Consciousness and the World*. Oxford: Clarendon Press, 2000.
Payne, B. Keith. "Weapon Bias: Split-Second Decisions and Unintended Stereotyping." *Current Directions in Psychological Science* 15, no. 6 (2006): 287–91.
Siegel, Susanna. *The Contents of Visual Experience*. Oxford: Oxford University Press, 2010.
———. *The Rationality of Perception*. New York: Oxford University Press, 2017.
Smith, Angela M. "Responsibility for Attitudes: Activity and Passivity in Mental Life." *Ethics* 115, no. 2 (2005): 236–71.
Thompson, Krissah and Lonnae O'Neal Parker. "For Trayvon Martin's Friend Rachel Jeantel, a 'Village' of Mentors Trying to Keep Her on Track." *Washington Post*. June 4, 2014. Accessed at https://www.washingtonpost.com/lifestyle/style/for-rachel-jeantel-travyon-martins-friend-the-journey-continues/2014/06/04/0135d5a2-ec11-11e3-93d2-edd4be1f5d9e_story.html?utm_term=.11c30fdf8abd.

Williams, Patricia. *Seeing a Color-Blind Future: The Paradox of Race*. New York: Farrar, Straus, and Giroux, 1997.
Yancy, George. *Black Bodies, White Gazes: The Continuing Significance of Race in America*. Lanham, MD: Rowman & Littlefield Publishers, 2008.
———. "Elevators, Social Spaces, and Racism: A Philosophical Analysis." *Philosophy & Social Criticism* 34, (2008): 843–76.

SIX
Embodiment and Oppression
Reflections on Haslanger, Gender, and Race

Erin Beeghly

> As I understand them, feminist and queer theory consist not only in giving an account of the meaning of lives of women and men in all their relational and sexual diversity.... Feminist and queer theories are also projects of social criticism. These are theoretical efforts to identify certain wrongful harms or injustices, locate and explain their sources in institutions and social relations, and propose directions for institutionally oriented action to change them. The latter set of tasks requires the theorist to have an account not only of individual experience, subjectivity and identity, but also of social structures.[1]

In *On Female Body Experience*, Iris Marion Young argues that a central aim of feminist and queer theory is social criticism. The goal is to understand oppression and how it functions: know thy enemy, so as to better resist. Much of Sally Haslanger's work shares this goal, and her newest article, "Cognition as a Social Skill," is no exception. In this essay, I will specify what I believe is special and insightful about Haslanger's theory of oppression and her most recent addition to it. However, I also explore what it is missing, namely an account of what Young calls "individual [embodied] experience, subjectivity, and identity." Echoing a chorus of critical voices, I argue that this omission undermines Haslanger's ability to effectively theorize group oppression and how to resist it. The core problem is that Haslanger privileges a third-person methodology that prioritizes social structures over all else. I conclude by amplifying a collective call to action: any adequate theory of oppression must attend to both the lived experiences of individuals and to social structures—that is, to the broad institutional and cultural underpinnings of oppression. A theory that does only one, or the other, will fail. Through this analysis, the chapter contributes to an overall aim of this volume, namely to push forward our understanding of racial and gender-based group oppressions by paying closer attention to facts about embodiment.

HASLANGER'S PROJECT: THE BIG PICTURE AND WHAT'S NEW

"Cognition as a Social Skill" begins with a pointed question: how does ideological oppression take root? Ideological forms of oppression are distinctive in that they are "enacted unthinkingly or even willingly by the subordinated and/or privileged."[2] The phenomenon is especially worth theorizing, in Haslanger's view, because ideological oppression is "insidious" and "far more difficult to identify and critique" than "directly coercive" and violent forms of oppression.[3] Her interest, in particular, is the way in which individuals' consciousness and agency are "colonized under conditions of injustice."[4] In previous work, Haslanger notes that humans have "psychological capacities . . . to be responsive to and learn from each other," and these capacities have a role to play in maintaining injustice.[5] This new article pushes the point further, elevating the concept of *mindshaping*.

In a 2001 article, Matteo Mameli introduced the term "mindshaping." He defines it as follows: "A mind-shaping effect is an effect on the development or structure of a mind. My telling you that I've broken your computer causes a mind-shaping effect in you. It makes you angry. My teaching a child how to tie his shoelaces causes a mind-shaping effect on him. It makes him able to tie his shoelaces."[6] According to this definition, any effect you have on someone else is an instance of the phenomenon. If I teach you a fact or a new skill, that's mindshaping. If I make you angry, happy, or sad, that's also mindshaping.

What Haslanger means by the term is more specific. Mindshaping is a handle for a revisionary theory of and approach to human cognition, advocated by philosophers like Victoria McGeer and Tadeusz Wiesław Zawidzki. It is also a label for a phenomenon central to their theories. McGeer and Zawidzki's theories are revisionary for the following reason: they reject standard assumptions about human cognition. According to standard views, cognition is conceptualized as "an individually realized epistemic capacity,"[7] and cognitive activity is understood on a scientific model. Babies are likened to tiny scientists in cribs, learning by way of hypothesis testing.[8] Similarly, adult mental life is described as proceeding in mainly predictive and explanatory modes. In contrast, advocates of mindshaping characterize human cognition as inherently social, and they emphasize the ways in which group interests and norms shape individuals' minds.

Had Haslanger exclusively discussed mindshaping in her article, it would still be worth reading. The mindshaping literature is fascinating, and it has yet to receive wide uptake, even among scholars who ought to be sympathetic to it. Advocates of mindshaping argue that human cognition is inherently interpersonal and embodied, and they also emphasize the kind of looping effects in which theorists of oppression have long been interested.[9]

Phenomenologists and theorists of mindshaping are potential allies, for example. Both groups have been avid critics of the view that humans' primary mode of cognition involves explanation and prediction. In *How the Body Shapes the Mind*, phenomenologist Shaun Gallagher calls attention to "our pragmatic way of 'being in the world'" and argues that "phenomenology tells us that explanation and prediction are relatively rare modes of understanding others, and that something like evaluative understanding about what someone means or about how I should respond in any particular situation best characterizes most of our interactions."[10] Additionally, phenomenologists have emphasized the value-laden, normative nature of perception and cognition, something that advocates of mindshaping also emphasize. For example, in *Visible Identities*, Linda Martín Alcoff argues, "Racism is manifest at the level of perception itself."[11] Her point is not just that racist predictions and explanations affect what we see and do not see. Rather, she suggests that perception involves epistemic practices and bodily habits, which embody a kind of *racial etiquette*.[12]

Consider an example discussed by Frantz Fanon. It's mid-twentieth-century France, and a Black man is travelling by train. He is not sure where the dining car is, so he asks someone. The person is white. "Excuse me," he says, "could you please tell me where the restaurant car is?"[13] The white passenger, only half paying attention, responds in pidgin: "Yes, sonny boy, you go corridor, you go straight, go one car, go two car, go three car, you there."[14] What has just happened? One possibility is that the white passenger perfectly heard every word spoken by the Black speaker but responded in pidgin in order to keep the man "in his place." A second possibility—and the one that interests me most in this context—is that the white passenger was failing to pay attention. He engaged in the bodily activity of judging someone quickly and mindlessly instead of stopping for a minute, listening to what a stranger has said, and responding based on the actual facts.[15] As a matter of fact, the Black stranger in front of him speaks fluent French. Fanon hints that there is a pattern here. Across France, he and a team of researchers observed white Europeans behaving in epistemically negligent ways when interacting with Black individuals. The pattern suggests a norm was at work: a racialized norm. For white Europeans in twentieth-century France, the norm was to expend minimal epistemic effort when interacting with Black folks in typical social contexts. Black folks were simply "of a type," and relying on racial generalizations was usually sufficient. The norm has consequences for the content of perception, for example, what white people hear or do not hear, see or do not see in the context of interracial social interactions. It also reveals that both the content of perception, and the behaviors that enable perception, are shaped by social roles. A racial hierarchy—supported by an ideology of Black inferiority and "otherness"—stands clearly in the background.

Fanon's example underscores a more general point. By emphasizing the impact of culture on perception and cognition, theorists call attention to the fact that humans are trained to see, think, and act in different ways. This differential training is tied to social roles, along with the stereotypes, scripts, and norms associated with them. The norm guided nature of social interactions guarantees that ideology and group hierarchy will shape people's perceptual and cognitive experiences.[16]

Given these convergences, mindshaping as discussed by Haslanger will be interesting to a range of antiracist and feminist theorists, including those with methodologies quite different than hers. Advocates of mindshaping provide a new kind of argument for claims that feminist and antiracist philosophers have traditionally wanted to defend. Mindshaping arguments are new because they are rooted in claims about the evolutionary development of humans.[17]

Nevertheless, before feminists and antiracists—or anyone else—can decide whether the mindshaping literature is ultimately useful, more information is required. While the approach sounds plausible enough, its details get controversial fast. According to Zawidzki, every instance of mindshaping has two components: "it aims at something, that is shaping minds," and "it requires representing that which it aims to accomplish, that is, shaping minds in a specific way."[18] Yet, as he notes, one must be careful. An advocate of mindshaping cannot interpret "representing" as something that requires language. Nor can one understand "aiming at" as something an agent does intentionally.

Here is why: mindshaping is supposed to be historically prior to mind reading. In other words, when it comes to our evolutionary history, humans must have had the capacity to shape others' minds before we had the ability to attribute beliefs or desires or emotions to others—that is, to read minds. Moreover, mindshaping mechanisms are supposed to explain why human beings have evolved to develop sophisticated language. As a result, the representations involved in mindshaping must be conceptualized nonlinguistically. Mindshaping must be able to occur, even if we take no view on what other people think, feel, or perceive and even if we had no language in which to conceptualize what they might think, feel, or perceive.

The alleged priority of mindshaping raises a puzzling question. How can one shape someone else's mind, and "aim" to do so, without having a view about what that person thinks or even a language in which to think?

As Zawidzki notes, this is a hard question. But it must have an answer if mindshaping is to be a viable model of cognition. Here is the key if he is right: "The goals, functions, purposes, or aims that help constitute mindshaping are [and must be] understood *teleofunctionally*, that is, in terms of what the mechanisms associated with mindshaping were selected for in evolution."[19] Accordingly, he defines mindshaping as follows:

> To state the definition formally, mechanism X mindshapes target Y to match model Z in relevant respects R, S, T . . . if and only if (1) effecting such matches is X's "proper function" in Millikan's (1984) sense; (2) X is performing its proper function, that is, causing Y to match Z in respect to R, S, T . . . (3) Y is a mind, understood as a set of behavioral dispositions or the categorical basis for them; (4) X's performance of its proper function is guided by representations of R, S, T . . . ; and (6) Z is or is somehow derived from an agent other than the agent to which Y belongs.[20]

This definition says a lot, and what it communicates to me is this: "Caution!" Though mindshaping resonates with claims that I find appealing, the required assumptions for endorsing the model are quite heavy. People do not mindshape; mechanisms do. Some of these mechanisms are subpersonal: they are exclusively "neural."[21] For example, Zawidzki discusses "a series of powerful yet counterintuitive experimental results in social psychology" that suggest "human beings automatically, unintentionally, and unconsciously match each other's non-functional behaviors."[22] These behaviors include "postures, mannerisms, gestures, facial expressions, and accents."[23] The finding sheds light on perceptual habits: how long we look at people, whether we look them in the eye or not, whether we look at people's lips when they are talking so we can hear them better, and so on. If humans naturally mimic one another, we may learn to be biased simply by being immersed in a culture and instinctively following the lead of others.[24] Other mechanisms are partially outside the brain and are "distributed across multiple agents, as in pedagogy or guided imitation, where a teacher can help the target match the model."[25] In all such cases, we must say that the mechanisms "have an aim" and "a proper function." Moreover, to get the model going, we must say that the relevant neural or extraneural mechanisms are guided by "representations" in a very specific *teleofunctional* sense. Furthermore, one must be willing to endorse an extremely controversial evolutionary story about how, when, and why these mechanisms were selected and the way in which language emerged out of mindshaping.

I am not, in principle, against endorsing controversial claims. My point is this: readers of Haslanger's article deserve to know the philosophical and empirical baggage associated with mindshaping. Since Haslanger cites Zawidzki approvingly and relies on his evolutionary story, she appears to be endorsing the above claims. As readers, we deserve to know whether she thinks that the mindshaping model (for example, as developed by other theorists like Victoria McGeer) requires such claims and why we ought to endorse them. Zawidzki is emphatic. Without an evolutionary story, there is no way to establish the priority of mindreading over mindshaping, or vice versa. "The distinction between mindreading and mindshaping," he writes, "cannot be captured in terms of simple empirical tests... no crucial experiment can vindicate one understanding at the expense of the other."[26] Both models of social cognition embrace the same empirical results; they just understand their significance differently.

Let me now briefly turn to a related issue. Haslanger's "Cognition as a Social Skill" is not just about mindshaping. Indeed, she is only interested in mindshaping for instrumental reasons, in particular, because it purports to explain why humans participate so naturally in oppressive patterns of thought and action. Haslanger writes, "I aim to show how social meanings shape thought and action and how this provides us with resources for thinking about ideology and ideology critique."[27] This way of putting her project takes the emphasis off of mindshaping and places it on culture. Culture, she explains elsewhere, "is a network of social meanings, tools, scripts, schemas, heuristics, principles, and the like, which we draw on in action, and which gives shape to our practices."[28] To better analyze culture's role in the colonization of consciousness, Haslanger deploys a new set of conceptual resources in her article, borrowed from sociologist Pierre Bourdieu and political scientist James Scott. The novel additions to her theory bring her account of oppression into deeper conversation with a wider set of literatures in sociology, history, and political science. They also serve to supplement her existing account of the ways in which people absorb—as well as resist—oppressive views and practices.

AN AESTHETIC AND POLITICAL INTERLUDE

Now that I have sketched what is new and provocative in Haslanger's article, something needs to be said about my experience of reading it. Haslanger quickly introduces five new concepts—mindshaping, doxa, heterodoxy, orthodoxy, and hidden transcripts—into a theory that already boasts an impressive amount of technical terminology. The article is also peppered with intricate, hard-to-follow diagrams.[29] Contemplating the images, my head spins—and not in a good way. Haslanger's theory is already complicated, and these new additions make it even more so. Her implicit promise to readers is this: "Bear with me. The tools of social science can explain ideological oppression." Yet the analysis often feels byzantine, and the payoff elusive. One cannot access what is interesting about it simply by reading. There is too much jargon, too many moving parts. Because of this, engaging with Haslanger's new article requires a costly investment. One must sink weeks and weeks, if not longer, into doing the research that illuminates the significance of the various distinctions, concepts, and arguments. Her main ideas do not jump off the page and explain themselves. The argument's lack of accessibility and transparency was a problem for me.

As I reflected more, I realized my reaction had feminist roots. Beautiful articles—articles that I aspire to write and read as a feminist philosopher—are not esoteric. They are both intellectually challenging and accessible. Accessibility is a paramount virtue, for which I am willing to sacrifice tremendously.

When I think of these virtues, I think of theorists like Iris Marion Young and bell hooks. I think, too, of what I call "the bell hooks rule." In her first book *ain't i a woman: black women and feminism*, hooks writes:

> I decided early on that I wanted to create books that could be read and understood across different class boundaries. In those days, feminist thinkers grappled with the question of audience: who did we want to reach with our work? To reach a broader audience required the writing of work that was clear and concise, that could be read by readers who had never attended college or even finished high school. Imagining my mother as my ideal audience—the reader that I most wanted to convert to feminist thinking—I cultivated a way of writing that could be understood by readers from diverse class backgrounds.[30]

As hooks notes, accessibility and clarity are crucial, aesthetically and politically. This is also writer Claudia Rankine's position. In a recent interview, Rankine talks about her first book, *Don't Let Me Be Lonely*, the predecessor of *Citizen*. She says:

> One of the things that I wanted in *Don't Let Me Be Lonely* was for the language to be transparent. I didn't want people to have to stop and think, I don't know what she means by that. I wanted it to feel simple, accessible, conversational. As a writer, this was the challenge—How do you get the ideas of Butler or Laurent Berlant or Derrida or all the reading you've done, inside the seven sentences that say, I saw this thing and it made me sad? And how do you do it in a way that the research material is not effaced, that trace elements are still present? That seems to me always to be the challenge—to create transparency and access without losing complexity.[31]

One might complain: Rankine writes poetry, not philosophy. Yet philosophers like hooks and others celebrate these same virtues.

Why, one might ask? Note what hooks says above. One cannot "convert" a broad audience to feminist or antiracist thinking if the texts that one writes are loaded down with jargon and written in ways that alienate even sympathetic, expert readers. To whatever extent it is possible, theorists who care about social liberation, and whose work supports antiracist and feminist values, must render their work accessible, clear, and compelling. The stakes of success are high. Understanding oppression is not a mere academic matter: people's lives, well-being, and freedom are on the line. The issue is not just persuading individuals that there is a problem but creating the social bases for collective action and institutional change.

All of this is to say I felt, and feel, conflicted about Haslanger's "Cognition as a Social Skill." While it is chock full of interesting concepts and insights, good feminist and antiracist theory ought to be accessible. However, this new piece drifts into obscurantism. Obscurity and complexity are not the same thing.

One might object that the subject matter requires a technical treatment and obscurity can be a virtue. An unsympathetic interlocutor might say, "Perhaps you are simply too stupid to understand, Beeghly! Or just plain lazy." Maybe, but I doubt that. I identify as a pluralist, trained in both the analytic and continental traditions. I am not against specialized terminology or theory, and I certainly am not opposed to rolling up my sleeves and digging into an unfamiliar literature. Despite all this, I found the article alienating. Its arguments felt cumbersome, the concepts opaque. The mode of address was impersonal and, from my perspective, it sent the wrong message about who the "insiders" and "outsiders" in the discussion really are.[32]

THE PROBLEM OF EMBODIMENT

As I thought about the accessibility of her new work, it began to dawn on me that there was another, related problem. Often Haslanger uses personal experience as a touchstone for theorizing. For example, in "Race & Gender: (What) Are They? (What) Do We Want Them to Be?," she begins her analysis by noting, "It is always awkward when someone asks me informally what I'm working on and I say that I'm trying to figure out what gender is."[33] Similarly, in "Changing the Ideology and Culture of Philosophy," she opens with a personal observation about her experience as a woman in philosophy, announcing, "There is a deep well of rage inside me. Rage about how I as an individual have been treated in philosophy; rage about how others I know have been treated; and rage about the conditions that I'm sure affect many women and minorities in philosophy, and have caused many others to leave."[34] When writing about adoption, family, and race, Haslanger also makes it clear that the subject matter is personal: she is an adoptive parent of two African-American children.[35] I love these personal moments. They are powerful and announce to readers the stakes of her philosophical work. However, personal reflections are absent in "Cognition as a Social Skill."

One could argue that the omission is coincidental and that she could add a few vivid examples to make the theory more accessible. I suspect the fix is not so easy. As far as I can tell, the failure to cite personal experience—hers or anyone else's—in the essay is a symptom of her methodology.

Consider the framework Haslanger uses to explain ideological oppression—a framework that constitutes one of her philosophical accomplishments and which she has developed carefully over the last decade. Four concepts are foundational: *social practices*, which are "patterns of behavior that enable us to coordinate and distribute resources";[36] *social structures*, or, "sets of interconnected practices";[37] *social relations*, that is, "links between nodes in a structure";[38] and *ideological formations*, described as "the practices, institutions, along with the thinking and acting shaped by ideology,"[39] which simultaneously justify and help constitute the system as a whole. Within this conceptual landscape, individuals are understood as "nodes" in social structures. As nodes, they are integral to the system. Yet there is no exploration of the ways in which individuals actually experience oppression in a phenomenological, embodied sense. Moreover, actual individuals (like you and me) are irrelevant to the theory; the theory is only interested in individuals qua abstract social types.[40]

Haslanger's view of gender and race fits nicely with this model. To be a woman, according to Haslanger, is to occupy a particular position in a social structure. She formulates the view as follows: "S is a woman if S is systematically subordinated along some dimension (economic, political, legal, social, etc.) and S is 'marked' as a target for this treatment by observed or imagined bodily features presumed to be evidence of a female's biological role in reproduction."[41] According to this view, what makes someone a woman is not her lived experience or relationship to gender norms. What makes someone a woman is that she is subordinated in particular ways due to her perceived reproductive function. Haslanger's account of race is analogous. To be Black, for example, is to be subordinated because of one's real or imagined bodily features—such as a person's skin color or hair texture—that serve as markers of African ancestry.[42]

There are problems with accounts like this, and they are not about accessibility per se. Haslanger's analysis of oppression, like her view of gender and race, lacks an account of what Young calls "individual [embodied] experience, subjectivity, and identity."[43] The omission is not accidental. When Haslanger explains ideological oppression, she intentionally frames her explanations in terms of social structures and the processes by which they are maintained. Such processes can be described without resorting to the nitty-gritty details of any particular individual's psychology, including facts about how it feels for someone to inhabit a certain kind of body.

Many feminists and critical race theorists will object here, and rightly so. Compare Haslanger's view with Iris Marion Young's. Like Haslanger, Young offers a structural analysis of gender. "What it means to say that individual persons are gendered," Young argues, "is that we all find ourselves passively grouped according to these structural relations, in ways too impersonal to ground identity."[44] However, Young does not end her analysis there. Instead she argues that a theory of gender—defined structurally—must be supplemented with an analysis of the lived body.[45] The addition is necessary to avoid the mistake of defining what it means to be a woman simply in terms of oppression. Being a woman ought to be a feature of oneself that can be lifted up and celebrated.

Young also sinks time and effort into understanding oppression from an embodied perspective. The lived body, she writes, "is a unified idea of a physical body acting and experiencing in a specific sociocultural context; it is a body-in-situation."[46] Drawing on research in the phenomenological tradition, including the work of Simone de Beauvoir and Toril Moi, she fills out the concept of a lived body in a vivid, relatable way. "Each person," Young writes, "is a distinctive body, with specific features, capacities, and desires . . . is born in a particular place and time, is raised in a particular family setting, and all these have specific sociocultural histories that stand in relation to the history of others in particular ways."[47] Each lived body is therefore unique. On the other hand, individuals face a range of limitations and possibilities that apply across the board to people like them. So there will be commonalities in how people live out their embodiment.

With the concept of the lived body, intentionality and agency rise to the forefront. "The most primordial intentional act," Young writes, "is the motion of the body orienting itself with respect to and moving within its surroundings."[48] We can choose to go this way or that, respond to an obstacle blocking our path in one way or another. Similarly, she argues, individuals have options in terms of how they respond to the "systems of evaluation and expectations" that shape and constrain them.[49] "The idea of a lived body," Young explains, "recognizes that a person's subjectivity is conditioned by sociocultural facts and the behavior and expectations of others in ways that she has not chosen. At the same time, the theory of the lived body says that each person takes up and acts in relation to these unchosen facts in her own way."[50] The interplay of choice and constraint is constant.

To better understand this interplay and its significance, we might look to other theorists who explore agency under conditions of oppression. Consider the work of Alisa Bierria.[51] Bierria is interested in "the experience and practice of disenfranchised subjects who act intentionally *despite/against/within* conditions of oppression and violence."[52] As a case study, she considers the experience of Janice Wells, a fifty-seven-year-old Black schoolteacher from Georgia. In Spring of 2012, Wells called the police to report a suspected would-be intruder. The officer who arrived at her home demanded that she provide the name of the person whom she believed to be prowling around. When Wells refused, the officer "proceeded to threaten to take her to jail, chase, handcuff, and pepper-spray her."[53] A second officer arrived and repeatedly tasered Wells, as she begged him to stop. In her analysis of the case, Bierria enumerates the ways in which Wells exercised agency throughout the encounter: calling the police to report someone on her property, withholding information from the officer who arrived after he behaved disrespectfully, moving to the front of her house perhaps in the hopes of making their conflict more visible, running when he grabbed her, and pleading with the second officer to stop assaulting her. The issue is not that Wells lacked agency, Bierria says. The problem lies in how the officers constrained her agency—harming her and violating her rights—and how they systematically distorted the meaning of her actions, viewing her actions through the lens of misogynistic and racist stereotypes. Bierria writes: "Instead of asking, how did Janice Wells' agency fail, we might ask, what kind of agency did Wells exercise before, during, and after the assault? How was her agency (dis)positioned with respect to institutional racism and sexism, and how might we describe her choice-making in those conditions?"[54] To accurately describe Wells's "choice making," her own, first-person view of the matter is invaluable.[55] Wells is not a passive agent, but someone who exercised a great deal of resistance when interacting with police. Bierria's heterogeneous model of agency reveals that Wells, and people like her, routinely exercise their agency in a variety of ways within and against oppressive social structures.

The work of María Lugones is similarly illuminating in this respect. Lugones—an immigrant to the U.S. from Argentina and a Latina philosopher—is particularly interested in "outsiders" like herself. Outsider existence, as she sees it, is defined by "perspectival flexibility."[56] As an outsider, one must perceive oneself through the lens of dominant groups, becoming fluent in their perspectives: the specific ways in which they tend to objectify you, how they stereotype or misinterpret you, and so on. However, outsiders also know that they are seen in alternative ways in social niches where they are more at home and have insider status. This perspectival knowledge—a kind of "double consciousness," as explored by Du Bois—is a product of the fact that one inhabits multiple worlds at once and must travel between worlds.[57] Famously, Lugones argues that outsider experience reveals a deep truth. All of us—insiders and outsiders—have more than one self: the self in this world and the self in other worlds. This multiplicity of selves makes agency possible even under conditions of oppression. One can see oneself in ways that are not sanctioned by dominant ideologies and the groups that create them, even in conditions where one's agency and individuality are seemingly quashed. Lugones writes: "The oppressed know themselves in realities in which they are able to form intentions that are not among the alternatives that are possible in the world in which they are brutalized and oppressed."[58]

Haslanger might interject: I, too, recognize the importance of individual agency and the way in which embodied experience reveals it! If individuals were not agents with particular identities and experiences, there would be nothing for culture to colonize. Hidden transcripts and heterodoxy would not be possible if humans had no choice but to conform. Moreover, embodiment is built into my theory of oppression via Bourdieu's notion of a *habitus*. A *habitus* consists in a set of bodily dispositions, which enable one to relate to and move through the world in particular ways. Haslanger even says as much, writing, "Social meanings are responsive to our embodied engagement with the world."[59]

Notice the difference, though. While Haslanger's theory of oppression presupposes the existence of embodied experience, she does not engage with embodied experience or individual agency on its own terms. Haslanger offers a top-down structural theory of oppression, supplemented by a discussion of mindshaping. Mindshaping mechanisms are "exclusively neural" or they are "socially distributed."[60] First-person experience is not central to the model. Nor does mindshaping provide any handle on how or why individuals could resist oppression and exercise their agency, for example, by creating hidden transcripts. Indeed, one of the upshots of mindshaping is that habitual actions and patterns of thought are constitutive of the social structure.[61]

The metaphor of colonization—freely invoked by Haslanger—is telling. Colonizers saw colonized peoples as passive and naïve. They sought to control them and appropriate their resources. According to Haslanger, social meanings do the same thing to you and me. Social meanings colonize our consciousness and agency via mindshaping mechanisms. Our inner resources are thus appropriated, taken over. This is precisely my point. In this picture, individual agency and embodied, first-person experience are things that have been coopted, usurped vessels used for social-structural purposes. It is thus unclear how humans could ever retain our agency in any meaningful sense and how a critical consciousness could emerge.

One is thus entitled to press Haslanger. How and why is resistance possible, if we accept her theory of oppression? How, exactly, do historically and socially situated individuals and their agency fit into the theory's explanations of how oppression works, both in general and in specific contexts? What is the justification for bracketing first-person, embodied experience? If these questions remain unanswered, we cannot be confident that Haslanger's theory satisfies an important desideratum for a theory of oppression. Lugones put it like this: any adequate theory of oppression must be liberatory. To fulfill this desideratum, a theory cannot leave the "ontological or metaphysical possibility of liberation" unargued for, uncovered, and unexplained, as Haslanger's theory does.[62] We must know how and why freedom and agency are able to unfold in conditions of oppression. Mere lip service to the possibility is not enough.

Without an explanation of how and why agency is possible, the theory is "useless from the perspective of the oppressed person."[63]

THE PROBLEM OF EMBODIMENT: THEORETICAL AND PRACTICAL RAMIFICATIONS

The fact that I am circling back to these concerns is not surprising. They constitute a constant thread in critical appraisals of Haslanger's recent work. Gathering these critical voices together, I amplify their call to action.

Criticism 1—Pigeonholing and Disrespect

One thread of criticism goes as follows. Because Haslanger's theory ignores embodied experience, it ends up pigeonholing individuals in problematic ways. Though Young could certainly lodge this criticism, one finds it articulated forcefully by other feminists and antiracist theorists. Katharine Jenkins, for example, argues that Haslanger's account of gender is disrespectful to transgender women.[64] Diagnosing why, she points to the purely structural nature of Haslanger's view. To count as a woman, according to Haslanger, you must be perceived as having a certain kind of body, namely one capable of fulfilling a female reproductive role. As Jenkins notes, some trans women will not be subordinated for this reason. They will be subordinated for other reasons. If so, they are not truly women, according to Haslanger. Jenkins objects: "The concept of *being classed as a woman* [in the structural sense] and *having a female gender identity*" should be given equal weight in feminist theory.[65] If feminists would give these concepts equal weight, they could craft an analysis of gender suitable for liberatory purposes. Haslanger cannot do this, Jenkins explains, because her analysis prioritizes social structures and excludes first-person, embodied experience.

A parallel criticism concerns Haslanger's account of race. According to Haslanger, to be Black is to be oppressed. However, as Janine Jones notes in her review of *Resisting Reality*, many ordinary Black individuals often understand being Black as something to be valued. They do not define their existence by their oppression, but rather, view Black identity as a source of pride.[66] Consider Imani Perry, who recounts the messages that she received on social media in the aftermath of protests against George Floyd's death at the hands of Minneapolis police. These messages seemed to presuppose that "Blackness is the most terrible of fates."[67] "Let me be clear," Perry says, "Racism is terrible. Blackness is not."[68] She writes:

> I cannot remember a time in my life when I wasn't earnestly happy about the fact of my blackness. When my cousins and I were small, we

would crowd in front of the mirrors in my grandmother's house, admiring our shining brown faces, the puffiness of our hair.

My elders taught me that I belonged to a tradition of resilience, of music that resonates across the globe, of spoken and written language that sings. If you've had the good fortune to experience a holiday with a large black American family, you have witnessed the masterful art of storytelling, the vitality of our laughter, and the everyday poetry of our experience.[69]

Perry also echoes the words of Zora Neale Hurston in her essay, "How It Feels to Be Colored Me." Hurston refuses to believe that she is "tragically colored" and has been given "a lowdown dirty deal" by nature.[70] She delights in her identity and heritage. "Sometimes I feel discriminated against," writes Hurston, "but it does not make me angry. It merely astonishes me. How *can* any deny themselves the pleasures of my company? It's beyond me."[71] Positive views of Blackness such as these are ignored by Haslanger's structural analysis. Jones puts the problem like this: Haslanger's methodology fails to recognize "that so many ordinary Black people who theorize their lived experience are experts on race."[72]

Once more, the political significance of Haslanger's third-person methodology rises into view. To write about oppression in a way that prioritizes structural analysis, and ignores first-person experience, is to send a message. The message is that everyday people are not experts when it comes to how oppression functions. A quite different message is conveyed when theorists recognize the value of lived experience and harness its insights in their work. By centering lived experience, they communicate to readers that individuals from historically marginalized groups have special knowledge about the harms of oppression, as well as how to resist oppression. Their experiences living in hierarchical social conditions, their emotions and their anger, constitute invaluable epistemic resources. To ignore such experiences is, arguably, to exercise a kind of disrespect.

Criticism 2 — Explanation & Agency

Remember that Haslanger characterizes individuals as nodes in a structure. One could perhaps argue that this way of describing human beings is disrespectful because it characterizes individuals as interchangeable, agency-deprived cogs. However, there are explanatory worries in the vicinity as well.

Consider this one. Theresa Lopez and Bryan Chambliss argue that Haslanger's explanations of individual choice are incomplete. According to Haslanger's theory, individuals act in certain ways because of their location within historically contingent, culturally specific social structures. Yet not all individuals react to the constraints of their social position in the same ways. Two similarly situated people might have radically different relationships to social norms; they may have conflicting values and preferences, as well as divergent attitudes toward risk. If so, structural explanations cannot tell the whole story about individual choice. What we need, Lopez and Chambliss argue, are explanations of choice that appeal both to unique features of individual psychology as well as social structures. They call these "integrative explanations of choice."[73]

Critical race theorists often argue for integrative explanations as well. There is a vast, rich literature here. I mention two recent examples from sociology. First, in "Producing Colorblindness: Everyday Mechanisms of White Ignorance," Jennifer Mueller criticizes structural models of colorblindness.[74] In her view, these models ignore the fact that white individuals minimize and deny their complicity in racial injustice in inventive and ever-resourceful ways.

To illustrate the point, Mueller offers empirical evidence. While teaching a course on racial inequality and intergenerational wealth, Mueller asked students to complete an assignment about their family history. "In terms of wealth and capital accumulation and transfer," she notes, "the full pool of papers documents over six times as many transfers of monetary assets across generations within white families than families of color. Intergenerational land, home, and business inheritances were similarly disproportionate."[75] White students also reported that their families historically benefited from state-sponsored policies designed to systematically benefit white people as a group.[76] As part of the assignment, Mueller required students to critically analyze the ways in which their family did or did not benefit from racist policies and institutions. When evaluating their responses, she noticed a pattern. White students were consistently evasive. They tended to twist the truth, create dubious narratives that absolved their families of racial guilt, and generally deflect responsibility. They did so in unique and inventive ways.

Consider an example. One student—Carmen—"began by suggesting how 'very difficult' it was 'to tie any of the course readings' to her data because her family had no 'large ties to slavery or oppression.'"[77] At the same time, Carmen noted that her family owned slaves prior to 1864. One might have expected this student to observe that her relatives enslaved and exploited Black labor for their own financial benefit and were, in this way, able to grow their wealth. Instead Carmen argued that slavery was "an expendable part of my family's wealth," hence, not very important in the overall scheme of things, because one of her relatives freed his slaves at the close of the Civil War. According to family lore, these freed slaves decided to keep working for the family, even though they could have struck out on their own. As Mueller notes, this student did something interesting that was not a mere matter of habit: she combined "an old racist stereotype [of the happy, loyal slave who loves his white master] with a *uniquely reasoned* color-blind argument to neutralize an inconvenient fact and reject course premises."[78] Such maneuvers need to be recognized for what they are, says Mueller: creative, resourceful attempts to maintain white ignorance that exceed generic colorblind narratives.

Second, consider Glenn Bracey and Wendy Moore's research on racial segregation in Evangelical churches.[79] Noting that structural explanations of segregation dominate the sociological literature, they argue that such explanations hide the ways in which Evangelicals in majority-white churches actively exclude potential Black congregants. Bracey—a Black man and devout Evangelical Christian—gathered the data himself. In his fieldwork, he found that spontaneous "race tests" functioned as invisible tools of segregation in white Evangelical churches. For example, at a majority-white mega church, he was introduced to a Black woman with an interracial child. Bracey's white host told him that he was a godsend. Congregants had been praying for someone who could serve as the boy's father.[80] The implication was that Bracey, because he was Black, was the answer to their prayers. At a different church, he was told that he would be a great addition to the church's choir, even after he explained that his background was in ministry and he would prefer a speaking role in church outreach.[81] To pass "utility-based" race tests such as these, Bracey and Moore argue, people of color must prove that they are content to play the role that white people envision for them and can be trusted not to disrupt white space. "Exclusionary" race tests function differently. To illustrate a second kind of race test, Bracey recounts arriving at the home of a congregant in a secluded, rural area for a prayer meeting. From how he was greeted, it is clear that the host had expected him to be white. She asks her husband to give Bracey a tour of their home, including their bedroom, chock full of Confederate memorabilia. In his field notes, Bracey writes: "They were clearly Confederate sympathizers, and they wanted me to know it. Evangelical Christian or not, I was not welcome in this home."[82] Fearful, he quickly left the property. "While we acknowledge the role that macrosocial forces play in maintaining segregation," Bracey and Moore argue, "we contend that structural relations require institutional dynamics and human actors."[83]

Though these sociologists do not engage with Haslanger's work specifically, their criticisms apply to her theory. Like Young, Bierria, and Lugones, they argue that one cannot adequately explain how oppression functions without paying close attention to embodied agents and the ways in which they exert their agency within social structures. Their distinctive contribution is to explore how individuals from dominant groups exert their agency in conditions of oppression in ways that reflect, and entrench, an unjust status quo.

Criticism 3 — Embodiment & Resistance

A final thread of criticism focuses on Haslanger's account of resistance. In "The Uses of the Erotic," Audre Lorde writes, "The erotic cannot be felt secondhand."[84] It can only be felt first-hand, from the inside. Explaining what she means, Lorde writes: "As a Black lesbian feminist, I have a particular feeling, knowledge, and understanding for those sisters with whom I have danced hard, played, or even fought. The deep participation has often been the forerunner for joint concerted actions not possible before."[85] As Lorde observes, being together with others in an embodied way—dancing, sweating, arguing—is a source of solidarity. However, this source of solidarity is obscured if we use a methodology that focuses exclusively on structural aspects of social reality, for example, habitual patterns of behavior or thought.

Alex Madva makes a complementary point. In addressing sexism, racism, and other forms of injustice, Haslanger recommends that we focus our activist energy on structural-level reforms. Madva thus dubs her a "structural prioritizer."[86] Structural prioritizers argue that we should reform social structures, and individual-level changes will follow. For example, if we better integrate neighborhoods using public policy, racial prejudices will decrease. Echoing the other critics mentioned so far, Madva takes issue with the strategy: "I believe that it is false and misleading to claim that we should prioritize structural over individual change."[87] While reforming social structures is critically important, we need both kinds of changes to fight oppression; moreover, structural-level interventions must be accompanied by individual-level interventions in order to be maximally stable and effective.

In a similar vein, Robin Zheng criticizes Haslanger's exclusive emphasis on structural reform. "It is all very well to say that we need structural solutions rather than reformed individuals," she writes, "but it is much less obvious what kind of collective action should be taken and how."[88] According to Zheng, justifying collective action to individuals requires convincing them that they should take personal responsibility for unjust social structures. However, questions of personal responsibility are "necessarily addressed from the first- and second-person practical perspective."[89]

CONCLUSION

Know thy enemy, so as to better resist. In Madva and Zheng, in Jenkins and Jones, in Lopez and Chambliss, as well as others, one hears the echo of Iris Marion Young. A purely structural theory of oppression, Young argues, cannot explain how oppression insinuates itself in the lived body, as well as the variety of ways in which individuals perpetuate and experience oppression. Nor can it explain how and why resistance is possible. To adequately explain oppression and to illuminate modes of resistance, a theory must incorporate both social structures and the lived experiences of individuals.[90]

One might object that lived experience resists theory. It is too varied and diffuse and personal. However, I would call attention to the numerous theorists of injustice who take seriously first-person, embodied experiences, while also keeping the structural in view. Think of Frantz Fanon, María Lugones, and bell hooks. Think of contemporary critical race theorists in sociology and psychology like Bracey, Moore, and Mueller.[91] The powerful work of such theorists—and many others—is a testament to the possibility, as well as the desirability, of a truly liberatory philosophy that attends to both social structures and lived experience.

Despite its new bells and whistles, "Cognition as a Social Skill" thus returns us to a basic problem. Haslanger deploys the third-person tools of social science—graphs and charts and a focus on abstract structures—to illuminate the phenomenon of ideological oppression. We even get an evolutionary story and new concepts added to the mix. Yet, as far as I can see, the resulting theory only underscores the need, more than ever, to give embodied experience its proper due. The way forward, I propose, is to pay closer attention to feminist and antiracist theorists who have lifted up lived experience as a crucial source of knowledge, while also analyzing the broad institutional and cultural underpinnings of oppression. Taking their cue, we can see how to effectively integrate these two modes of inquiry and, in so doing, how to better understand the means by which individuals and groups may contribute to, or resist, social injustice.

ACKNOWLEDGMENTS

For helpful feedback on this essay, I thank Janine Jones, Brock Bahler, Alex Madva, Sally Haslanger, Céline Leboeuf, Katherine Tullman, Gabby Yearwood, Robin Zheng, Mari Mikkola, Nancy McKitrick, Natalie Stoljar, Dan Kelly, Keota Fields, and Joshua Rivkin.

NOTES

1. Young, *On Female Body Experience*, 20.
2. Haslanger, "Cognition as a Social Skill," 1.
3. Ibid., 1.
4. Ibid., 1n2.
5. Haslanger, "Culture and Critique," 156–57. See also Haslanger, "Racism, Ideology, and Social Movements," 14.
6. Mameli, "Mindreading, Mindshaping, and Evolution," 608.
7. McGeer, "Mind-Making Practices," 263.
8. See, for example, Gopnik, Meltzoff, and Kuhl, *The Scientist and the Crib*.
9. Mameli, "Mindreading, Mindshaping, and Evolution," 613.

10. Gallagher, *How the Body Shapes the Mind*, 212.
11. Alcoff, *Visible Identities*, 184.
12. Ibid., 184–85.
13. Fanon, *Black Skin, White Masks*, 18.
14. Ibid.
15. For various ways of interpreting what is happening, see Siegel, "Bias and Perception."
16. For additional analysis on this point and examples, see Yancy, *Black Bodies, White Gazes*.
17. It is worth mentioning a related complaint here, namely that many of the theorists just cited already discuss and document the phenomenon of mindshaping (in McGeer's sense), just not under that name. These theorists go unmentioned in the article. Indeed, Haslanger talks about mindshaping as if McGeer and Zawidzki invented it. However, critical race theorists have long noted the ways in which culture shapes individuals' thinking. Thanks to Janine Jones for this observation. Jones also argues elsewhere that Haslanger's work would benefit from deeper engagement with historically important antiracist thinkers such as Du Bois (Jones, "Review of *Resisting Reality*," 24–25).
18. Zawidzki, *Mindshaping*, 30.
19. Ibid., 31.
20. Ibid., 32.
21. Ibid., 60.
22. Ibid., 50.
23. Ibid., 60.
24. Similar arguments are made by Davidson and Kelly, "Minding the Gap"; Leboeuf, "The Embodied Biased Mind," 47; Ngo, *The Habits of Racism*; Sullivan: *Revealing Whiteness*.
25. Zawidzki, *Mindshaping*, 31.
26. Ibid., xii.
27. Haslanger, "Cognition as a Social Skill," 7.
28. Haslanger, "Culture and Critique," 155.
29. For figures, see Haslanger, "Cognition as a Social Skill."
30. hooks, *ain't i a woman*, 26.
31. Rankine, "Claudia Rankine."
32. See Roelofs, *The Cultural Promise of the Aesthetic* for more on the role of promises and modes of address in aesthetic creations. Roelofs argues that particular modes of address create and sustain certain kinds of relationships, hence can work in favor, or against, the status quo.
33. Haslanger, "Race & Gender," 31.
34. Haslanger, "Changing the Ideology and Culture of Philosophy," 1.
35. Haslanger, "You Mixed?," 265–66; Haslanger, "Exploring *Race* In Life," 7.
36. Haslanger, "Racism, Ideology, and Social Movements," 3.
37. Haslanger, "Cognition as a Social Skill," 4.
38. Ibid., 2.
39. Ibid., 7.
40. Haslanger, "What Is a (Social) Structure Explanation?" 121.
41. Haslanger, "Race & Gender," 39.
42. Ibid., 44.
43. Young, *On Female Body Experience*, 20.
44. Ibid., 22.
45. For a feminist critique of the lived body see Leboeuf, "Bodily Alienation and Feminist Social Critique."
46. Young, *On Female Body Experience*, 16.
47. Ibid., 18.
48. Ibid., 35. See also Ahmed, *Queer Phenomenology*.
49. Ibid., 17.

50. Ibid., 18.
51. Bierria, "Missing in Action," 135.
52. Ibid., emphasis in the original.
53. Ibid., 133.
54. Ibid., 137.
55. As documented by Cook, "2 Officers out of Jobs."
56. Lugones, *Pilgramages/Peregrinajes*, 77.
57. Du Bois, *The Souls of Black Folk*.
58. Ibid., 59.
59. Haslanger, "Cognition as a Social Skill," 7.
60. Zawidzki, *Mindshaping*, 62.
61. See also Zheng, "Bias, Structure, and Injustice."
62. Lugones, *Pilgramages/Peregrinajes*, 55.
63. Ibid., 55.
64. Jenkins, "Amelioration and Inclusion," 396.
65. Ibid., 416.
66. For a parallel criticism about gender, see Mikkola, "Ontological Commitments, Sex and Gender," 75.
67. Perry, "Racism is Terrible. Blackness is Not."
68. Ibid.
69. Ibid.
70. Hurston, "How It Feels to Be Colored Me," 153.
71. Ibid., 155.
72. Jones, "Review of *Resisting Reality*," 25.
73. Chambliss and Lopez, "Social Structures and Individual Wrongdoing," ms.
74. Mueller, "Producing Colorblindness."
75. Ibid., 224–25.
76. Rothstein, *The Color of the Law*; Taylor, *Race for Profit*.
77. Mueller, "Producing Colorblindness," 227.
78. Ibid., 228.
79. Ibid., 282.
80. Ibid. 290.
81. Ibid., 291.
82. Ibid., 295.
83. Ibid., 284.
84. Lorde, "The Uses of the Erotic," 59.
85. Ibid., 59.
86. Madva, "A Plea for Anti-Anti Individualism," 703.
87. Ibid., 702.
88. Zheng, "Bias, Structure, and Injustice," 6.
89. Ibid., 5.
90. For further arguments, see Ayala-López and Beeghly, "Explaining Injustice."
91. Obasogie, *Blinded by Sight*; Salter and Adams, "Towards a Critical Race Psychology."

BIBLIOGRAPHY

Ahmed, Sara. *Queer Phenomenology: Orientations, Objections, and Others*. Durham: Duke University Press, 2006.

Alcoff, Linda Martín. *Visible Identities: Race, Gender, and the Self*. Oxford: Oxford University Press, 2006.

Ayala-López, Saray and Erin Beeghly. "Explaining Injustice: Structural Analysis, Bias, and Individuals." In *Introduction to Implicit Bias: Knowledge, Justice, and the Social Mind*. Edited by Erin Beeghly and Alex Madva, 211–32. New York: Routledge, 2020.

Bierria, Alisa. "Missing in Action: Violence, Power, and Discerning Agency." *Hypatia* 29 (2014): 129–45.

Bracey, Glenn E. and Wendy Leo Moore. "'Race Tests': Racial Boundary Maintenance in the White Evangelical Church." *Sociological Inquiry* 87 (2017): 282–302.

Chambliss, Brian and Theresa Lopez. "Social Structures and Individual Wrongdoing: The Need for an Integrative Account of Social Injustice." Manuscript.

Cook, Rhonda. "2 Officers Out of Jobs in Wake of Repeated Tasering of Woman." *The Atlanta Journal Constitution.* August 11, 2012. Accessed at https://www.ajc.com/news/local/officers-out-jobs-wake-repeated-tasering-woman/LLXob5uAAFH9j6bEw4ggkI/.

Davidson, Lacey and Dan Kelly. "Minding the Gap: Bias, Soft Structures, and the Double Life of Social Norms." *Journal of Applied Philosophy* 37 (2020): 190–210.

Du Bois, W. E. B. *The Souls of Black Folk.* Mineaola, NY: Dover Thrift Press, 1994.

Fanon, Frantz. *Black Skin, White Masks.* Translated by Richard Philcox. New York: Grove Press, 2008.

Gallagher, Shaun. *How the Body Shapes the Mind.* Oxford: Oxford University Press, 2005.

Gopnik, Alison, Andrew Meltzoff, and Patricia Kuhl. *The Scientist in the Crib: What Early Learning Tells Us about the Mind.* New York: William Morrow Paperbacks, 2000.

Haslanger, Sally. "Changing the Ideology and Culture of Philosophy: Not by Reason (Alone)." *Hypatia* 23 (2008): 210–33.

———. "Cognition as a Social Skill." *Australasian Philosophical Review* 3 (2019): 5–25.

———. "Culture and Critique." *Proceedings of the Aristotelian Society Supplementary Volume* 91 (2017): 149–73.

———. "Exploring *Race* in Life, in Speech, and in Philosophy: Comments on Josh Glasgow's *A Theory of Race.*" *Symposia on Gender, Race, and Philosophy* 5 (2009): 1–9.

———. "Race & Gender: (What) Are They? (What) Do We Want Them to Be?" *Noûs* 34 (2000): 31–55.

———. "Racism, Ideology, and Social Movements." *Res Philosophica* 94 (2017): 1–22.

———. "Social Structure, Narrative, and Explanation." *Canadian Journal of Philosophy* 45 (2015): 1–15.

———. "You Mixed? Racial Identity without Racial Biology." *Adoption Matters: Philosophical and Feminist Essays.* Edited by Sally Haslanger and Charlotte Witt, 265–90. Ithaca: Cornell University Press, 2005.

———. "What Is a (Social) Structural Explanation?" *Philosophical Studies* 173 (2016): 113–30.

———. "What Is a Social Practice?" *Royal Institute of Philosophy Supplement* 82 (2018): 231–47.

hooks, bell. *ain't i a woman: black women and feminism.* New York: Routledge, 2015.

Hurston, Zora Neale. "How It Feels to Be Colored Me." In *I Love Myself When I am Laughing: A Zora Neale Hurston Reader,* 152–54. New York: The Feminist Press at the City University of New York, 1979.

Jenkins, Katharine. "Amelioration and Inclusion: Gender Identity and the Concept of Woman." *Ethics* 126 (2016): 394–421.

Jones, Janine. "Review of *Resisting Reality: Social Construction and Social Critique.*" *Newsletter on Philosophy and the Black Experience, American Philosophical Association* 13 (2013): 19–25.

Leboeuf, Céline. "Bodily Alienation and Feminist Social Critique." Manuscript.

———. "The Embodied Biased Mind." In *Introduction to Implicit Bias: Knowledge, Justice, and the Social Mind.* Edited by Erin Beeghly and Alex Madva, 41–57. New York: Routledge, 2020.

Lorde, Audre. "The Uses of the Erotic." *Sister Outsider: Essays & Speeches by Audre Lorde.* New York: Random House, 2007.

Lugones, María. *Pilgramages/Peregrinajes: Theorizing Coalition Against Multiple Oppressions.* Lanham, MD: Rowman & Littlefield, 2003.

Madva, Alex. "A Plea for Anti-Anti Individualism: How Oversimple Psychology Misleads Social Policy." *Ergo* 27 (2016): 701–28.
Mameli, Matteo. "Mindreading, Mindshaping, and Evolution." *Biology and Philosophy* 16 (2001): 597–628.
McGeer, Victoria. "Mind-Making Practices: The Social Infrastructure of Self-Knowing Agency and Responsibility." *Philosophical Explorations* 18 (2015): 259–81.
Mikkola, Mari. "Ontological Commitments, Sex and Gender." In *Feminist Metaphysics*. Edited by Charlotte Witt, 67–84. New York: Springer, 2011.
Mueller, Jennifer C. "Producing Colorblindness: Everyday Mechanisms of White Ignorance." *Social Problems* 64 (2017): 219–38.
Ngo, Helen. *The Habits of Racism: A Phenomenology of Racism and Racialized Embodiment*. Lanham, MD: Lexington Books, 2012.
Obasogie, Osagie. *Blinded by Sight: Seeing Race Through The Eyes of the Blind*. Palo Alto: Stanford Law Books, 2013.
Perry, Imani. "Racism is Terrible. Blackness is Not." *The Atlantic*. June 15, 2020. Accessed at https://www.theatlantic.com/ideas/archive/2020/06/racism-terrible-blackness-not/613039/.
Rankine, Claudia. Interview with David Ulin. "Claudia Rankine: The Art of Poetry No. 102." *The Paris Review* 219 (Winter 2016).
Roelofs, Monique. *The Cultural Promise of the Aesthetic*. New York: Bloomsbury, 2014.
Rothstein, Richard. *The Color of the Law: A Forgotten History of How Our Government Segregated America*. New York: Norton, 2017.
Salter, Phia and Glenn Adams. "Towards a Critical Race Psychology." *Social and Personality Psychology Compass* 7, no. 11 (2013): 781–93.
Siegel, Susanna. "Bias and Perception." In *Introduction to Implicit Bias: Knowledge, Justice, and the Social Mind*. Edited by Erin Beeghly and Alex Madva, 99–115. New York: Routledge, 2020.
Sullivan, Shannon. *Revealing Whiteness: The Unconscious Habits of White Privilege*. Bloomington: Indiana University Press, 2006.
Taylor, Keeanga-Yamahtta. *Race for Profit: How Banks and the Real Estate Industry Undermined Black Homeownership*. Chapel Hill: University of Chapel Hill University Press, 2019.
Yancy, George. *Black Bodies, White Gazes: The Continuing Significance of Race in America*. 2nd edition. Lanham, MD: Rowman & Littlefield, 2017.
Young, Iris Marion. *On Female Body Experience: Throwing Like a Girl & Other Essays*. Oxford: Oxford University Press, 2007.
Zawidzki, Tadeusz Wiesław. *Mindshaping: A New Framework for Understanding Human Social Cognition*. Cambridge, MA: MIT Press, 2013.
Zheng, Robin. "Bias, Structure, and Injustice: A Reply to Haslanger." *Feminist Philosophy Quarterly* 4, no. 1 (2018): 1–29. Accessed at https://ojs.lib.uwo.ca/index.php/fpq/article/view/3125/2390.

SEVEN

The Embodied Practices of Whiteness

Unpacking One's White Supremacist Education

Brock Bahler

In "White Crisis and the Value of Losing One's Way," George Yancy writes:

> By the time White students have arrived in our classrooms, they have already been shaped by White ways of being-in-the-world, White ways of avoiding the issue of White privilege, White ways of constructing nonwhite bodies as "different," White ways of seeing themselves as "innocent" of White racism, and White ways of taking up space and moving through that space in the capacity of ownership and possession.[1]

But what does it look like to receive a white supremacist K–12 education? I ask this to my college students prior to studying James Cone or Martin Luther King Jr. or Delores Williams. Most of them look at me wide-eyed, as if I've just asked a question so unfathomable, I might as well have asked them what it was like growing up on Mars. But some get it. They say:

- A white supremacist education is being told your entire childhood that Christopher Columbus was an all-around good guy who deserves having his own holiday.
- A white supremacist education is being told your entire childhood that Thomas Jefferson is a great role model and worthy of emulating, and no one telling you he owned over 600 slaves.
- A white supremacist education is never noticing how Christians automatically get a day off for Good Friday or have a Christmas

vacation, while Jews or Muslims have to out themselves to get an excused absence for their religious holidays.
- A white supremacist education is interpreting all of world history through the lens of Europe as the center.
- A white supremacist education is being told the Civil War was fought over states' rights.

In my introductory lecture to "Letter from Birmingham Jail," I ask them how many have read anything by Martin Luther King Jr. before. About half raise their hands. I ask if they're familiar with the practice of redlining. Maybe seven in a class of 45 raise their hands. I ask if they've heard of the bombing of Black Wall Street in Tulsa in 1921. Three students hold up their hands. I show them the words of *Dum Diversas* where the Pope officially sanctioned the kidnapping and enslavement of Africans in 1453 and every student is shocked. A Catholic student preparing for the priesthood asks, "Why didn't anyone ever tell me about this before?"

What are the long-term effects of yearly being taught a white supremacist education? Of course, few of us are taught white supremacy *explicitly*; rather, it is *implied* by what appears in the curriculum, by *how* that material is presented, by *who* writes textbooks, and by what information is regularly *excluded* from the textbooks. Hence, while racist assumptions and stereotypes can be an epistemological datum—that is, it a belief or idea one merely mentally assents to or conceptualizes with his or her prefrontal cortex—what we tend to find is that racist assumptions and stereotypes are "caught" and habituated throughout our educations less so by what is said but by what is unsaid or mis-said.

In this chapter, I argue that racism is a cultural and personal disposition that one is habituated and ritualized into on the social, somatic, affective, and narrative levels of human existence. Somewhat similarly to how we are habituated into virtues, white supremacy is first and foremost a *practice*, a praxis. To be clear, habituation is not always on the level of conscious, intentional awareness; rather, we often unconsciously, unmeditatively become habituated into various ways of being-in-the-world. White supremacy functions as a set of rhythms and repertoires that we enact that shape how we perceive the world. Hence, in a parallel to how Emmanuel Levinas writes that Jewish assimilation into "secular" France resulted in an "unconscious Christianization,"[2] as an American it is virtually impossible to resist white supremacist assumptions because they function as the unstated norm of American society, which are embedded into the founding documents and institutions of America itself. As a result, these unconscious white supremacist habits and codified presuppositions provide a depth of meaning (note, that *meaning* can be derived regardless of whether the information is true or false) that we instantly and seamlessly ascertain without having to go through the time that self-reflective cognition requires.

In my view, this provides the best explanation for two of the features that manifest themselves in theories about what constitutes implicit bias: *dissociation* and *introspective opacity*. According to Daniel Kelly and Natalia Washington *dissociation* means that "implicit biases can coexist with explicit racial attitudes that are diametrically opposed to them."[3] And *introspective opacity* means that "a person who is only implicitly biased has tendencies whose presence and influence on thought and behavior is not easily detectable via introspection."[4] In short, implicit biases betray one's expressed epistemological beliefs about racism and are resistant to investigation because they function at the level of the unconscious, or, at the level of pretheoretical embodied activity. In a word, racism is not first an ideology articulated from one's self-reflective, conceptually oriented prefrontal cortex; rather, it is pretheoretical as Merleau-Ponty would put it. It is habituated into one's historicity, running along "under the hood," so to speak, of one's embodied lived experience.

The phenomenological method claims that a descriptive, first-person account of our lived experience can reveal essential structures about human existence. In contrast to the derivative nature of scientific measurement, phenomenology pays attention to how humans encounter the world in the immediate and habitual modes of being, which we regularly take for granted. This method can, thus, be useful for describing the essential fundamental structures of the human that make us prone to developing implicit bias or racist habits. How do implicit biases form within a white person—that is, *me*—who was raised in a family that, on the surface, would explicitly decry racist convictions? How are racial biases embedded, cultivated, confirmed, and practiced within *this* white body? What are the fundamental structures of embodied whiteness and how does one make them manifest and address them in oneself?

In the following, I will propose that we take up "white ways of being-in-the-world," not through abstract arguments, but primarily through (a) the *imitation* of models (mimesis), which over time become codified through (b) a *habituation* of practices and rituals. Somewhat anachronistically, I will begin with an inquiry into my own children and work backward to my own upbringing. Since our children are often a reflection of our own lives—like it or not, we regularly pass on how we live and think to the next generation—beginning with an inquiry into what models my children have with regard to issues related to race allows me to better interrogate what models I had—whether they are similar or different—that have become habituated into my own being-in-the-world.

PHENOMENOLOGY OF INFANT LEARNING: WHITE SUPREMACY AND IMITATING EXEMPLARS

We do not begin life as autonomous, self-reflective thinkers, or as fully formed adults (indeed, the idea of autonomous rationality is likely a myth); rather, we are movers attuned to an environment and embodied actors at play in an intersocial world. As newborns, we do not start out as self-reflective cogitators; rather, we learn primarily through imitating models and by physically engaging with our environment. Indeed, one could make the case that learning would be impossible were it not for what René Girard calls "mimetic desire," which enables humans to express more than an animal instinct by mimicking, responding to, *and* modulating human behavior.[5]

Infant Learning

In his pioneering work, child psychologist Andrew Meltzoff was able to demonstrate that less than an hour after birth, infants can inspect and imitate facial expressions.[6] Neonates instinctually imitate a variety of facial gestures, and they can do so with increasing precision. After working with each neonate, the next day Meltzoff entered the room, and the infants would immediately recognize him and initiated the "game" by trying to perfect the facial gestures they had learned the previous day. There's much to be said here about infant intelligence, but for my purposes I'm interested in its implications for how imitation can (unfortunately) contribute to our racialized dispositions.[7]

First, infant imitation reveals a capacity to anticipate intentions in the actions of others. An infant cannot recognize his or her own self in a mirror until about 12 months of age. Hence, long before humans self-reflectively can say "I" or "me," or *cogito sum*, infant have already engaged in a meaningfully oriented prereflective understanding of the world that is constituted by their imitative behavior of the people in their small circle of influence. For over 300 days, infants—which means all of us—are ritualized into a repertoire of routines that profoundly shapes their embodiment for the rest of their lives—what to eat, how to walk, how to speak, how to feel, how to love. We have already developed a narrative about what the world is like, not one based on formal arguments, but based on our affective, bodily encounters with others. Hence, as René Girard writes, thinking about myth and religious practices, but particularly appropriate in this context: "The true guide of human beings is not abstract reason but ritual."[8] These rituals and narratives are *not* irrational—even if they are partial or mythical—but rather, provide one with a sensible framework for moving and being-in-the-world.

Without a formal conception of the self, the infant has an innate perceptual capacity for empathically mapping the expressions of others onto his or her own body by means of a fundamental corporeal schema and capacity for movement.[9] The infant's engagement with the world is not borne out of a conceptual theory of mind; rather, it is propelled by a discovery of his or her own possibilities *through* the faces and bodies of others.[10] Our bodily, affective, and intellectual comportment toward other humans is formed by how our caregivers comport themselves to others. Hence, given how fundamental the first five years of brain development—but *especially* the first one to two years—are in shaping human social skills, emotional response to stimuli, nonconceptual sensory understanding of the world (e.g., hearing, vision, proprioception), and habitual ways of comporting to others and the world, the wiring of the neurons in our brains is largely conditioned by the imitation of a very small sample size of individuals.[11]

Second, Meltzoff stresses, babies often learn from their caregivers "even when we do not deliberately teach them."[12] This is sometimes called "unsupervised learning" where what is learned is "caught" through a situation rather than "taught" in a didactic manner. Stated otherwise, at the same time the infant imitates the facial gestures of the adult, the infant learns a vast assortment of other lessons about intersocial behavior that are not explicitly intended, and in doing so, develops a gestalt of how human interaction works.[13]

Third, imitation is intrinsically value laden. The infant is *born* with an attunement to a shared world, with a capacity to create a mutually meaningful world with others and discern the *interests* of others. This is consistent with René Girard's account of mimetic desire, which suggests that not only is most learning imitative, but desire is triadic[14]—that is, I imitate others' interest in an object not because I believe the object itself to be intrinsically valuable but because I desire the same relationship the other person has with the object. Infants quickly learn that the world is already laden with value by the amount of time and attention their caregivers give to various objects. As Meltzoff observes, toddlers readily take up the capacity to turn a banana into a telephone or place a phone up to their ear and talk to an imaginary person. Children perceive the value we place upon objects without having that value explicitly stated.[15] I observed this in my daughter when she was five months old—she did not want to play with the fake toy phone or toy keys I gave her; she wanted to play with my phone and set of keys, because she could discern that they were more valuable than the toy keys given the amount of time and attention I gave to them.

INFANT LEARNING AND RACIAL BIAS

These conclusions provide a general model for understanding how imitation can foster dispositions as early as infancy that may later lead to racial bias. And while significant scientific and psychological studies are trying to analyze data that reveals racial bias in infants—often reduced in the media to provocative titles such as "Your Baby Is a Racist"[16]—for the purposes of this essay, I'm interested in explicating how the lived experiences of my own children have led them to pick up racialized cues about human behavior. To be clear, these cues are not immediately discernible because they are often picked up tacitly; rather, they become made manifest later on by explicit behavior or verbal statements that reflect the process of codifying their lived impressions about the world.

Vignette #1: I'm driving home after picking up my four-year-old daughter from preschool. Out of the blue, she announces emphatically from her car seat in the back: "Black and white people can't marry each other." I immediately pulled over the car, thinking to myself, "Oh shit!" My response, in and of itself, is telling. I did not want my daughter to grow up embodying racist assumptions. I did not want to believe that my daughter had been formed into racist assumptions by my parenting choices. My next response was to resort to logical facts: I told her what she said wasn't true, but abstract statistics and facts rarely have the same power as one's affective lived experience. When we went home, I showed her pictures of all my friends on Facebook that had racially diverse family makeups. We talked about how one of her babysitters is a person of color whose husband is white. I pointed out to her that two of her other babysitters are part of a transracial family (they are from China adopted by parents of European descent). And I pointed out the three biracial families that we know who live on our block.

So where did this line of thinking come from? What were the unstated views that led to this conclusion? And how long did she take part in an embodied formation of this perspective before she was able to verbally articulate it? No one had explicitly stated this idea to her. She had not read anything that made this proclamation. Indeed, quite the opposite, we have told our children that people can marry whoever they want. We have been intentional about incorporating children's books into their repertoire that include people of color (and more than just the stereotypical tropes Black characters are typically afforded—that of an athlete, former slave, or Civil Rights activist).

She didn't arrive at this conclusion by any explicit statement or by a preschool teacher intentionally showing her monolithic family portraits. Her conclusion about the impossibility of biracial marriages was a conclusion drawn entirely from the implicit messages that she garnered from her isolated, yet powerful, educational environment. As best as I can now discern, it appears to have been an inference she drew from observing the pictorial family trees that all of her preschool classmates had made several months prior to her proclamation. This affective, visual, lived encounter with whiteness—there was only one African-American family in her preschool and no biracial or transracial families (and all of her preschool teachers were white)—was far more powerful than any Black History Month lesson, Doc McStuffins episode, or reading of Ezra Jack Keats's *Snowy Day*. Indeed, precisely due to the paucity of such exposure, she had already imbibed a predominately white world and spaces where white people are the norm. Growing up in a predominately white world, her limited exposure to biracial or transracial families functioned as exceptions to the rule, as aberrations to the norm.

Vignette #2: From ages three to five, my son went to a public school in Pittsburgh that was about 60 percent white and had a staff that was predominately white. His kindergarten teacher was a white woman who had been teaching for nearly three decades. Generally speaking, she was supportive of our son's education, creative in her teaching methods, and encouraged her students to learn. At the same time, some of the ways in which she was biased against certain students were obvious. In the few times we volunteered in the classroom it was clear her expectations for the handful of Black students were lower than they were for the majority of the white kids in the class. Her tone of voice with them was harsher, quicker to scold. Invariably, while some energetic and talkative white children also got the label of troublemakers, it regularly seemed as if *all* of the African-American children in the class were seen as troublemakers and were rarely deemed the bright students in the classroom. None of these ideas were ever explicitly stated by the teacher. No one pronounced in explicit terms the claim that white kids are smart and Black students are troublemakers.

That my son picked up on these social cues, even though we never explicitly discussed our concerns about them in his presence, later became quite clear. In first grade, we moved him to another school, one that was 66 percent African-American, had a far more diverse teaching staff, including an African-American principal, and was known for cultivating a tight-knit community.[17] Going to a new school had its own share of difficulties, yet it led to a profound transformation in his perceptions about his social reality. This coalesced one day near the end of first grade, when, as we were walking home from the bus stop, my seven-year-old said to me, "Dad, I used to think that kids who get in trouble at school were just bad kids, but now I think that maybe they are just having a bad day, or maybe they're having a hard time dealing with something at home."

Again, while this statement is a reflective articulation, I believe it is the *product* of the change in his environment which produced an entirely different social narrative on the level of his embodiment and intersubjective interaction with others. In contrast to his first educational experience, his relationships with peers that did not look like himself were now encouraged. The representation of a diversity of teachers and leaders in his school communicated an implicit message about the possibility that all students, regardless of their race or ethnic background, can be successful. The ways in which students were perceived and disciplined was notably different. The walls at the new school, emblazoned with images and flags from prominent HBCU schools—Howard, Morehouse, Spelman—told him, without any explicit explanation, that Black people take pride in their education, in their culture, and in themselves.

Vignette #3: It's April 2018, and we're watching TV at a hotel. A commercial comes on about a TV special that will air on April 4, which will consider the life and legacy of Dr. Martin Luther King Jr., in memory of the 50th anniversary of his assassination. At the sight of the commercial, my nine-year-old son—who, as I previously noted, attends a predominately African-American public school—remarks off-handedly, "What? Why would they be talking about Martin Luther King? It's not February!" February, of course, in the United States is Black History Month.

This third vignette powerfully illuminates the distinction between intention and impact. The intentional efforts of his African-American principal and African-American third grade teacher to highlight the achievements of Black activists, scientists, artists, and writers during one month of the year, in some respects, actually had the opposite effect. My annual act of pulling out a children's book about Martin Luther King Jr. on his birthday likely had a similar effect. These activities, rather than *enhancing* the importance of bringing traditionally marginalized voices into the mainstream, communicated to him that those voices were supposed to be quarantined and cordoned off to one month out of the year, that they were special exceptions to average, everyday American life. The net result was a tacit communication that one's racial conscience was only to be pricked occasionally. Like a nominal Christian who attends church only on Easter and Christmas, he was being told that discussions about race and racism should be limited to sentimentalist readings, reduced to a holiday one celebrates without any substantial change to the institutional policies that perpetuate racism or the personal habits that assume whiteness as the norm.

In our own activities, we have sought to combat this by taking our children to events throughout the year that will raise their awareness on a whole host of issues related to white supremacy, racism, and diversity. Last summer, I took my children to a protest after the death of Antwon Rose, an unarmed Black teenager shot in the back and killed by a police officer (who was later acquitted). We took them to the National Underground Railroad Museum in Cincinnati. We visited the National Museum of African-American History and Culture in D.C. They've cultivated friendships with a diverse group of kids through playdates, birthday parties, and sports teams. No doubt, their public school education about race *is* substantially different from our own—to my surprise, our children have nothing positive to say about Christopher Columbus and colonialism—but try as we might, none of these singular activities can wholly thwart the constant barrage of messages they receive from a culture that regularly communicates a Zeitgeist of white supremacy, such as unstated norms about standards of beauty (white women with straight blonde hair).

In sum, the lived experiences of my children suggest that growing up in America, we don't have to be explicitly taught racial stereotypes or given a concept for racism, for we are thrown into a white supremacist social milieu. In this regard, George Yancy aptly speaks of the "historical sedimentation or encrustation of white supremacy."[18] Even the child of white parents committed to antiracism may intuitively take up the long history of systemic racist assumptions that are embedded within American society. Through imitation and ritualization, my children have, in a relatively unconscious manner, inferred racialized assumptions about human engagement.

HABITUS: INHABITING THE HABITS OF WHITENESS

Our imitations of others, then, become codified through another important process of personal and social formation: habit. Both on the social and individual level, the narrative we construct to make sense of our world and encounters with others, including the racialized lens by which we perceive them, are shaped through a performative process of habituation, ritualization, and practice. Here both Pierre Bourdieu's pioneering work on the notion of *habitus* and Maurice Merleau-Ponty's account of the lived body are particularly instructive.

Bourdieu and Merleau-Ponty on Habits

According to Pierre Bourdieu, a *habitus* reflects structured, orienting bodily dispositions that we live into—that are often passed down to us—which bring about a familiarity and attunement with our world.[19] A *habitus* reflects the influence of the "cultural milieu"[20] in which we live: "a habitus is always sort of bigger than me—it is a communal, collective disposition that gets inscribed in me."[21] It is "a kind of embodied tradition" and a "handed-down way of being."[22] While Bourdieu was primarily interested in studying how meaning is derived through embodied participation in religious practices, his assessment can be applied more broadly. As a whole, society—the institutions, cultural artifacts, and social circles that demarcate our daily lives—cultivates myths and narratives that are embedded into our cultural memory and our collective consciousness, ones that shape each one of us unconsciously.

Two aspects of *habitus* are particularly instructive for my purposes. First, a *habitus* is not conceptually thought but is lived. Praxis precedes theory. Bourdieu speaks of "a reason immanent in practices."[23] Bourdieu writes, "We don't 'decide' our way into every action. Our being-in-the-world is characterized by inclinations that propel us to all sorts of action 'without thinking.'"[24] That is, we don't have to form a theoretical concept or linguistically express a propositional belief in order to perform such tasks; rather, we are directly attuned to them on the level of the body, enacting them with what might be called an "embodied know-how."[25] We intuitively immerse ourselves into these practices, and we remain largely unconscious to such practical logic as to how they conform and train our perceptions, behaviors, and attitudes.[26] We don't have to be explicitly told to live into these practices but implicitly take them up in order to seamlessly, masterfully make our way through the world.

Second, a *habitus* is a deeply meaningful practice even if I cannot adequately articulate or conceptualize its significance. A *habitus* provides an orientation (the French: *sens*), direction, purposefulness, and structure to everyday life. Bourdieu describes *habitus* as "a way of *meaning* the world, a way of 'making sense of' the world. But it is a 'making sense' that is not consciously, mentally processed or even thought about."[27] In fact, a *habitus* is *more* meaningful than an abstract, logical concept. The symbols we encounter and rituals we regularly perform—whether in a religious environment (e.g., the sign of the cross) or as a product of a highly marketed capitalist society (the Nike swoosh)—appeal to us on a more holistic register than abstract concepts. They are encountered via the body, affects, imagination, and mind, and in an intersocial context; they are *enacted* through my participation with them. Hence, they become deeply meaningful to the point that they need no explanation, for our engagement with the symbol or practices reveals their meaning in the very process of (re)enacting them.[28]

We can add to Bourdieu's account of *habitus* Maurice Merleau-Ponty's account of the lived body—which actually shaped Bourdieu's own work.[29] The world is encountered through the lived body—that is, a self that takes up a particular *style* or comportment while it inhabits space. Merleau-Ponty, clearly in response to Descartes's dictum *cogito sum*, stresses that *I am my body*. This means that "consciousness is in the first place not a matter of 'I think that' but of 'I can.' . . . Consciousness is being-toward-the-thing through the intermediary of the body."[30] Praxis precedes philosophical reflection, and while the development of theory is important, and goes on to shape other practices, the time it takes to perform theoretical self-reflection is also tedious labor. Habits allow me to not only seamlessly participate in the world, but also to creatively attune myself to new possibilities. My everyday activities, reflecting thousands of repeated interactions—driving a car, picking up my coffee mug, discerning emotions by looking at someone's eyes, running down the street, or typing on my computer—allow me to develop a kind of thinking that is delegated to and understood on the level of the body. But this form of thinking is not only quick and agile (imagine how difficult life would be if you had to literally think about each step you took), it is deeply meaningful in that it gives me a performative and malleable structure to modulate and improvise in related contexts. Knowing how to comport myself to a door handle I've never encountered parallels the adept skills of a premier athlete or musician.

As Merleau-Ponty puts it, habit is a "form of [practical] intelligence [that] is not conscious of itself," which resides in my corporeal posture toward the world.[31] It is a kind of "knowledge in the hands, which is forthcoming only when bodily effort is made."[32] Merleau-Ponty uses the example of typing. I personally can type around 90 words per minute, and such a speed requires a thorough intimacy with the location of the letters on the keyboard that is only learned through extensive practice and experience. When I type words at this speed, I do not have time to make a mental representation of each letter of each word that I type, nor do I have a mental image of the location and image of each key on the keypad. I don't need to. In fact, focusing on the image of each key will likely make my typing worse. Rather, the keys are an extension of my fingers, which work in intimate connection with my entire body. As Merleau-Ponty writes, "When I sit at my typewriter, a motor space opens up beneath my hands, in which I am about to 'play' what I have read.... It is the body which 'understands' in the acquisition of habit.... To understand is to experience the harmony between what we aim at and what is given, between the intention and the performance—and the body is our anchorage in a world."[33] Habit is a movement or practice that has been learned by the body, when the body has "absorbed a new meaning, and assimilated a fresh core of significance."[34] Thus, habit allows me to smoothly, intuitively, and uniquely interact with my surroundings and others.

But habits are not dormant artifacts from our past; rather we *inhabit* them. We don't possess our habits so much as they possess us, as they provide us with a meaningful orientation to our lived experience.[35] Drawing on Merleau-Ponty, in her book *The Habits of Racism*, Helen Ngo observes that habits are not only sedimentations from the *past* that we passively take up, but are also active structures that shape our *future*. Our habits "attest to the weightiness of the past in the present lived body,"[36] they reveal the historical and systemic structures that follow along in our wake, which anchor us in the world, but they are also "inherently futural.... They also look forward, at once serving as both a medium and gateway to that which we may incorporate into our body schemata."[37] Our embedded past experiences shape what we perceive in our present and anticipate the future.

It is important to stress that even if we come to theoretically *disagree* with our past, it still shapes how we perceive the world and our future possibilities. We may ultimately disagree with our parents on matters of religion, politics, or social issues, but we cannot erase our history. Monica Coleman observes, even if "we decide not to repeat that aspect of [our] past, its imprint stays with us. . . . Even if we 'negatively' incorporate our past, we still bear the traces of that aspect of the past. Just the consideration and rejection of the past give it a kind of life beyond itself. We are shaped by what we do not do just as much as we are shaped by what we do."[38] Indeed, deciding to take up a new way of being-in-the-world requires being exposed to new models one can imitate and learning new rituals and rhythms one can embody, which are often absent in our families of origin. Hence, prior to taking up new models and rhythms, it is important to analyze how our past educational environments habituate white supremacist assumptions into us.

The Habits of Whiteness: William Henry Harrison High School

In her 2005 *New York Times* bestselling memoir, entitled *Jesus Land,* Julia Scheeres describes what it was like growing up white with an adopted African-American brother named David in a rural setting in Indiana. In one scene, Scheeres recounts the first day of riding the bus with her brother to the rural, (almost) entirely white high school as freshmen in 1985. As they walk down the aisle of the bus, she writes,

> Rows of white faces point in our direction. A pocket of space materializes at the back of the bus. . . . Two rows before we reach the empty bench, a black boot slams down in front of me, heel first. My eyes sweep over it and up the jean-clad leg and the United Methodist T-shirt to the orange hair of the boy wearing it. . . . "[N****r] lover," he snarls. . . . The bus lurches forward and I stumble over his leg and fall onto the empty bench. When I look up, David's swaying in the middle of the aisle, gawking down at the boot. . . . He gingerly lifts his foot over the boot and when he's mid-stride, the boot rockets up and slams into his crotch. Laughter clatters around us.[39]

Julia walks into Harrison High School with David, but "a moment later he's engulfed by a wave of white bodies."[40] After a few days of faithfully staying next to David's side while entering the gauntlet, the taunts become too much for Julia. She concludes:

> After hearing "[n****r] lover" and "there goes [n****r] and his sister" hurled at our backs too many times, I stop walking into school with him. . . . As I rush down the sidewalk ahead of him, I feel a pinch of guilt, but a greater relief as I melt into the sea of white bodies. . . . Why do I always have to be the "black boy's sister" anyway? Why can't I be my own person? It's not fair. . . . Sometimes I run into him between classes, always alone, always rushing and looking straight ahead, his face a blank mask. He's easy enough to spot because he's the only black kid at Harrison. A couple of times, he's rushed right by me without seeing me—I must have been just another white face to him, blurring by.[41]

There is much to discuss in these excerpts,[42] but I want to focus on two observations: first, the various kinds of white privilege at work in Julia's desire to assimilate into the "sea of white bodies," and second, the habitual ways of being white that both Julia and other white actors in this story express.

In his introduction to *Christology and Whiteness*, George Yancy speaks about the feeling of alienation he undergoes when he is in predominately white spaces, such as academic philosophy conferences or liberal mainline churches. In what he also describes as the "sea of whiteness" that marks such spaces, he notes how white bodies express an "ease of movement" that is taken for granted, whereas the Black body feels a "peculiar sense of alienation" because it stands out.[43] He writes, "Such spaces are perceived by whites as open spaces, even if unconsciously. Unlike bodies of color within the context of predominately white spaces, a white body is able to extend itself into spaces."[44] Like the father of the house sprawling out on the family room easy chair after a long day of work, in spaces where whiteness functions as the presumed norm, white bodies feel relaxed, at ease, familiar, at home. This ease grants white bodies permission to be comfortable—an ability to be themselves, without fear of scrutiny or of being singled out. Such ease also implicitly grants permission to white bodies an openness and expansiveness to fill that space, and especially for white males, an expectation to take up as much of that space as possible. Shannon Sullivan speaks similarly of what she calls "ontological expansiveness," where "white people tend to act and think as if all spaces—whether geographical, psychical, linguistic, economic, spiritual, bodily, or otherwise—are or should be available for them to move in and out of as they wish."[45] The ease and at-homeness whiteness affords provides a sense of entitlement and ownership—an assumed right to raid and colonize—an assumption that this space, this school, this religion, this tradition, this government building, this country is *mine*, that there is thus no space in which I don't have the right to roam, no word that I am not allowed to say. And conversely, people of color are perceived as anomalies—or worse, as unwelcome—in these spaces.

Julia desires to identify with the sea of white bodies due to the protection that such anonymity provides. This is clearly a different kind of anonymity than we observe in David's "blank mask." Whereas David's anonymity is a work of dehumanization—to not be seen is to be denied his human dignity—and reflects one who has already been rejected by the crowd, Julia's pursuit of anonymity is a coping strategy, reflecting a desire to be accepted and the safety that comes with fitting in with the They. David's anonymity reflects one who is not given permission to be at home in his own body, whereas Julia's anonymity affords her the permission not only to like her body but to expand it. David is rendered invisible by the visibility of his black skin; Julia seeks invisibility not only through her disassociation from her brother but by the camouflage of whiteness. Ironically, it's precisely through identification with the crowd that Julia is allowed to be her "own person"; it's precisely through being a part of a community that she can receive her subjectivity, precisely through following the crowd that she is granted her individuality.[46]

If it is not already obvious, the ease, familiarity, openness, entitlement, ownership, relief, and protection that are afforded to Julia by this sea of whiteness are all benefits of white privilege that are not offered to David. They are made available to Julia not because of any personal merit or willful choice she has made, but simply because she lives in a society that has presumed and codified whiteness as the norm. And in contrast, David is left constrained, obstructed, constricted, rendered suspicious.

Second, we can observe a number of racial habits that are at work in this scene which, I argue, can be understood on both the social and individual levels. When the students laugh at the act of violence toward David, when the white students conform to the patterns of the "sea of white bodies," when the white students repeatedly do not acknowledge David as he walks through the halls, or when the school community regularly accept racial stereotypes as the norm, these are not merely instinctual, knee-jerk responses, and nor are they behaviors having the mark of conceptual, theoretical reflection. Rather, they are learned practices that have become meaningful, embodied ways of being-in-the-world as a result of repetition and ritualization of the models they have at their disposal—their parents, relatives, bus drivers, teachers, religious leaders, and so on. As George Yancy maintains, racism in the white self involves taking up "racist practices," which are "habitual, somatically ingrained ways of whitely-being-in-the-world."[47] These racist habits reflect a prereflective unconscious, which "are long-standing and constitute historical racist sedimentation."[48] Because cultural practices are so powerful, because they are so easy to adopt and unthinkingly embody, whiteness becomes a meaningful yet unanalyzed lens by which we perceive the world and can take up with ease.

Thus, before Julia sets foot into Harrison, the rural high school has already been presumed as a *white* space where white cultural norms and ways of living are not only accepted but considered normative. The machinations of whiteness in Midwest America already predetermined that laughing at racist actions is socially acceptable. For decades, the silent anonymity of the sea of white bodies had provided white people with the impression that they are not complicit in racism because they do not perform any explicit acts of racist hate. Before Julia has been exposed to a context in which her participation in white supremacy can be questioned, and despite having a brother that is African-American, she has already been habituated into years of unconscious, unreflective patterns that perpetuate it.

Julia and David attended William Henry Harrison High School in 1985.

I started there in 1996.

I cannot recall any extensive, explicit acts of racism occurring while I was there—they probably did occur (I do recall subtle instances of Islamophobia and anti-Semitism), but I simply did not notice them since I was not the target—looking back I can see how I too was unconsciously habituated into a repertoire of racist practices, of racist liturgies, one might say. As Helen Ngo writes, "Racism finds expression not only in public discourse, overt acts of racial violence, hatred, or discrimination, but also and perhaps more potently in the subtle bodily gestures, reactions, and behaviors—not always explicitly intended—that are routinely enacted in response to an encounter with the racialized 'other.'"[49] Such subtle habits are all the more difficult to recognize and root out, all the more easy to deny and deflect, and all the more powerful because they provide a simplistic yet meaningful orientation to one's world.

What are some of the subtle messages—both by what was said and what was left unsaid—I heard that contributed to my white supremacist education? The school, named after President William Henry Harrison, is located only a few miles down the road, where, in November of 1811, Harrison led 1,000 soldiers through the Battle of Tippecanoe where he defeated Tenskwatawa ("the Prophet"), the brother of famed Shawnee leader Tecumseh. During my childhood, I hiked through the woods of the state park and gazed at the national monuments that now reside where the town of Prophetstown once stood and the Shawnee defended themselves against invading white men. I was taught to revere William Henry Harrison. Not until well into my 30s did I learn that there on that soil, Harrison's soldiers burned the Native American town of Prophetstown to the ground, that his soldiers scalped the bodies of the fallen Native American warriors, that they further proceeded to dig up the graves of the indigenous people to scalp them and mutilate their bodies, or that Harrison not only enslaved Black people but sought to expand slavery in the Indiana territories. Not once was I challenged to stop to think about my brother's blood that cries out to me from that ground.

The school's mascot is the Raiders. We commemorated ourselves, played sports, and rooted for Harrison's Raiders. Throughout the school, the symbolism of raiding, marauding, pillaging, attacking, and colonizing was normalized. As the school's "militia band" played at halftime at football games, they wore attire that was designed to look like the clothing worn by Harrison and his officers. Not once were we challenged to question this obvious reference to the murder and genocide of indigenous people, to the legacy of colonialism.[50]

The rural high school has an annual "bring your tractor to school" day, a seemingly innocuous event until one learns that 98 percent of all agricultural farm land in America is owned by white people, that, in fact, the five wealthiest white farmers in America own more farmland than all African-Americans combined,[51] that there were more Black farmers at the turn of the twentieth century than there are now in the twenty-first. Like the support for the Confederate Flag on the basis of some alleged white rebel heritage, in this context, the tractor functions as code or symbol for the preservation of a mythological construction of a white America.

While I attended, there were about 1,500 students, yet not a single staff member—not even a janitor—was a person of color. There were four Black students in my graduating class of 325 students. In all the years throughout elementary and middle school that I played baseball and basketball, in the years in high school I wrestled and ran cross-country, not once did I have a coach or even a teammate that was a person of color. I was that sea of white bodies. It never occurred to me to confront the racist undertones of the team mascot. It never occurred to me—even as we read *To Kill a Mockingbird* or *Huck Finn*—to consider the implicit structures of racism that surrounded me, for racism, I was taught, was something that was over, something we had solved by freeing slaves and passing Civil Rights legislation, something that a town in Indiana never had to address.

One more story: I love baseball, and I devour statistics and stories related to the sport. Even in middle school, I read biographies about Mickey Mantle, Gil Hodges, Ernie Banks, and even Negro Leagues legend Josh Gibson (I was a catcher myself). But a white supremacist education is being a Cubs fan my entire life and not learning until 2019 that the first Black player in Major League Baseball was not Jackie Robinson in 1947 but several players, including Moses Fleetwood Walker, who, in 1884, was forced out because Hall of Famer Cubs player Cap Anson refused to play against Black people.

The past shapes our present, and we carry the history of white supremacy in our bodies. The habits of whiteness[52] not only reflect a history I'm thrown into but offer a future horizon of possibilities. The history of white supremacy not only provides a context in which—unlike people of color—my citizenship, religious sincerity, or patriotism are not placed under suspicion, but it also provides me with the capacities and flexibility to freely express my national or religious identity in ways that are considered acceptable.

Because the sea of whiteness never felt physically and psychologically oppressive to me, I never stopped to imagine the feeling of alienation and suffocation the smattering of people of color in our school likely regularly felt. In sharp contrast, as a white male, the structures of whiteness (over)expanded my sense of futural possibilities. We often say that "representation matters," but representation does not matter only for people of color or marginalized groups. The *absence* of people of color and the prevalence of white bodies in places of prominence shape the collective consciousness of white people.

THE IMPLICATIONS OF EMBODIED PRACTICES OF WHITENESS

I end by again emphasizing the nature of embodied practices and habits and how they might be able to help bring about transformation regarding the issues of racism and implicit bias.

First, we must think of habit on a far more fundamental level. Before we cognizantly choose to take up habits—whether that is to exercise, meditate on a daily basis, attendly weekly religious services, or read certain kinds of books, we have already initiated a set of fundamental habits that inform our comportment toward others and the world. Speaking about the importance of religious practices and rituals, philosopher James K. A. Smith remarks that the human is not a "rational animal" as the entire Western philosophical tradition would have it, but rather, to be human is to be a "liturgical animal."[53] We do not *become* ritual-making or habitual beings; we already are. Our most basic movements and engagements with others—our interactions with others on the sidewalk, our speech and what we perceive qualifies as normal speech or standard English, what kinds of food we eat, how we comport ourselves on public transportation, where we live (or who we live by), and so on—already reflect habits and behaviors that are not only fundamental to our daily lives but also reflect deeply ingrained attitudes and assumptions about the world, about ourselves, and about other people that are regularly shaped by the construct of race. In this vein, much of the staying power of white supremacy, despite our explicit rejection of it, is precisely because of its capacity to function as a ritualized assumed norm, the default, continually running silently behind the scenes.

Second, what most fundamentally drives our beliefs and behaviors are often *not* conscious thoughts but are the stories and mythologies that we tell. And as white people, as James Baldwin put it, we are only "dimly or vividly aware that the history [we] have fed [our]selves is mainly a lie."[54] What motivates us, what shapes us, are not logical syllogisms, but myths, unconscious habits, and the models of others who we unwittingly imitate. We intuitively orient ourselves to the world through certain narratives and practices that largely function on the pretheoretical level. And contrary to the commonly held view that repetitious activities are rote, meaningless, and lifeless, the actions we regularly perform, the practices that we *inhabit* and that inhabit us, are often the *most* meaningful and significant behaviors precisely because we do not have to think about them. As Lakoff and Turner write, we assume "that those things in our cognition that are most alive and most active are those that are conscious. On the contrary, those that are most alive and most deeply entrenched, efficient, and powerful are those that are so automatic as to be unconscious and effortless."[55] What gives white supremacy its power is precisely its ubiquity, our failure to recognize its profound effect throughout all of American life.

Third, beliefs (whether about race, religion, or anything else) are not merely mentally known. They are not merely propositional, doctrinal, or epistemological, but are lived, incarnational and participatory. And thus, they are seemingly effortless to maintain or perform. Our practices or rituals are part and parcel of the beliefs we hold. We do not begin with theorizing about pure ideas and then develop a practice for how we live and move in the world; our theories already reflect a pattern of movement and perceiving the world that is already value laden and reveals an ethical comportment toward others. Hence, the more we live into a set of rituals and practices the more they shape our everyday comportment toward others and the world. Most significantly, this means that changing the racist behaviors and attitudes of a society will *not* happen by simply learning a fresh set of statistics about racial injustice in America, by taking a college course in Africana studies, by learning the results of an implicit association test, or by being told that implicit bias is bad at the end of an implicit bias workshop. As important as all of these things are, their value primarily remains on the level of theoretical reflection. Rather, change in implicit bias and racist dispositions will only come through changing our narrative of reality, changing our embodied practices, and changing the perceptual and social cues that continually shape our unconscious ways of being-in-the-world—that is to say, changing an entire cultural and social milieu that has been built to prop up white supremacy for roughly five hundred years.[56]

NOTES

1. Yancy, "White Crisis and the Value of Losing One's Way," 12.
2. Levinas, "Assimilation Today," 257.
3. Washington and Kelly, "Who's Responsible for This?" 2, 17.
4. Ibid., 17.
5. "We should not conclude that mimetic desire is bad in itself. If our desires were not mimetic, they would be forever fixed on predetermined objects. . . . Human beings could no more change their desire than cows their appetite for grass. Without mimetic desire there would be neither freedom nor humanity. Mimetic desire is intrinsically good" (Girard, *I See Satan Fall Like Lightning*, 15).
6. Meltzoff, "Born to Learn," figure 7, page 8.
7. For more on the sophistication of the neonate, see Bahler, *Childlike Peace in Merleau-Ponty and Levinas*, ch. 2.
8. Girard, *I See Satan Fall Like Lightning*, 92.
9. Decety and Meltzoff, "Empathy, Imitation, and the Social Brain," 61–63.
10. See Merleau-Ponty, "The Child's Relations with Others."
11. "The problem with formulating our hypotheses . . . when we are so young is that at that time in life our sample size for collecting data is quite small. We may interact with caregivers, a few siblings, and some relatives or neighbors—but not a very large sample. Nonetheless from this inadequate data base, we formulate *the most elementary, enduring, and far-reaching hypotheses of our lives*" (Wagner, *Nine Lenses on the World*, 68). Thanks to Kerry O'Donnell for pointing me to this quotation.
12. Meltzoff, "Born to Learn," 2.

13. Indeed, leading experts in artificial intelligence admit that AI will only advance if they take better stock of the implicit and tacit modes of learning that are essential to human development rather than the application of explicit, linear rules. The *majority* of how infants learn is tacitly "caught" rather than didactically taught. This was discussed at length at a lecture I attended at the Pittsburgh office of Google on February 21, 2018.

14. Girard, *I See Satan Fall Like Lightning,* 9. One should note that such mimetic desire is "intrinsically good" (ibid., 15).

15. "Some of us carry telephones in our cars, on our belts, or in our purses. They must be important objects to command so much attention" (Meltzoff, "Born to Learn," 6).

16. See for example, Jeffrey Kluger, "Your Baby Is a Racist—and Why You Can Live With That," *Time.* April 17, 2014. http://time.com/67092/baby-racists-survival-strategy. Or Molly Shea, "Your baby is a little bit racist, science says," *NY Post.* April 13, 2017. https://nypost.com/2017/04/13/your-baby-is-a-little-bit-racist-science-says/. For some of the more formal research on this subject, see Kang Lee in Craig, "Racial Bias Begins in Infancy" and Xiao et al., "Infants Rely More on Gaze Cues from Own-Race than Other-Race Adults." This study found that infants between 6–8 months of age were more likely to favor the social cues of adults, such as tracking the direction of their facial and eye movements, when they looked like themselves. However, this conclusion is deeply problematic given that infants cannot perceive themselves in a mirror until they are about a year old. Hence it seems more accurate to say that what is more likely happening here is that most children prefer receiving information from people that look like *their caregivers*, and most infants are born into environments lacking any racial diversity. A study with interracial families or transracial adoptive families would likely produce very different results.

17. As my friends have pointed out, there's a certain level of white privilege still functioning here in my capacity to transfer my son and place him into another school.

18. Yancy, *Black Skin, White Gazes,* 5. He continues: "This white self is prereflectively constituted through various racial and racist discursive regimes, the sedimentation of experience shapes perceptions of, and mediates embodied transactions with, the social world in ways that reinforce the social order of things as normative and stable" (223).

19. Bourdieu, *The Logic of Practice,* 81. Cf. 59, 60, 66, 68, 80–85. See also Smith, *Imagining the Kingdom,* 80, 81, 85.

20. Bourdieu "considers how social and cultural milieu profoundly shape our behavior, actions, and attitudes. Grounding his analysis is the proposition that habits are acquired and operative in a collective or group environment. For Bourdieu, our socialization entails acquiring and acting through a collectively intelligible *habitus*, and in fact, that we do so is the *condition* upon which social life is possible at all" (Ngo, *The Habits of Racism,* 10). Ngo goes on to stress that, on the whole, Bourdieu's account is only on the social level and is a deterministic, sedimented structure. However, Bourdieu himself is adamant that a *habitus* is "always both personal and political" and that despite such conditioning, our actions can "be spontaneous and improvised" (Bourdieu, *The Logic of Practice,* 81, 84). Similar to Merleau-Ponty, who I will discuss below, Bourdieu speaks of *habitus* as "a kind of compatibilism" between freedom and determinism (84).

21. Bourdieu, *The Logic of Practice,* 81.
22. Ibid., 81.
23. Ibid., 50.
24. Ibid., 79–80.
25. Smith, *Imagining the Kingdom,* 80.
26. "Practical sense is not an intellectual or mental processing of objective inputs; it is more a kind of adept immersion in an environment. . . . Practical sense is not that sort of knowledge; it is more a kind of proficiency, a mastery" (ibid., 85). "Practical sense, then, is a communal habitus that has been absorbed to such an extent that it now orients my perception of the world without me realizing it" (88).

27. Bourdieu, *The Logic of Practice*, 87.

28. Eastern Orthodox and Catholic religious practices around Easter provide especially illuminating examples, as these churches often perform liturgies or services where they literally reenact the last days of Jesus. Here, theology is clearly not rationalized or theorized but is embodied and lived.

29. Some literature contrasts Bourdieu versus Merleau-Ponty, as if Bourdieu is strictly concerned about collective practices that are merely passively taken up while Merleau-Ponty is strictly concerned about individual habits that are actively expressed (see Ngo, *The Habits of Racism*, 10–11). While there are certainly differences in their approaches, such a sharp bifurcation seems untenable as Bourdieu describes a *habitus* that "has a history that is both collective and individual" (Bourdieu, *The Logic of Practice*, 83) and Merleau-Ponty explicitly discusses not just individual behaviors but how my bodily comportment is shaped by a "cultural world" of artifacts and tools such as "villages, streets, churches, implements, a bell, a spoon, a pipe" (Merleau-Ponty, *Phenomenology of Perception*, 405).

30. Merleau-Ponty, *Phenomenology of Perception*, 159, 160.

31. Merleau-Ponty, *Child Psychology and Pedagogy*, 212. He also calls habit a "communion with the environment" (*Child Psychology and Pedagogy*, 140) and "an aptitude to invent a valuable solution to a situation" (ibid., 196).

32. Merleau-Ponty, *Phenomenology of Perception*, 166.

33. Ibid., 166–67.

34. Ibid., 169. See also 160, 166, 167.

35. Drawing on a quotation by Merleau-Ponty, Ngo writes, "That is, we accumulate habits and it is through these habits that we live in or inhabit the world, but at the same time, so to do these habits come to inhabit us" (ibid., 8).

36. Ngo, *The Habits of Racism*, 3.

37. Ibid., 4.

38. Coleman, *Making a Way out of No Way*, 103.

39. Scheeres, *Jesus Land*, 46–47.

40. Ibid., 49.

41. Ibid., 54, 55.

42. There are, for example, clearly parallels between this bus scene and the history of Black bodies being forced to the back of public transportation buses. There are the significant details that the white teen who commits the hate crime identifies himself with a Christian organization, not to mention his orange hair, which may connote that he is Irish—a group of people who were also similarly the subject of ethnic discrimination and at one point in America's history were not considered "white." Clearly, Scheeres also seeks to point out the rural dimensions of the source of the racist actions. There is also the clear trauma and subsequent coping mechanisms that David enacts in order to merely survive in this environment.

43. Yancy, Introduction to *Christology and Whiteness*, 2.

44. Ibid.

45. Sullivan, *Revealing Whiteness*, 10. For a helpful overview, see Ngo, *The Habits of Racism*, 80–82.

46. Bessel van der Kolk writes, "Our culture teaches us to focus on personal uniqueness, but at a deeper level we barely exist as individual organisms. Our brains are built to help us function as members of a tribe. We are part of that tribe even when we are by ourselves. . . . Most of our energy is devoted to connecting with others" (van der Kolk, *The Body Keeps the Score*, 78). Girard similarly grounds human freedom in the modeling others' behaviors (Girard, *I See Satan Fall Like Lightning*, 16, 17).

47. Yancy, *Black Skin, White Gazes*, 40.

48. Ibid., 224; see 223, 235.

49. Ngo, *The Habits of Racism*, 13.

50. In July 2020, I wrote a petition to rename my high school and its mascot. Despite receiving a significant amount of co-signatories, the opposition to it was immediate

and fierce. To read the petition, go to https://www.change.org/p/rename-w-h-harrison-high-school-remove-the-raider-mascot-in-greater-lafayette-in.

51. See Antonio Moore, "Who Owns Almost All America's Land? A USDA Report is Exposing a Massive Disparity Between White and Black Land Ownership in the United States," Inequality.org, February 15, 2016, https://inequality.org/research/owns-land/.

52. Here, I allude to Terrence MacMullan's *The Habits of Whiteness.*

53. Smith, *Imagining the Kingdom,* 12.

54. James Baldwin, "The White Man's Guilt" (1964). Quoted in Aanerud, "Humility and Whiteness," 103. Baldwin's thought here echoes Enrique Dussel's extensive work that has shown that the narrative undergirding the concept of "Europe" in modernity as an unbroken genealogy to Greek philosophy and continual process of advancing civilization is also effectively a myth. See Dussel, "Europe, Modernity, and Eurocentrism."

55. Lakoff and Turner, *More than Cool Reason,* 129.

56. As Father Richard Rohr writes (here thinking about religious practices), "We do not think ourselves into a new way of living; we live ourselves into a new way of thinking" (Rohr, *Everything Belongs,* 19).

BIBLIOGRAPHY

Aanerud, Rebecca. "Humility and Whiteness: How Did I Look without Seeing, Hear without Listening?" In *White Self-Criticality beyond Anti-Racism: How Does It Feel to Be a White Problem?* Edited by George Yancy, 101–14. Lanham, MD: Lexington Books, 2015.

Bahler, Brock. "Merleau-Ponty on Embodied Cognition: A Phenomenological Interpretation of Spinal Cord Epidural Stimulation and Paralysis." *Essays in Philosophy* 17, no. 2 (July 2016): 69–93.

Bourdieu, Pierre. *The Logic of Practice.* Translated by Richard Nice. Stanford: Stanford University Press, 1990.

Craig, Lindsey. "Racial Bias Begins in Infancy, New Insight on Cause." University of Ontario Institute for Studies of Education. April 11, 2017. Accessed at: http://www.oise.utoronto.ca/oise/News/racial_bias_begins_in_infancy_new_research_reveals.html.

Decety, Jean and Andrew N. Meltzoff. "Empathy, Imitation, and the Social Brain." In *Empathy: Philosophical and Psychological Perspectives.* Edited by Amy Coplan and Peter Goldie, 58–81. Oxford: Oxford University Press, 2011.

Dussel, Enrique. "Europe, Modernity, and Eurocentrism." *Nepantla: Views from the South* 1, no. 3 (2000): 465–78.

Girard, René. *I See Satan Fall Like Lightning.* Translated by James G. Williams Maryknoll, NY: Orbis, 2001.

Lakoff, George and Mark Turner. *More than Cool Reason: A Field Guide to Poetic Metaphor.* Chicago: The University of Chicago Press, 1989.

Levinas, Emmanuel. "Assimilation Today." *Difficult Freedom.* Translated by Seán Hand, 255–58. Baltimore: Johns Hopkins University Press, 1990.

Meltzoff, Andrew. "Born to Learn: What Infants Learn from Watching Us." Originally from Fox, N. and J. G. Worhol (eds.), *The Role of Early Experience in Infant Development.* Skillman, NJ: Pediatric Institute Publications, 1999. Accessed at http://ilabs.washington.edu/meltzoff/pdf/99Meltzoff_BornToLearn.pdf.

Merleau-Ponty, Maurice. *Child Psychology and Pedagogy: The Sorbonne Lectures, 1949–1952.* Evanston: Northwestern University Press, 2010.

———. "The Child's Relations with Others." In *The Primacy of Perception and Other Essays on Phenomenological Psychology, the Philosophy of Art, History and Politics.* Edited by James M. Edie. Translated by John Wild, 96–155. Evanston: Northwestern University Press, 1964.

———. *Phenomenology of Perception.* Translated by Colin Smith. London: Routledge, 2010.

Ngo, Helen. *The Habits of Racism: A Phenomenology of Racism and Racialized Embodiment.* Lanham, MD: Lexington Books, 2017.

Rohr, Richard. *Everything Belongs: The Gift of Contemplative Prayer.* New York: Crossroad Publishing Co., 2003.

Scheeres, Julia. *Jesus Land: A Memoir.* Berkeley: Counterpoint, 2005.

Smith, James K. A. *Imagining the Kingdom: How Worship Works.* Grand Rapids: Baker Academic, 2013.

Sullivan, Shannon. *Revealing Whiteness: The Unconscious Habits of Racial Privilege.* Bloomington: Indiana University Press, 2006.

van der Kolk, Bessel A. *The Body Keeps the Score: Brain, Mind, and Body in the Healing of Trauma.* New York: Viking, 2014.

Wagner, Jerome. *Nine Lenses on the World: The Enneagram Perspective.* Evanston: NineLens Press, 2010.

Washington, Natalia and Daniel Kelly, "Who's Responsible for This? Moral Responsibility, Externalism, and Knowledge about Implicit Bias." In *Implicit Bias and Philosophy Volume 2: Moral Responsibility, Structural Injustice, and Ethics.* Edited by Michael Brownstein and Jennifer Saul, 11–36. Oxford: Oxford University Press, 2016.

Xiao, Naiqi G., Rachel Wu, Paul C. Quinn, Shaoying Liu, Kristen S. Tummeltshammer, Natasha Z. Kirkham, Liezhong Ge, Olivier Pascalis, Kang Lee. "Infants Rely More on Gaze Cues from Own-Race Than Other-Race Adults for Learning Under Uncertainty." *Child Development* 89, no. 3 (May 2018): e229–e244.

Yancy, George. *Black Bodies, White Gazes: The Continuing Significance of Race.* 2nd Edition. Lanham, MD: Rowman & Littlefield, 2016.

———. "Introduction: Framing the Problem." In *Christology and Whiteness: What Would Jesus Do?* Edited by George Yancy, 1–13. New York: Routledge, 2013.

———. "Introduction: White Crisis and the Value of Losing One's Way." In *Exploring Race in Predominantly White Classrooms: Scholars of Color Reflect.* Edited by George Yancy and Maria del Guadalupe Davidson, 1–16. New York: Routledge, 2014.

EIGHT

Racialized Habitus in Criminal Immigration Defense Attorneys

Jessie K. Finch

The reality of structural racism, despite its far-reaching impact on our culture and ourselves, is all too often unnoticed by the majority of individuals, particularly among those of privileged groups. In his critical work *Racism without Racists: Color-Blind Racism and the Persistence of Racial Inequality in America*, Eduardo Bonilla-Silva explains that "whereas for most whites racism is prejudice, for most people of color racism is systemic or institutionalized."[1] Bonilla-Silva argues that "the new racism" that has developed in the post–Civil Rights era includes a color-blind, individually focused *mis*conception of racial reality in the United States, particularly for whites. As such, there is often a fundamental misunderstanding for whites that racism is, in fact, still deeply embedded and frequently reproduced in our most central societal systems and structures.

Nowhere is institutional racial inequality clearer than in the criminal justice system. Michelle Alexander's *The New Jim Crow: Mass Incarceration in the Age of Color-Blindness* documents the long history of racial caste systems and racial bribes in the United States, from slavery to mass incarceration. Her central argument is that "few Americans today recognize mass incarceration for what it is: a new caste system thinly veiled by the cloak of color-blindness."[2] While her argument specifically examines systemic racism against African-Americans in the criminal justice system, the institutional criminalization of dark skin extends to other racial/ethnic groups in the United States as well.

Growing literatures on "making immigrants into criminals,"[3] "crimmigration,"[4] and the "criminalization of immigration"[5] show the powerful structural interplay of race, immigration, law, and the criminal justice system, particularly for Latinx people. The militarization and criminalization of migration that has occurred in the past half century has been a clear indication that the institutions, laws, and policies that govern migration into the United States are part of a larger structurally racist society. In particular, Latinx people who have made up the growing share of immigrants into the United States in the past fifty years, have been subject to increased racialization, and thus, increased discrimination and criminalization in the United States immigration system.

Social scientists suggest that, in particular, Latinx people who may be more easily identifiable to outsiders based on darker skin or other phenotypic markers, as well as visible cultural and language distinctions, are more subject to identity ascription[6] and are thus becoming more racialized.[7] Given the ever-evolving social construction of racial groups, it is worth noting that "Hispanic Origin" is still primarily seen as an ethnic group for official purposes. For example, on the 2010 US Census, respondents were asked in Question 5, "Is this person of Hispanic, Latino, or Spanish origin?" and in Question 6, "What is this person's race?"[8] In response to these questions, then, 53 percent of people who identify as of Hispanic, Latino, or Spanish origin also identify racially as white.[9] However, the current literature on the racialization of Latinx people[10] also suggests that this group is more and more frequently subject to the same structural and systemic racism faced by other minority groups in the United States. This racialization of Latinx people and their subsequent permeation into structurally racist systems is also demonstrated by the increased criminalization of US immigration policy.

As such, the common—though often unrecognized—structural racism that is at play in society at large manifests both in the criminal justice system as well as in US immigration policies. In combining these areas, we see that the criminalization of immigration is just one more example of how minority groups are systemically and legally oppressed—in this case, Latinx people have been particularly targeted based on immigration and demographic trends.

But how do these broad, abstract, societal-level forces play out in individuals' embodied practices? In this essay, I argue that structural racism becomes habituated and, in turn, embodied through continued exposure to racialized institutional practices. Specifically, I explore the reinforced racialized habitus and resultant embodied practices of criminal defense attorneys who participate in a systemically racialized, criminal immigration proceeding called Operation Streamline. Through examining attorneys' own descriptions of how they "just got used to seeing 70 clients at a time in chains" (Barney,[11] non-Latino, CJA) as well as observing their embodied interactions with these migrant clients, I argue that structural racism in the US criminal immigration system not only perpetuates symbolic violence onto clients, it normalizes and rehabituates racism in attorneys. The racialized habitus and embodied practices of these attorneys, however, seems to differ among Latinx and non-Latinx attorneys who are involved in these proceedings.

CONNECTING THE STRUCTURAL AND EMBODIED: RACIALIZED HABITUS

In connecting macro- and micro-levels of racism, many scholars have suggested a socialized, cognitive disposition toward racism through a variety of means, from early definitions of stereotypes[12] to more expansive understandings of racial schemas.[13] Cognitively habituated racism—learned from broader structurally racist systems—is not a new concept, but the concept of racialized habitus is particularly useful in linking this micro-level, cognitive racial structuring to individuals' resultant racialized behaviors.

Bourdieu suggests, "The habitus . . . enables an intelligible and necessary relation to be established between practices and a situation, the meaning of which is produced by the habitus through categories of perception and appreciation that are themselves produced by an observable condition."[14] Zavisca and Sallaz, in their analysis of how Bourdieu's work has been interpreted by American sociologists, propose that understanding habitus as the connection between individuals and their structural reality is a tripart task:

> First as a disposition, habitus is less a set of conscious strategies and preferences than an embodied sense of the world and one's place within it—a tacit "feel for the game." Second, because it is internalized in individuals through early socialization in the family or primary group, habitus is durable (although never immutable). Third, habitus is transposable, in that people carry their dispositions with them as they enter new settings.[15]

As such, individuals' behaviors are habituated through early socialization, embodying in them certain modes of thought as well as behavioral tactics that play out in a variety of contexts.

Using a frame of racialized habitus in attempting to explain individuals' racialized practices, then, we must take into account the situations, or observable conditions, within which they are regularly placed and how they perceive and understand those situations based on their prior racial socialization. Racialized habitus can provide an understanding of individuals' cognitive structures—socialized through racial hierarchy in society—and then played out in their everyday practices. Perry argues:

> While Bourdieu's application of habitus centered primarily on class, more recently, race theorists have suggested that the structural and cultural conditions associated with an actor's location within the racialized social system of the United States also produce a habitus unique to different racial groups or a "racial habitus": a matrix of tastes, perceptions, and cognitive frameworks that are often unconscious (particularly for whites), and that regulate the racial practices of actors such that they tend to reproduce the very racial distinctions and inequalities that produced them.[16]

Racialized habitus has been discussed in a variety of contexts: residential and social segregation through a white habitus;[17] racial habitus durability after the end of South African Apartheid;[18] racial conflict and domination within interracial religious organizations through racialized habitus;[19] identity construction of Chinese-Canadian immigrant youth related to racial habitus;[20] and the role of racial habitus in creating color-blind ideologies in white children.[21] These diverse settings demonstrate that the idea of a racialized habitus can be pivotal in linking racialized behaviors to racialized modes of thinking in a variety of organizational fields.

Importantly, those of different racial/ethnic groups will be socialized differently, resulting in various racial habitus by race/ethnicity. While white habitus has been more frequently studied, different racialized habitus based on differential racial socialization has been less explored. Hagerman compares her study of white habitus development in children with other types of racial lessons learned by minority groups, such as African-American parents who "offer strategies for countering racism, building resilience, and fostering empowerment" to their African-American children.[22] Cui also suggests that "contemporary forms of racism are not only systemic and institutional but are also individual, in the sense that they perform as categorical differentiations, explanatory schema, and terms of reference that frame the thinking, doing, and being of not only the dominant white group but also racialized minorities themselves."[23] This suggests that minority groups will have a different racialized habitus that affects their behaviors differently. Given the differential socialization as well as social location of different racial/ethnic groups in larger societies' racial hierarchy, we can see why individuals of different racial groups come to have different "tacit feels for the game."

Additionally, these dispositions may be somewhat malleable beyond early socialization, adjusting along with changing experiences of the individual. Cui focuses on Chinese-Canadian immigrant youth and proposes that racialized habitus "functions as durable dispositions that have been structured by racism in the past and is continually structuring social agents' current and future racist practices."[24] As such, this continual structuring can link racial socialization in early life as well as embodied racialized behaviors later in life through different racial experiences in the past for different racial groups.

The development of racialized habitus goes beyond just early socialization. Using data from attorneys involved with criminal immigration court proceedings, I find that certain situations reinforce individuals' racialized habitus through prolonged exposure and the ultimate acceptance of systemically racialized contexts. That is, racialized habitus is not only developed early on in our society through embedded racism, but it is also supported and rehabituated through later continued contextual exposure to systemic racism.

I also find that different racial/ethnic groups exhibit different behavioral responses to the structurally racist experiences in which they are regularly involved. Thus, through extensive involvement in situations that uphold structural racism, the habitus of an individual can become further racialized, but this contact results in different embodied practices for different racial/ethnic groups, supporting the idea of distinct racialized habitus by each racial/ethnic group.

I support this argument with data from interviews with forty-five criminal defense attorneys who explain that a once shocking, racialized criminal immigration proceeding (Operation Streamline) has become mundane, a reinforcement of their racialized habitus that accepts systemic racism as normal. Given the internalized and somewhat unrecognized nature of racialized habitus, however, I also specifically look for the embodied practices that would confirm racialized habitus has been reinforced. I observe these embodied forms of racialized habitus through courtroom observations and attorneys' physical interactions with their migrant clients. I find that these embodiments are different between different racial/ethnic groups—specifically non-Latinx and Latinx criminal defense attorneys. Thus, while structural racism is reinforced through Operation Streamline, those of the minority racial/ethnic group may resist in small behavioral ways.

OPERATION STREAMLINE

Between April of 2013 and September of 2014, I observed 66 sessions of a criminal immigration program called Operation Streamline at the Tucson federal courthouse. I also interviewed forty-five criminal defense attorneys who participated in these proceedings either as Federal Public Defenders, appointed by the court, or as private Criminal Justice Act attorneys who voluntarily contracted with the court to represent defendants.

Operation Streamline began under the George W. Bush administration in 2005 in Del Rio, Texas, and quickly spread throughout Texas as well as to New Mexico and Arizona. In Tucson, it was officially known as the "Arizona Denial Prosecution Initiative" and began its trademark *en masse* prosecutions in 2008, with up to seventy defendants prosecuted in one proceeding. Interestingly, following heavy controversy (which continues to this day), the federal courthouse calendar lists the public court session only as "Special Proceedings Duty."

Operation Streamline is a joint venture between the Department of Homeland Security and the Department of Justice, whereby Federal Prosecutors are employed under the Department of Justice but are paid by Customs and Border Protection to specially work with Border Patrol officers. Approximately seventy defendants are brought to the Evo A. DeConcini US Courthouse each weekday for a "streamlined" criminal prosecution. In my eighteen months of observations, I personally saw over 4,200 women and mostly men convicted under United States Criminal Code, Title 8, Subsection 1325: Improper Entry by Alien (commonly called "illegal entry") and Subsection 1326: Reentry of Removed Aliens (commonly referred to as "illegal re-entry"). Though these criminal codes have been on the books since 1952, it was not until the advent of Operation Streamline in 2005 that they were systematically enforced.

Frequently challenged for its lack of due process, Operation Streamline combines what regularly includes three to five court appearances (initial appearance, preliminary hearing, detention hearing, change-of-plea proceeding, and sentencing) into one court appearance (lasting less than a half day) for not just a single defendant but for a large group of defendants (up to seventy people). This has made the procedure extremely controversial, with critics calling it "assembly-line justice,"[25] "an inferior standard of due process,"[26] and "a bastardization of the American legal system" (End Operation Streamline Coalition Activist, Fieldnotes August 25, 2014).

This "zero tolerance policy" starting with the Bush administration but continuing through Obama and Trump, has led to a surge in US prosecutions. For example, in 2012, immigration-related offenses—such as illegal entry or reentry after removal—accounted for 40.6 percent of all federal criminal cases in the United States—up from just 13.4 percent the previous decade in 2002.[27] In 2018, the percentage has risen up to 61 percent of all federal criminal cases.[28] Between 2000 and 2010, federal prosecutions for petty, immigration-related criminal misdemeanor offenses increased by over 330 percent.[29] Operation Streamline, thus, represents the most extreme institutionalization of the criminalizing of migrants in US history, with hundreds of thousands of migrants being prosecuted over its nearly fifteen-year lifespan.

While the institutionalization of criminalization is clear in this process, the racialization is more subtle. Jason Hannan, a federal public defender who worked in Operation Streamline for some time, was interviewed by Dan Rather and claimed, "To have to work in Operation Streamline is like being a puppet, it's not being a lawyer. You have two so-called criminal justice systems: you have Operation Streamline and you have the normal criminal justice system and it's separate and it's for Mexicans charged with illegal entry and it's certainly unequal."[30] Current legal challenges to Operation Streamline in San Diego also argue that Operation Streamline violates the Equal Protection Clause of the US Constitution.[31]

Indeed, while there is no nationality requirement for someone to be placed in Operation Streamline, there is a language requirement, as the proceedings are only translated in Spanish. As such, a very specific group of migrants are selected for Operation Streamline, primarily men from Mexico and Central American countries—Guatemala, Honduras, and El Salvador being most commonly represented in my observations in Tucson. Given the previously mentioned due process concerns as well as the specific Latinx population that almost exclusively is processed through Operation Streamline, there is no shortage of evidence to support the "separate and unequal" claim about this program and its exemplification of systemic racism both in US immigration policies and in the criminal justice system.

Though there is no explicit racial motivation stated in any material on Operation Streamline, as one attorney I interviewed explained it, "race covers the border" (Mickey, non-Latinx, CJA). Prior literature on race, law, and immigration has discussed the underlying systemic racism as it has both influenced and been influenced by racial hierarchy in the United States. Molina suggests that historical forces in the midcentury also created "immigration regimes" that have influenced the racial categorization of Mexicans in particular.[32] Other work has shown this is not specific to Mexicans, but also to other Latinx people such as Central Americans who are subject to increased racialization based on immigration polices rooted in white nativism.[33] This literature has even gone as far to suggest that the Illegal Immigration Reform and Immigration Responsibility Act of 1996 (IIRIRA), may as well have been called "The Latino Exclusion Act."[34] This allusion to the 1882 Chinese Exclusion Act highlights the racialized nature of this immigration policy's true aim as well as the historic underpinnings of racialized immigration law in general. IIRIRA also laid the groundwork for the mass criminalization of migrants that is seen in Operation Streamline,[35] linking the systemically racist immigration and criminal justice systems.

These racist subtexts, though not explicitly stated in many immigration laws themselves, can be further explained by looking at the lawmakers behind these acts. For example, the initial development of United States Criminal Code, Title 8, Subsection 1325: Improper Entry by Alien (commonly called "illegal entry") was started by Senator Coleman Livingstone Blease of South Carolina as far back as 1929.[36] A well-known white supremacist who endorsed lynching and favored segregation, Blease set up the legal defense for criminalizing migrants by highlighting unauthorized border crossings by Mexicans in particular. He then "became the broker of a compromise between nativists and a faction protective of business interests that required cheap labor."[37] As such, the initial criminal prosecution of migrants—and almost exclusively Mexican migrants at the time—was based on the same Jim Crow racial milieu of the 1920s that brought the 1924 Immigration Reform Act which included the Asian Exclusion Act, both of which were endorsed by the Ku Klux Klan. These racist subtexts continue to shape the debate around immigration today.

Indeed, some attorneys who I interviewed[38] understood the structurally racist aspects of Operation Streamline and called them out as problematic. Usually, this was second-generation Latinx attorneys who themselves had experienced racialization. In a prime example, Valentina explains:

> How can we say that this [OSL] isn't violative of the constitution when we are specifically impacting a specific population of foreign nationals? It may not be a violation of due process because there's a neutrality in the law, but in its application, it's illegal . . . it's an evolution of racism, but no one will call it racist, because on its face, the law is [gives air quotes] "race neutral." So, I mean, it's just disgusting. (Valentina, Latina, FPD)

This quote helps to support the idea of a differential racialized habitus for Latinx attorneys in particular. Nationally, throughout 2006–2010, only 4.2 percent of lawyers, judges, magistrates, and other judicial workers were categorized as Hispanic or Latino/a, while Arizona had a slightly higher rate at 6.6 percent.[39] The Tucson Metro Area has a 5.9 percent rate of Hispanic judicial workers.

Strikingly, for my attorney respondents involved in Operation Streamline, the breakdown was 64 percent Latinx. This suggests that a larger proportion of Latinx attorneys end up working in federal criminal defense generally and in Operation Streamline specifically. This overrepresentation of Latinx attorneys in OSL is partially because Latinx lawyers have fewer alternatives for legal work and they are perhaps thought to have a competitive advantage for Operation Streamline, given their potential cultural and language overlap with the migrant clients in Operation Streamline.

As such, observing Operation Streamline and interviewing the attorneys involved can help us to understand how institutionalized racism through these *en masse*, criminal immigration proceedings becomes habituated in the attorneys' practices and may allow us to discern if there are differences among various racial/ethnic groups.

HABITUATING ONESELF TO RACIALIZED STRUCTURES

Many attorneys had a lot of reservations about Operation Streamline when they first began participating in the program. Over time, these reservations were rationalized, justified, or otherwise neutralized by these attorneys in order to continue to participate. Certainly, my sample represents a selection bias, whereby people who did not become accustomed to the problems with Operation Streamline would have weeded themselves out by no longer participating as late as 2013, six years after the start of the program.

Nonetheless, in my interviews with attorneys who were still participating, it was very common (thirty-two out of forty-five) for attorneys, among those who identified as Latinx and non-Latinx alike, to suggest that they had immediate negative feelings about Operation Streamline when they first began that then became normalized throughout their continued participation.

In viewing this normalization through a lens of racialized habitus, then, we can see how Operation Streamline both supports and reinforces the racialized habitus of the attorneys involved. This aligns with Bonilla-Silva, Goar, and Embrick's conception of the white habitus as an "uninterrupted socialization process"[40] that not only occurs in early childhood but is continually evolving and may be reinforced in different social settings.

There is something deeply problematic, and yet deeply human, about the fact that after prolonged exposure to racist and dehumanizing processes, it becomes a new normal. Perhaps it was in order to cope with the stress of the Operation Streamline proceedings, but most attorneys described how they became habituated to the dehumanization they faced every week.

In my interviews, I particularly asked about attorneys' first experiences with Operation Streamline and a general theme of acceptance of a tragic reality was shared. For example,

> INTERVIEWER: How did you feel about Streamline when you first started seeing it, or when you first came?
>
> ANDREW: That's a good question because it—well, I don't have any sort of the same bad feelings the way I did when I first went and saw it. I think when you first go and see it, it's—I don't know it's, it's—shocking, you know? To see that many people chained up and looking dejected. I think, because I had worked in State Court—I don't know, for some reason they don't have the same quantity in the courtroom. They have, you know, groups of maybe five or six guys chained together at max, but they're in orange suits, and it's different when you see people in sort of civilian clothes, the clothes they've been in the desert in for days, and they're all chained up and—and they just don't look that great. They look like they need a shower and it's a little depressing.

> So, I'd say maybe the first few days, I think, were difficult mentally. And now it's just—it's same old, same old. It's totally different now and I mean, but I can still remember that impression that it left from the very beginning. Then, you know, that just left over time. Then that's not the impression that I get anymore. My focus has totally changed. Now it's more like, you know, I need to get the information from my clients and to my clients. I need to let them know what's going on. And then, and then, you know, we'll have time to chat a little bit about, you know, where are they going with their lives in the future? Because these doors [entering the United States] may be closing permanently for them and they may be realizing that with the amount of time that they're doing in jail. And then after they finish that time, it may become more of a reality, like this is not going to happen for me in the future, either. (Andrew, Latino, CJA)

Andrew explicitly describes how his understanding of Operation Streamline went from "shocking" to "same old, same old." This normalization of the proceedings leads to a strictly business separation of the emotional impact of the proceedings on him personally to a professional need to share information with the migrant clients about the real impact of this proceeding on their future opportunities. Because convictions in Operation Streamline leave migrants with a criminal record in the United States, their future prospects for entering the country legally are essentially nonexistent.

In another example of how Operation Streamline participation went from monstrous to monotonous, Jesús explains his resistance and eventual acceptance of the procedure, but with the caveat that he doesn't agree with the law overall:

> When Operation Streamline first came out, I was totally against it. I was totally against it because the information I had was information gleaned from 30 seconds of just looking in there and just seeing these poor brown people lined up, chained, dirty, sad. I didn't understand what it was they were doing, really.
>
> And I'll be the first one to tell you that, to somebody who is unfamiliar with that program and unfamiliar with court proceedings at all, like someone who has just seen courts on television and there's all the niceties about our rights and stuff. When you pile up nine guys before microphones to take guilty pleas all at once and the judge—and he does 70 people in one hour, it seems . . . it has the appearance of just being goddamned railroading.
>
> But, the fact of the matter is that you do have all morning to talk to them. And you can tell if there are going to be problems. It really isn't any different from the flip-flops, except for the fact you have increased numbers. After a while it's sort of boring, but these guys are going to go to prison anyway.
>
> I'm not lauding the immigration law that permits this sort of procedure—that criminalizes them all just coming in. I mean, I can under-

stand trying to keep out felons. But, you know, these guys just want to work. But what the better answer is? I don't know. The guys that are working on immigration reform better come up with a better answer, because this is not working. (Jesús, Latino, CJA)

Jesús is not the only attorney to link his own eventual acceptance of his work with Operation Streamline while still holding a disagreement with the law and policy that permits the program to exist. For example, Carlita explained that she didn't like the idea of Operation Streamline when it was proposed, but she realized, from an institutional perspective, these prosecutions were bound to become the norm:

> Yah, I was there from the very beginning when they first talked about the initiative they were going to begin, and I think we all were pretty concerned about the fact that they decided to prosecute the number they were going to prosecute this way. And now of course, with how long it's been in process, you know, that's just part of our legal reality, given that they've made this firm decision to prosecute them, we are just playing our part in the larger system. (Carlita, Latina, CJA)

Carlita's initial hesitations for participating in such a proceeding were assuaged by knowing this was not her individual choice, per se, but that she was merely part of a larger system. This demonstrates a reinforcement of a previously understood racial habitus that accepts structural racism as the norm.

In supporting this reinforcement of racialized habitus, there were many examples of attorneys expressing their work as mechanical through the use of "a cog in the machine"–style metaphor:

> Streamline is really just terribly sad and offensive. We're just a cog in this big machine of locking people up. (Soledad, Latina, CJA)

> Sometimes you go in there, or I go in there, thinking, "Okay, I'm here as a lawyer," but you don't feel like a lawyer. You kind of feel like a pawn for the government, you're just there for show. I mean they probably would have made the decision to take the plea on their own. It's a safeguard to ensure that it's not you know, they take this and they're really not a citizen and it's not just like someone said just sign here but that's pretty much it. Just a cog in the wheel. (Santana, Latina, CJA, emphasis added)

Valentina explains her own rationalization of the process, specifically calling in the idea of witnessing the problematic acts firsthand and doing as much as she can to help:

> My first reaction to doing Streamline was, "Not in a million fucking years. I will never go in there. I did not get my law degree to do this. No fucking way." That was my first reaction. And then I saw what was happening. And I saw how attorneys weren't taking the time, and I saw how people were not understanding, and I saw that because it was

so expedited, most of the attorneys devalued and diminished them as clients. And I felt like, "I have to do this. I have to. I mean even if it's one person, I have to do this."

More broadly, I think that we have an obligation to bear witness, because in 20 years, or 30 years, or who knows when, because now things take so little time, but when we go back and we look at Operation Streamline historically, I don't want to say, what happened? Because it'll be gone in memory. I don't know if this morning you were— if you listen to NPR but they were talking on Arizona Spotlight. They were talking about Mr. Hirabayashi who was interned at the Japanese internment camp here on the Catalina Mountains because he violated the curfew law. And I, like I said to the class, I don't see this as being any different.

When we have a world that is so interconnected by the economies of scale that we're going through, when we see how we treated other populations of people from other countries, with the connections getting so much smaller and distances being so insignificant now, I think we're going to look back and we're going to say, "Oh, my God, this is so shameful." And there was a professor from ASU that was talking on the radio this morning. Her name was, I think was Carolina Leon, who was talking about how this historically has happened in the United States. And I think it's something, like she said that wasn't the first time, and what's happening now is not going to be the last. And we need to document, and we need to do this. That's how I ended up doing Streamline. (Valentina, Latina, FPD)

Despite her continued distaste for the program, she does see her individual work with migrant clients as helpful to those individuals and she links her larger involvement in Operation Streamline to trying to keep the government accountable for their own poor behavior. Certainly, the allusion to Japanese internment camps speaks to the racialized and inequitable nature of Operation Streamline as she understands it, but she nonetheless finds a way to justify her continued participation.

Overall, then, many attorneys habituate the institutionally racist behavior of the system into their own understandings of their work. This adjustment represents the reinforcement of a racialized habitus that has come to accept the systemically racist and legally problematic proceeding as "normal." This is similar to how George Yancy speaks of white supremacy and anti-Black racism as a "transcendental norm."[41] Hence, the discourse surrounding criminality and immigration functions within a system in which white supremacy is normative, in which everyone who is not "white" is seen as a deviation from the norm. Cognitively, these attorneys come to understand that they are complicit in this system, but they fail to assign any moral implications to themselves by seeing their work as "just a cog in the machine" or seeing themselves as "pawns." They are but part of the structural racism they have been habituated to.

However, beyond their own cognitive justifications, they still come to embody the racism and dehumanization of their migrant clients.

In becoming normalized, participation in Operation Streamline then supports and reinforces an already developed racialized habitus of attorneys that supports their "tacit feel for the game." Given that structurally embedded racism is already aligned with their early racialized habitus, prolonged exposure to Operation Streamline or similarly dehumanizing and systemically racist settings thus makes embodied racialized practices, the result of racialized habitus, all the more observable.

EMBODIED RACIALIZED PRACTICES IN OPERATION STREAMLINE

The embodiment of racialized habitus by attorneys involved in Operation Streamline during court proceedings took several forms. In particular, the major conclusion came from seeing differences between Latinx and non-Latinx attorneys, suggesting a difference in racialized habitus despite a shared acceptance of Operation Streamline as normalized systemic racism. I argue that while both Latinx and non-Latinx attorneys habituated themselves to the structurally racist Operation Streamline court proceedings, their embodied practices differed, with Latinx attorneys showing less embodied racialized practices. This is likely a small form of resistance to the structural racism that Latinx attorneys themselves may be subjected to in different contexts.

In a set of fieldnotes from early January 2014 until May 2014, I began noting the physical interaction of attorneys with their migrant clients. Using a list of the attorneys assigned for the day, I would watch for any time the attorneys would make physical contact with a client and I would note the location and type of contact made. The different types of physical contact included all forms of meaningful touch, from shaking the client's hand, to removing their headset for them, to patting them on the back, to helping pull up a client's sagging pants to avoid tripping (as clients' belts had been taken from them in processing).

In a demonstration of racialized habitus embodied, these "tallies of touch" showed that non-Latinx attorneys were less likely to touch their migrant clients than Latinx attorneys. In contrast, specifically as they were being ushered out of the courtroom, Latinx attorneys were more likely to shake their clients' hands and provide some kind of physical comfort such as a hand on the back or shoulder or a light squeeze of the forearm. A total of 58 percent of Latinx attorneys (twenty-one out of observed thirty-six) who were observed more than once during this time regularly engaged in physical contact—which I defined as more than three tallies of touch in one courtroom session—with their clients. In contrast, only 37 percent (seven out of the observed nineteen) non-Latinx attorneys had more than three instances of touching a client in a given court proceeding.

While I collected these "tallies of touch" regularly for several months, not all attorneys were included in the tallies, specifically if they missed several of their regularly scheduled days. Additionally, I did not interview all of the attorneys who were included in the tallies. However, the overall pattern appears to be quite clear—nearly two-thirds of the Latinx attorneys (especially the women) regularly engaged in physical contact while only about one-third of the non-Latinx attorneys did so. This demonstrates a potential difference in the embodied behaviors of different racial/ethnic groups. When faced with the same habituated and structurally racist context, it is possible to interpret this data that Latinx attorneys embody a more physically compassionate reality for their migrant clients.

In addition to making tallies of physical contact in the early part of 2014, I also made tallies of attorneys' use of hand sanitizer in the courtroom. In the courtrooms I observed, alcohol-based antibacterial sanitizer was regularly made readily available on the many tables. The use of sanitizer is, of course, for hygienic purposes, but it may also be interpreted symbolically as "echoing a long history of anti-immigrant disease hysteria"[42] that views immigrants and migrants as "unclean," which is encoded in a much larger white supremacist narrative that depicts black and brown bodies as by nature impure, stained, and sinful. I argue this is another embodied, behavioral demonstration of different racialized habitus. I observed that non-Latinx attorneys, while less likely to make physical contact with migrant clients, were *more* likely to use the hand sanitizer after doing so. About 79 percent of non-Latinx attorneys (fifteen of nineteen) used sanitizer at any time while in the courtroom, while only about 64 percent (twenty-three of thirty-six) of Latinx attorneys did so.

Given the racial breakdown in touching and the use of hand sanitizer in Latinx versus non-Latinx attorneys, there certainly appears to be a contrast in racially differentiated embodied practices in the courtroom. That is, Latinx attorneys had markedly different client interactions in court proceedings, and thus, a notedly different racialized habitus from their non-Latinx counterparts. I argue that this is a form of resistance, whereby those Latinx attorneys who share the same racial/ethnic identity as their migrant clients, demonstrate a slightly more personable and considerate version of participation in Operation Streamline to their clients.

Interestingly, the difference in physical touch was also a gendered habit, potentially suggesting a gendered habitus as well as a racialized one. In interviews, female attorneys described their empathy for their migrant clients more often than males, but they also demonstrated it more clearly in courtroom interactions. For example, female attorneys were most likely to make physical contact with defendants. In revisiting my "tallies of touch" analysis, I found that female attorneys (64 percent) were more likely to engage in physical contact than male attorneys (38 percent), regardless of race, demonstrating extra attachment and sympathy for migrant clients as they hoped to comfort them through pats on the back or rubs of the shoulder, help them with taking off the translating headphones, or guide them with soft touches on the shoulder or back.

RACIALIZED HABITUS IN INDIVIDUALS AS INTERNALIZED FROM INSTITUTIONS

While Bourdieu most consistently discussed habitus as the structuring structure from early socialization with friends and family, I argue here that while a racialized habitus of the Operation Streamline attorneys previously existed, it was further normalized and habituated through consistent and long-term exposure *and participation in* racialized and dehumanizing court proceedings that represent the structural racism of the current trend in criminalizing migration. This is evidenced in the attorneys' initial distastes for the proceedings that eventually became less problematic for them over time.

Additionally, there were racial differences in the embodiment of this habituated racialized practice. Latinx attorneys consistently showed more physical empathy through touch and were less likely to use hand sanitizer than non-Latinx attorneys. As such, there seems to be a racialized habitus difference in embodied behaviors toward individual migrant clients. It seems likely that because the Latinx attorneys are themselves socially situated closer to their migrant clients, they behaviorally resist the structurally racist reality of Operation Streamline by trying to put a personalized "touch" on it for their clients.

For example, Bridget suggests her physical contact with her migrant clients is part of making the process more humane, even though she knows the larger migration system is flawed. In her description of her work she said,

> My personal motivation is, given that these clients are going to be prosecuted, processed this way through Streamline, you know, I try to do what I can to make it as humane a process as possible for them on an individual level. I try to make sure they are comfortable in the seat when we are talking. I always offer them a glass of water, I ask if they are feeling OK. And I always try to shake their hands when we are done, so they know I am sincere. Obviously, I know that doesn't address the real issue behind this, with the fact that the government has decided to prosecute them for crossing, and we're not going to back down from it anytime soon, apparently. (Bridget, Latina, CJA)

While a kind touch on the shoulder or a handshake may not have any practical effect on the migrant clients who go through Operation Streamline, these embodied behaviors do show a symbolic difference. As one attorney specifically spoke to the "bad optics" and the symbolic nature of the Operation Streamline proceedings:

> I think the optics of it are just so alarming. People see them come in and they see them and they're dirty and they're in chains and that sort of thing. It's all very symbolic of how we're treating them like just a number and not a person.
>
> I almost feel like, if in Border Patrol custody, they could give them a shower and like put them in orange jumpsuits, and then bring them to the court, like you know, there's just a symbolic aspect to that. . . . When people came in and saw them in orange jumpsuits and chains, they'd be less inclined to think, "Oh, these poor people who've just gotten dragged out of the desert." They'd think "Oh, they're in orange jumpsuits, like orange jumpsuit equals criminal." You know, they would automatically be, which is sad that they would automatically be less sympathetic to like an audience, you know.
>
> So, there's things that, you know, they could do to change the bad optics of it. And I think it would be a lot more humane to give them a shower and some time to, you know, compose themselves certainly. But there's a lot of it that's just sort of, you know, symbolic, that it has this name and the emphasis is on streamlining it and it just sounds not great for the, (laughs) I mean, for the justice system in general. (Emilio, Latino, CJA)

In recognizing the symbolic problems associated with Operation Streamline, Emilio attempts to at least suggest superficial adjustments to make it less shocking, though he acknowledges the inhuman process the clients are still facing. The immediate description of clients as "dirty" has implications linking back to the use of hand sanitizer in the courtroom and the racial stereotypes of the "uncleanliness" of brown and black bodies. Additionally, his suggested adjustment of using orange jumpsuits highlights systemic inequality, given that he would rather detained migrants be automatically perceived as criminals.

Emilio's attempts to correct the "bad optics" of the situation emphasize the ways in which a racialized habitus is unconscious. Emilio thinks that short of systemic reform, it is *more* meaningful that migrants instead be perceived as criminals on the symbolic level than it is to correct this system on a literal or explicit level. In other words, Emilio does not have to explicitly lay out to others that "orange jumpsuit equals criminal" or "migrants are dirty," for the very nature of a symbol (for Bourdieu) is that it is always already meaningful in the very participation with it, or in the reenactment of the ritual itself.[43]

The habituation of a structurally inhuman procedure, then, becomes embodied in the attorneys who regularly participate in it, but does so differently based on race. This was seen in the "tallies of touch" where there were racial differences in who would and who would not physically interact with migrant clients. The higher percentage of Latinx attorneys compared to non-Latinx attorneys who engage in physical contact suggests an embodied racialized practice differentiated by race. That is, given the likely different racial socialization in earlier years for Latinx and non-Latinx attorneys, we would expect Latinx attorneys to be more likely to make physical contact with migrant clients, despite the same habituation to the structurally racist court proceeding that is Operation Streamline.

The attorneys involved in this program had implicit racialized practices instilled in them not only through their early socialization and personal lives, but consistently through their professional practices. This then resulted in different embodiments of racialized habitus for Latinx and non-Latinx attorneys. It was through the institutionalization of racism in our criminal justice system, as well as in dealings with structurally racist immigration policy, that these instilled racialized habits of the attorneys in Operation Streamline became the new normal, and so it is to these same systems that we must turn for change.

If, as I have sought to show in this chapter, institutions habituate racism, how then can we dehabituate them? Presumably, given the nature of structural racism, institutional level change would be needed to deinstitutionalize and thus dehabituate racism in criminal immigration proceedings in particular. And certainly, beyond Operation Streamline, this dehabituation of racism could be more largely applied to deracializing our immigration policies as well as deracializing broader criminal justice efforts.

How would such change be possible? Systemically, there would need to be large-scale overhaul that decriminalized migrants and deracialized the criminal justice system. Imagine a court proceeding in the opposite symbolic context of Operation Streamline—perhaps redubbed Operation Personalized. Removed from criminal court and returned to civil proceedings, these individualized hearings would take into account the more nuanced and root causes of economic inequality that cause so many to migrate to the United States in the first place. Being able to hear each individual case and understand the larger systems of global inequality that drive immigration would help.

Beyond Operation Streamline proceedings in particular, imagine a criminal justice policy that actually treated individuals as humans, particularly individuals of color, so long dehumanized and targeted by America's criminal justice policies. Decriminalization of immigration as well, would be better achieved through policy-level changes that focus only on migrants with criminal records in contrast to the "zero-tolerance" policies such as Operation Streamline that criminalize a whole category of people. Broader social movements dealing with the humanitarian crisis at the Mexico-US border would do well to join forces with #BlackLivesMatter and other criminal justice reform groups in recognizing a shared goal of the decriminalization of dark skin. In order to disrupt the differential racialized habitus of individuals, such as the attorneys who participated in Operation Streamline, the broader racial hierarchy currently enshrined and upheld through racist immigration and criminal justice policies must be changed.

NOTES

1. Bonilla-Silva, *Racism without Racists*, 8.
2. Alexander, *The New Jim Crow*, 223.
3. Abrego et al., "Making Immigrants into Criminals."
4. García Hernández, *Crimmigration Law*; Stumpf, "The Crimmigration Crisis."
5. Morris, "Zero Tolerance"; Ewing, Martínez, and Rumbaut, *The Criminalization of Immigration in the United States*; Douglas and Sáenz, "The Criminalization of Immigrants & the Immigration-Industrial Complex."
6. Lee and Bean, "Reinventing the Color Line."
7. Frank, Akresh, and Lu, "Latino/a Immigrants and the U.S. Racial Order."
8. US Census Bureau. "Overview of Race and Hispanic Origin: 2010."
9. Ibid.
10. Bonilla-Silva "Rethinking Racism"; Itzigsohn and Dore-Cabral, "Competing Identities"; Omi and Winant, *Racial Formation in the United States*; Roth, *Race Migrations*; Cobas, Duany and Feagin, *How the United States Racializes Latinos*.
11. All interviewee's names have been changed to protect their confidentiality in line with the Institutional Review Board of the University of Arizona who approved this project in 2013.
12. Peffley, Hurwitz and Sniderman, "Racial Stereotypes," 31.
13. Roth, *Race Migrations*.
14. Bourdieu, *Distinction*, 101.
15. Zavisca and Sallaz, "Bourdieu in American Sociology," 25.
16. Perry, "Racial Habitus, Moral Conflict, and White Moral Hegemony," 90.
17. Bonilla-Silva, Goar, and Embrick, "When Whites Flock Together."
18. Sallaz, "Talking Race, Marketing Culture."
19. Perry, "Racial Habitus, Moral Conflict, and White Moral Hegemony within Interracial Evangelical Organizations."
20. Cui, "Capital, Distinction, and Racialized Habitus."
21. Hagerman, "Reproducing and Reworking Colorblind Racial Ideology."
22. Ibid., 60.
23. Cui, "Capital, Distinction, and Racialized Habitus," 1165.
24. Ibid.
25. Lydgate, "Assembly-Line Justice."
26. Grassroots Leadership, "Operation Streamline: Costs and Consequences."
27. US Attorney's Office, "Annual Statistical Report, Fiscal Year 2002"; "Annual Statistical Report, Fiscal Year 2012."
28. Transactional Records Access Clearinghouse, "Federal Prosecution Levels Remain at Historic Highs."
29. Lydgate, "Assembly-Line Justice."
30. Rather, "Dan Rather Reports: Operation Streamline."
31. Hartzler, "Appeal to the Ninth Circuit in U.S. v. Oscar Chavez-Diaz."
32. Molina, *How Race Is Made in America*.
33. Rodriguez and Menjívar, "Central American Immigrants and Racialization in a Post–Civil Rights Era."
34. Ibid., 195.
35. Abrego et al., "Making Immigrants into Criminals."
36. Stanley-Becker, "Who's Behind the Law Making Undocumented Immigrants Criminals?"

37. Ibid.
38. In the following statements from the attorneys I interviewed, the names of participants have been changed and kept anonymous.
39. US Census Bureau, "Detailed Census Occupation by Industry."
40. Bonilla-Silva, Goar, and Embrick, "When Whites Flock Together," 152.
41. Yancy, *Whitness and Christology*, 7.
42. Cohen, "Witnessing Racism in the American and Israeli Borderlands."
43. Bourdieu, *The Logic of Practice*, 69, 86, 96.

BIBLIOGRAPHY

Abrego, Leisy, Mat Coleman, Daniel Martínez, Cecilia Menjívar and Jeremy Slack. "Making Immigrants into Criminals: Legal Processes of Criminalization in the Post-IIRIRA Era." *Journal on Migration and Human Security*, 5, no. 3 (2017): 694–715.

Alexander, Michelle. *The New Jim Crow: Mass Incarceration in the Age of Color-Blindness*. New York: The New Press, 2012.

Bonilla-Silva, Eduardo. *Racism without Racists: Color-Blind Racism and the Persistence of Racial Inequality in America*. 4th Edition. Lanham, MD: Rowman & Littlefield, 2014.

———. "Rethinking Racism: Toward a Structural Interpretation." *American Sociological Review* 62, no. 3 (1997): 465–80.

Bonilla-Silva, Eduardo, Carla Goar, and David G. Embrick. "When Whites Flock Together: The Social Psychology of White Habitus." *Critical Sociology* 32, nos. 2–3 (2006): 229–53.

Bourdieu, Pierre. *Distinction: A Social Critique of the Judgement of Taste*. Cambridge, MA: Harvard University Press, 1984.

———. *The Logic of Practice*. Translated by Richard Nice. Stanford: Stanford University Press, 1990.

Cantú, Francisco. *The Line Becomes A River: Dispatches from the Border*. New York: Riverhead Books, 2018.

Cobas, José A., Jorge Duany and Joe R. Feagin. *How the United States Racializes Latinos: White Hegemony and Its Consequences*. Boulder: Paradigm Publishers, 2009.

Cohen, Dan. "From Nogales, Arizona to Ofer Prison: Witnessing Racism in the American and Israeli Borderlands." *Mondoweiss*. Retrieved March 21, 2015. Accessed at http://mondoweiss.net/2015/03/witnessing-american-borderlands.

Cui, Dan. "Capital, Distinction, and Racialized Habitus: Immigrant Youth in the Educational Field." *Journal of Youth Studies* 18, no. 9 (2015): 1154–69.

Douglas, Karen M. and Rogelio Sáenz. "The Criminalization of Immigrants & the Immigration-Industrial Complex." *Daedalus* 142, no. 3 (2013): 199–227.

Ewing, Walter, Daniel E. Martínez and Rubén G. Rumbaut. *The Criminalization of Immigration in the United States*. Washington: American Immigration Council, 2015.

Frank, Reanne, Ilana Redstone Akresh and Bo Lu. "Latino/a Immigrants and the U.S. Racial Order: How and Where Do They Fit In?" *American Sociological Review* 75, no. 3 (2010): 378–401.

García Hernández, Cesar Cuauhtemoc. *Crimmigration Law*. Chicago: American Bar Association, 2015.

Grassroots Leadership. "Operation Streamline: Costs and Consequences." Accessed at http://grassrootsleadership.org/sites/default/files/uploads/GRL_Sept2012_Reportfinal.Pdf.

Hagerman, Margaret A. "Reproducing and Reworking Colorblind Racial Ideology: Acknowledging Children's Agency in the White Habitus." *Sociology of Race and Ethnicity*, 2, no. 1 (2016): 58–71.

Hartzler, Kara. "Appeal to the Ninth Circuit in U.S. v. Oscar Chavez-Diaz." Accessed at https://www.voiceofsandiego.org/wp-content/uploads/2019/12/AOB-Chavez-FINAL-FILED-002.pdf.

Itzigsohn, Jose and Carlos Dore-Cabral. "Competing Identities? Race, Ethnicity and Panethnicity among Dominicans in the United States." *Sociological Forum* 15, no 2 (2000): 225–47.

Lee, Jennifer and Frank D. Bean. "Reinventing the Color Line: Immigration and America's New Racial/Ethnic Divide." Social Forces 86, no. 2 (2007): 561–86.

Lydgate, Joanna Jacobbi. "Assembly-Line Justice: A Review of Operation Streamline." Chief Justice Earl Warren Institute on Race, Ethnicity, and Diversity. University of California, Berkley Law School, 2010. Accessed at http://www.law.berkeley.edu/files/Operation_Streamline_Policy_Brief.pdf.

Molina, Natalia. *How Race Is Made in America: Immigration, Citizenship, and the Historical Power of Racial Scripts*. Los Angeles: University of California Press, 2014.

Morris, Helen. "Zero Tolerance: The Increasing Criminalization of Immigration Law." *Interpreter Releases* 74 (1997): 1317–26.

Omi, Michael and Howard Winant. *Racial Formation in the United States: From the 1960s to the 1990s*. New York: Routledge & Kegan Paul, 1986.

Peffley, Mark, Jon Hurwitz and Paul Sniderman. "Racial Stereotypes and Whites' Political Views of Blacks in the Context of Welfare and Crime." *American Journal of Political Science* 41, no. 1 (1997): 30–60.

Perry, Samuel. 2012. "Racial Habitus, Moral Conflict, and White Moral Hegemony Within Interracial Evangelical Organizations." *Qualitative Sociology* 35, no. 1: 89–108.

Rather, Dan. "Dan Rather Reports: Operation Streamline." CBS/AXS TV. May 14, 2013.

Rodriguez, Nestor P. and Cecilia Menjívar. "Central American Immigrants and Racialization in a Post–Civil Rights Era." In *How the United States Racializes Latinos: White Hegemony and Its consequences*. Edited by José A. Cobas, Jorge Duany and Joe R. Feagin, 183–99. Boulder: Paradigm Publishers, 2009.

Roth, Wendy D. *Race Migrations: Latino/as and the Cultural Transformation of Race*. Stanford: Stanford University Press, 2012.

Sallaz, Jeffrey J. "Talking Race, Marketing Culture: The Racial Habitus in and out of Apartheid." *Social Problems* 57, no. 2 (2010): 294–314.

Sallaz, Jeffrey J. and Jane Zavisca. "Bourdieu in American Sociology, 1980–2004." *Annual Review of Sociology*: 33, no. 1 (2007): 21–41.

Stanley-Becker, Isaac. "Who's Behind the Law Making Undocumented Immigrants Criminals? An 'Unrepentant White Supremacist.'" *Washington Post*. June 27, 2019. Accessed at https://www.washingtonpost.com/nation/2019/06/27/julian-castro-beto-orourke-section-immigration-illegal-coleman-livingstone-blease/.

Stumpf, Juliet. "The Crimmigration Crisis: Immigrants, Crime and Sovereign Power." *American University Law Review* 56, no. 2 (2006): 367–419.

Transactional Records Access Clearinghouse (TRAC). 2018. "Federal Prosecution Levels Remain at Historic Highs." Accessed at https://trac.syr.edu/tracreports/crim/540/.

US Attorneys' Office. "Annual Statistical Report, Fiscal Year 2002." Accessed at http://www.justice.gov/usao/reading_room/reports/asr2004/asr2004.pdf.

———. "Annual Statistical Report, Fiscal Year 2012." Accessed at http://www.justice.gov/usao/reading_room/reports/asr2012/12statrpt.pdf.

US Census Bureau. "EEO 10w K. Detailed Census Occupation by Industry (Services-Professional, Scientific 54, Management 55, and Administrative and Waste Management 56), Sex, and Race/Ethnicity for Worksite Geography, Total Population; Universe: Civilians employed at work 16 years and over; EEO Tabulation 2006-2010 (5-year ACS data)." *Tables for Geographic Regions: United States; Arizona; Tucson, AZ Metro Area*. Accessed at http://factfinder.census.gov/faces/tableservices/jsf/pages/productview.xhtml?pid=EEO_10_5YR_EEOALL10WK&prodType=table.

———. "Overview of Race and Hispanic Origin: 2010." *2010 Census Briefs*. Accessed at https://www.census.gov/prod/cen2010/briefs/c2010br-02.pdf.

Yancy, George. "Introduction: Framing the Problem." In *Christology and Whiteness: What Would Jesus Do?* Edited by George Yancy, 1–13. New York: Routledge, 2013.

NINE

Three Kinds of Racialized Disgust in Film

Dan Flory

In director John Ford's Western *The Searchers* (1956), there is a famous shot of the character Ethan Edwards (John Wayne) as he reacts to a white woman whose captivity by the Comanche has allegedly driven her insane. To emphasize its importance, Ford dollies up the camera to the Wayne character for a rare close-up and lingers on his face as he cycles through a series of troubled and troubling reactions. As philosopher Robert Pippin has argued, in making a point that I believe is not often appreciated, the Wayne character responds to this madwoman not simply in hatred—although that is definitely a component of his response—but rather with a complex mixture of emotions. Moreover, this character does not merely reflect his own affective confusion, but an analogous confusion on the part of many white audience members, both at the time of the film's original release as well as now. Pippin notes that Edwards shows not simply hatred toward this woman because he sees her as defiled by her intimate association with the Comanche, but also anger, sadness, self-hatred, and moral confusion.[1] I would further add that this shot portrays Edwards as seeing the woman as a powerfully disgusting but pitiable object of compassion. Through these confused feelings, and perhaps a touch of shame that seems to momentarily flash across Wayne's face, is raised the possibility that the complexity and contradictory nature of all these emotions might be worth contemplating. However, the Edwards character quickly brushes aside this possibility.

Because Ford has allowed the camera to linger on this character's face in order to register all of these complicated and conflicting emotions (and alludes to them repeatedly over the course of the movie), viewers are clearly meant to discern them. This shot thus reveals a number of dimensions pivotal to the film's narrative, and various discussions in the critical literature on *The Searchers* reflect the fact that the shot has successfully done its work. Essays such as Pippin's illustrate how this film evokes realizations in thoughtful viewers that American attitudes toward race are not simple, straightforward, and clear, but rather are exceedingly complex, inconsistent, and difficult to analyze. Furthermore, such essays underscore that the possibility for reflection about race that Ethan brushes aside needs to be taken seriously.[2]

The emotional complexity of this shot also raises important questions concerning race and the affect of disgust. For example, how are they related? How do they play themselves out generally in audience reactions to film? And how could we possibly change the racist reactions often generated so that people would no longer be enthralled by them? What I hope to discuss in this chapter are some conceptual tools that might begin to help us answer these questions.

Some arresting theorization concerning evolution and the philosophy of affect has recently argued that Western conceptions of race are in certain respects entangled with disgust.[3] In a different vein, other theorists have argued that disgust can be such a powerful reaction that it makes imagining itself difficult or impossible. As Noël Carroll observes, "Moral revulsion can . . . stop the imagination in its tracks."[4] In addition, provocations of disgust are frequently evident in movies, a point underscored by film theorist Carl Plantinga.[5] I will consider a cluster of concerns that these diverse theoretical claims raise by arguing that the cinematic intersection of race and disgust may be preliminarily categorized into three broad types. Over the course of this chapter, I will articulate these types and argue that they constitute a spectrum of reactions that, once formulated, can then permit us to begin devising strategies to counteract racist reactions to cinema. I will also offer some theoretical background concerning these categories, provide illustrations and reasons why such categories are not only useful but also need to be further studied and analyzed, and sketch how we might begin going about eliminating cinematic reactions toward race based in disgust—as well, perhaps, as how these reactions might be addressed in the real world.

DISGUST IN GENERAL

Researchers in psychology and the cognitive sciences are by no means in agreement concerning how to divide up the affect of disgust. As philosopher Daniel Kelly notes, "At present there is no single received view."[6] However, he argues that the best way to make sense of all the data on disgust that has accumulated over the last forty-plus years is to think of it as an "affect program" that is "complex and highly coordinated," "reflex-like," and is "often triggered automatically and [has] a quick onset and brief duration."[7] Its "core," Kelly continues, consists of various components and features that we typically identify as characteristic of disgust, such as "a sense of oral incorporation, a sense of offensiveness, and contamination sensitivity."[8] In addition, one "downstream effect" of this affect is an astonishing and powerful influence over evaluative judgments, especially moral judgments, which can persist even after the rational justifications for these assessments have been refuted.[9]

In his book *Yuck!* Kelly argues that disgust consists of the entanglement of two cognitive mechanisms provided through evolution, one being "an adaptive response to the ingestion of toxins and harmful substances," the other, "an adaptive response to the presence of disease and parasites."[10] Crucial to this characterization of entangled evolutionary mechanisms is "gene-culture coevolutionary theory" (GCC), which places "culture, biology, cultural evolution, and biological evolution all within a single overarching framework."[11] Rather than having a conception of evolution that is brutely biological, Kelly (like many other recent theorists of evolution) argues that "genetic information and cultural information can be seen as constituting two distinct *inheritance systems*" that have combined to shape human beings as they developed over enormous stretches of time and that have had an especially profound effect on "human psychology and cognitive architecture."[12] Our ways of thinking and reacting to the world, to put it bluntly, have been shaped collectively by culture and biology, which codetermine our interactions with the environment and function together to shape human responses.

Where these factors become relevant to the affect of disgust and the phenomenon of race is through the ways in which disgust became linked to what Kelly and others call "tribal instincts." He argues, "One result of our species' immersion in culture has been that humans are now innately disposed to see their social world in tribal terms and to react accordingly."[13] In other words, our sensitivity to "particular types of cultural information . . . that structure and facilitate living within the context of small-scale societies, groups that can be thought of as 'tribes'" came to be paramount in our evolutionary development, so this sensitivity co-opted "dedicated cognitive mechanisms" such as disgust that were already on hand in order to do the work.[14] Our "human *ultrasociality*," which is fundamentally governed by social norms, meant that the ability to pick up as quickly as possible on culturally transmitted information came to be heavily favored by GCC, and the disgust response, as an already available mechanism, was drafted into being one of the chief detection devices for this ability.[15]

The boundaries between tribes, according to Kelly, had enormous importance for humans because it demarcated those with whom one might readily and easily cooperate as well as coordinate, in contrast to those with whom one would have far greater difficulties.[16] Disgust was thus coopted into being a means through which social norms and boundaries were detected and enforced because it was quick, often effective, and could be readily detected by others. This cooptation in turn gave rise to various forms of sociomoral disgust. Such a development enabled disgust to become "the emotion recruited to fill" the roles of demarcating ethnic boundaries and ethnic actors, and thus, was "instrumental in shaping and sustaining ethnocentrism, xenophobia, and many forms of out-group biases and discrimination."[17] Much later, when the concept of race arose, disgust was therefore ready to hand as a dedicated detection mechanism for implementing and imposing this idea's limits and quickly became conscripted to demarcate where its boundaries lay. Evolutionarily speaking, race was merely another difference bounded by social norms that came to be sensed and prescribed by moral disgust. Kelly's speculative evolutionary theory thus explains how disgust came to be linked to race and places that connection at the forefront of how humans might respond to their social environment.

Five points need to be made about this excursus into Kelly's explanation articulating the relation between race and disgust. First, Kelly outlines a conception of disgust that in typical cases circumvents any need for what we usually think of as mental processes. Rather than requiring high-level, belief-based cogitation, no belief, intention, or other thoughtful cognition is required. Disgust is instead a direct affect that in most cases circumvents conscious mental operations and functions autonomically—it is "largely automatic and potentially unconscious," as he notes.[18] Second, for Kelly disgust is not a straightforward, simple type of response, but rather comprises a complex group of reactions that admit of no easy, essentialistic characterization. Moreover, this complexity applies not only to core-type disgust responses but also to moral ones. Third, his view of moral disgust in particular is that it is a "kludge"—"a clumsy, piecemeal, or inelegant" response on the part of humans to their environment that was gerrymandered together by GCC "to fix problems that were themselves unanticipated," so that human responses resulting from it often imperfectly and ham-handedly fit the circumstances to which they were conscripted.[19] Thus, moral disgust's link to race is contingent, ad hoc, and a deeply flawed development in humans that was partly the "by-product" of disgust's imperfect fit to the purposes into which it was originally coopted.[20] Nonetheless, in many other contexts moral disgust and its enforcement of social norms had overall evolutionary utility, which outweighed its drawbacks and allowed for its ongoing continuation and development, application as well as misapplication. Fourth, moral disgust is deeply embedded in automatized, embodied responses that are inculcated and enculturated into individuals through habit and habituation, as these latter elements will be among the prime "social learning mechanisms" that allow for the training and passing on of socially accepted disgust responses through culture.[21] As Kelly notes, "We are instinctual imitators," and one of the things humans inevitably imitate are the culturally transmitted habits of others, including, unfortunately, those involving race.[22] Fifth and finally, given the way he describes moral disgust Kelly would agree with Plantinga that this kind of response is "largely a matter of social construction" that may also have a "political dimension" and can be "used to maintain social hierarchies" as well as "demonize certain groups."[23] Such uses, Plantinga notes, could include marginalization, stigmatization, and even the justification of murder.[24] Clearly, then, Kelly believes that moral disgust is deeply flawed and untrustworthy. For these and other reasons, understanding the nature of moral disgust and its link to race in the way Kelly outlines offers us avenues for diagnosing how we might treat and remedy their connection, which will at least partly reside in possibilities for changing flawed, automatized, embodied responses, especially insofar as disgust amounts to a kind of racialized habit.

DISGUST AND PHILOSOPHY OF ART

Carolyn Korsmeyer's work carries disgust forward into aesthetics by examining how this affect operates in art. Analogous to Kelly and Plantinga, she argues that disgust is "built up from education and habit," but she also notes that if we are willing and able to reflect on our disgust responses and their artistic origins, we may come to grasp why some art so disturbs us and conceive of disgust's significance in meaningful new ways.[25] Her introduction of reflection into the experience of disgust is crucial, for it shows that disgust in art can also lead us to think differently about our responses of revulsion and perhaps even promote social and moral change, as long as we consider the source of our "disturbation" to be serious enough.[26] In this way Korsmeyer lays the foundation for what she calls "aesthetic disgust," which, as I will explain below, is applicable to certain movies insofar as they encourage reflections about race.

Like Kelly and Plantinga, Korsmeyer notes various continuities as well as differences between basic core disgust responses and their more complicated sibling, moral disgust. In general, she argues that the latter builds upon and extends the former into the social as well as the moral realm, offering us automatized shortcuts to sociomoral reaction. Thus her discussion in many ways parallels these other thinkers' theoretical commitments regarding the heterogeneous nature of disgust.[27] She likewise believes that moral disgust is often flawed and not trustworthy. However, most significantly, Korsmeyer develops a philosophical account of this affect that is designed to capture a variety of ways in which we can be disgusted by art, points to the very different nature of some disgust reactions, and distinguishes her account from more mainstream work, such as that by Tamar Gendler and Kendall Walton, who require higher-level cognitive functions to be at work in imagining or engaging art.[28] Instead, Korsmeyer theorizes that sometimes our imaginations may be engaged directly by art in ways that circumvent belief, thought, and other high-level cogitation, thus opening the way for disgust responses that do not (initially) require that we consciously ratiocinate about what our aesthetic response will be.

Plantinga's above-mentioned effort to apply disgust to the movies illustrates how this artform has developed a sophisticated repertory of techniques to elicit forms of visceral revulsion. In particular, Plantinga notes the need for "direct exposure" to the stimulus, and like Martha Nussbaum and many others (such as Kelly) he notes that disgust is "not a sympathetic emotion," but instead characteristically distances us from its object.[29] In addition, Plantinga's brief reference to Hollywood's Hays Code of self-imposed censorship from the 1930s in connection with disgust indicates how filmmakers recognized even then that alluding to this affect in connection with race would elicit strong white audience reactions of aversion.[30] Moreover, as Plantinga also argues and I will illustrate shortly, for some white viewers the imagining of certain nonwhite characters' appearances and actions can be fraught with fears of impurity and feelings of contamination. Having such responses will typically distance viewers from raced cinematic characters in ways that preclude sympathetic response, making it easier for these viewers to laugh at them, withhold compassion, or see violence and revenge wreaked upon them.[31]

THREE TYPES OF RACIALIZED DISGUST IN CINEMA

With this conceptual account of disgust as a backdrop, I will now outline three types of racialized disgust that we observe in movies. As I stated at the outset, the goal of articulating these types is to show that they seek to produce a variety of affective responses that, once acknowledged and understood, might allow us to imagine strategies to counteract racist reactions.

First Type: White Racialized Disgust

This form of disgust is the main variety through which such affective responses have been manifested for much of mainstream cinema's history. This type has dominated standard presentations of nonwhite characters for much of film's existence and continues to exert considerable influence on viewers. As a form of moral disgust that many whites have traditionally felt—at the idea of sharing drinking fountains and other forms of "race mixing," for example—it can be seen as having been manifested in perhaps its most extreme form in contemporary white moviegoers' reactions to the character Gus in *The Birth of a Nation* (1915). Consistent with widespread beliefs about race at the time, most white viewers were appalled and at times even sickened by this black character's lustful appetites for a young white girl.[32] Such an extreme form of white racialized disgust might be usefully termed "white supremacist racialized disgust,"[33] as it presumes zealous adherence to modes of white racial hierarchy and supremacy that were part and parcel of the early twentieth century's White Anglo-Saxon Protestant (WASP) sensibilities, which powerfully linked many forms of contact with nonwhiteness to disgust, but especially singles out certain forms of intimate contact as sites of aversion.

This form of disgust also helps us to understand the look that Ethan Edwards gives to the white woman captive in *The Searchers*. He is disgusted by her contaminated and defiled intimate association with the Comanche, and responds accordingly with a sense of aversion and repulsion toward her. Such responses were pervasive among whites for a long time in the U.S. and arguably underlay much of the institutionalization of segregation from the late nineteenth and into the twentieth centuries.[34] Thus, it seems reasonable to infer that whole generations of white people grew up and were enculturated into a society where adverse reactions to racial others were typically linked to automatized disgust responses.[35] Trained and habituated into many individuals were disgust reactions that encoded white supremacy into automatized, embodied reactions, well below the level of conscious thought.

Of course, not all forms of white racialized disgust were as extreme as those found in *The Birth of a Nation* or *The Searchers*. More muted forms of white racialized disgust were common in the form of reactions to disgusting "comic relief" provided, for example, by the antics of African-American actors Lincoln Perry ("Stepin Fetchit"), Willie Best ("Sleep n' Eat"), Mantan Moreland, and others before, during, and after Hollywood's "classic" period. On this point, one might consider the presumed contemporary audience reactions on the part of whites to such scenes as when Perry soaks his aching feet in the same tub of warm water that his wife is washing the family dishes in *David Harum* (1934), or to Moreland's nervously verbalized fear that cannibals might prefer "dark meat" when he and his white companions are captured in *Law of the Jungle* (1942).[36] Laughter and amused responses to such scenes evince milder forms of revulsion toward nonwhites and their behavior than did, say, the character Gus, and plausibly admit a kind of tolerance toward some forms of sensory contact. Nonetheless, these reactions remain rooted in white racialized disgust, as that is the source of their humor.[37]

As I have argued in greater detail elsewhere, it is also worth noting that the stock depiction of Native American characters in many Westerns was aimed at eliciting white racialized disgust and therefore a distinct lack of sympathy and readiness to see violence or revenge wreaked upon them.[38] In Howard Hawks's famous *Red River* (1948), for example, Native Americans enter into the narrative as screaming "savages" who communicate with each other by means of animal sounds and inexplicably ambush white settlers, attacking and burning wagons full of allegedly blameless pioneers looking for a better life. Native Americans also wantonly kill women, good cattle, and steal family jewelry, thereby flaunting additional white audience social norms. At the beginning of the film they are foreshadowed as a threatening, unseen presence, liable to mount unprovoked, vicious assaults at any moment. These violations of standard social norms held by most white audience members make Native American characters morally disgusting, as such acts demonize them, placing them outside the fully human and rendering them morally repellent. Later in the film Native Americans are also a source of disgusting humor, as when the Cherokee character Quo (Chief Yowlatchie) wins half-interest in Nadine Groot's (Walter Brennan) false teeth, which must then be passed back and forth in order for Groot to eat. When viewers see Native Americans shot or injured in the film's battle scenes, therefore, they are prepared to feel little or no compassion toward them, as well as a certain amount of satisfaction that they are receiving "appropriate" treatment by being hurt or killed. In general, white racialized disgust has been used in movie Westerns to limit viewer imaginings of Native American characters by placing them outside the realm of the fully human. Thus, when these films present unsympathetic narrative fates for them, those fates are much more palatable and in many cases even pleasurable for viewers.

An analogous case can be made for many black characters in film. Recently such depictions have become more symbolic and metaphorized, but it still seems fairly obvious, on reflection, that certain characters are coded as black so that they may be treated unsympathetically, and in many cases hurt or killed. For example, the fearsome Uruk-hai warriors that the wizard Saruman (Christopher Lee) conjures in the *Lord of the Rings* trilogy (2001–2003) are coded as black—in sharp contrast to the virtually all-white cast of humans, hobbits, elves, and dwarves. Not only is their skin literally black, but as film studies scholar Sean Redmond argues, the birth scene of the first Uruk-hai contains symbolic representations that racially code this creature: "Shot in close-up, his blazing nostrils, dreadlock hair and animalistic posturing directly recall the stereotype of the all-body/no-brain black buck of racist imagination."[39] Later, as Redmond notes, this Uruk-hai and his cohort adorn themselves with tribal paint and go out hunting for white man-flesh, alluding to cannibalism and other social violations.[40] Thus when viewers see these creatures hacked and slaughtered by the white heroes of the narrative, they feel no remorse. Rather, they feel that these creatures' bestial and not so subtly racialized nature calls for such treatment.[41]

Similar points about racialized black coding can be made regarding depictions of disgusting racialized humor. For example, the character Jar Jar Binks in *Star Wars: Episode I—The Phantom Menace* (1999), with his whipping tongue and bumbling ways, has been identified by critics from the *Wall Street Journal* to the *Nation* as a racist stereotype, a "Rastafarian Stepin Fetchit," to recall the former newspaper's description.[42] Black film studies scholar Ed Guerrero rightly places this character in the blackface minstrel category of the "coon."[43] There are also the characters Skids and Mudflap in *Transformers: Revenge of the Fallen* (2009). In spite of being robots, these two seem like twenty-first-century hip-hop versions of Amos 'n' Andy. As illiterate, jive-talking, gold-toothed autobots, they, too, illustrate how minstrelsy remains alive and well in the current era, as *New York Times* critic Manohla Dargis noted.[44]

Efforts to elicit reactions across the range of white racialized disgust have thus been common throughout the last century and continue into the current one. Some might wish to understand more recent occurrences of this phenomenon as merely unfortunate instances of what black film historian Donald Bogle describes as "throwbacks to the past."[45] However, I disagree that this way of categorizing these contemporary instances is accurate, for such reactions continue to manifest themselves much more regularly than that stance can satisfactorily accommodate. White racialized disgust can be detected, for example, in reactions to popular mainstream films such as *Avatar* (2009), *Machete* (2010), the 2012 release of the first *Hunger Games* films, and the 2015 release of *Star Wars: Episode VII—The Force Awakens* featuring British Nigerian actor John Boyega in a major role; moreover, similar arguments could be mounted regarding the recent remake of *Ghostbusters* (2016) with Leslie Jones and *Star Wars: Episode VIII—The Last Jedi* (2017) with Kelly Marie Tran.[46] The frequency of such reactions better supports the idea that white racialized disgust remains a depressingly familiar and enduring response on the part of many viewers and therefore something much more serious than merely an unfortunate throwback to the past.

Additional examples could be cataloged, but the point I hope to have conveyed here is that the presence of white racialized disgust in reaction to many nonwhite cinematic characters is not a thing of the past but continues to occur with jaw-dropping frequency. The phenomenon of white racialized disgust thus seems not to be a problem that is merely confined to the "bad old days" of open racism and white supremacy, but dogs us contemporaneously as well.

Second Type: Moral Disgust at Racism

By contrast, a second type of racialized disgust, moral disgust at racism, can be readily seen to be elicited by movies such as *Fruitvale Station* (2013), *Selma* (2014), or *Hidden Figures* (2016), where the filmmakers like

Ryan Coogler, Ava DuVernay, and Theodore Melfi have clearly aimed to provoke disgust at racist white characters. Yet moral disgust at racism has a far longer and more substantial history than many of us might think. It may surprise some readers that moral disgust at racism has been around almost as long as white racialized disgust. For example, it is evident in black filmmaker Oscar Micheaux's *Within Our Gates*, his 1920 response to *The Birth of a Nation*, which includes a sequence where an older white man lustfully pursues the young mixed-race heroine of the story, only to find after subduing her that she is his daughter from an earlier relationship. Through its allusion to incest, Michaeux's scenario is clearly meant to encourage viewer moral disgust at the sexual lust white men have often had for black women. *Within Our Gates* also encourages moral disgust at racialized lynching, which is here depicted as indiscriminately committed by the white community as a whole (including participation by women and children) against innocent men, women, and children as well as criminal suspects. Micheaux even underscores the moral disgust at racism that audiences are to feel through his intertitles. For example, one title card in this silent film notes that a woman being hunted by the lynch mob, "though a Negro, was a HUMAN BEING," an explicit reminder of her moral status as well as the fundamental immorality of lynching as a form of extrajudicial execution.

Of course, more mainstream Hollywood films have often explicitly rejected white racialized disgust as well. For example, from a historical perspective it is worth noting that expressing a moral disgust at racism became a part of Humphrey Bogart's star persona during the 1940s and was used consistently through the latter part of his movie career in order to motivate audiences to feel similarly. For example, in his World War II film *Sahara* (1943), when a captured Nazi pilot objects to being searched by a Sudanese soldier (Rex Ingram), the film urges viewers to side with the Bogart character, who dismisses the Nazi's concerns about being touched by an "inferior race" with a wisecrack to the effect that the black soldier's skin color won't come off on the German's pretty uniform. Through the Bogart character's righteous stance, we are encouraged to respond with approval to his rejection of this Nazi's white racialized disgust. During the previous year, audiences also heard Bogart's character Rick Blaine state that he doesn't "buy or sell human beings" in response to Signor Ferrari's (Sydney Greenstreet) offer to buy Sam (Dooley Wilson) in *Casablanca* (1942). Moments where Bogart's characters aimed to elicit moral disgust at racism also arise in *Key Largo* (1948), *Knock on Any Door* (1949), and *The Harder They Fall* (1956).

Encouraging this kind of response can also be found in a number of mid-twentieth-century social problem films, such as *Gentleman's Agreement* (1947), *Lost Boundaries* (1949), and *No Way Out* (1950); and there is a whole subclass of classic American films noirs that similarly evoke moments of moral disgust at racism, such as *Crossfire* (1947), *The Lawless*

(1950), and *The Killing* (1956). During the late 1960s and early 1970s, Hollywood began to more forcefully elicit this type of response through films like *Guess Who's Coming to Dinner* (1967), *Soldier Blue* (1970), and *Little Big Man* (1970). Blaxploitation films enjoyed a brief vogue at around this time as well and often encouraged audience disgust at the racist behavior of whites, as in *Sweet Sweetback's Baadasssss Song* (1971). Although we may now find fault with some of these earlier depictions of race due to our understanding of this concept having substantially evolved during the intervening decades, for their time these depictions were progressive advances that actively promoted fairer treatment of nonwhites by encouraging audiences to feel a moral disgust at white racist behavior. More recently, of course, filmmakers such as those mentioned above, Spike Lee, Jordan Peele, Boots Riley, and others have placed moral disgust toward racism at the forefront of their work.

With its aim to provoke viewers into negative responses to racism based on relatively conventional audience presumptions, this form of racialized disgust should not, upon reflection, seem especially rare or uncommon. However, to an extent it is limited as an affective reaction by its reliance on conventional default presumptions and predispositions. In general, because it is immediate, direct, and typically produces a straightforward negative response, moral disgust at racism does not ordinarily require viewers to go further than how they already normally think, feel, or act. While at times it can and has been employed to encourage audience members to expand their cognitive, affective, or action-tendency horizons, in most cases it does not require them to seriously rethink their presumptions, perceptions, or actions regarding race, but instead reaffirms their rejection of racist positions they already regard negatively or modestly extends them to a new case. To go significantly beyond this type of response, a different technique is needed.

Third Type: Aesthetic Disgust

This form of racialized disgust at film can encourage thoughtful reflection about race. While in some ways similar to moral disgust at racism, it differs in the sense that it aims to elicit a more deeply shocked response and induce viewers into thinking critically about race due to a more strongly core disgust reaction. In this sense aesthetic disgust is a distinct type of response that aims to upset and outrage moviegoers to the point of critically engaging in thoughtful reconsideration of elements linked to race, unlike moral disgust at racism, which relies primarily on conventional presumptions and therefore does not typically so strongly challenge viewers. By contrast, aesthetic disgust, when used in connection with race, typically aims to encourage thoughtful and extended critical reflection on the part of filmgoers by disturbing them to the point of making them think meditatively about their experience.

While by no means a foolproof method, aesthetic disgust linked to race in film can be seen as borrowing from a trend in recent avant-garde fine art in order to force audiences to think critically about their presumptions, perceptions, and predispositions.[47] Again, Korsmeyer generally develops this idea by analyzing how it can often disturb audiences sufficiently to provoke them into questioning the grounds for their aesthetic reactions. By exploiting the way that the "profoundly repulsive may also fascinate" and "rivet our attention," she argues that art can be put to positive moral and political uses by means of disrupting ordinary ways of thinking, upsetting and unsettling "comfortable attitudes and conceptual frameworks."[48] As such, art that is aesthetically disgusting can motivate audiences to become reflective. Through forcing repulsive experiences on cinemagoers, the use of racialized aesthetic disgust can thus aim to challenge as well as promote alterations in ordinary stances toward race by throwing into question the viewer's capacity to incorporate the disgusting images depicted. While at times difficult to accommodate, depictions of disgusting images in film can amount to opportunities to rethink and possibly overcome flawed default presumptions, attitudes, and action tendencies toward race, and thereby achieve more enlightened perspectives.

As I have argued elsewhere, this shift to a reflective metaresponse to art is precisely the response Steve McQueen aims to generate in *12 Years a Slave* (2013); that is, to not only disgust his audience at the racism of antebellum American slavery, but also to encourage them to reflect on how its brutality, excess, and gross injustice fit into their existing attitudes and conceptual frameworks.[49] McQueen exploits the qualities of aesthetic disgust in order to compel audience members to reflect on complaisant default conceptions, attitudes, and predispositions concerning race. This aim is why he lingers for far longer than narratively necessary over such shots as the main character, Solomon Northrup (Chiwetel Eijofor), hanging precariously by his neck after having been nearly lynched, or of Patsey's (Lupita Nyong'o) suppurating wounds from a brutal whipping. McQueen wants his viewers to be strongly and viscerally disgusted, but he does so in order to shock them into thinking critically about race in a way that mere moral disgust at racism typically fails to do.

Nor is McQueen the only film artist to take advantage of this potential reflective impetus motivated by racialized aesthetic disgust. Arguably writer/director Bill Gunn deploys it in *Ganja and Hess* (1973) to motivate viewer reflection by means of linking blood and vampirism to race, as does Spike Lee in his reinterpretation of Gunn's work, *Da Sweet Blood of Jesus* (2014). Cary Fukanaga does something similar by lingering over the appalling acts West African child soldiers are forced to perform in *Beasts of No Nation* (2015), encouraging viewers to reflect on the horror of youngsters committing war atrocities and how such actions might be possible in the wake of European colonialism and racial exploitation.

Another example worth mentioning in this context is Lee's *Bamboozled* (2000), which I would argue so overwhelms our sensibilities with the sounds and images of blackface minstrelsy that it elicits not only moral disgust at racism, but also encourages responses of reflective aesthetic disgust aimed at not only repelling us, but also at being disgusted with ourselves and the ways in which we often continue to respond positively (e.g., through laughter, pleasure, and amusement) to minstrel songs, routines, images, and jokes.[50]

A SUMMARY OF THE THREE TYPES

This three-part categorization of cinematic racialized disgust has been offered as a preliminary way to distinguish between its basic varieties. No doubt it will require subsequent revision, refinement, and supplementation. However, the reason that these different forms of racialized disgust seem worth explaining is that they hold out the prospect of telling us a great deal about our nonconscious affective attitudes toward race as well as film. Furthermore, not only have movies apparently elicited such affects over much of this art form's existence, but there continue to be underappreciated peculiarities in many filmgoers' resistances and refusals to imagine race. Those peculiarities further suggest that our understanding of the intersection between race, cinematic imagining, and forms of embodied cognition such as disgust remains inadequate and in need of greater exploration. However, through these categories, even as currently formulated, I would argue that we can gain a better sense of not only why imagining race was, but also remains, such a persistent and perplexing phenomenon. The reason is that these categories allow us to better understand many commonplace cinematic responses.

In general, for example, it is important to understand how disgust, race, and cinematic character intersect in the ways outlined above because they can reveal in greater detail how a viewer's habituated, embodied responses to the perceived race of a character are configured. A whole raft of automatized default attitudes, preconceived appraisals, and action dispositions that accompany the perception of race and manifest themselves through embodied reactions to film become clearer. In terms of default presumptions, for instance, people begin with a bundle of preliminary values, dispositions, assessments, and ideas affectively encoded into our bodies by repetition and cultural practice regarding what another person's character will be like, which in many individuals will be partly dependent on what race they perceive an individual to be, which in turn heavily determines one's reaction. Of course, these values, predispositions, and so on may vary greatly from individual to individual, but the point here is an old one that art historian E. H. Gombrich made decades ago, applied to race, namely that "the innocent eye is a myth," and that this absence of innocence extends to the perception of racialized cinematic narrative figures.[51] As subjects enculturated into the modern, Westernized world we enter into movie watching with a full complement of racialized presumptions, culturally molded cognitive/affective mechanisms, and action tendencies regarding the figures we might encounter, and those racialized presumptions, mechanisms, and tendencies get played out in the noninnocent embodied reactions we have to movies and especially the characters we see in them.

This new twist on an old Gombrichian point, then, presumes that some of our lack of innocence is embodied as well as raced—that is, some of our default values, presumptions, action tendencies, and so on are ingrained into their bodies as acquired habits and action dispositions that partly guide our imaginings of cinematic characters. Typically, those imaginings will possess a racialized dimension, as our training and enculturation lead us to expect. This aspect of our imaginings being partly body based and rooted in habit has a profound impact on how we understand aesthetic responses to race in film. For example, just as many whites unconsciously tense up when riding alone in an elevator with a black man or woman, so will they respond in similar physiological ways to racialized images onscreen.[52] The sorts of reactions involving race that we have in our day-to-day lives often carry over into our aesthetic appreciation and appraisal of movie characters, and vice versa. Thus, when disgust is elicited by the movies, such reactions immediately and automatically generate approval, disapproval, or occasionally reflection, depending on the type of disgust evoked and the subsequent audience response that is triggered. These insights, based on the taxonomy offered above, mean that disgust is a lot more complicated than many of us had previously thought, and that our embodied habits are profoundly implicated in the creation, maintenance, and possible alteration of attitudes concerning race. Such an insight presents us with a number of useful potential avenues for coming to better terms with our affective reactions to race in film—and in our everyday lives.

TRAINING OURSELVES OUT OF BAD RACIAL CINEMATIC HABITS

In this final section I briefly sketch how the understanding of race and disgust proposed here might prove helpful in the fight against racism. One way in which it would be useful, of course, would be in how it helps us to recognize and understand various ways in which race and disgust arise in film. For example, recognizing white racialized disgust, in spite of a viewer's denial of being racist and perhaps even having some commitment to ideals such as equality and justice, would be facilitated by the insight that one may be racist in their embodied affective reactions, in spite of conscious, rationalistic allegiances to ideals and beliefs to the contrary. Some evaluative moral assessments based on disgust survive the refutation of their justifications, as Kelly notes, so the application of this observation to film viewing should be relatively straightforward, allowing us to see that assessments based on race and their rational justification may be detached.[53]

The types of racialized disgust outlined here also allow for the circumvention of problematic theoretical presumptions such as those required by psychoanalytic theories. The contentious Freudian idea of the "unconscious," for instance, a relic of thoroughly discredited, nineteenth-century philosophy of mind, may be left to one side and replaced with a more acceptable and benign sense of what is not conscious. Similarly, commitment to the implausible Lacanian "mirror stage" could be avoided. Such insights would greatly benefit dominant film theory as it is currently used and taught.

Another benefit of this categorization would be the way in which we might come to recognize cinematic techniques for influencing or changing moral stances toward race by modulating and modifying moral disgust responses. Noël Carroll has recently outlined how such moral change is possible through a technique that redirects audience emotional responses in more positive directions. By associating characters who are objects of disgust with more positively regarded objects, ideas, or scenarios, audience imaginings might be recalibrated to consider objects of disgust more favorably. Through outweighing a negative bias "with an even more firmly entrenched [positive] one," filmmakers could redirect viewers to think and feel differently about characters they had previously perceived as disgusting.[54]

Carroll's argument fits well with the above described taxonomy. As he notes, the technique he describes is rooted in "preexisting moral commitments," namely "norms of communal order" such as respect for the integrity of good, loving families and the desire to eliminate unjust conditions that tear them apart.[55] Thus, what he outlines could readily be used to counteract forms of white racialized disgust by redirecting viewers' affective responses in more positive directions, namely toward a moral disgust at racism. Carroll describes how Harriet Beecher Stowe's novel *Uncle Tom's Cabin* (1852) and its pre–Civil War theatrical presentations did just that by virtue of associating black slaves with being loving family members whose lives are torn apart by slave auctions. As Carroll observes, "Stowe takes every opportunity to stress how genuine the family love is among the slaves," which marshals "the pro-family sentiment of the reader in such a way that the sundering of families, which Stowe represents as one of the primary features of slavery, erupts into not only sympathy for the slaves but indignation about their treatment."[56] Thus "the slaves are recalibrated under the image of the good family" and "approval and alignment with the slave family is supported by the audience's preexisting moral commitments to the value of the [good] family unit."⁵⁷ This recalibration fits readily into how white racialized disgust might be transformed into moral disgust at racism. It also clearly applies to not only literature and theater but also film—and this application is clearly Carroll's intention. In his essay he applies this explanation to the 1993 movie *Philadelphia* and argues that such recalibrations are more broadly generalizable. I have extended his theory of moral change in order to analyze *Moonlight* (2016), and would add that it is analogously an element of many films mentioned above, such as *Sahara* and *Guess Who's Coming to Dinner*.⁵⁸

The three categories proposed above also connect to the vast literature on disgust, embodied cognition, implicit bias, antibias training, habit, imaginative resistance, and a variety of other topics, thereby making a whole matrix of adjunct theorizing available for the purposes of devising additional strategies to counteract racism. For example, Michael Brownstein argues in his book *The Implicit Mind*, "It is by treating our implicit attitudes as if they were habits—packages of thought, feeling, and behavior—that we can make them better."⁵⁹ By realizing that white racialized disgust is akin to implicit racial attitudes and therefore that it, too, might be treated as if it were a habit, we might find additional strategies to change it, such as "nudging," managing context and goals, the importance of internal motivations for changing one's habits, and other aspects of debiasing.⁶⁰

I would also note in passing that aesthetic disgust in particular allows us to better analyze complicated cinematic works that contain racist as well as antiracist elements, such as *The Searchers*, as well as offering us a better perspective from which to understand works that clearly use aesthetic disgust to generate reflections about race, such as *12 Years a Slave*, *Bamboozled*, and other movies mentioned above.⁶¹

In the foregoing essay I have outlined a taxonomy for cinematic racialized disgust, indicated its applicability regarding various films, and suggested some additional benefits that it might offer. However, by no means do I believe that this chapter has been exhaustive: much more remains to be done regarding these ideas, their refinement, and their use. But my hope is that with this first stab at outlining various forms of racialized disgust in film, further research, development, application, and discussion will be produced. Only in these ways might we better understand racism in art and thereby formulate improved strategies against it, as well as coming to better terms regarding how it operates in our everyday lives.

NOTES

1. Pippin, "What Is a Western?" 236. In slight disagreement with Pippin I reject the claim that Ethan's look in this close-up is "almost completely ambiguous" (236). Rather, as I will argue, it is extremely complex.

2. See Pippin, "What Is a Western?" 236–46, which in many ways is structured around an analysis of this shot. For other analyses of Ethan's look, see Wilson, *Narration in Light*, 47–48; Roth, "'Yes, My Darling Daughter,'" 69; Pye, "Double Vision,"233; Eckstein, "Darkening Ethan," 11–12.
3. See Boyd and Richerson, *The Origin and Evolution of Cultures*, 99–131; Kelly, *Yuck!*, 101–36.
4. Carroll, *Humour*, 113.
5. Plantinga, "Disgusted at the Movies" and *Moving Viewers*, 203–17.
6. Kelly, *Yuck!*, 12.
7. Ibid., 15.
8. Ibid., 17.
9. Ibid., 23–24.
10. Ibid., 45.
11. Ibid., 103.
12. Ibid., *Yuck!*, 103, 106. Other theorists who have argued similarly include Boyd and Richerson, *The Origin and Evolution of Cultures*.
13. Kelly, *Yuck!*, 103.
14. Ibid., 106, 107.
15. Ibid., *Yuck!*, 107.
16. Ibid., 107.
17. Ibid., 124.
18. Ibid., 5.
19. Kelly, "Moral Disgust and the Tribal Instincts Hypothesis," 509, 513, 517n4.
20. Kelly, *Yuck!*, 133.
21. Ibid., 38, 78–86, 104–5.
22. Ibid., 82.
23. Plantinga, *Moving Viewers*, 207, 206, 207.
24. Ibid., 207.
25. Korsmeyer, *Savoring Disgust*, 6, 37–38, 52.
26. Ibid., 90. Korsmeyer borrows the idea of "disturbation" from Danto, "Art and Disturbation."
27. Kelly, *Yuck!* 6–7; Korsmeyer, *Savoring Disgust*, 31–35.
28. See Gendler, "Imaginative Resistance Revisited" and Walton, "On the (So-called) Puzzle of Imaginative Resistance."
29. Plantinga, *Moving Viewers*, 210; Nussbaum, *Hiding from Humanity*, 71–171. Kelly, for example, notes how disgust can cause an individual to be "dehumanized" and "not even be cognized as a *person*" (*Yuck!*, 125).
30. Plantinga, *Moving Viewers*, 208. The "Hays Code" was the informal name for the Motion Picture Production Code, which the U.S. film industry formulated in order to avoid state and federally imposed censorship. It was adopted in 1930, strictly enforced after May 1934, and guided Hollywood filmmaking (albeit, in less and less effective ways) until its abandonment in 1968.
31. Ibid., 207, 210–13.
32. See, for example, the contemporary reviews reprinted in Lang, *The Birth of a Nation*, 176, 178, 179, 184.
33. Thanks to Rebecca Giordano for suggesting this term to me.
34. For example, Stephen Jay Gould notes how famous nineteenth-century naturalist Louis Agassiz had a "pronounced visceral revulsion" to being in close proximity with blacks and considered racial intermarriage a "sin," "repugnant," and "a perversion of every natural sentiment" (Gould, *The Mismeasure of Man*, 76, 80). Agassiz also vehemently argued for segregation and institutionalized social inequality (ibid., 80–82). George Yancy has more recently explored relations between disgust and race, linking it to Fanon's famous description of the lived experience of being black (Yancy, *Look, a White!*, 28–50; Yancy, *Black Bodies, White Gazes*, 7–8, 30, 67, 243–62). Finally, Fanon himself speaks of the "revulsion" and nausea that many whites feel at close proximity with Blackness and points to its influence on South African *apartheid* and the

ways in which disgust-based reactions had an impact on colonialism (Fanon, *Black Skin, White Masks*, 68, 133–62, 178).

35. See Gould, *The Mismeasure of Man*, 80–82. For additional historical examples that link disgust with race, see Gossett, *Race*, 60, 100, 188, 221; Hannaford, *Race*, 217; Saxton, *The Rise and Fall of the White Republic*, 88–89; and Lott, *Love and Theft*, 98,145–50. For ways in which racist habits may be passed on generationally, see Shannon Sullivan, *Good White People*, 85–115.

36. For more on these actors and the sorts of reactions they encouraged, see Bogle, *Toms, Coons, Mulattoes, Mammies, and Bucks*, 41–42, 71–75.

37. See also Carroll, *Humour*, 112–13. (Of course, as Carroll's remarks reveal, our reactions can be quite complicated.)

38. See Flory, "Racialized Disgust and Character in Film."

39. Redmond, "The Whiteness of the *Rings*," 97.

40. Ibid., 97.

41. I should note in passing that the racial codifications in these films are by no means exhausted by the points just described. See Redmond, "The Whiteness of the *Rings*" for further analysis.

42. Morgenstern, "Our Inner Child Meets Young Darth Vader"; Williams, "Racial Ventriloquism."

43. Guerrero, "*Bamboozled*," 113.

44. Dargis, "Invasion of the Robot Toys, Redux."

45. Bogle, *Toms, Coons, Mulattoes, Mammies, and Bucks*, 429–31.

46. For specific references and analyses of these white racialized disgust reactions, see Flory, "Race and Imaginative Resistance in James Cameron's *Avatar*"; Flory, "Imaginative Resistance and the White Gaze in *Machete* and *The Help*"; Flory, "Racialized Disgust and Character in Film"; Rogers, "Leslie Jones, Star of *Ghostbusters*, Becomes a Target of Online Trolls"; and Tran, "I Won't Be Marginalized by Online Harassment."

47. Regarding this link between avant-garde art and film, see Flory, "Imaginative Resistance, Racialized Disgust, and *12 Years A Slave*," 86–89.

48. Korsmeyer, *Savoring Disgust*, 37, 96–97, 120.

49. See Flory, "Imaginative Resistance, Racialized Disgust, and *12 Years A Slave*." For a deeper sense of how bad antebellum American slavery really was, see Baptist, *The Half Has Never Been Told*.

50. I touch on these issues in more depth (but still rather superficially) in Flory, "*Bamboozled*: Philosophy through Blackface."

51. E. H. Gombrich, *Art and Illusion*, 298.

52. See also Yancy, *Black Bodies, White Gazes*, 17–49, 243–59.

53. Kelly, *Yuck!*, 24–26.

54. Carroll, "Moral Change," 54.

55. Ibid., 49, 50.

56. Ibid., 48, 49.

57. Ibid., 49.

58. See ibid., 51–55; Flory, "*Moonlight, Film Noir*, and Melodrama."

59. Brownstein, *The Implicit Mind*, 205.

60. See ibid., 191–95; Correia, "Contextual Debiasing and Critical Thinking." As noted, this three-part formulation for understanding cinematic racialized disgust would also seem amenable to aspects of recent work on embodiment, race, and habit, as well as implicit bias. See Sullivan, *Revealing Whiteness*; Sullivan, *Good White People*, 85–115; Sullivan, *The Physiology of Sexist and Racist Oppression*; Al-Saji, "A Phenomenology of Hesitation"; Ngo, "Racist Habits"; Ngo, *The Habits of Racism*; Brownstein and Saul, *Implicit Bias and Philosophy*; Chakrabarti, "Refining the Repulsive," 160–63.

61. Regarding the application of aesthetic disgust to *The Searchers*, see Flory, "Racialized Disgust and Character in Film." Regarding *12 Years a Slave*, see Flory, "Imaginative Resistance, Racialized Disgust, and *12 Years a Slave*."

BIBLIOGRAPHY

Al-Saji, Alia. "A Phenomenology of Hesitation: Interrupting Racializing Habits of Seeing." In *Living Alterities: Phenomenology, Embodiment, and Race*. Edited by Emily S. Lee, 133–72. Albany: State University of New York Press, 2014.
Baptist, Edward E. *The Half Has Never Been Told: Slavery and the Making of American Capitalism*. New York: Basic Books, 2014.
Bogle, Donald. *Toms, Coons, Mulattoes, Mammies, and Bucks: An Interpretive History of Blacks in American Films*. Fourth Edition. New York and London: Continuum, 2001.
Boyd, Robert and Peter Richerson. *The Origin and Evolution of Cultures*. New York: Oxford University Press, 2005.
Brownstein, Michael. *The Implicit Mind: Cognitive Architecture, the Self, and Ethics*. New York: Oxford University Press, 2018.
Brownstein, Michael and Jennifer Saul, eds. *Implicit Bias and Philosophy*, two volumes. Oxford: Oxford University Press, 2016.
Carroll, Noël. *Humour: A Very Short Introduction*. Oxford: Oxford University Press, 2014.
———. "Moral Change: Fiction, Film, and Family." In *Cine-Ethics: Ethical Dimensions of Film Theory, Practice, and Spectatorship*. Edited by Jinhee Choi and Mattias Frey, 43–56. London: Routledge, 2014.
Chakrabarti, Arindam. "Refining the Repulsive: Toward an Indian Aesthetics of the Ugly and the Disgusting." In *The Bloomsbury Research Handbook of Indian Aesthetics and the Philosophy of Art*. Edited by Arindam Chakrabarti, 149–65. London: Bloomsbury, 2016.
Correia, Vasco. "Contextual Debiasing and Critical Thinking: Reasons for Optimism." *Topoi* 37, no. 1 (2018): 103–11.
Danto, Arthur. "Art and Disturbance." In *The Philosophical Disenfranchisement of Art*, 117–33. New York: Columbia University Press, 1986.
Dargis, Manohla. "Invasion of the Robot Toys, Redux." *New York Times*. June 23, 2009. Accessed at https://www.nytimes.com/2009/06/24/movies/24transform.html?hpw.
Eckstein, Arthur M. "Darkening Ethan: John Ford's *The Searchers* (1956) from Novel to Screenplay to Screen." *Cinema Journal* 38 (1998): 3–24.
Fanon, Frantz. *Black Skin, White Masks*. Translated by Richard Philcox. New York: Grove Press, 2008.
Flory, Dan. "*Bamboozled*: Philosophy through Blackface." In *The Philosophy of Spike Lee*. Edited Mark Conard, 164–83. Lexington: University Press of Kentucky, 2011.
———. "Imaginative Resistance and the White Gaze in *Machete* and *The Help*." In *Race, Philosophy, and Film*. Edited by. Mary K. Bloodsworth-Lugo and Dan Flory, 17–34. London and New York: Routledge, 2013.
———. "Imaginative Resistance, Racialized Disgust, and *12 Years A Slave*." *Film and Philosophy* 19 (2015), 75–95.
———. "*Moonlight*, Film Noir, and Melodrama." *Western Journal of Black Studies* 43, no. 3/4 (Fall/Winter 2019): 104–13.
———. "Race and Imaginative Resistance in James Cameron's *Avatar*." *Projections: The Journal for Movies and Mind* 7, no. 2 (Winter 2013): 41–63.
———. "Racialized Disgust and Character in Film." In *Screening Characters: Theories of Character in Film, Television, and Interactive Media*. Edited by Johannes Riis and Aaron Taylor, 110–26. London: Routledge, 2019. DOI: https://doi.org/10.4324/9780429422508.
Gendler, Tamar Szabó. "Imaginative Resistance Revisited." In *The Architecture of the Imagination: New Essays on Pretence, Possibility, and Fiction*. Edited by Shaun Nichols, 149–73. Oxford: Clarendon Press, 2006.
Gombrich, E. H. *Art and Illusion: A Study in the Psychology of Pictorial Representation*. Second Edition. Princeton: Princeton University Press, 1972.
Gossett, Thomas. *Race: The History of an Idea in America*. New Edition. New York and Oxford: Oxford University Press, 1997.

Gould, Stephen Jay. *The Mismeasure of Man.* Revised and Expanded Edition. New York: W. W. Norton, 1996.
Guerrero, Ed. "*Bamboozled*: In the Mirror of Abjection." In *Contemporary Black American Cinema: Race, Gender, and Sexuality at the Movies.* Edited by Mia Mask, 109–27. London: Routledge, 2012.
Hannaford, Ivan. *Race: The History of an Idea in the West.* Baltimore: Johns Hopkins University Press, 1996.
Kelly, Daniel. "Moral Disgust and the Tribal Instincts Hypothesis." In *Cooperation and Its Evolution.* Edited by Kim Sterelny, Richard Joyce, Brett Calcott, and Ben Fraser, 503–23. Cambridge, MA: MIT Press, 2013.
———. *Yuck! The Nature and Moral Significance of Disgust.* Cambridge, MA: MIT Press, 2011.
Korsmeyer, Carolyn. *Savoring Disgust: The Foul and the Fair in Aesthetics.* Oxford: Oxford University Press, 2011.
Lang, Robert, ed. *The Birth of a Nation.* New Brunswick: Rutgers University Press, 1994.
Lott, Eric. *Love and Theft: Blackface Minstrelsy and the American Working Class.* New York: Oxford University Press, 1993.
Morgenstern, Joe. "Our Inner Child Meets Young Darth Vader." *Wall Street Journal.* May 19, 1999. Accessed at https://www.wsj.com/articles/SB927082592439077365.
Ngo, Helen. *The Habits of Racism: A Phenomenology of Racism and Racialized Embodiment.* Lanham, MD: Lexington Books, 2017.
———. "Racist Habits: A Phenomenological Analysis of Racism and the Habitual Body." *Philosophy and Social Criticism* 42 (2016): 847–72.
Nussbaum, Martha. *Hiding from Humanity: Shame, Disgust, and the Law.* Princeton: Princeton University Press, 2004.
Pippin, Robert. "What Is a Western? Politics and Self-Knowledge in John Ford's *The Searchers.*" *Critical Inquiry* 35, no. 2 (2009): 223–53.
Plantinga, Carl., "Disgusted at the Movies." *Film Studies* 8 (2006): 81–92.
———. *Moving Viewers: American Film and the Spectator's Experience.* Berkeley and Los Angeles: University of California Press, 2009.
Pye, Douglas. "Double Vision: Miscegenation and Point of View in *The Searchers.*" In *The Book of Westerns.* Edited by Ian Cameron and Douglas Pye, 229–35. New York: Continuum, 1996.
Redmond, Sean. "The Whiteness of the *Rings.*" In *The Persistence of Whiteness: Race and Contemporary Hollywood Cinema.* Edited by Daniel Bernardi, 91–101. London: Routledge, 2008.
Rogers, Katie. "Leslie Jones, Star of *Ghostbusters*, Becomes a Target of Online Trolls." *New York Times.* July 20, 2016. Accessed at https://www.nytimes.com/2016/07/20/movies/leslie-jones-star-of-ghostbusters-becomes-a-target-of-online-trolls.html.
Roth, Marty. "'Yes, My Darling Daughter': Gender, Miscegenation, and Generation in John Ford's *The Searchers.*" *New Orleans Review* 18, no.4 (1991): 65–73.
Saxton, Alexander. *The Rise and Fall of the White Republic.* London: Verso, 1990.
Sullivan, Shannon. *Good White People: The Problem with Middle-Class White Anti-Racism.* Albany: State University of New York Press, 2014.
———. *The Physiology of Sexist and Racist Oppression.* New York: Oxford University Press, 2015.
———. *Revealing Whiteness: The Unconscious Habits of Racial Privilege.* Bloomington: Indiana University Press, 2006.
Tran, Kelly Marie. "I Won't Be Marginalized by Online Harassment." *New York Times.* August 21, 2018. Accessed at https://www.nytimes.com/2018/08/21/movies/kelly-marie-tran.html?hpw&rref=movies&action=click&pgtype=Homepage&module=well-region&region=bottom-well&WT.nav=bottom-well.
Walton, Kendall. "On the (So-called) Puzzle of Imaginative Resistance." In *The Architecture of the Imagination: New Essays on Pretence, Possibility, and Fiction.* Edited by Shaun Nichols, 137–48. Oxford: Clarendon Press, 2006.

Williams, Patricia. "Racial Ventriloquism." *The Nation.* June 17, 1999. Accessed at https://web.archive.org/web/20060920011550/http://www.thenation.com/doc/19990705/williams.
Wilson, George M. *Narration in Light: Studies in Cinematic Point of View.* Baltimore: Johns Hopkins University Press, 1986.
Yancy, George. *Black Bodies, White Gazes: The Continuing Significance of Race.* Second Edition. Lanham, MD: Rowman & Littlefield, 2016.
———. *Look, a White! Philosophical Essays on Whiteness.* Philadelphia: Temple University Press, 2012.

TEN

Disappearance, or, the Neat Punctuation of an Invisible Sentence

James B. Haile

I picked up the newspaper as I usually do each morning; I snapped open the pages against the sun-cracked light whispering through and around the draperies over my shoulder, greeting each new page, each new headline—pronouncing each disaster, each local story, and every job available to the men of our times—as I had done each and every morning, punctuating the start of the day. The kettle on the stove squealed, insisting upon itself, as usual. I sat and waited for the bacon to pop and begin smoking, as with every morning. But, on this day, I found waiting for me a punctuated silence, the front-page story titled in uppercase lettering, "DISAPPEARANCE," accompanied with this letter:

To Whom It May Concern,

It is a Tuesday, in this year of our Lord and the African-Americans have disappeared. If you will allow me to explain; it has, of recent, been noticed that they are gone, and left in their place are a series of gestures and articulations that, until this very moment, had been taken to *be* "Black people." In other words, it cannot really be known *when* they left, or *where* they have gone. What we do know is that seven days ago, we at this newspaper received a flood of calls and letters alerting us that the Blacks had indeed disappeared and that their disappearance has led to much confusion and anxiety. While we are not quite sure where they have gone, or what these various gestures and articulations mean, please do rest assured that law enforcement has consulted various experts to solve this dilemma. In the meantime, please continue living your life as usual.

> Mercifully yours,
> Chief Editor

I read this headline and the letter in a bit of shock. I went to the front door and looked out, seeing a passing garbage truck filled with Black men picking up and putting down garbage cans, and thought to myself, "We all *know* that this cannot be true; Black people had not disappeared." This had to be a hoax, a ruse of some kind. But, what kind of ruse was this? I read the letter again, like the punctuation of an invisible sentence, asking myself: Why cause such confusion? Why reassure us at the end? Why even think that this news would cause any concern? Why? Why? Why?

INTRODUCTION TO AN ELABORATION OF SPECULATIVE REALISM AFOOT

In their respective fantasy works, "Day of Absence" (1965) and "The Other Foot," (1951) Douglas Ward Turner and Ray Bradbury played around with the idea that Black people may one day disappear or leave the planet altogether. In Turner's piece, we encounter this scene:

> ONE. Henry—they vanished!
>
> TWO. Disappeared into thin air!
>
> THREE. Gone wit'out a trace! . . .
>
> MAYOR. Wait a minute!! . . . Hold your water! Calm down—!
>
> ONE. But they've gone, Henry—GONE! All of 'em!
>
> MAYOR. What the hell you talking 'bout? Gone? Who's gone—?
>
> ONE. The Nigras, Henry! They gone!
>
> MAYOR. Gone? . . . Gone where?[1]

In his seminal work, "What America Would Be Like Without Blacks" (1970), Ralph Ellison argued that it was, indeed, a white fantasy that Black people would disappear or leave the Earth, or any other scenario on which, borne "of petulance, exasperation and moral fatigue," America would be able to keep hidden from itself what is "inescapably tragic about the cost of achieving our democratic ideals."[2] He continued:

> The fantasy of an America free of blacks is at least as old as the dream of creating a truly democratic society. . . . There is something so embar-

rassingly absurd about the notion of purging the nation of blacks that it seems hardly a product of thought at all. It is more like a primitive reflex, a throw-back to the dim past of tribal experience, which we rationalize and try to make respectable by dressing it up in the gaudy and highly questionable trappings of what we call the "concept of race."[3]

Just twenty years earlier, Ellison had written in *Invisible Man* (1952) that Black invisibility was a result of a willfulness of this evasion. "I am invisible, understand, simply because people refuse to see me."[4] Ellison further explained that this invisibility is not "a matter of a bio-chemical accident to my epidermis. That invisibility to which I refer occurs because of a peculiar disposition of the eyes of those with whom I come in contact. A matter of the construction of their inner eyes, those eyes with which they look through their physical eyes upon reality."[5] But, perhaps, still, it is more than Turner or Bradbury or Ellison had proposed. Perhaps the problem—or better, the difficulty—arises not because of willfulness or evasion, or some desire to imagine what the Earth would be like, what America would be like, without Black people. Perhaps the difficulty is in the fact that, at bottom, there aren't any "Blacks" at all—at least, not as they have been described and understood. Perhaps what has been surmised is what Sheree R. Thomas calls "dark matter": "Scientists believe that the amount of 'visible' matter in the universe is not enough to account for the tremendous gravitational forces around us"; perhaps this "missing" or "invisible" matter was not missing or invisible at all. For her, the issue isn't that "dark matter" is, itself, invisible, it's that we don't have an adequate "method for detecting the components of dark matter."[6] There may be Black people, but perhaps the difficulty is in the fact that we have yet to develop a method for understanding the nature of "the tremendous gravitational forces around us." Perhaps, the difficulty is not so much in what we have termed racism, or invisibility, or desire for disappearance but the fact that we can only approximate Black life *through* the products of Black life, but have yet to really come to terms with the reality of actual Black people.

Some fifty years after these publications, Fred Moten posed similar questions, not in the realm of fantasy, but of *phantasy*—that inescapable realm of cognitive order and disorder. Moten tells us that the very idea of "Blackness" is a phantasmic construction of "wretchedness," which "emerges from a standpoint that is not ours, that is not only one we cannot have and ought not want, but that is, in general, held within the logic of im/possibility that delineates what subjects and citizens call the real world."[7] For Moten, *this* Blackness is the boundary that marks the Manichean oppositions—human/nonhuman, civilized/savage, order/disorder, citizen/foreigner, thought/unthought, and so on—and, as such, cannot be ours because it does not, cannot, and must not articulate the actual existences of actual persons. What, then, is necessary is another method for understanding those persons demarcated as liminal through this term, one that is, "from the outset," not "the construction of a necessarily fictive standpoint of our own," but one that will "*begin* to explore not just the absence but the *refusal* of standpoint, to actually explore and to inhabit and to think . . . from no standpoint." In other words, if Blackness as the demarcation of boundaries offers us the only perspective or standpoint through which we can think ourselves in the world as subjects, citizens, or free, rational persons, why not, as Moten suggests, simply refuse a standpoint altogether—refuse, as it were, the boundaries created by Blackness, and Blackness itself as the demarcation of those boundaries? As Moten further questions in the form of an assertion, "What would it be, deeper still, what is it to think from no standpoint; to think outside the desire for a standpoint?"[8]

What, though, would it mean, as Zakiyyah Iman Jackson notes, to "theorize in a void" or from a positionless or subjectless position? For Jackson, it would mean coming to terms with the "demonic," not as object of "religious hierarchies and the supernatural," but in the sense of "mathematics, physics, and computer science," namely "a working system that cannot have a determined or knowable outcome."[9] This "demonic theory" is one of sublimity wherein the void, or a Blackness that is not itself a boundary, reifies itself as it confronts and contends with the possibility of its impossibility. The formal expression of this, then, would be something like theorizing dark matter—a speculative sur/realism of the im/possibility of thought only detectable by its own gravitational effects, or its capacity to galvanize matter around itself. It would "point toward the epochal threshold of a mode of being/feeling/knowing with the capacity to rupture the current order's consolidated field of meaning, affect- and behavior-regulating schemas, and order-replicating hermeneutics."[10]

Is this the realm of speculative studies which has been termed fantasy or science fiction? Is this what Mos Def terms, "so real, it's surreal" or what Hal Bennett notes as "distort[ing] in order to see reality"?[11] Would Black theory as the subjectless refusal of a standpoint always appear as fantasy in that it contests the given reality with another kind of realism from another dimensional space? If taken seriously, does it, then, always create another reality altogether? And, if so, does it always carry within it the unintended consequence of revealing that the boundaries, the constructed notions of the subject, the citizen, freedom, and the nation-state are merely and tragically fictive?

A man awakens, rises and moves into the kitchen to sit at a table. The water in the kettle on the stove is in midboil, and the bacon is just beginning to pop, before it smokes. A newspaper awaits him, folded crisply on a table. He sits at the table, and snaps open the newspaper, looking over each page, turning it slowly, moving from story to story. He does this every morning to announce, to annunciate his day, as a sort of ritual. On this particular day, he comes across a headline and a letter, and exclaims to himself that it cannot be true; he looks out of the window and *sees* Black people. They are not mere cloaks and hats? He does see them, right? Right?

A man awakens and sees the world, makes mention of it in his mechanical motions—swinging his right, then left leg over the edge of the bed to meet awaiting slippers, walking down the hall from his bedroom, past the bathroom, and into the kitchen, sitting at a table, always already hissing pot of water on the stove, and bacon cooking itself out of habit in a pan, his face "a face you seen many times," that of a man whose "ancestors conquered a continent, pushing across death-laden plains, until they came to an ocean which faced away from Europe into a darker past."[12]

A man awakens one morning, has his cup of coffee and reads through the newspaper, tragedy after tragedy while he cuts bacon into his mouth, and thinks about the balance of his day. See . . . they are *already* gone, but he does not know it, yet. See . . . he cannot *understand* and does not know he cannot understand, but still thinks that he *must* understand. Where have they gone? Do you see? He is searching for what cannot be found.

> Man cannot enquire either about that which he knows, or about that which he does not know; for if he knows, he has no need to enquire; and if not, he cannot; for he does not know the very subject about which he is to enquire. . . . The soul, then, as being immortal, and having been born again many times, and having seen all things that exist, whether in this world or in the world below, has knowledge of them all; and it is no wonder that she should be able to remember all that she ever knew about virtue, and about everything; for as all nature is akin, and the soul has learned all things; there is no difficulty in her eliciting or as men say learning, out of a single recollection.[13]

Is there any way to think about, talk about "race," about "Blackness"—this *boundary* which surrounds and envelops each and every *thing*—in a way that is not pseudoscientific, or in terms that are not overtly speculative, or in terms of the *phantasy* of that which is not yet, at least not yet in *this* temporal frame? Is *this* why Danez Smith tells us, "I've left Earth. . . . I'm giving the stars their right names and this life, *this* new story and history you cannot steal or sell or cast overboard or hang or beat . . . if only *this* one is ours,"[14] and why Elizabeth Alexander questions, "If black people are the subconscious of the Western mind, where is 'the black subconscious,' both individually and collectively articulated? . . . If black people in the mainstream imaginary exist as fixed properties deemed 'real,' what is possible in the space we might call surreal?"[15] Are there searching words and thoughts that might be said or heard or capable of being heard that can find that which we can only note by their affect? Can we find a way into that which is not really *here*? "Blackness," Fred Moten chimes in, "is the site of absolute dereliction at the level of the Real.... Blackness is the site of absolute dereliction at the level of the Imaginary."[16] But, here Moten is not bold enough. If it is true that "statelessness is our terribly beautiful open secret, the unnatural habitat, and habitus of analytic engines with synthetic capacities,"[17] it is not because *we are* stateless, but because the state itself, as the central organizing principle of human existence, is not the material order of *our* existence. In other words, we may be here, but what if *we* are not meant to *be* "here"?

This is the very essence of inutterability—that which is said cannot be made sensical within a given logical structure of space and time; that which is heard comes in direct conflict with the body out of which it is said, and the words as sound and meaning cluster around this flesh, causing the system to fail on all fronts. In this condition, what, *really*, can be said of the Black political imagination—that is, questions of freedom, and justice, and progress, and so forth—other than what Moten has suggested: a disavowal of form and a subjectless standpoint position. What, in the pre- and post-Industrial material experiences which negate the possibility of Black existence, but navigate its imagination and understanding on Black flesh, is the meaning of a *Black* freedom that is not *really* freedom at all—liberation, marronage, flight? This is what it means to disappear and leave behind gestures and articulations, and why it is not difficult to detect, but when detected, causes such a stir. The inutterable made material through the nonlegibility of a body that refuses labor or commerce. But, this has always been the case, so, when did this become a problem?

I received a phone call. Before I could begin my coffee and bacon, the voice on the other end had tasked me with investigating the story. In this moment, hovering over the newspaper, the strangeness of the letter staring back, the adjoining page advertising a new, state-of-the-art vacuum cleaner with the promise that it can "make it look like the mess was never there," I felt like I had been transformed, as it were, into a kind of maverick, like John Howard Griffin, but instead of clothing myself in the skin of another, I found myself staring at the page, hearing the voice and its words, "David, you have to get on this. There's definitely a story here. I'm not sure what it is, but you've gotta figure it out." Searching beneath what was written, combined with the voice I heard and my head and the presence of these Black men right outside my window, I was confronted by a mystery that needed to be solved.

As I puzzled it over, Nina Simone's classic song, "Pirate Jenny," came on and played against the background of the whistle of the kettle and the popping flesh—the opening verse moved slowly as if on 33 instead of 45, the words blurring, reminding me I'll never be able to guess who I'm talking to.[18] What was *meant* by "left in their place is a series of gestures and articulations"? What have I been seeing, what have *we* been seeing all along—what are we seeing now? Is it what has been shown to me— these various gestures and articulations, or something else? And, *why* have I, *we*, not noticed this very fact—of absence, of the gestures and articulations—until *right now*?

That which occludes epistemology—what is seen, and how it is seen—for the "demonic ground" of occlusion is that which "bypass[es] an examination of the very conditions not only of visual epistemologies of 'evidence' but also of representability itself."[19]

I began my work combing through archives of texts that were recommended to me by a professor at the nearby university. I started with Ray Bradbury's "The Other Foot." The professor recounted Bradbury's story: "One day out of the blue, every Negro in town left, one by one, by bus out of the city. The year was unknown, but the year doesn't matter, here. It just marks a specific moment but has no bearing on the event itself." He continued, "Actually, time and dates get in the way of thinking about what exactly happened. The white members of the town were left wondering why they—the Blacks—were leaving—though they *knew* why— and where they might be going—of this, they had no clue." He paused, looking out of his office window before continuing. "They only knew that *it* was happening, that *it* was an Event—a unique, nonrepeatable, significant moment that it, itself, marked time, much more than a simple date—and that this Event could not be stopped."

I gathered and read every account I could about stories like these— George Schuyler's *Black No More*, Douglas Ward Turner's "Day of Absence," Toni Morrison's *Song of Solomon*. I went through all the folkloric elements I could from Virginia Hamilton's story, "The People Could Fly" and W. E. B. Du Bois's "The Comet," and finally went through all of the first-person accountings of migrations, emigrations, *petit* and *grande marronage* to try to understand how people function, to see if there were any clues as to what was going on. I read Richard Wright's *Black Boy*, Du Bois's *The Souls of Black Folk* and "The Souls of White Folk," Martin Delany's *Blake, or the Huts of Africa* and Daniel Sayers's *A Desolate Place for a Defiant People*. I read material histories and philosophies of race, racialization, and racism; I tried to record as much "truth" as I could, but discovered I was no closer, for how could *I* read about *this*, and truly understand what it meant to be physically present, but somehow absent and just *what* it would mean to be left with gestures and articulations?

RACE, BLACKNESS, AND SPECULATIVE WRITING

Can the imaginative rendering of the present and possible futures, the "now" and all possible, alternate "nows" or speculative theories of the past be racist? That is, can the imagination itself, the realm in which we understand and differentiate the *real* from the *nonreal* be racist? Are the present and possible worlds that we inhabit, the real as well as the nonreal, somehow habitable for Black expressive products, but uninhabitable to and for Black life? Is it at all conceivable that we can imagine a past, present, or future that is itself not always already involved with our contemporary problems, thoughts, and solutions?

C. Wright Mills tells us that the problem with the contemporary sociological imagination is that it "has become the accumulation of facts for the purpose of facilitating administrative decisions." This, though, becomes problematic in that it does not take into account the "quality of mind" wherein we come to grasp "history and biography and the relations between the two within society"[20] that constitutes and interprets these "facts." For Mills, engaging the social world means also engaging how the world is constructed, and how we as subjects of this world help to construct it, and are, in turn, constructed by it. In particular, it means engaging the contemporary U.S. social world as a racial project constituted by whiteness, and constituted by an anti-Black racism against those who would be deemed "Black."

It is for this reason that Albert Murray refers to contemporary U.S. social sciences as social science fiction fiction in that they are often predicated upon racial assumptions that are, in themselves, never really acknowledged and very rarely challenged. For this reason, not only is our scientific gaze impoverished, but so is our imagination as well. Murray writes, most "American readers . . . regard fiction as being little more than a very special extension of the social science case study."[21] For Murray, fiction itself is reflective of how we see, understand, and interpret the world. If our view of the world itself is limited and skewed, our imagination and, by extension, our fiction will be limited and skewed. The difficulty we are presented with, then, is two-fold: generally, white Americans cannot see the reality of their own racial project, and, thus, cannot understand the full extent of their imagination; but also, they cannot disregard their own racialized reality in order to engage Black people as people rather than as *ideas*. At the same time, Black Americans cannot see themselves as individuals or as a collective within this social scientific fiction fiction that regards itself as truth. Between these two worlds stands a science that is a fiction—a fiction that fictionalizes the already existing racialized-fiction-presented-as-fact—that is best understood through speculative studies. Is it no wonder that *most* Black intellectuals, no matter their pursuits, are also somehow concerned with the production of what we traditionally term science fiction narrative writing?

Charles S. Saunders has argued that Black people should write science fiction, noting,

> There's a reason for blacks to read and write science fiction that goes beyond the number of black writers in the field, or the number of black characters who can break dance on the head of a micrometeorite in someone's hard-science plot line. Science fiction serves as the mythology of our technological culture. . . . The human imagination manifests itself in stories. These stories become legends, myths, the defining elements of a culture.[22]

For Saunders, like Murray, the human imagination structures how the world is not only interpreted, but how it is materially organized—the myths and legends informing and structuring the technological and social innovation. Blacks should read and write science fiction to be part of this building. If we put Saunders and Murray together, what we discover is that Black people write science fiction because the world they exist in is itself fictional and their existence as "Black" people in this world is equally as fictive.

As void itself, and existing within a void in the literature, the Black science fiction writer is markedly different from their white counterpart. Rather than fictionalizing the contemporary world, the Black writer, in general, and science fiction writer in particular, demonstrates that the contemporary world itself is already a fictional space. That is, writing from/in the void, the Black writer is always already in the space of fiction—the space already outside of the contemporary world as it has been constituted by whiteness. Given this fact, the Black writer is always already in the realm of the speculative—the theorization of what is not yet present, or what is present but unaccounted for and illegible—even when not overtly writing science fiction work.

Samuel Delany argues that because racism exists in the science fiction and fantasy writing world, this particular voice and its mode of communication is difficult to articulate and discern. Delany recounts the first time he had encountered "direct" racism as a science fiction writer: he submits a portion of a novel to a well-established science fiction magazine to receive not only a letter, but a personal phone call from the editor to explain that "while he liked pretty much everything else about it, he didn't feel his readership would be able to relate to a black main character." The imaginative realm of transposition—that is, self-projection into a nonexistent, mythical or possible realm of existence—had been exhausted at the limits of its own possibility. The possibility of embarkation was only interposed with the reality that this Blackness not only tainted the imagination, but, as Toni Morrison noted in *Playing in the Dark*, was the American imagination, an imagination which both actively denied and actively asserted.[23]

Charles Mills tells us, "This notion is hard to tease out; it is a pretheoretical intuition, and as with all intuitions, it can be hard to convey to those who do not, in this case because of their color, spontaneously feel it in the first place."[24] Mills further elaborates, "the source for blacks of a likely feeling of alienness, strangeness, of not being entirely at home in this conceptual world" has to be engaged at "another level, in a taxonomy of different kinds of silences and invisibility."[25] That is, the fictive racialized world of whiteness and anti-Blackness has to be revealed—that is, disclosed—through an enactment of the imagination through what has been denied therein—the identification *and* mis-identification of ontological types.

What is critical to this investigation is not merely what is said or how something appears, but the very insight into which language, and meaning, and bodies and flesh are interpreted—that is, theorizing the material order as an epistemic contour. As Mills puts it, "For the inhabitants of this universe [the African-American experience], the standard geometries are of limited cartographic use, conceptual apparatuses predicated on assumptions that do not hold true. It is not a question of minor deviations, which, with a bending and twisting here and there, can be accommodated within the framework . . . a reconceptualization is necessary because the structure logic is different. . . . And those who have grown up in such a universe, asked to pretend that they are living in the other. . . . They know that what is in the books is largely mythical as a *general* statement of principles."[26]

Mills is pointing out the dimensional gap at the heart of the Black speculative and literary traditions where the phantasm of *this* "demonic ground" of unaccounted for alternate logical structure exists, not as mode of negation or for the sake of recognition, but as an insight into im/possible possibility of an/other time and space.

THE VIBRATO OF BLACK VOICE IN SPECULATIVE WRITING

After we hung up the phone, I wondered, aloud, *why me?* There must be other reporters, most of whom are Black, who sympathized with those particular issues. It's not like I'm *not* sympathetic, but it's just not where I land my boat on shore, as it were. I'd written some pieces in the past about local singers, and a couple of jazz clubs after hours and the haunting syncopation of the "sound," but that wouldn't have made me think of me for this kind of piece. Nevertheless, it was here, in front of me, with me, daring itself to be answered: why would a newspaper print such a letter if anyone looking outside their window could contradict its claims? And, if they *could* be contradicted so easily, why did the letter produce so much panic? Just *who* were those concerned letters from? All I knew was that I was being sent to "gather the facts," and write them up in "proper journalistic fashion." But there seemed to be something beyond simple facts here.

There are many ways one can approach a story such as this. It could be understood largely in terms of some natural or biological or biosocial phenomena, akin to a Negro "sink hole": a thing that appears overnight without explanation. All one would need to do is interview a few scientists to give a scientific explanation to ease our anxieties—there is no forethought to the disappearance; it's just something that happened. It could be handled as one would a special interest or community story—interviewing a few folks on some particular subject; edit the answers down to a few minutes and drop it in between the sports plays of the week and the weather report. But, and perhaps less obviously so, it could be understood in terms of what is missed on the registry of the human—that is, what is misunderstood and mischaracterized because of how we've understood and characterized the world. In this case, there would be no easy solution, no easy answer to simply "report." In this case, it would call for an evaluation. I decided that this would be the best approach, especially since I, too, was confused by the whole ordeal.

I wondered what I was missing, what I was seeing, incorrectly, and how, if at all, I could begin to unravel the riddle of space and time—that is, the enigma of the *real*—to tap into the vibrato of what is clearly another language, another tone, another registry of voice and another mode of existence . . . the unseen, unheard logic of disappearance.

I sat there for a few moments until the smoke from the bacon filled the dim space near the ceiling of my kitchen, and the spittle from the kettle kissed hotly against the back of my neck. How am I going to get at *this*? How would I know what I was missing—suddenly, in midthought, my cat announced its presence, jumping into my lap, perhaps to alert me to the fire bubbling, popping in the pan, and began to purr, giving me something of an answer: while there is no scientific explanation as to exactly *how* a cat purrs—it isn't in the vocal chords, but in the separation of the vocal chords during breathing—here, in my lap, *is* my cat, purring.[27] And, it struck me. It's in the separation, not in either side, in either dimensional existence, but the distance between them that necessitates a multiverse.

To begin this task, I decided to begin with the people themselves. I would not try to solve the dilemma, but simply record their words. I then remembered a series of interviews I had done previously on workers' rights, which, when I interviewed Black workers, no matter the field, the discussion turned into one centered on racism and rights. I went through all the recordings of Black workers I could find and have noted them here. These were interviews in which I merely asked them an opening question, "What do you think of when you hear the phrase, 'workers' rights or political economy'," and stepped away from the microphone. I recorded a wide range of Black workers from every facet of the economy and realized that the "economy" was a designation through which one could track political *and* racial aspects or facets of social life—it was a portal, of sorts, between our world and theirs.

I began writing up my notes, keeping in mind that they were all somehow false as soon as I recorded them, but nonetheless true given that they spoke aloud something beyond themselves. Below is a case study of the answers I received. I've decided, as a way to approach this problem, to curate the words and ideas that I had collected along the way to help navigate the discussion, to be as anonymous and invisible as I can be in the process, and to let these words and ideas tell the story, *become* the story to explain the "disappearance." As Updike put it, "On the single strand of wire strung to bring our house electricity, grackles and starlings neatly punctuated an invisible sentence."[28]

THE NEAT PUNCTUATION OF AN INVISIBLE SENTENCE

"Albert," Physicist

When I first met "Albert," he was jogging slowly across the yard of his campus. He was running late for our meeting and didn't see me heading in his cross-direction. We almost ran into one another on the steps leading to his building. Albert, a portly man standing about five feet, eight inches, stammered as we whizzed by one another in what must have looked like a choreographed dance.

"Mr. David," he began midtwirl. "Albert. Sorry I'm running late, and into you. But you know what they say, when two bodies occupy the same space at the same time . . . they dance," and, then he smiled. Albert is a physicist—what he terms, a "maker of science-reality"—who argued loudly, and unprompted, that what he did had little to do with provable facts, but the annunciation of the imagination toward the possible realms of human existence.

"I was a philosophy minor," he told me, and, would have been a major if not for his father, who thought he would never be employed with a philosophy degree. "I'm still a philosopher, but my father would never know," he said with a wink. "Or, my colleagues."

We began our conversation about political economy with what he thought science largely, but physics in particular, could offer to our understanding of our current situation. Our conversation began with the economy as a kind of "mental projection" of human desire. "You know," he began, "the economy is a lot like theoretical physics and the multiverse—do you think in an alternate dimension of possible selves we still have a capital framework based on future consumption; or, do you think the other "me" and "you" figured out new ideas of how to organize our lives better, differently?" He smiled brightly, as if the very thought of it was enough, flashing a large gap between his two front teeth that somehow rounded out his cheeks on both sides.

"The economy itself is a projection of desires," he began again. "Theoretical physics can help us to understand that each and every one of our decisions is a combination of choices we've already made before we made them because we could have always done things differently, and in theory we *have* done things differently."

"What about 'race,' then," I interjected. "People argue that it's constructed too—"

"A projection of our desires and anxieties brought to life," Albert said, finishing my question, "given life, really—like *all* of our material world; like a virtual reality machine that translates the electrical impulses in our brains into the material world we experience *as* real. 'Race,' of course, as one part of the material world, mirrors our political economy."

He then looked at me very sternly and seriously, the smile missing from his mouth. He continued, "If time and space are experiences as much as they are real facts outside of us; and, if as experiences, they are shaped by certain histories and ways that we navigate the world because of these histories, then it seems different people may be existing in different dimensions occupying the *same* physical plane of spatial reality. You know what that means? The implications of what I'm telling you?"

We had been talking as we walked up the stairs to the third floor to his office. We arrived at his office door, and he stopped in front of it, looking through his pants and jacket pockets for his keys. After looking through his bag, he pulled out a ring of keys, and looked through them to find the exact key, put it in the lock, and turned it. The room opened brightly, revealing a desk with piles of papers and books, and chairs with equally large piles. Albert picked up one of the piles from a chair nearest his desk, looked at me, and said, "Sit. Sit. Where were we?" Before I could answer, he walked to his window and said, "Yes." He stopped, looking out of the window, a red bird landing on a branch closest to his face. "You, know, blue birds are the prettiest, but they're also the meanest. You think how they act has something to do with the fact they know I think they're the prettiest? You think if I didn't *think* they were pretty they'd be nicer?" He laughed, and mentioned something of "observer bias," and scientific method, before finishing.

"Sometimes these dimensions might overlap, and in those moments, we can see one another, but when they are out of alignment, we pass right by and sometimes *through* one another. Now, imagine if these dimensional fields are nonphysical, but psychical, existential, and that while we may all *appear* present in our moments of shared spatial existence, we are all really existing in multiple and different dimensions?

Take, for example, Malcolm Jenkins—the football player for the Eagles who kneeled before games to protest police brutality."

He turned around, and took out his wallet, and opened it. I watched while he quietly unfolded a photograph as any proud father would of his children, but instead of a small person who looked slightly like him, it was a photograph of a man holding a placard reading, "You're not listening." He continued as if uninterrupted.

"Over the past year he was asked about his protest after *every game* and he answered in terms of police brutality of Black community members. And, after *every game* a reporter asked him why he protested the American flag. At the end of the season, Jenkins brought two placards to his interviews, one with his reason for his protest and one with the phrase, 'You're not listening' scrawled across it. When asked time and again, he would hold up one sign of explanation and then the other sign of assertion. Maybe, they could see the signs, even if they could not hear *him*? Temporal spatial dissonance. Gives a different sense of 'C. P. time,' huh?"

Albert laughed, slapping his knee until tears fill up his eyes. "But, in all seriousness," he continued, "this is, perhaps, the trouble with your question: we're never really talking about what we think we're talking about." Albert's eyes were piercing.

"It has never been a question of *when*—the triangulation of location from three points of reference (past, present, and future), even though this is how we've understood, and what we've meant by 'Black people.' Rather, it's been about *where* we locate 'Black people,'—transatlantic slave trade, abolition, Reconstruction, Civil Rights, Obama; you get the story; it's been given in a linear way—the 'when' understood through the 'where'—but what we've *really* been talking about is absence and presence; what and where things are absent and present—what makes them absent or present—and the process by which things (and people, and people as things) are made to be available and made to be missing. See what I mean?"

He stopped and walked back to the desk and sat down, disappearing behind a stack of papers. "Always where, and never when; always present, and always absent; always invisible, and always visible. But this does not tell us much about 'Black' people, or those people we've tried to trap within this triangulation. Where or how they actually *exist*. We've always known that there have been problems in the world that have been called social, political, and economic, sometimes aesthetic when dealing with the impact of social and political and economic concerns on *ideas* of beauty and value. We have always thought of these as residing *in* Black people since they seem to follow us around, generation after generation, country after country, continent after continent. We've thought of these problems in contemporary terms such as urban renewal, but we have not really thought of this problem in terms of theoretical physics, or in terms of dimensional spaces—that is, in more than just the three dimensional spaces of here and there, and now."

"C. K.," Poet

I walked into a sun-filled room. "C. K." had told me to meet her in her office, although she was running a bit late. C. K.'s assistant let me in; her office was filled with books on one wall, a desk filling the other wall, and lastly, two walls filled floor to ceiling with windows. She arrived about ten minutes later, finding me drifting over the poetry section of her collection, "Etai-Eke" I whispered to myself. "Seeds of singing," she said. "They're the most significant elements in human beings." She continued, "It's what we mean when we say, 'soul.' A discovery that a door between one's insides and the outside is not necessarily there."[29] I turned around to find a bright face meeting mine. "Nice to meet you." When one meets C. K. for the first time, you cannot help but notice the brightness that surrounds her. She's a petite woman, about five feet, six inches, and has short hair cropped neatly around her face and ears. She's wearing a thin brown sweater and carrying a stack of student papers. She invites me to have a seat on a chair across from her desk, next to her bookcase.

I begin by asking her what she thinks poetry has to offer, what insights it might bring to a conversation about political economy. She begins by taking a book from her desk, opening it, and reading from it. "It's from my first collection," she says. "I could have written this yesterday; I couldn't have written this yesterday. It is urgent; it disrupts and takes apart. It is a formal invention. It dances and sings along/side inventing new ways; it is inventing new days to meander through like city tunnels, and bridges down the streets and over the buildings, over and under and through and around the blood, veins, bowels, limbs and appendages of its body."

"You see," she says, "what could be said today or yesterday is not about language itself, but about what is and is not available to us at a particular time. We don't always have the words to say how we feel or what is happening to us. Sometimes we have to invent a language, invent words for these things. And sometimes that means breaking apart what we already have and seeing what's left. You see, that's what's urgent in words. In language itself. It's a calling; an urgent calling." She continues reading, "I remembered a faceless painting, a black blur in a sea of white lines crisscrossing across and through its countenance with a placard that reads, 'the other of myself, the other to myself is myself.'"

C. K. stopped reading for a moment, putting the book in front of me, face down. "Toyin Ojih Odutola created a collection a few years ago," she began. "She positioned prominent white figures with blackened skin. Everything was the same—the seated or standing position; the facial features, hair texture, and clothing—except this one detail. She wanted to see if how we 'saw' these men and women would be the same if we changed just one detail. It's about the imagination," she paused and looked away. "And, how we understand reality—or the *real* of the real. Our imagination is poetic; it's centered on how we construct, break down, and reconstruct reality, like poetry does with language.

She picked the book back up and continued reading. "And, I don't remember painting this or saying that, or myself in this title; it is me, but somehow not. It is to be sold, given away, really, as the source of my existence. How do I/we break from the past—from our memory; how do we break our memory? We cannot live 30 years in the future, but we can live 30 years in the past. How can I write this placard or be this placard or find myself in the words of another? Is there no other place to be than in the words of another?

"What begets what? When? Or, where?

"Those are the facts. What do those facts mean? To how things are made? To how life is lived?" She stands up, and walks around the room, the book dangling under her armpit. She walks over to the window and looks out, her back to me. "They think they know me because they hear the rhythm of the work," she says, almost to herself. "A figure on a canvas, what they think is brought to an end. They think they see me. But I am never hear/here, never their/there, always here and always there. We're always meandering in and through the body of these different identities—like cities—these different modes of existence." She turns back around, and sits at her desk, opens her book, and begins reading again.

> A rose is a rose is a rose is a rose, a rose, a rose, I arose /
> S/he commands us to play for the dance and I arose alongside Stein's nigger-grin, like the bright moon /
> I arose outside, outside language loses itself in itself, for itself outside/
> outside in the nigger-moon grin bright smile.

"See," she says looking over her book closely into my eyes, not breaking her gaze. "Whenever we begin, we're always beginning anew, even with old things, with old ideas. We're always lost, really, within language, within ourselves, within past traditions. We don't find ourselves in the language of others, in traditions either. We find ourselves by losing ourselves and creating ourselves again, and again and again. Tradition, language, identity if it's done right, should be about losing and finding ourselves. Nothing does or can happen." She continues reading,

> The weather does nothing
> More than tide or title or
> The sound of
> Words rushing back at
> The base of the neck....

Tear into this flesh, tightly sewn; tightly as one's own; tightly tightly tightly again down and through and over and around the flesh of the city
The flesh of language, and identity
Roaring flesh on fire screaming itself AAAAWWWW! Tear flesh from bone; bone from flesh
Without indignation?
Of course!
Pleasant?
Always!
Always! There/their tightly sewn together inside outside of it/self
A rose arose Gertrude Stein's Manet
Harnessing the white power captured in pretty...

When she finished reading, she placed the book back on her desk, and looked at me, silently with her eyes. I told her I wasn't really sure that she had answered my question and asked if she could be more specific about what she thought of the relationship between poetry and political economy. "You see, political economy," she began, more professorially now, "should be about the imagination and creating, breaking down, and re-creating—putting together, establishing and giving, really, disseminating, redistributing a set of ideas, a set of ideals about how things should be. That's what the government is really about—a set of ideals and practices of those ideals. That's why it's really an issue of the imagination, an issue of language, an issue of poetry." She stopped and looked, as if to see if I was paying attention, since I'd asked for a formal answer to my question. She paused, and started again, "It's really about identity and human personality and engaging them. But it's never really been about engaging them—the way we've done it; rather, it's been about controlling them. As a result, we've never really dealt with ourselves, with race—only, anything and everything around it as a kind of distraction through desire; not *real* desire, but the absence of it." She stopped and looked seriously at me. "Do you see what I mean? There's nothing less imaginative than race." I nodded, but, again, she didn't seem convinced.

She continued, this time revisiting her original voice, and her original brightness returned. "The things that we do, the things that we become; and, in between those are the voices we inhabit. Our techno-scientific culture, in other words, is predicated on a kind of primitivism—not Native American or African or even Protestant paganism, ha!—but the kind of tribalism that we've decided to call 'American values,' or the principles of democratic faith—those things that determine who is what, and who gets what, and who deserves what. How we've decided on those things is really prepolitical. Really, it's in *how* we've decided to talk about them."

"You see, political revolution is a fiction; political order is a fiction. The citizen, the foreigner, the nation-state, the stateless, are all fictions.

All science fictions, or fictions of technological innovations, innovations in what we would call "science," the systematic study of a thing, its essential features, and maybe even 'nature/s' — all fictions created to look like stable, absolute and permanent truths. Let's talk more on that!"

C. K. looks at me. She is being insistent, but persistent in thought, as if reinforcing her words, her thoughts for herself, and I am simply witnessing the monologue. "We gotta start reading more and writing more poetry — it's where truth comes from as we live it. We're only lost if we think the world is what takes place within what we already see and feel and think; if we believe that, what we get as truth is the reasonable exchange of what is and its existing framework. We forget that it is this process and believe — act as if — the world is really a *real* place, and not a fiction created and *made* real through thought, or will — expressions of our imagination. I think we've forgotten what exists beyond the possible, at the edges of the impossible, which is the realm of the understanding unfettered by the real as given — the imagination is necessary for this extension, contradiction, and extraction of thought or will. *Politics, the economy — they're curated fantasy!*"

"Jim" and "John," Community Organizers

I met "Jim" and "John" at a barbershop. It is a small shop on the corner, with two large windows overlooking the sidewalk as it made an L, bending First Street and Martin Luther King Boulevard together. The shop is small, but it seems bigger with the light coming from the windows. The floors are dingy red and white squares. On the walls are posters of different haircuts with numbers in the lower right-hand corner. There are six barber chairs, and fifteen seats for customers, but many more barbers and customers than there are chairs. All the barbers and customers are Black men ranging in age from about ten to seventy. Jim was getting his hair cut, while John waited in one of a long line of black chairs along the wall. Jim had invited me here, thinking it would be better suited to our conversation, more so than his office, a converted warehouse — up a long flight of stairs, glass windows overlooking the factory floor of rusted out assembly line belts, and a graveyard of tall beige metallic boxes, running to no end, like an industrial horizon. I ask Jim about the jobless rate in the community, up 2 percent since President Obama took office.

Jim tells me, his voice animated, "There really ain't no explanation [of political economy] — not one you'd take anyway, not as truth. Maybe myth or something like that, but certainly nothing as certain as *your* truth. So, I'll tell you the best way I know, in a way that you'll accept."

"You see," Jim says, riding forward in his chair, getting excited. The barber stops cutting his hair, as if he knew Jim was going to move forward. "Black labor has always been invisible. But, its invisibility is a necessary component to the US economy. So, Black unemployment would, necessarily, be invisible, too. No one sees or really *knows* about our unemployment because no one ever really comes here—"

"—except when it's election time!" John says. The men laugh uncomfortably. "No, really. We're invisible until we're not; or until we're needed. Like right now." John walks over to the window and points to a white man across the street. "You see that man over there? He could be a recruiter coming to look at some kids playing basketball; he could be a real estate investor coming to scope the future; or, he could be a design rep from some designer looking for a new look. We can't really know just by looking. But, we can guarantee he ain't here just to be here. He wants something. So he can see us—just enough to get what he wants. Then he'll leave. And we'll never see him—well, some variety of him, but not *him*—ever again. Kinda like you," he says pointing to me.

Jim interrupts to bring the conversation back to what he was saying. "You ever read Frederick Douglass? Not the slave narratives." Everyone in the room is silent, as if they knew Jim didn't want to be interrupted. "Douglass wrote a fictional story about slave rebellion. If you read it, you think you're getting something about slave rebellion and Douglass's ideas of freedom. But you're not." Jim pauses, almost to slow down to teach the younger men—but not me. "You get all caught up in the words, in the story [of slave rebellion], in deciding if you trust how Douglass is telling the story—from the perspective of a white man, and not from the perspective of the main character, a Black man. You find yourself cheering for these Black men and miss that the story is being told from a white man's perspective. Think about what Douglass is telling us about freedom—it's a white man's idea that we're imposing on Black men. But, what does Black freedom look like? We can't see it because the white perspective is in the way."

He stops midsentence and looks around to me and the others. "But there's another point made here. The Black perspective disappears. Think about it. Douglass, a Black man, writes from a white perspective to cover a Black perspective about freedom. He's really writing about *his* perspective to sell it to a white audience as if it was *their* perspective. Man, Douglass was a magician—he disappeared right in front of our eyes, just like that!" He snaps his fingers. "How could a man disappear right in front of us?" He smiles and asks me if I think the barber is doing a good job. I nod approval.

"Like Obama," an older man interjects as if he's heard this story before. Jim nods, and looks over to John, who smiles.

Jim continues his thought, unbroken, "And, you have Barack Obama in that critical moment. You remember, they *had* him. Jeremiah Wright's 'Goddamn America' speech. They *had* him right there." Jim slaps his hands closed and holds his hands high over his head as if to show us all the finality of how Obama was trapped. "And Obama gave that speech—

my grandmother was racist but loved me speech. And, it was all gone. He disappeared, right there, in front of us all, in front of all those cameras, the man made himself vanish. He took his white grandmother's voice to cover his own voice, and all we saw was her whiteness; and, all we heard was his voice. He left a pile of clothes holding his shape behind. That's what you don't get." Jim looked at me to explain what he seemed to assume everyone else already knew: "Black folks know they're invisible. They know you only come when you want something, and only see why you're there. Black folks don't really ever leave, they vanish and leave behind, dressed in their clothes, all *your* expectations!"

John interrupts, "'Goddamn America; Goddamn, America,' we all heard it. We heard it all! The Democratic primaries, 2008 against Hillary. And, we all thought the same thing: 'No way he recovers from this. They've *made* him Black, even if he isn't *really* Black; they've created him into one. It was Jessie Jackson all over again. He was cooked. You know? Then he gave that speech. Man, that speech. I can't really explain it."

The room exploded in voices, some talking about Obama's "Blackness" — "You know he's gotta be Black. Do you think Michelle would be with some phony ass Black dude?" — to talk about Obama's nascent racial consciousness — "If he didn't know he was Black before, he certainly does now."

John raised his hands and the room quickly quieted — a clear indication of his authority of age. "We all heard it," he turned to the barber and asked him to pull up the speech on his phone for us all to listen to it. Within minutes, Obama's voice sprang to life.

> Why associate myself with Reverend Wright in the first place, they may ask? Why not join another church? And I confess that if all that I knew of Reverend Wright were the snippets of those sermons that have run in an endless loop on the television sets and YouTube, or if Trinity United Church of Christ conformed to the caricatures being peddled by some commentators, there is no doubt that I would react in much the same way.
>
> But the truth is, that isn't all that I know of the man. The man I met more than 20 years ago is a man who helped introduce me to my Christian faith, a man who spoke to me about our obligations to love one another, to care for the sick and lift up the poor.
>
> I can no more disown him than I can disown the Black community. I can no more disown him than I can disown my white grandmother — a woman who helped raise me, a woman who sacrificed again and again for me, a woman who loves me as much as she loves anything in this world, but a woman who once confessed her fear of Black men who passed her by on the street, and who on more than one occasion has uttered racial or ethnic stereotypes that made me cringe.[30]

John started to laugh, but not a laugh of amusement; it was more of immense sadness. Then he spoke, "Why compare Reverend Wright with his racist grandmother? Are they really saying the same thing? Just what is he trying to do with this?"

Jim interrupted. "*That* is how he disappeared! He used *us* to disappear; he used us to hide right out in the open!" His smile was no longer a smile but something else; a crack just beneath his nose and above his chin, but rather than opening up his face, it seemed to collapse on itself, like a sink hole and with it his very countenance. "You wouldn't believe it unless you were there. He gave a majestic speech, one that all but separated him from his past, from himself, from all others in his category and made him something new, forbidden and smoke-filled twilight; a shadowed presence just behind the steamed fog of a manhole cover, rising to gossamer. I tell you, you had to be there to believe it. Never seen nothing like that my whole life. Right before my eyes. It was almost like he was saying to us, to all of us, without us really knowing it, if 'some commentators have deemed me either "too Black" or "not Black enough," I will show you my Blackness.' And, then, he vanished."

"Man, I've seen that plenty," John inserted.

"Where?"

"The unemployment line." An eruption of laughter followed.

"James," University Professor

I met "James" at a café, a short distance from the campus. He asked to meet here rather than his office. The café was large and nondescript. There was a bar at one end of the room, opposite the door, and a series of tables scattered throughout. The music playing was all but background muzak. James was already at a table near the bar with a white mug filled to the rim with coffee. He stood up when he saw me come in and waited until I got to the table to shake my hand. He was dressed in a blue, pin-striped, collared shirt, and a gray vest. His beard was closely shaven, as was his hair. His glasses, round and black, magnified his large brown eyes, which, under magnification belied something else that made his gesture of standing up and watching me cross the floor all the more odd. We sat. When I arrived, I was initially going to go to the bar and place my order but didn't want to leave James standing at the table by himself. So, I sat there without a drink and began recording. Our conversation began with a discussion of political economy—as had all the other interviews I had done. Though James did not profess to be an expert on the subject—he did aesthetics and politics—I thought that he, the only Black faculty in the college of Arts and Sciences, might have a unique and interesting take on the politics of labor. I asked him his experience of being newly hired at the university and what the job market and job interview process was like for him. He began, as I had expected, with a sort of rehearsed answer, "The job market is grueling, especially after the market crash of 2008—even places like Harvard lost their shirts and suspended searches."

But, as he talked, he seemed to talk himself into more and more detail, less rehearsed. He tells me about the first department meeting he had: "We were discussing potential curricular overhaul given the paucity of undergraduate majors, and the new mandate the university had—really our new dean had—for us to increase our majors to a certain number by a certain time. We have to increase our image . . . add some sexy classes with pizazz to attract the students." James's voice changed; his tone became a bit more nasally, and his intonation a bit tighter in his throat. I wondered if he was aware that he seemed to be imitating someone else—his posture changed, his arms shrank into his body, and his left leg began to thump.

"'Well, how do we do that?'

"'We have to add some classes at the introductory level that are going to draw them in.'"

James was now having what appeared to be an internal dialogue between members of the department. With each new perspective came a different voice of sorts. He then returned to his original voice and posture, shifting his upper torso back in my direction and extending his arms toward me. "I raised my hand. . . I'm not really sure why I did that—kinda like I'm not sure why I stood up when you walked into the door; I'm not really sure why I'm telling you this now. Anyway, I raised my hand and waited to be called. It was my turn. I suggested that we keep the courses as they were, in terms of content, and simply thematize them."

James, while still in the conversation, still in the meeting, as it were, turned to me to give me an example of what he had in mind. "'We could, for example, take the social/political course and thematize it around the idea of individual rights, free will, and the carceral state.'"

James had begun with another accent and bodily position. "'What, exactly, does that mean? Thematize—'

"'Well, it simply means we read the history of philosophy through a particular lens. One of the lenses could be incarceration or state oppression.'

"'Well, I simply don't see that as *philosophy*. We can't attract students simply by dumbing down the curriculum to *current* issues.'"

"I remember thinking," James said to me, returning to himself, "this is, again, one of those moments. There are always 'one of those moments'—the ones where you have to make a choice, to *become*, as it were, what you needed to *be* (not what you are, but what you're going to have to be in that moment) to . . ." James seemed a bit lost for words. He stopped, looked down at his coffee. His right leg started to move, rhythmically up and down, rapidly. He continued without looking up. "I'm simply refusing the privilege of death. It's a privilege, you see, to get such an invitation. A call, really, to address your own negation, to give, as it were, the eulogy at your own funeral to defend the *way* that you decided to die. And, to answer *this* call, which is all there really is, is one of the greatest callings a man can have."

He must have felt my confusion. Without looking up, he stopped midthought and answered my face. "I know that sounds radical," he continued, "but, you see, there's nothing more radical than being yourself. Especially for me." James looked up from his coffee again, as if he hadn't interrupted his own story, and continued,

[*In a different voice*] "'Quite honestly, if this is what you're going to do in your classes, I'm not sure why you're here.'

"I looked around the table to my other colleagues. Their bodies shrank, some *into* their hands, others into the doodle on the page in front of them. I asked, 'Is someone going to address this, or do I need to?' No one answered, so I took the call. 'Can you explain what it means to dumb down philosophy?'

"'Well, philosophy is about larger issues than what can be understood by anyone and should not be limited to contemporary issues.'

"'What makes you think incarceration and state oppression is a contemporary issue?'

"'Well, I know about the marches against police brutality—'

"'What makes you think I'm talking about those things—Black Lives Matter and all?' He was quiet. The whole room was quiet.

"'Well, I heard incarceration—'

"'How did Socrates die?' Again silence. I continued, 'Wasn't he killed by the state? By the tyrants of the state for teaching what he thought was the truth? And, Descartes—who were the *Meditations* written to? Wasn't it the cardinals of the church? Didn't he beg not to be excommunicated for not establishing God as the center of knowledge, replacing God with human consciousness? How is this a *contemporary* issue?'

"Again silence. And, then he spoke. 'I see your point.'"

James then turns to me, reflecting on the moment, "I have to tell you, there is nothing more hollow than addressing preconceived notions. Even though he conceded the point, it wasn't enough. I was invited to death and had to answer the call. I tell you, I sunk in my chair—really, I'm not being figurative with language. . ." He stopped, and looked at me, almost to get me on his side. "But, really it's all in the language. *I'm* figurative, so are you and this building and this room. I'm forced to see it. They're not. After all, *I'm* the only one being counted in official documents. 'As far as diversity, one fourth of our employees are *of color*, far better than many departments our size.'"

James laughed, looked around the room as if to see who was listening to our conversation, and turned back to me. "So, I sank in my chair, sank back into it, how a vanishing twin might sink into his other wombmate—the chair simply absorbed me, and I left the room. I went back to my office to read a book and listen to Miles Davis, then Kendrick Lamar; I called my wife and we chatted about our daughter; then I called my father to chat about LeBron James. All the while, I left something of a facsimile of myself in the chair for the meeting, 'Nod gently forward and backward an approval,' I told the other James."

"Is this why we're meeting here, instead of your office?" I asked James.

"Distance is always a good thing," he said, never fully answering. "Just a good getaway, I guess. There's always something troubling about proximity, about closeness that leads to conflict." James leaned forward, his face serious. "What's ironic," he began, "is that in my own department, all they can see is what you saw when you walked in the café, before you talked to me, if someone was to ask you how to identify me. But—and I can recall, a job interview I went on when they told me that I wasn't Black *enough* for the same reasons that I am *too* Black for my department. So, I go on this job interview, in a suit and tie. I give a presentation on prestidigitation and the Black novel form."

James interrupts himself again. His face brightens, as if to bring himself back to the present, in the coffee shop with me. "Man, I love this essay—philosophical form and content and theories of theatrical magic and masking in the written word." He continues, "They were kind enough. But, after the interview, I am told, confidentially, that I didn't 'wow' them enough. That they were used to 'traditional philosophical presentation of ideas,' but had 'expected *more*. Expected something additional to what is standard practice.' It reminded me of a time where, in graduate school being told that my work simply wasn't 'Black enough,' which roughly translated into, 'not enough pain and frustration with racial discrimination.'"

"And, true, I don't write directly on those things," James said, blowing gently on his coffee cup, almost out of habit—we'd been talking for about an hour at that point, the point by which his coffee would have been cold—then sipping from his cup, "which are largely seen as *my* interest—or, what *should* be my interest. And that's the problem," he said, putting down his cup to free up his hands. "A lack of imagination. We," he said, pointing to himself and, more specifically, his sweater, "sit across from largely white audiences who have come to some conclusion about what it *means* to be 'Black' in order to understand what it is they take me to be doing, to understand *me*—as if that's the goal of this world—and they expect it should show in my demeanor, either angry or demure."

James then reaches into his bag and takes out a book. "Turn to page 7, and read," he says handing me the book.

I read aloud, "Ntozake Shange writes: 'As black people we exist metaphorically and literally as the underside, the underclass. We are the unconscious of the entire Western world. If this is in fact true, then where do we go? Where are our dreams? Where is our pain? Where do we heal?' If black people are the subconscious of the Western mind, where is 'the black subconscious,' both individually and collectively articulated?"[31]

"What do you make of this?" he asks. It was the first time that the interview became a conversation—a *mutual* interview. I'm not sure what to make of it, and since James seems to have something in mind with the question itself, I sit blankly and stare at him. He begins again, "I'll tell you. The very idea of 'Blackness' is ubiquitous and dispersed. I'm expected to be both-and, all the time—angry *and* demur. It's an invitation that is demanded—you can see it in their eyes when you walk into a room. I saw it in your eyes when you walked in. That's why I stood up. Almost out of instinct—like how you saw me and wondered what I might be on the registry of race or Blackness. It's in the question you asked me about the job market, and my 'experience' at the university. It's all an invitation to death. And, I'll tell you—" he interrupted himself once more.

"Hell, I'm doing it again," he said. "Like I can tell you. My father once told me that there's nothing you can really learn from dissecting a frog that a frog doesn't already know. And, there's a whole lot you can't know that a frog already knows. But, we do it anyway. All the time. All throughout the nation—in every middling biology class. Dissect frogs, ask kids stuff about what they see. But we also learned along the way that they must still be alive, somewhere, somehow and participate in the process. So we numbed them to see the hearts beating—"

"The kids or the frogs?" I asked before I realized I had spoken.

James smiled. "Exactly." He hands me another book. "Page 153," he says.

I read a line from Zora Neil Hurston, "BUT I AM NOT tragically colored. There is no great sorrow dammed up in my soul, nor lurking behind my eyes. I do not mind at all. I do not belong to the sobbing school of Negrohood who hold that nature somehow has given them a lowdown dirty deal and whose feelings are all but about it. Even in the helter skelter skirmish that is my life, I have seen that the world is to the strong regardless of a little pigmentation more or less. No, I do not weep at the world—I am too busy sharpening my oyster knife."

"Sometimes, I feel discriminated against, but it does not make me angry. It merely astonishes me. How can any deny themselves the pleasure of my company? It's beyond me."[32]

Again, I stare blankly, wanting James to fill in the gap. "See, it's always assumed that Black people are being denied something simply because we can't be around white people because they're racist. That the goal is somehow, somewhere, to get closer." James stops and looks all around him. He continues, "But we all know there ain't no magic there; just force of will. And, it is also assumed that all we do is sit around and talk *about* white people and what they've done to us. And, it's also assumed—and this is the real disingenuous part—that when they're reading Hegel and Kant, they're finding themselves *there*—"

James points down forcefully at an imaginary book on the table without interrupting himself. "Calling yourself Hegelian or Kantian, or whatever other -ian you can be, that you're not involved in a racial project, but one concerned with some abstract issue. But Hegel and Kant were German, or more properly, from specific towns and regions in what is called 'Germany'—and this was important to them. It's just not important to *us*, because we don't do regional or town specific identities in this country—not really, any more than we have convenient ethnicities where we drink green beer on St. Patty's day, but can't speak Gaelic! But they think ignoring history and place and language and culture for the sake of universal sameness *isn't a racial project!* Man, come on. Some white kid sitting in his room in Iowa thinks he's Platonic, and you want me to show you something 'authentically Black.' That shit is perverse!"

"Amina," Science Fiction Writer, Freelance Journalist, Blogger

I met "Amina" at her loft. It was brick with exposed duct work and concrete floors. Amina looked how you might imagine an Afrofuturist blogger might look. Amina had a cleanly buzzed head, a gold ring through the center of her nose; she had on a pair of jeans covered in paint, and a t-shirt that read, "There are Black people in the future."[33] We began discussing what her shirt meant.

"Why do you ask?" Amina said. "Would you have asked if I had on a *Star Trek* shirt, or a *Lord of the Rings* shirt, where there are literally *no* Black characters? What do you think those plot lines are saying with this absence—what does *their* future look like? What are *their* central concerns—is it not with the specific issues that may emerge from a specific experience? Look, I'm not saying these shows and movies are white," Amina says. "It might be that they didn't think about us, or just that they couldn't figure out to how include us into their fictive world—it seems like the only way we know how to tell a 'Black story' is to place it within what we think is a 'Black setting'," Amina said, giving rabbit-eared air quotations. "My t-shirt only means that whatever the future may look like—whether it be like it is today or radically different, in either case, *I* will still exist in some form, and that this form will still consistently be *me*."

I asked Amina, given the presence of advertisers on most blogs and the need to attract views and downloads to monetize thoughts, "What does it mean to be a blogger on Afrofuturism, given its disavowal of linear time and space for alternate frames of knowledge, to monetize itself?" Amina looked at me gracefully, her mouth something like a grin. She told me, "You know even Ray Bradbury saw this coming, way back in 1951! But it had already been told before. The people could fly..."

Amina trailed off slightly, her voice shrinking in her mouth, still open, still waiting to tell; she paused, midmaw, and then started again—"with the folk myth of Flying Africans, replicated by a Toni Morrison novel, and Frank Ocean." Amina paused, then continued. "Frank Ocean talked about this, too. 'Super Rich Kids.'" Amina walked over to her stereo sitting on the second shelf of a five-shelf floating installation of steel and birch. Elton John's "Rocket Man," came on, but slower, more deliberate, different. *"We end our day up on the roof/I say I'll jump, I never do/But when I'm drunk I act a fool/Talking 'bout, do they sew wings on tailored suits."*[34] Amina smiled. The light cut through the window, articulating a beam of dancing particles, "a portal, a transport of the soul interdimensionally—like that great pyramid-machine. If we only knew how to harness the power in a single beam of light. You see, Frank Ocean could only harness his own beauty, could only harness the power to hold open the portal between himself and the world when he was drunk."

Amina appeared momentarily sad, then perked up and continued, "Bradbury imagined a scenario where Black folks left Earth to go to Mars and start over—and, of course, white folks, after having destroyed the world, followed us there, too!" She stopped and laughed. I watched her watching me for my reaction—I couldn't tell if it was for what she said about white folks destroying the world, or, for white folks following Black people to Mars. "But he missed it—it's not out there [*points to the sky*], it's in here [*points toward the chest*]. Bradbury thought that Black life without white people would be *Black American* life without white people; but on Mars, they wouldn't even *be* 'Black,' even if they still built pyramids, a sphynx, just like in Egypt. The Egyptians weren't 'Black'; they were cosmic; their gods were cosmic, their structures were cosmic. Frank Ocean is cosmic."

Amina paused, then continued, "We're then same way—you think we're terrestrial, as if everything that *is* is always what we see. But you missed it. Mahalia. Aretha. 'Black' people ain't 'black.' We're cosmic(ally oriented). Zora tried to tell us, but y'all didn't listen. We did. We know; we've always known. If we are Black, what is *Black* about us ain't our situation, but how we step in-*between* what is seen and heard in vibrations—this isn't music or culture, as in Black people are musical people; vibrations are something different. The space inside is farther and harder to reach than any planet, anywhere. It's really quantum, if you know what I mean."

I nod my head in agreement, but Amina continues without looking at me. "If you listen to *A Love Supreme* nothing else seems to matter. Have you heard Alice Coltrane's *Journey to Satchidananda*? Or, Cecil Talyor's *Unit Structure*—they're trying to give us a map. They found John Coltrane's letter to Yusef Lateef—it was literally a map. Quantum mechanics—Einstein's relativity, and his Einstein-Rosen bridge, not out in space, but *between* spaces, *here*, in music form."

Amina stops, returning circuitously back to Bradbury. "Bradbury seems to think as long as we're all shitty, we're all even—Black people ran from Earth; white people destroyed Earth; and, white people came to Mars to be with the Black people, because we're *all* shitty. That 'Blackness' has always been shitty, and if he can make whiteness shitty, too, all that has happened *here* will be evened out, and 'we' can start over again, on the same level. But what stays with us, though, from historical consciousness? Anything? What did we carry with us to Mars? *Has* Black life really always *been* shitty? Are we just holding on to shit and calling it 'culture'? Is there anything else to leaving the Earth than to relieve ourselves and let the white folks kill themselves off instead of always killing us?"

Amina hands me a newspaper clipping. I look down to see Amina is holding a book with a caption titled, "The Afrofuture is Here!" She points to a paragraph that's been highlighted. Amina reads,

> *Can a community whose past has been deliberately rubbed out, and whose energies have subsequently been consumed by the search for legible traces of its history, imagine possible futures? Furthermore, isn't the unreal estate of the future already owned by the technocrats, futurologists, streamliners, and set designers—white, to a man—who have engineered our collective fantasies?*[35]

"These aren't my words," she said. "They're from Mark Drey. You see, Mark Drey told us that the future and the past belong to white people, and that the only way for Black people to imagine ourselves is in science fiction and fantasy, which are both controlled by the white imagination. So Black people cannot really *be* anywhere or anything at all—and Mark isn't alone in this belief. We're not connected to the future. But what is there about Black people that make people like Drey say that we have no future?" She stopped and walked back toward the window. "It's because Drey misunderstood and mistook the white impression of reality *as reality itself*. But, the white past is as fictive as any speculative fiction, science fiction, or fantasy. Black existence in past and future already exists, but in a way that is not detectable by whatever Drey uses to understand and interpret reality. Black people have already left, already abandoned Drey's world and no one seems to know where to look for it, but they busy themselves searching. *You're searching, too,*" Amina said, looking at me. But, like Eryka Badu says, 'we ain't dead yet; we're on the internet.'"

Amina flashes the light kissed off the brick that I saw when I first walked into her loft, and finishes her thought. "We didn't really believe we could go to the moon until we did it. And, it was, from the movies and books and popular ideas, a group of unassuming Black women that helped to get us there. That's a hell of a phrase, 'helped to get us there'— could be used as the slogan of Black women in America. Unassuming propensity to help 'us' get 'there,' to find out, when they got there, their restrooms were in the other building, down a dirty hall, and a dark flight of stairs. But there *is* a bathroom, and isn't that the point?"

Amina's voice cut like hard distorting glass. "But, we didn't think that could happen until it did; and we still don't really know the names of *all* these Black women that made it happen—maybe some of them are still lost in the halls trying to find the restroom? And that's just it. You think because you ain't looking for it, it don't exist. And, you think you don't need to look for it, because you know what it is anyway. It's not circular, it's a spiral. Black girl magic, right? There's a space between the 'hashtag' and that phrase. Did you know that? There's always a space where you think there's not one; and never a space where you think there is one."

I stare blankly. Amina laughs, reaches out and touches my arm.

"Ed," Independent Scholar

I can't recall much from my meeting with "Ed." Though my notes tell me that we met on the corner of 125th and Lexington, I can't recall, in the moment, exactly what happened as we walked the streets of the city. I can't recall what he was wearing, his individual expressions or the tone of his voice as he spoke. I am recalling, here, what he said, and what I transcribed.

"We can't begin to have a conversation about political economy without a conversation about race," Ed began. "*We* were the first mode of economic exchange, the first *embodied* capital in this country." He pauses, as if an accusation has been made. I remember not moving, not wanting to create new ideas or to inhabit any old ones. "There is a grand irony here. Before currency, you had *our* womb—this was the original moment of 'printing money'; and, then, before the federal mint, you had the currency backed by *our bodies*. We were both the currency and the national backing assuring the currency held its value!"

He paused again. "What do you know about para-ontology?" Before I could respond, he amended his question. "Para- anything really—about what comes before, and stabilizes everything around it? What would you *give*—and *take*—for such assurances of life, *your* life, its meaning and value? *What* would *you* give for *that*? A series of questions? A claim about and for *this* interview? What are you going to give *me* to answer these questions? An advance for you, but what for me? Why would I *do* this honestly? Why would I ever give you anything of use *for* you to advance yourself again—on *my* back. Still currency and national backing, huh?"

Ed's voice started trailing off. I could—if you can imagine—*see* his words melting away into a swirling, counterclockwise vortex. I stared at him. This time, not as an interviewer, though. I had never been spoken to this way, by anyone. It was not so much an accusation, but a review, a reflection and introspection—how *can* I know *why* I'm asking this question, really? Is there anything that can reorient it—my questions, myself—to justify these years and all of our relationships?

"In history's ass pocket," I heard Baldwin whispering in my ear, to discover it was Ed's voice mumbling to himself.[36] Baldwin's voice in Ed's mouth snapped me back to Ed, who was mysteriously still talking. "We understand *Blackness* as a name given to the general antagonism, one that operates as a dialectic between racial capitalism and Black radicalism, since the opening of the modern projects of racial slavery and colonialism. In other words, we understand Blackness *historically*, as the external imposition of a racial ontology which is particular to populations racialized as Black. At the same time, the internal production of racial ontologies of Blackness by Black diasporas have destabilized the claim that any racial category is given, or natural."[37]

But I couldn't hear him beyond his words. "The modality of whiteness in its construction as the central iteration of racial capitalism is exclusionary and exploitative."[38] It was Ed's voice, but somehow not. I knew what each of the words meant individually, but was caught, ensnared, snagged by the words that wouldn't leave my thoughts alone—"embodied capital," and what had been invested, like currency in the body or the federal reserve of the womb. I broke my usual protocol, cutting the interview short—at least in my mind—while Ed was still talking, the recorder still running. Ed was being recorded, not by me, but by a small black and silver rectangular box with a gleaming red eye that somehow stood between us.

"Damien," Government Employee

I met "Damien" at a local staffers bar for happy hour. Damien walks into the room wearing a navy-blue suit with a crisp white shirt, red tie, and silver cufflinks. His shoes are black and slightly scuffed. He gives the appearance of a government worker, high up enough to need to wear a power tie, but busy enough to have on shoes slightly scuffed to indicate he still walks the streets with the people. The only thing that seems to be out of place is his hair and his beard. His hair is longer at the top than on the sides, and his beard, though neatly trimmed, is longer than I would expect from a government employee. We are meeting right after his workday to discuss his perspective as a policy analyst on the political economy. He begins with a story about James Baldwin's interview (1963 "Take this Hammer" Interview).

"Baldwin sits in front of the camera as only Baldwin does. He looks so absolutely serious, but also melancholy, not for himself, but always for the ill gotten gains ignorance of whiteness. He listens to the interviewer's question, takes a drag of his cigarette and attempts to offer a civil, humane answer to an absurdly reaching 'The Negro question . . .' His answer breathes out of his mouth and nostrils and lingers in the air, like the smoke from his cigarette. 'What you say about anybody else, reveals you.'"

Damien seems unaware, but he is offering the same gestured response as Baldwin himself, waving his hand in front of his face as if to wave away ignorance and stupidity, or as one does a bad smell or a fly. "Baldwin finishes his thought," Damien notes. "I'm not describing you, when I talk about you. I'm describing me. . . . I've always known . . . I am not a nigger. But if I am not the nigger . . . then who is the nigger?"

Damien laughs uncomfortably.

"White people seem to think these things are where I am. That at night, when I am putting my babies to bed, and looking them in their eyes, and seeing the glint and glimmering of a forever possibility that is always there, right in front of my own face, that all I can gather is the idea that what *you* see is all that there is. You might have thought that when Baldwin told us that we are not niggers, that white people needed the nigger—still need the nigger—he was being glib, or even provincial. But something else was going on there, beneath his wide eyes, wide mouth and 'serious' brow. It's right there in front of us, captured on camera. In that space between the tip of his cigarette and the smoke, that's where it is, like a smokeless fire—the truth."

Damien leans back in his chair and laughs, this time to himself, sipping his Old Fashioned. "There. Shit, man. Right there. Baldwin is right there, like a jinn. He's supernatural. He's gone somewhere else, and when he looks into that camera, and says, 'I'm not the nigger, baby. You are,' we can hear in that 'baby' our grandmother's 'bless your heart' and know that something really transformative has just happened. Man, she ain't there no more. Not right in front of you to see: you think you just received a blessing, but you've just been given a sentence."

Curtis Mayfield is playing in the background, *"We people who are darker than blue."* A strange choice for 6:00 p.m. The sky just outside is beginning to darken, highlighting the fog cutting against the yellowish glow from the lamp post. Damien makes note of it all.

"See, Baldwin was trying to tell us that when all the signifying and gestures have dried up, you're gonna have to be ready to fight. See that fog out there? [*Damien points to the window*]. You see how it cuts across and against the light and presses against the window? With enough pressure, the window could break. But, everyone in here thinks they're safe, but no one in here would even ask the question of the pounds of pressurization that the glass is calibrated. They just assume it to be true. Just like, at just the right amount of density, something as thin and ephemeral as the fog can cause blindness. See, we're all vulnerable at some point, but we condition ourselves not to see it. That's really the function of the law—to hide anxiety behind the shield of the *idea* of control. But, under just the right conditions, everything can break and we could be blinded. That's why we have to be ready to fight."

Damien looks at me directly, then looks away. "I see it all the time—the fractures in the law, that breaking point. Not just because I'm Black and we live in those rupture points. But also because I review policy; I see the loopholes and tricks to make it look whole and sturdy. But, at just the right angle, you can see it all—all the gaps, holes, the breaking points where the glass is not pressurized correctly, the fog rolling in, dense and thick. Baldwin was trying to tell us . . . we're all inside this building surrounded by glass, surrounded by fog. And, we all gotta look out and see. Some of us simply refuse to see the glass or the fog, and only want to see the beauty, like some 1930s movie with Humphry Bogart. But, Baldwin tried, Baraka tried, too. Also, Malcolm and Stockley. And on and on and on—that right at the edge of beauty is the uncontrolled chaos of disorder."

Damien leaned back and closed his eyes, apparently listening to the music play. *"This ain't no time for segregatin'/I'm talking 'bout brown and yellow two / High yellow girl, can't you tell / "You're just the surface of our dark deep well."* [39]

Damien quickly opened his eyes and picked up his drink and took a sip. He rolled out his hands in front of him, like he was giving a piece of candy to a child. "But where are you gonna go when it all breaks and the fog comes rolling in? The moon? Mars? You got a gas mask? Night vision goggles? A spaceship?"

CONCLUSION: THAT WHICH IS GIVEN AND THAT WHICH IS TAKEN

Over sixty years ago Frantz Fanon told us that the "folklore of Martinique is meager," and as a result, though it may be strange to hear, "as late as 1940 no Antillean found it possible to think of himself as a Negro." In other words, because there were (little to) no central mythological frameworks through which to think oneself as positively "Negro," only leaving as the possibility of positive being, white characters and "whiteness" as "human," no Black children in Martinique, in Fanon's view, could or wanted to imagine themselves as Black. "It was only with the appearance of Aimé Césaire," Fanon finishes, "that the acceptance of negritude and the statement of its claims began to be perceptible."[40] For Fanon, the narratives in which and through which we can imagine ourselves inscribes our practices of hearing, seeing, and reading and are modes of transformation and transfiguration of our central claims and concerns alerting us to the fact that politics and our political imaginations and political understandings are (largely) aesthetic, and must be thought of in terms of these aesthetic elements.

So, when Hillary Putnam, or any other Anglo or European philosopher, begins a conversation about truth, in this case, semantic externalism—that is, the idea that meanings are tied to context, and that, with a change of context, we also see a change in the meaning of words that we may potentially understand—we can begin to have a clear understanding of the role of folklore. But, in order to understand meaning in *this* Earth, Putnam demands we leave it for another Earth, a twin Earth. In other words, to understand the construction of meaning and value within language and human communities, he had to somehow create a new, fictive human community. But, if he really wanted to understand the central role of context in meaning and value, he didn't need to leave this Earth to do it. He could have just read Douglass's "What to the Slave Is the Fourth of July?" or any Black theorist discussing freedom, rights, democracy or any other liberal concept to see if they are the same as when spoken by John Locke or Thomas Jefferson. That is to say, he could have stayed on *this* Earth and found an alternate view of reality to see if meaning and value crosses context or is context specific. The fact that he did not—refused or could not—tells us something of the mythological foundation of truth, but what is more, of ourselves.

There must have been a reason he evaded this obvious fact. And, this is the point. One can look out the window and see Black bodies, but still not really see them—Black people, it must be said, are not Black bodies nor the condition of simply being meat. But, if only seen as such, not only do they become invisible, but their perspective recedes underneath the flesh. This is what Putnam really does, and what is really being discussed here is not knowledge acquisition—that is merely a shadow of the central issue: the formation of community.

The example of Putnam really reveals that white communities are formed largely on an implicit agreement of what they will see and *how* they will see, and therefore, interact with and *experience* the world. But, this is how all communities are formed. It is in this way that all truth is itself speculative, surrealistic, and governed by a specific mythos of articulation—it is all science fiction, a fiction that presents itself under the rigors of "science." The difficulty, then, is seeing and thinking beyond our boundaries to what exists outside of them, what has been placed outside of them, and learning how to think at the borders. In other words, this means learning how to think both what is mythologically placed inside and outside. The trouble, though, is in the paralocation of Blackness, as both that which is *placed* outside and necessary for integrity inside, *and*, that which *places* itself outside, each predicated within the speculative fiction of "inclusion" (integration) and "amelioration" (remuneration) of the post–Civil Rights epistemology. This means that we all think we "know" the spatial and temporal location of our politics, which is never really where it appears. It also means that no matter what the ontological registry—of resistance or displacement—we are always somewhere else in approximating Blackness and its meaning to white political life.

We may hate to admit it, but we still buy houses, cars, and clothes, and drive down roads into gated spaces, and live our lives. We all agree by living our lives that this is the meaning of "freedom" or "rights" or "humanity," and ignore having to think about what it all means.

It seems that this letter was written by the chief editor in some haste and was not fully thought out. It was meant to be reassuring—that *if* Black people were to someday vanish, that is, stop pretending, it should not be cause for alarm. Somehow it created the opposite. When I was assigned this story, I didn't know what to think, didn't really know where it would go. But it turns out, I learned more about myself than really about those I had previously interviewed. Mostly of our dependence on Black people, not just for labor, but for something else a bit more primitive—the very idea of ourselves, the psychic order of our reality. We've come to rely on them as the one knowable, unchangeable, understandable thing in our world—an Archimedean point in the storm. Without them, we would lose ourselves to the chaos. Without them, we would lose the gravity that ties us to the Earth. Bradbury was on to something, even if he didn't know it, when he wrote that if Black people had left the Earth, white people would build a ship to see where they had gone, what they are doing, and if we could join them. At the end, I discovered that it is not the material order of the world we need to control, but the order which is not material at all, that must be navigated and controlled. This is the realm of the imagination and the understanding out of which we and all that surrounds us is manifested. After combing through my notes, reflecting on the letter and the response, this is what I have learned, what I have gathered, and what I leave you, the reader, with. My hope is that it gives you a glimpse into race and racism in America, but what is more, a glimpse into yourself.

David finished typing his findings, which began, ostensibly, to discover what it means that Black people have disappeared and left in their wake a series of articulations, gestures, and ended, as it were, with a conversation about the imagination and understanding, and the principle idea that what we consider to be real and true is but an extension of other, formative phantasms of thought—in other words, speculative fiction given material life. He pushed himself away from the table, crossed his legs at the knee, placed his hands behind his neck and stared at the screen.

"The world is a virtual reality, and we're just beginning to realize this," David whispered to himself, closing the top of his computer. Simone's song still lingered in the air, beckoning him to wonder who that could have been.[41] The bacon still burned behind him, the kettle still flicked water from its lips.

NOTES

1. Turner, "Day of Absence," 39.
2. Ellison, "What America Would Be Like Without Blacks," 581.
3. Ibid.
4. Ellison, *Invisible Man*, 3.
5. Ibid., 3.
6. Thomas, "Introduction," x.
7. Moten, "Blackness and Nothingness (Mysticism in the Flesh)," 738.
8. Ibid., 738.
9. Jackson, "'Theorizing in a Void,'" 618.
10. Ibid., 620.
11. Mos Def, "You Already Knew"; Nelson, ed., "Hal Bennett," 38.
12. James Baldwin, *Giovanni's Room*, 3.
13. Plato, *Meno*, 360.
14. Smith, "Dear White America," 25.
15. Alexander, *The Black Interior*, 6.
16. Moten, "The Subprime and the Beautiful," 240.
17. Ibid., 239.
18. Simone, "Pirate Jenny."
19. Jackson, "'Theorizing in a Void,'" 620.
20. Elwell, "C. Wright Mills on the Sociological Imagination."
21. Murray, *Omni-Americans*, 121.
22. Saunders, "Why Blacks Should Read (and Write) Science Fiction, 403–04.
23. Morrison, *Playing in the Dark*, 15.
24. Mills, *Blackness Visible*, 2.
25. Ibid., 3.
26. Mills, *Blackness Visible*, 225–26.
27. Stuart, "Why Cats Purr."
28. Updike quoted in Dill, "Little Plentitudes," 1.
29. Horton, "'The Structure, then the Music,'" 27, 38.
30. Obama, "A More Perfect Union."
31. Alexander, *The Black Interior*, 6.
32. Hurston, "How It Feels to Be Colored Me."
33. Wormsley, "There Are Black People in the Future."
34. Ocean, "Super Rich Kids."
35. Broadnax, "What the Heck Is Afrofuturism."
36. Baldwin, *No Name in the Street*, 61–62.
37. The Black Study Group, "The Movement of Black Thought: Study Notes."
38. Ibid.
39. Mayfield, "We People Who Are Darker than Blue."
40. Fanon, *Black Skin, White Masks*, 118.
41. Simone, "Pirate Jenny."

BIBLIOGRAPHY

Alexander, Elizabeth. *The Black Interior*. Minneapolis: Graywolf Press, 2004.
Baldwin, James. *Giovanni's Room*. New York: Random House, 2013.
———. *No Name in the Street*. New York: Vintage, 2007.
The Black Study Group, "The Movement of Black Thought: Study Notes." *Dark Matter: In the Ruins of Imperial Culture*. September 29, 2015. Accessed at http://www.darkmatter101.org/site/2015/09/29/the-movement-of-black-thought-study-notes/.

Bradbury, Ray. "The Other Foot." In *The Illustrated Man*, 40–47. New York: Doubleday, 1951.
Broadnax, Jamie. "What the Heck Is Afrofuturism." *The Huffington Post*. February 16, 2018. Accessed at https://www.huffingtonpost.com/entry/opinion-broadnax-afrofuturism-black-panther_us_5a85f1b9e4b004fc31903b95.
Def, Mos [Yaslin Bey] and Talib Kweli. "You Already Knew." *Black Star: Aretha*. Javotti Media, 2011.
Delany, Samuel. "Racism and Science Fiction." In *Dark Matter: A Century of Speculative Fiction from the African Diaspora*. Edited by Sheree Renee Thomas, 383–98. New York: Warner, 2000.
Dill, Scott. "Little Plentitudes: John Updike's Affective Ontology of the Image." *The John Updike Review* 3 (2011): 1–28. Accessed at http://www.updikereview.com/wp-content/uploads/2011/03/Dill-1.pdf.
Ellison, Ralph. *Invisible Man*. New York: Vintage, 1952.
———. "What America Would Be Like without Blacks." In *The Collected Essays of Ralph Ellison*, 581–89. New York: Modern Library, 2003.
Elwell, Frank W. "C. Wright Mills on the Sociological Imagination." Accessed at http://www.faculty.rsu.edu/users/f/felwell/www/Theorists/Essays/Mills3.htm.
Fanon, Frantz. *Black Skin, White Masks*. Translated by Richard Philcox. New York: Grove Press, 2008.
Griffin, John Howard. *Black Like Me*. New York: Signet, 1977.
Horton, Randall. "'The Structure, then the Music': Interview with Ed Roberson" *Callaloo* 33, no. 3 (Summer 2010): 762–69.
Hurston, Zora Neale. "How It Feels to Be Colored Me." *The World Tomorrow* (May 1928).
Jackson, Zakiyyah Iman. "'Theorizing in a Void': Sublimity, Matter, and Physics in Black Feminist Poetics." *The South Atlantic Quarterly* 117, no. 3 (July 2018): 617–48.
Mayfield, Curtis. "We People Who Are Darker than Blue." *New World Order*. Sound Recording. Warner Brothers, 1996.
Mills, Charles. *Blackness Visible: Essays on Philosophy and Race*. Ithaca: Cornell University Press, 1998.
Morrison, Toni. *Playing in the Dark: Whiteness and the Literary Imagination*. New York: Vintage, 1993.
Moten, Fred. "Blackness and Nothingness (Mysticism in the Flesh)." *The South Atlantic Quarterly* 112, no. 4 (2013): 737–80.
———. "The Subprime and the Beautiful." *African Identities* 11, no. 2 (2013): 237–45.
Murray, Albert. *Omni-Americans: New Perspectives on Black Experience and American Culture*. New York: Da Capo Press, 1990.
Nelson, Emmanuel Sampath, ed. "Hal Bennett." In *Contemporary African American Novelists: A Bio-bibliographical Critical Sourcebook*, 36–42. Westport: Greenwood Press, 1999.
Obama, Barack. "A More Perfect Union." Transcript. *NPR*. March 18, 2008. Accessed at https://www.npr.org/templates/story/story.php?storyId=88478467.
Ocean, Frank. "Super Rich Kids." *Channel Orange*. Def Jam Recordings, 2012.
Plato. *The Dialogues of Plato, Volume 1*. New York: Random House Publishing, 1937.
———. *Republic*. Indianapolis, IN: Hackett Publishing, 1992.
Putnam, Hilary. "Meaning and Reference." *The Journal of Philosophy* 70, no. 19 (November 1973): 699–711.
———. "The Meaning of 'Meaning.'" *Minnesota Studies in Philosophy of Science* 7 (1975): 131–93.
Saunders, Charles. "Why Blacks Should Read (and Write) Science Fiction." In *Dark Matter: A Century of Speculative Fiction from the African Diaspora*. Edited by Sheree Renee Thomas, 398–405. New York: Warner, 2000.
Simone, Nina. "Pirate Jenny." *The Best of Nina Simone*. PolyGram, 1969.
Smith, Danez. "Dear White America." In *Don't Call Us Dead*. Minneapolis: Graywolf Press, 2017.

Stuart, Annie. "Why Cats Purr." *Pets WebMD*. April 21, 2012. Accessed at https://pets.webmd.com/cats/features/why-cats-purr#1.

Thomas, Sheree Renee. "Introduction: Looking for the Invisible." In *Dark Matter: A Century of Speculative Fiction from the African Diaspora*. Edited by Sheree Renee Thomas. ix–xiv. New York: Warner, 2000.

Turner, Douglas Ward. "Day of Absence." In *Happy Ending and Day of Absence: Two Plays by Douglas Ward Turner*, 31-–61. New York: Dramatists Play Service, Inc., 1996.

Wormsley, Alisha. "There Are Black People in the Future." Art Installation. Accessed at http://www.alishabwormsley.com/there-are-black-people-in-the-future/.

Index

affordances, xxiii, xxiv, xxvi, xxxiin25
agency, viii, xix, xxix, 5, 9, 34, 55, 70, 71, 91, 122, 130–132, 134, 135, 136. *See also* epistemic agency
Alcoff, Linda Martín, 97, 101, 115, 116, 123
alienation, 4, 155, 158
anger. *See* anger-silencing spirals; attributive anger; knowing resistant anger
anger-silencing spirals, xxviii, 79, 80, 81, 82, 85, 89, 90–93
anti-Black racism, viii, ix–x, 4, 26, 176
Anzaldúa, Gloria, 63–64, 70, 71
Apartheid, 168, 196
Asian, xxviii, 25, 28, 32, 35, 39–40, 44, 46, 57, 59, 62, 65, 68, 69. *See also* Asian-American
Asian-American, xxviii, 55, 56, 58–59, 66, 67–68, 71–72. *See also* Asian
attributive anger, 80, 81
attunement, xxiii, 147, 151

Baldwin, James, vii, 15–16, 159, 236, 236–237
The Birth of a Nation , xxiii, 190, 191, 193
Black body memory, xxvii, 2, 9–10, 11, 17, 18, 19. *See also* body memory
Black Lives Matter, 44, 92, 229
Black Wall Street, xviii, 144
body memory, 6, 7–9. *See also* Black body memory; sedimentation
Bogart, Humphrey, 194, 237
Bourdieu, Pierre, xix, xxiii, 126, 151–152, 161n20, 162n29, 167, 168, 179
Bradbury, Ray, xxx, 208, 209, 213, 232, 233, 240

Christianity, xin6, xx, xxxin13, xxxin14, 136, 143, 144, 150, 162n28, 162n42, 226. *See also* religious practices
Civil Rights, 12, 13, 14, 26, 220
cognitive penetration of perception, 104, 105–106, 107, 109. *See also* perception; racialized seeing
colonialism, 4, 56, 57, 150, 157, 196, 236
colorblindness, xxviii, 97–99, 101, 115, 116
confirmation bias, 57, 109. *See also* implicit bias; stereotypes
contextualism, 101, 102, 103, 107, 114. *See also* social construction of race
criminalization, xxvi, xxxin17, 16, 19, 63, 72n3, 94n3, 100, 113, 174, 176, 179, 180. *See also* criminal justice system
criminal justice system, xxix, 166, 169, 170–171, 172, 181
critical race theory, 15, 18, 99, 129, 135, 138, 139n17

dark matter, 209, 210
despair, 16, 57, 93
Diallo, Amadou, 113
disgust, xxix, 186, 187–188; aesthetic disgust, 189–190, 195–196, 198, 200, 202n61; moral disgust, 186, 187–188, 189, 190, 191, 193–195, 196, 199; racialized disgust, 190, 191, 193–194, 197, 198, 199–200
Dotson, Kristie, 77, 78, 93, 94n3, 111
double consciousness, xxviii, 14, 62, 131
Du Bois, W. E. B., 14, 18, 58, 62, 72n1, 131, 213

Ellison, Ralph, xxx, 208–209

245

embodied cognition, xviii, xxxin5, 8, 11, 123, 197, 200
embodied practices. *See* racism; religious practices
epistemic agency, 108, 111, 112. *See also* agency
epistemic harm, viii, 61, 79, 82, 84, 90, 99, 108–110, 111, 115. *See also* epistemic injustice
epistemic injustice, xxviii, 77–78, 79, 85, 89, 91, 92–93. *See also* epistemic harm
epistemic oppression, 93, 111, 112. *See also* oppression
epistemic violence. *See* epistemic harm
essentialism, 73n12, 101, 102
ethnicity, 13, 26, 28–29, 44, 168
ethno-racial homogamy, 25, 26–28, 28–29, 30, 32, 36, 39, 44, 48, 49n3
Eurocentrism, 55, 72n2, 163n54

Fanon, Frantz, vii, 2, 4, 11, 68, 70, 123–124, 201n34, 238
fantasy, 81, 208, 209, 210, 215, 224, 234
feminist theory, 85, 88, 89, 92, 99, 121, 123, 124, 127, 128, 129, 133, 137, 138
film, xxix, 67, 185–186, 191–193, 194, 196, 198, 199

gaslighting, 77, 82

habit. *See* habituation; *habitus*; racialized habitus
habituation, xx, 7, 107, 144, 145, 151, 159, 180, 181, 188. *See also* sedimentation
habitus, xix, xxix, 132, 151–152, 161n20, 161n26, 162n29, 166–169, 172, 173, 175, 176, 177, 178, 179, 180, 181, 212. *See also* racialized habits; racism
Haslanger, Sally, xxix, 122–123, 124, 125–127, 128, 129, 132–133, 134, 137, 138
hermeneutical injustice, 85, 89, 90, 93
Hispanic, xxix, 65, 166, 172. *See also* Latina/Latinx
hooks, bell, 72n2, 127, 138

ideological oppression, 122, 126, 129, 138. *See also* oppression
imagination, xxii, 6, 56, 152, 186, 192, 212, 214–215, 216, 218, 223, 234, 240
imitation, xxix, 70, 125, 145–146, 147, 151, 153, 159, 188
immigration, xxix, 42, 166, 170, 171, 174, 178, 180, 181. *See also* criminalization; criminal justice system
implicit bias, xviii, xix, xxiv, 8, 57, 60. *See also* confirmation bias; stereotypes
incarceration, 5, 87, 165, 228, 229
institutionalized racism, xvii, xviii, xxx, 56, 60, 97, 150, 165, 172, 201n34. *See also* oppression; segregation; structural racism
intentionality, 61, 69, 130
invisibility, 37, 38, 57, 60, 79, 98, 155, 209, 216, 220, 224. *See also* veil

Jim Crow. *See* segregation

King Jr., Martin Luther, 143, 144, 150
knowing resistant anger, 77, 78, 79, 83–85, 86, 87–93, 95n47

Latina/Latinx, xxviii, 25, 32, 33, 35–36, 42, 46, 65–66, 131, 175, 176, 180. *See also* Hispanic
lived body, 3, 4, 6–7, 8–9, 10, 19, 129–130, 137, 152, 153
lived experience, x, xix, 4, 5, 17, 26, 38, 42, 47, 58, 66, 67, 72, 77, 121, 129, 134, 137, 145, 147, 151, 201n34
Lorde, Audre, 79, 80, 82, 84, 87–89, 92, 137
lynching, xvii, xxv, 5, 14, 87, 171, 193

Martin, Trayvon, xvii, 16, 73n27
Merleau-Ponty, Maurice, xviii, 6, 145, 151, 152–153, 162n29, 162n35
migrants. *See* immigration
Mills, Charles, 94n3, 110, 216
mindshaping, xxix, 122–123, 124–126, 132, 139n17
model minority, xxviii, 66

myth, 4, 14, 19, 56, 60, 63, 100, 146, 157, 159, 197, 215, 216, 232, 238, 239

Native American, xvii, 68, 71, 157, 191
natural kinds, x, 102, 104
neuroscience, xviii, xxiii
nominalism, 101

Obama, Barack, xxi, 44, 170, 220, 224, 225–226
Operation Streamline, 166, 169–173, 174–175, 176–177, 178, 179–180, 181
oppression, xxviii, xxix, 10, 12, 25, 28, 34, 37, 38, 63, 71, 79, 86, 121–122, 126, 127, 129, 132, 134, 136, 137, 229. *See also* ideological oppression; structural racism

perception 3, 6, 8, 9, 17, 99, 107, 109, 114, 123, 161n18, 161n26, 197; racialized, viii, xxix, 57, 61, 62. *See also* cognitive penetration of perception; perceptual learning; racialized seeing
perceptual learning, xxviii, 103, 104, 105–107, 109–110, 113–114, 115. *See also* perception
phenomenology, viii, x, xxvii, xxxiin25, 2–4, 5, 6, 9, 11, 18, 64, 72n1, 105, 123, 145, 146
philosophy, x, 3, 71, 92, 99, 128, 155, 159, 163n54, 186, 228–229
police, xvii, xxv, xxvi, 1, 2, 14, 15, 17, 30, 37, 45, 87, 92, 113, 130, 133, 219, 220
political ideology homophily, 25, 28–29, 41, 44, 48, 49n4
prereflective, ix, xxix, 146, 156, 161n18. *See also* unconscious

racial formation, x, 4, 101, 148
racialized habits, x, xviii, 39, 98, 123, 156, 188, 191, 198; *See also habitus;* racism; sedimentation; stereotypes
racialized seeing, xxii, xxv, xxviii, 98–102, 103–104, 106, 107, 108–116; diachronic penetration, 105, 107. *See also* cognitive penetration of perception; perception; perceptual learning; stereotypes
racialized socialization, viii, x, xix, xxvi, 167, 168, 173, 180
racism, embodied practices of, viii, ix, x, xxvii, xxix, xxx, 144, 145, 151, 156, 159, 160, 161n18, 166, 168, 169, 177, 178, 180; *See also habitus;* sedimentation
racism as performance, x, xix, 67, 68
religious practices, xviii, xx, xxxin14, 143, 146, 151, 152, 158, 159, 160, 162n28, 163n56. *See also* Christianity
resistance, forms of, 27, 34, 47, 58, 64, 68, 71, 79, 91, 132, 137, 178
responsibility, 56, 61, 63, 99, 115, 135, 137
ritual. *See* habituation; *habitus*; racism; religious practices
Rose II, Antwon, 17, 150

science fiction, xxx, 210, 214, 215, 223, 234, 239, 240. *See also* speculative fiction
sedimentation, viii, xviii, 7–9, 116, 151, 153, 156, 161n18. *See also* body memory; habituation; racialized habits; racism
segregation, x, xxv, 15, 26, 37, 72n1, 136, 168, 171, 191, 201n34. *See also* institutionalized racism
slavery, xin6, 4, 10, 12, 15, 17, 34, 38, 60, 135, 157, 165, 196, 199, 202n49, 236
social construction of race, xxv, xxvii, xxix, xxx, 4, 5, 10, 19, 25, 62, 63, 69, 166, 188. *See also* contextualism
speculative fiction, xxx, 208, 210, 215, 216, 234, 239, 240. *See also* science fiction
stereotypes, xix, xxx, xxxin17, 4, 13, 14, 34, 35, 37, 44, 56, 62, 69, 72, 97, 100, 106, 108, 109, 110–111, 113–114, 124, 130, 135, 144, 148, 151, 156, 167, 180, 192, 193, 226. *See also* confirmation bias; implicit bias; unconscious; racialized habits; racialized seeing
structural racism, ix, xix, 26, 40, 60, 66, 72n1, 135, 136, 137, 165–167, 169, 175, 177, 179, 181. *See also* institutionalized racism; oppression

systemic racism. *See* institutionalized racism; oppression; structural racism

"the talk", xxiv, xxvii, 1–2, 11, 15, 16–18, 19

testimonial smothering, 78, 83, 94n26, 95n47

tone policing, xxviii, 77, 80, 81, 84, 92

tone vigilance, 77, 79, 81, 84

trauma, xvii, xviii, 6, 10, 37, 63, 70, 82, 87, 162n42

Trump, Donald, xxviii, xxxin17, 26, 28–30, 34, 42, 43, 46–48, 170

unconscious, xviii, xix–xx, xxii, xxiv, 8, 9, 33, 98, 100, 103, 107, 109, 113–114, 116, 144–145, 151, 155, 156, 157, 159, 168, 180, 188, 198. *See also* prereflective; stereotypes

unlevel knowing field, 78, 90, 92

veil, 14, 56, 57, 70, 72, 72n1. *See also* invisibility

white fragility, xix, 82

white gaze, vii, ix, xxv, xxvii, xxviii, 11, 13, 56, 57, 60–64, 66, 68, 70, 72. *See also* whiteness; white supremacy

whiteness, vii–viii, ix, xvii, xx, xxii, xxiv, xxix, 3, 48, 60–61, 63, 66, 68, 70, 72, 72n1, 102, 103, 145, 148, 151, 154, 155–156, 158–159, 214, 215, 216, 225, 233, 236, 238. *See also* white gaze; white privilege; white supremacy

white privilege, x, xviii, xxii, xxiv, xxvi, 61, 72n8, 98, 110, 143, 155, 156, 161n17. *See also* whiteness; white supremacy

white space, vii, viii, ix–x, xvii, xxvi, 60, 64, 69, 136, 143, 148, 155, 156

white supremacy, x, xviii, xxi, xxiv, xxvii, xxix, xxx, 5, 34, 38, 48, 60–64, 70, 73n12, 98, 144, 146, 150–151, 156, 158, 159, 160, 176, 191, 193. *See also* white gaze; whiteness; white privilege

Yancy, George, xxv, xxxiin27, 3, 5, 10, 60–61, 62, 69, 100, 112, 143, 151, 155, 156, 161n18, 176, 201n34

About the Editor and Contributors

Brock Bahler is associate teaching professor and director of undergraduate studies in religious studies at the University of Pittsburgh. With a PhD in philosophy (Duquesne University), his research is interdisciplinary in scope, investigating the nature of habit, ritual, and embodiment at the intersections of religious studies, continental philosophy, developmental psychology, and cognitive neuroscience. He is the author of *Childlike Peace in Merleau-Ponty and Levinas: Intersubjectivity as Dialectical Spiral* (2016, Lexington) and coeditor (with David Kennedy) of *Philosophy of Childhood Today: Exploring the Boundaries* (2017, Lexington).

***

Sarah Adeyinka-Skold (PhD, University of Pennsylvania) is assistant professor of sociology at Furman University. Her dissertation considers how race and gender shape relationship seeking in online dating spaces and apps. She has published essays in the journals *Sociology of Race and Ethnicity* and *Du Bois Review: Social Science Research on Race*.

Alison Bailey (PhD, University of Cincinnati) is a professor of philosophy at Illinois State University where she directs the Women's, Gender, and Sexuality Studies Program. Her scholarship engages issues at the intersections of feminist theories, philosophy of race, critical whiteness studies, and social epistemology (especially epistemic injustice and ignorance). She coedited *The Feminist Philosophy Reader* (2007) with Chris J. Cuomo. Her forthcoming book, *The Weight of Whiteness: A Feminist Engagement with Privilege, Race, and Ignorance* (2021, Lexington) is framed as a series of invitations to wade slowly and mindfully into the inherited weight of whiteness and to hold space with the ways that white supremacy works to anesthetize white people from the damage it does to our collective humanity.

Erin Beeghly (PhD, philosophy, UC Berkeley) is associate professor of philosophy at the University of Utah. Her research analyzes stereotyping, discrimination, and group oppression and their intersections with ethics and epistemology. She is the coeditor (with Alex Madva) of *An Introduction to Implicit Bias: Knowledge, Justice, and the Social Mind* (2020). Her current book project, *What's Wrong with Stereotyping?* examines the conditions under which judging people by group membership is wrong.

Jessie K. Finch (PhD, University of Arizona) is undergraduate coordinator and lecturer in sociology at Northern Arizona University. Her research focuses on migration, racial/ethnic identity, social psychology, and deviance. She is a coeditor of *Migrant Deaths in the Arizona Desert* (2016). She has also published in *Teaching Sociology*, *Race and Social Problems*, and *Sociological Spectrum*.

Dan Flory is professor of philosophy at Montana State University. He is the author of *Philosophy, Black Film, Film Noir* (2008) and coeditor (with Mary K. Bloodsworth-Lugo) of *Race, Philosophy, and Film* (2013). He has also written over thirty essays on philosophy, critical race theory, film, and the history of philosophy, which have appeared in venues such as the *Western Journal of Black Studies*, *The Philosophy of Spike Lee*, *On Race: 34 Conversations in a Time of Crisis*, *Journal of World Philosophies*, *Journal of Aesthetics and Art Criticism*, *Projections: The Journal for Movies and Mind*, *Film and Philosophy*, *The Routledge Companion to Philosophy and Film*, and *The Blackwell Companion to Film Noir*.

James B. Haile (PhD, philosophy, Duquesne University) works at the intersection of philosophy, literary criticism, and Africana studies to bring together living challenges surrounding the meaning of Blackness and experiences and complexities of Black life. Haile is the editor of *Philosophical Meditations on Richard Wright* (2012, Lexington), a collection of essays on the philosophical insights and value of Richard Wright. His current book, *The Buck, the Black, and the Existential Hero* (2020), is a meditative analysis of the Black male literary voice to investigate Black male lives in Western modernity, to, as it were, shape the silence around their existence and the hypervisibility of their death. Haile is currently working on a book on jazz improvisation and the relationship between Black cultural forms and Continental philosophy (most notably, the under-researched aspects of the dependency of twentieth-century Continental philosophy on Black American cultural forms).

Autumn Redcross, PhD, is visiting assistant professor of psychology at Point Park University. Her research interests include restorative justice, Black existentialism, and democratic engagement. She is the author of "Death Passes Twice" in *Our Black Sons Matter* (2016, Rowman & Littlefield).

Nora Tsou is a graduate student in philosophy at San Jose State University. She received her BA in Humanities and Cultural Studies at Dominican University where she developed a thesis project on the Asian-

American experience grounded in the scholarship of Gloria Anzaldúa and George Yancy.

Katie Tullmann is assistant professor of philosophy at Northern Arizona University. She completed her PhD in philosophy at the CUNY Graduate Center. Katie works at the intersection of philosophy of mind and value theory. Her current research applies recent work in cognitive science and the philosophy of perception to questions on gender, race, and sexuality.

George Yancy is the Samuel Candler Dobbs Professor of Philosophy at Emory University and a Montgomery Fellow at Dartmouth College, one of the college's highest honors. He is also the University of Pennsylvania's Inaugural Fellow in the Provost's Distinguished Faculty Fellowship Program (2019–2020 academic year). Yancy is the author, editor, and co-editor of over twenty books, including *Black Bodies, White Gazes* (2016, Rowman & Littlefield); *Look, A White! Philosophical Essays on Whiteness* (2012); *Backlash: What Happens When We Talk Honestly about Racism in America* (2018, Rowman & Littlefield); and *Across Black Spaces: Essays and Interviews from an American Philosopher* (2020, Rowman & Littlefield). He is known for his influential essays and interviews in the *New York Times* philosophy column "The Stone," and is the "Philosophy of Race" book series editor at Lexington Books.